Building Culturally Responsive Family–School Relationships

Ellen S. Amatea
University of Florida

PEARSON

Upper Saddle River, New Jersey
Columbus, Ohio

Library of Congress Cataloging-in-Publication Data

Building culturally responsive family-school relationships / [edited by] Ellen S. Amatea.
    p. cm.
    ISBN 0-205-52364-1
    1. Home and school—United States.   2. Academic achievement—United
States.   I. Amatea, Ellen S., 1944-
    LC225.3.B769 2009
    371.19'2—dc22

                                                                              2008000939

Photo Credits: p. 3: Michael Newman/PhotoEdit; p. 19: Nancy Sheehan Photography; p. 51: Ellen B. Senisi;
p. 81: VStock LLC/IndexOpen; p. 115: Assunta Del Buono/John Birdsall Archive/The Image Works;
p. 144: Nancy Sheehan Photography; p. 169: Corbis RF; p. 201: Ellen B. Senisi; p. 231: IndexOpen;
p. 252: Michael Newman/PhotoEdit; p. 279: Bob Daemmrich Photography; p. 308: Lori Whitley/Merrill
Education; p. 337: Andrea Booher/FEMA; p. 364: Digital Vision/Getty Images

Series Editor: Kelly Villella Canton
Series Editorial Assistant: Christine Pratt Swayne
Director of Marketing: Quinn Perkson
Marketing Manager: Danae April
Production Editor: Paula Carroll
Editorial Production Service: Black Dot Group/NK Graphics
Composition Buyer: Linda Cox
Manufacturing Buyer: Linda Morris
Electronic Composition: NK Graphics
Interior Design: Black Dot Group
Photo Researcher: Annie Pickert
Cover Administrator: Joel Gendron

This book was set in Bembo 11/13 by NK Graphics. It was printed and bound by R.R. Donnelley &
Sons/Harrisonburg. The cover was printed by Phoenix Color Corporation/Haggerstown.

Pearson Education Ltd.   Pearson Education Australia Pty. Limited
Pearson Education Singapore Pte. Ltd.   Pearson Education North Asia Ltd.
Pearson Education Canada, Ltd.   Pearson Educación de Mexico, S.A. de C.V.
Pearson Education—Japan   Pearson Education Malaysia Pte. Ltd.

Merrill
is an imprint of

www.pearsonhighered.com

10 9 8 7 6 5 4 3 2 1
ISBN-13: 978-0-205-52364-1
ISBN-10:   0-205-52364-1

CONTENTS

PREFACE

These days teachers are likely to see a classroom of faces unlike their own, faces of children who speak languages not their own, and who live lives far different from their own. They are the children whom teachers most need to learn about. Yet the families of these children are often the most hesitant to approach the school, and the most unsure about how they might help in the education of their children. These are also the families whom teachers find most difficult to approach. Yet the research evidence is clear. Whether poor or well-to-do, whether English is their first or second (or third) language, or whether from a mainstream or marginalized cultural group—when families are engaged in their children's school learning, children are more successful academically. When teacher and family work together to pool their wisdom about the children they share, they build a clearer structure of expectations and activities that foster children's learning and development. Hence, building positive relationships with students' families not only expands the resources that teachers can bring to bear to facilitate student learning, but also it helps teachers learn more effective ways to personalize their teaching. In this book we discuss the changing context of schooling in the United States. We then examine how families, schools, and communities interact to influence children's school success. Next, we describe the revolutionary changes in teacher beliefs and practices that undergird educators' efforts to build more culturally responsive relationships with students and their families.

We believe that interacting with families is a means toward the end of improving students' learning and school achievement, not just an end in itself. In addition, we do not offer one approach that we assume will work for everyone. Hence, you will see many different ideas showcased about how you might change your teaching practices. Because these ways of working with students and their families are a radical departure from traditional practices and beliefs, information about these new teaching practices, the research on their effectiveness, and the theory that underlies their development have not been a standard part of teacher preparation programs. Consequently, most beginning education professionals continue to have an exceedingly narrow conception of the role that families might play in their children's schooling—conceptions that all too often keep families in a marginalized, disempowered position.

This book is designed to acquaint you with these new ideas and practices in the field of family–school relationship building and highlight the changes in thinking that underly these new educational practices. Our goals for this book are to describe

- The changing context of schooling in the United States and the challenges to traditional beliefs and practices about how we as educators should interact with students, their families, and their communities

- What practitioners and researchers are learning about how families' beliefs, values, and interactions contribute to children's success in school
- A new approach to family–school relations, the family–school collaboration approach, and the distinctive beliefs and practices that characterize it
- Everyday instructional and noninstructional routines that individual teachers use to communicate, build collaborative partnerships, and forge a sense of co-ownership and connection with students' families and the larger community
- How school staffs are changing the school-wide norms and routines of their schools to support a more collaborative way of working with students, their families, and their communities

How This Book Is Organized

We have organized this book into four parts. Part I, *Changing Family–School Roles and Relationships,* discusses the changing beliefs and policies about how family–school roles and relationships should be structured. Educators' ideas about the roles that families should play in students' lives have changed significantly over the past fifty years. In Chapter 1, we briefly describe these shifts in thinking and practice and discuss the benefits and barriers to this new way of working with students' families. In Chapter 2 we describe the historical shifts in beliefs and expectations as to how family–school roles and relationships should be structured and the federal education policies that have shaped these changing beliefs. In Chapter 3 we describe the beliefs and actions of educators committed to building more culturally responsive and collaborative relationships with students' families. This perspective is essential to your understanding of how to partner with families.

Families vary significantly from one another, not only in terms of their surface characteristics, but also in terms of their ways of interacting, their cultural traditions, and their economic and social resources. Part II, *Understanding Families in Their Sociocultural Context,* explores how family members may interact with one another and with schools and the impact of cultural and community conditions on these interactions. In Chapter 4 we look at how family members interact with one another and the functions they perform together as families. Chapter 5 explores the varying family forms and how they move through various stages of the families' lives. Chapter 6 examines the diverse cultural and socioeconomic backgrounds of families, and Chapter 7 further explores the neighborhood and community conditions that influence the day-to-day lives of families and schools.

Educators need strategies for building effective partnerships with families, not only for the purpose of solving student problems, but also for maximizing student learning. In Part III, *Building Family–School Relationships to Maximize Student Learning,* we describe strategies that educators use that focus on creating stronger connections with families to maximize student learning and development. In Chapter 8 we focus on the communication skills and practices that educators can routinely use to build a sense of connection with their students' families. In Chapter

9 we examine the unique challenges faced by second language learners and their families, and the instructional and noninstructional strategies educators can utilize to build working relationships with families. In Chapter 10 we describe the use of student-led parent conferences as a powerful tool for establishing relationships with students and their families that gives students a greater voice in their assessment of their learning.

To effectively partner with students' families, educators must include families in their decision making and problem solving concerning a student. In Part IV, *Building Family–School Relationships through Joint Decision Making and Problem Solving,* educators describe strategies for joint problem solving with families so as to solve student problems, to determine whether their child requires special education services, or to assist a family in accessing needed outside resources. Chapter 11 describes a process of joint problem solving with families. Chapter 12 depicts how educators can partner with families when deciding whether a student needs special education services and developing and implementing an educational plan for the student. Chapter 13 considers how educators can assist families who face crisis situations that affect their capacity to care for their children. Chapter 14 considers how educators might work together in a school to create more culturally responsive ways of relating to the families of their students.

Distinctive Features of the Book

Several features of the content and format of this book differentiate it from existing textbooks in this field. This book

- Depicts a collaborative approach to working with parents and students in promoting student learning and resolving student problems
- Encourages educators to examine their personal beliefs and assumptions about their involvement with families
- Views families and their influence on children's learning through a strength-based framework
- Cultivates an appreciation for the diverse cultural, social, and economic circumstances that impact families, schools, and communities
- Showcases instructional methods that teachers use to link students' home and school worlds
- Showcases everyday routines that teachers use to communicate with families, including those difficult to engage, and to create opportunities for meaningful family–school interaction
- Describes effective strategies for managing the conflict and blaming endemic to many family–school interactions

Teaching and Learning Aids

We have included the following teaching and learning aids that we hope will assist you in understanding the ideas and practices we are promoting in this book.

- **First-person Stories** are numerous first-person accounts from innovative teachers, administrators, counselors, students, and parents that reflect how their own thinking and practices have changed as they have embraced more collaborative ways of working.
- **Chapter Summaries** will help you focus on the central issues of the chapter in preparing for exams.
- **Reflective Exercises** are activities in the reading that invite your self-reflection, application, and critique of personal beliefs, attitudes, and personalization of knowledge.
- **Case Studies** will be used to illustrate common situations in which educators interact with families, the emotional reactions resulting from them, and a range of effective responses to these situations.

ABOUT THE AUTHORS

Editor

Ellen S. Amatea is a professor in the Department of Counselor Education at the University of Florida. She is a psychologist and a marriage and family therapist and maintains a private practice specializing in the treatment of children and adolescents and their families. She has authored two books, *Brief Strategic Intervention for School Behavior Problems* and *The Yellow Brick Road: A Career Guidance Program for Elementary School Counselors and Teachers,* coauthored a second book, *Love and Intimate Relationships,* written chapters for other books, and written over forty articles. Dr. Amatea's research interests include the processes and outcomes of family involvement for the development of children and youth, particularly underserved low-income children; interventions for child and adolescent behavior problems; and the preparation of educators in family involvement in education. Prior to arriving at the University of Florida, she was a school counselor and a vocational rehabilitation counselor specializing in working with low-income youth with special needs. Dr. Amatea teaches graduate courses in school counseling and in marriage and family counseling. In addition, she teaches an undergraduate course in teacher education on family and community involvement in education.

Contributing Authors

Linda S. Behar-Horenstein is a Distinguished University Teaching Scholar and professor in the Department of Educational Administration and Policy and an affiliate in the College of Dentistry at the University of Florida. She teaches graduate courses in instructional leadership, curriculum, evaluation, and research design. Her recent research examines theory-practice connections and instructional practices among faculty in public schools, professional and clinical learning environments, teachers' beliefs and use of instructional strategies, and the impact of faculty development.

Mary Ann Clark is an associate professor in the Department of Counselor Education at the University of Florida, where she has served as the coordinator of the School Counseling Program and teaches graduate courses in school counseling and career development. She has worked as a school counselor and administrator in stateside and overseas schools before entering higher education. Her research areas include university–school partnerships, gender issues in educational achievement, and school success factors of low-income and culturally diverse students.

Maria R. Coady is an assistant professor in the School of Teaching and Learning at the University of Florida. She teaches graduate courses and specializes in English for Speakers of Other Languages (ESOL) and bilingual education. Dr. Coady teaches courses related to second language acquisition and the sociocultural context of education for English language learners. Her research interests include bilingualism and biliteracy development for language minority (mainly Spanish-speaking) students in U. S. public schools.

Kelly L. Dolan is a university–school assistant professor at the P. K. Yonge Developmental Research School at the University of Florida. She earned her bachelor's and master's degrees in Elementary Education from the University of Florida and has been an elementary school teacher for the past twenty-five years. She has supervised pre-service teachers and consulted with a variety of school districts participating in the Florida Reading Initiative to improve literacy instruction.

Silvia Echevarria-Doan is an associate professor in the Department of Counselor Education at the University of Florida, where she serves as the coordinator of the Marriage and Family Counseling Program. She teaches graduate courses in family therapy and family violence. Her research and writing interests include strength-based family therapy approaches, family narratives, parenting capacities, multicultural issues in family therapy, and qualitative research methodology. She has received awards for excellence in teaching and her work associated with cultural diversity issues.

Heather L. Hanney, Ed.S., N.C.C., is a doctoral candidate in the Department of Counselor Education at the University of Florida. She is currently employed as a children's therapist, working with children in therapeutic foster care. Her research interests include family–school collaboration, the impact of infertility on couple's marital adjustment and satisfaction, and the impact on the emotional development of children of involvement in the foster care system.

Crystal N. Ladwig is an independent educational consultant and an adjunct faculty member in the School of Education and Social Science at Saint Leo University. She teaches graduate courses in special education, with an emphasis on family involvement, instructional methodologies, and assessment. Her research interests have focused on family literacy, family involvement, and addressing the social/emotional development of young children at risk for developmental delays. She is especially interested in researching approaches for addressing the behaviors of young children with autism.

Teresa N. Leibforth, Ed.S., NCC, OTR/L is a school counselor and a doctoral candidate in the Department of Counselor Education at the University of Florida. She is also a practicing occupational therapist with advanced training and specialization in sensory processing disorders. Her areas of interest include clinical supervision, preparing school counselors to work with students in exceptional student education, and family–school collaboration.

Ann A. Rai earned a doctorate in Counselor Education from the University of Florida. Dr. Rai developed and taught a course in teacher education called Family and Community Involvement in Education while at the University of Florida. In addition, Dr. Rai has had fourteen years of experience in counseling with children and youth in a variety of settings, including five years as a school counselor. She is currently working as a middle school counselor at Wichita Collegiate School in Wichita, Kansas.

Sondra Smith-Adcock is an associate professor in the Department of Counselor Education at the University of Florida. She teaches graduate courses in school counseling and mental health counseling, with a specialization in counseling children and adolescents. Her research interests have focused on addressing children's and adolescents' social, emotional, and behavioral needs in schools. Individual and contextual issues related to children and adolescents' conduct problems have been a primary interest in her work. She also has studied how school, family, and community partnerships work to facilitate the needs of underrepresented populations in schools.

Catherine Tucker is an assistant professor in the Department of Communication Disorders, Counseling, and School and Educational Psychology at Indiana State University. Her research focuses on family–school–community relationships in the United States and internationally. Catherine also conducts research on the impact of poverty and race on schooling and mental health service delivery.

Frances M. Vandiver is the director of the P. K. Yonge Developmental Research School at the University of Florida. She is also a member of the Department of Educational Leadership and Policy Studies and teaches in the graduate program. She has worked with schools and school leaders across the country, focusing on the areas of instructional leadership, school change, and building teacher leadership.

Cirecie A. West-Olatunji is an assistant professor in the Department of Counselor Education at the University of Florida. Her current research focuses on exploring the schooling experiences of African American children that affect their educational achievement and psychosocial development. She teaches graduate courses in multicultural counseling and community counseling and is licensed as a professional counselor and a marriage and family therapist. She is also a nationally recognized speaker, practitioner, and author in the area of culture-centered theory, research, and practice.

ACKNOWLEDGMENTS

This book is dedicated to the many educators and families who are deeply committed to enhancing the school success of children from all walks of life. I especially want to thank the authors who contributed their perspectives and insights. It is an honor to work closely with such a talented and committed group of scholars and practitioners. As for myself, I owe much of my current thinking and perspective to the many conversations I have had with my colleagues and students. I am especially thankful to Dr. Howard Weiss, Dr. Fran Vandiver and Dr. Harry Daniels for their stimulating conversations and overall support. I also want to thank my mother, Vivian Sherlock, and my sister, Dr. Kathryn Sherlock, who as long-time educators, patiently listened and reviewed much of the text as it was being written.

Kelly Villella Canton, my project editor at Pearson Allyn and Bacon, deserves a special thanks for her unwavering support throughout the development and completion of this project. I am also grateful to the reviewers: William Flechtner, *Warner Pacific College*; Carole Kurtines-Becker, *University of North Carolina at Asheville*; Cindy Boettcher, *Texas A&M*; Carolyn Barber, *University of Maryland*; Harry Morgan, *University of West Georgia*; Linda Garris Christian, *Adams State College*; Donna Rafanello, *Long Beach City College*; Deborah A. Farrer, *California University of Pennsylvania*; Amy J. Malkus, *East Tennessee University*; and Jane Tingle Broderick, *East Tennessee University*. Their comments were instructive and essential to refining the book. Finally, I thank my husband, Frank, and my sons, Christian and John, for their patience, support, and shared belief in the importance of this project. They continue to teach me much about how families support their members' achievement efforts. I truly hope this book makes a difference for administrators, teachers, counselors, their students and their families as they work together to facilitate children's academic and personal success.

Part I

Changing Family–School Roles and Relationships

Chapter 1   Connecting with Families: A Nice or Necessary Practice?
Ellen S. Amatea

Chapter 2   From Separation to Collaboration: The Changing Paradigms of Family–School Relations
Ellen S. Amatea

Chapter 3   Building Culturally Responsive Family–School Partnerships: Essential Beliefs, Strategies, and Skills
Ellen S. Amatea

Educators' ideas about the roles that families should play in students' lives have changed significantly over the past fifty years. In Chapter 1 we briefly describe these shifts in thinking and discuss the benefits and barriers to implementing this new way of working with students' families. In Chapter 2 we describe the historical context for these changing beliefs and expectations as to how family–school roles and relationships should be structured and the federal education policies that have shaped these changing beliefs. In Chapter 3 we describe the beliefs and actions of educators committed to building more culturally responsive and collaborative relationships with students' families.

Chapter 1

Connecting with Families: A Nice or Necessary Practice?

Ellen S. Amatea

Learning Objectives

After reading this chapter, you will be able to:

- Describe the changing demographics of the student body and teacher workforce in U.S. schools.
- Summarize the research documenting the differences in educational outcomes and school conditions among low-income, racially and ethnically diverse students, and middle-income student populations.

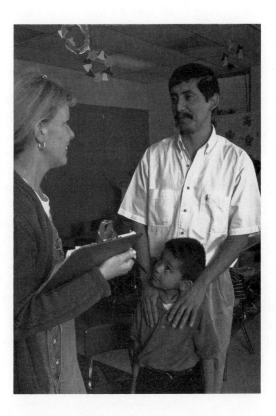

■ Describe the influence of families on children's learning and the influence of schools on families.

■ Describe the fundamental changes in how educators who seek to make schools more responsive to culturally diverse students and their families teach and structure their relations with students, their families, and other persons in the community.

■ Explain the basis of the belief that undergirds the development of this book—that working with students' families is a necessary, not simply a nice, aspect of educational practice.

■ Outline the benefits of these new ways of interacting with students and their families and the challenges to traditional family–school roles and practices that these ways imply.

> *In all likelihood, today's teachers will work with students whose back-grounds and lives are quite different from their own. Drawing on information collected from Census 2000, Villegas and Lucas (2002) predicted that,* **although some 40 percent of the school population is now from racially and culturally diverse groups, by 2035 children of color will be in the majority, and by 2050 they will represent 57 percent of the school population.** *However, many researchers have predicted that this population growth would be uneven across the United States. According to Hodgkinson (2002), "Sixty-one percent of the population growth in the next 20 years will be Hispanic and Asian, about 40% Hispanic and 20% Asian; but then, as now, 10 states will contain 90% of the Hispanic population, 10 will contain 90% of the Asian population, and 7 will do both" (103).*

A comparison of the racial/ethnic background of U.S. children ages five to seventeen for 1980 and for 2004 (Digest of Education Statistics, 2005) illustrates how this segment of our population is shifting. As seen in Figure 1.1, in 1980, White, non-Hispanic children comprised 74.6 percent of this population, but by 2004 they made up only 59.9 percent of all U.S. children ages five to seventeen. Whereas in 1980 only 14.5 percent of U.S. children were Black/non-Hispanic, by 2004 there were 14.9 percent in that category. The most dramatic population growth occurred among Hispanic children. In 1980 they comprised 8.5 percent of U.S. children, but by 2004 they comprised 18.2 percent of all children in the five-to-seventeen age bracket. Similarly, although 1.7 percent of U.S. children were Asian or Pacific Islanders in 1980, by 2004 they made up 3.8 percent of this group. Moreover, in 1980 only 0.8 percent of students were American Indian/Alaska Native, and by 2004 they comprised 0.9 percent. However, the distribution of these demographic changes has occurred unevenly across the country. In only six states (California, Hawaii, Louisiana, Mississippi, New Mexico, and Texas) and the District of Columbia, 50 percent or more of students are non-White. Not only does Figure 1.1 depict the percentage of U.S. children from birth to seventeen years by race and Hispanic origin from 1980 to 2006, but also the projected percentage from 2007 to 2020. For example, by 2020, the White, non-

Figure 1.1   Percentage of U.S. Children Ages Birth to Seventeen Years by Race and Hispanic Origin, 1980–2004, and Projected 2005–2020.

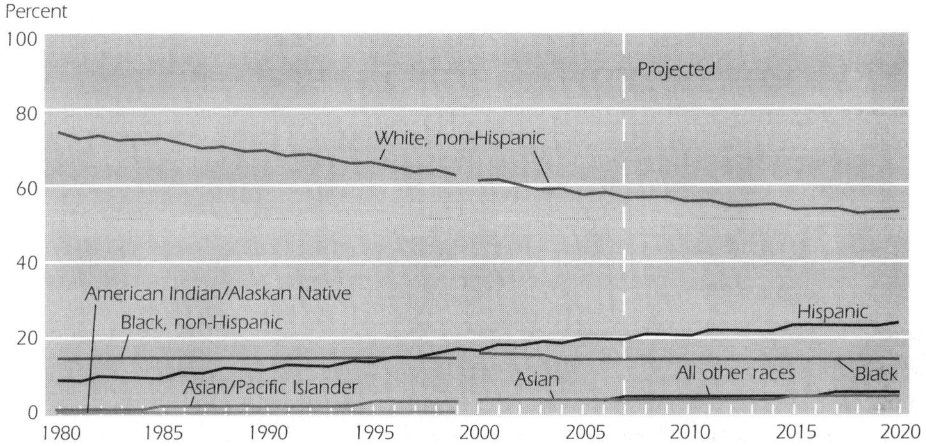

Source: Childstats.gov. (2006). America's children in brief: Key national indicators of well-being, 2006. Retrieved June 18, 2007, from www.childstats.gov/americaschildren/pop3.asp.

Note: Data from 2000 onward are not directly comparable with data from earlier years. Data on race and Hispanic origin are collected separately; Hispanics may be any race. In 1980 and 1990, following the 1977 OMB standards for collecting and presenting data on race, the decennial census gave respondents the option to identify with one race from the following: White, Black, American Indian or Alaskan Native, or Asian or Pacific Islander. The Census Bureau also offered an "Other" category. Beginning in 2000, following the 1977 OMB standards for collecting and presenting data on race, the decennial census gave respondents the option to identify with one or more races from the following: White, Black, Asian, American Indian or Alaska Native, and Native Hawaiian or Other Pacific Islander. In addition, "Some other race" category was included with OMB approval. Those who chose more than one race were classified as "Two or more races." Except for the "All other races" category, all race groups discussed from 2000 onward refer to people who indicated only one racial identity. (Those who were "Two or more races" were included in the "All other races" category, along with American Indians or Alaska Natives and Native Hawaiians or Other Pacific Islanders).

Hispanic population is projected to decrease to approximately 55 percent, and the Hispanic population is projected to increase to about 25 percent.

Meanwhile, due to the declining enrollments of Hispanics, Asians, and African Americans in teacher education, today's teaching force is becoming increasingly White European American. White teachers currently account for some 86 percent of the teaching force, and teachers of color collectively account for only 14 percent. Moreover, most teachers are White European Americans from middle-class backgrounds and speak English only, yet they have many students who are people of color, live in poverty, and/or speak a first language that is not English (National Center for Education Statistics 2005). Because of these differing life circumstances, teachers find that they do not have the same cultural frames of reference or points of view as their students, and they live in "different existential worlds" (Gay 2000). As a result, teachers often label such children and their families as deficient and have difficulty serving as role models for their students (Villegas & Lucas 2002) or as cultural brokers helping students bridge the differences between their home and school worlds (Gay 2000; Goodwin 2000). Teachers also have difficulty in developing curriculum, instruction, and classroom interactions that are culturally responsive (Ladson-Billings 1995).

Indicative of the difficulties that White, middle-class educators have had in effectively teaching students who are not like themselves is the staggering disparity in the educational outcomes and conditions for students from diverse cultural groups who are poor. The United States has the highest rate of children who live in poverty among advanced nations worldwide (Children's Defense Fund 2005), and the percentage of Black and Hispanic children who live in poverty (42 percent and 40 percent, respectively) far exceeds the percentage of White children (16 percent). Further, the achievement levels of Blacks and Hispanic students on the National Assessment of Educational Progress (NAEP) mathematics and reading assessments are markedly lower than levels for White students (National Center for Education Statistics 2005), as are high school graduation rates (Orfield 2004). Villegas and Lucas (2002) assert: "The consistent gap between racial/ethnic minority and poor students and their White, middle-class peers . . . is indicative of the inability of the educational system to effectively teach students of color as schools have been traditionally structured" (9).

In addition to the staggering differences in educational outcomes are major differences in the allocation of resources (e.g., teacher quality, equipment, supplies, physical facilities, books, access to computer technology, and class size) to urban, suburban, and rural schools (Darling-Hammond & Young 2002). In addition, growing evidence shows that children of color and children who live in urban or poor areas are the most likely to have teachers who are not fully qualified or licensed to teach (Darling-Hammond & Young 2002; Darling-Hammond & Sclan 1996). Take a moment and consider your expectations for the children you will teach by completing Reflective Exercise 1.1.

Reflective Exercise 1.1

Your Vision of Your Future Life as a Teacher

Imagine yourself five years from now. You may be starting your third or fourth year as a teacher and are reflecting on your previous experience as you prepare for the new school year. Describe the following:

1. Whom do you envision you will be teaching? (Student grade level? Type of student population in terms of race, SES, disability?)
2. Where do you envision you will be teaching? (i.e., geographic location and school site, such as urban or rural; private/public school/parochial school)
3. What will you be teaching? (What subjects do you most enjoy? Why? What subjects do you least enjoy? Why?)

4. How will you be teaching? (What does your classroom look like? How is it equipped? How are you interacting with students?)

5. Are you interacting with anyone else?

6. How and when are you interacting with adults from students' homes? How and when are you interacting with other adults at your school? What do you most appreciate about your relationships with these other adults?

7. Why are you teaching? (i.e., What are the personal results you want to create in the world? What is the legacy you want to leave to the children, other educators, or community with whom you work?)

Reflection: What was it like creating your answer to this assignment? What was the hardest part to imagine? The easiest?

From this picture, what can you infer are your assumptions or underlying beliefs about:

What your classroom of students will be like (e.g., how will the students learn)?

How you should teach so that your students learn?

How students' families should be involved with you?

How other school staff should be involved with you?

What information do you have about the present and future that supports or contradicts your assumptions? Which assumptions need to be examined more carefully?

The Influence of Families on Children's School Success

What does all of this mean? Are children from poor or culturally diverse families destined to fail in school? Are such families incapable and/or unwilling to help their children succeed in school? As early as the 1980s, researchers who studied the family's impact on children's academic achievement began reporting that some children from low-income, culturally diverse families did very well in school. They found that neither family socioeconomic status, cultural group membership, nor type of family structure (e.g., single-parent versus two-parent) was the main predictor of children's school success or failure (Clark 1983; Dornbush, Ritter, Leiderman, Roberts & Fraleigh 1987). What appeared to make the difference was not the families' social class position but their engagement in their children's learning and development. As Clarke (1990) asserted: "It was not class position that determined a family's ability to support their children's learning, rather it was the child's development of 'survival knowledge' for competent classroom role enactment resulting from the positive attitudes and communication encounters they had with family members" (121).

Over the past two decades, many more researchers (Bempechat 1998; Collignon, Men & Tan 2001; Dornbush & Ritter 1992; Eccles & Harold 1996; Edin & Lein 1997; Furstenburg, Cook, Eccles, Elder & Sameroff 1999; Jeynes 2003; Murry, Brody, Brown, Wisenbaker, Cutrona & Simons 2002) have studied the specific ways that non-White, low-income families function together to positively influence their children's school achievements. Edin and Lein (1997), for example, in their interviews with 379 low-income, single mothers, discovered families living in extreme poverty and deprivation who demonstrated surprising resilience and creativity in building strategies to help their children overcome poor life conditions. Even with low incomes and the struggles of getting and keeping public assistance, a high proportion of these economically disadvantaged families was able to keep their children in school, set family rules, get children to school on time, monitor their children's whereabouts, organize their households, and engage their children in developmentally appropriate activities. As a result, children in these families had higher grades and test scores, better long-term academic achievement (Eccles & Harold 1996; Henderson & Mapp 2002; Jeynes 2003), better student attendance and attitudes about school, greater maturation, and more positive self-concepts (Bempechat 1998; Cox 2005; Sheldon & Epstein 2002; Swap 1995).

What does all of this add up to? First, teachers and schools do not educate alone. Instead, a child's family can make the difference in whether the child succeeds in gaining an education from schools. Second, educators cannot simply blame families or invoke income or social class as an explanation for children's failure to learn. Instead, educators need to connect with families to bridge the chasm between the school and life experiences of those without social, cultural, racial, and economic advantages. Such an effort requires fundamental changes in the ways teachers teach and structure their relations with students, their families, and other persons in the community (Cochran-Smith 2004).

Changing Models of Teaching and Learning

Historically, teachers and schools have been expected to be the exclusive experts at "delivering" education to children. They are supposed to be all-knowing, make no mistakes, be completely organized, have everything "under control," and have all students "on task" (McCaleb 1994). Children's social, economic, and cultural backgrounds have often been viewed as obstacles to be addressed or overcome outside the classroom through provision of parent education or specialized mental health or social services (Dryfoos 1994). The basic structure of roles in schools has been top-down and bureaucratic. Teachers and schools have not placed much value or invested much effort in building collaborative relationships with students or with their families. Instead, students and parents have been expected to accommodate to the school and "follow its lead." Those parents who do not "come when called" by the school for various events or conferences are viewed as "not caring," "deficient" (i.e., lacking time, interest, or competence), "hard to reach," and "having little to offer to the education of their children" (Lott 2001; Pianta & Walsh 1996).

Yet there is now overwhelming evidence that parents from all income groups care about their children, want them to succeed in school, talk about the importance of schools, and say they would like to be more involved in the school or at home in helping their children. However, many parents, especially those from lower socio-economic groups, feel reticent about communicating with the school. These parents report feeling unsure about how to help their children succeed in school because they lack confidence, communication skills, and knowledge about the teaching and learning processes used in schools (Hoover-Dempsey, Walker, Sandler, Whetsel, Green, Wilkins & Closson 2005; Lareau & Horvat 1999; Lott 2001).

In contrast to affluent parents, the communication that low-income parents have with schools is typically negative and problem-focused. Most of these parents perceive themselves as being talked down to and blamed when required to interact with school staff. Despite wanting an equal, person-to-person relationship and not a "professional–client" relationship with school staff, many parents report that they are often dissatisfied with school personnel who are "too business-like" or "patronizing" or who "talk down" to them. Culturally disenfranchised groups are particularly vulnerable to feelings of judgment and blame. As a result, parents often avoid contact with school staff or view them as adversaries (Lareau 1989; Lareau & Horvat 1999; Lott 2001).

As schools have grown larger, and busing has become a fact of life for most students, many schools have become distant, impersonal organizations for families. Although some schools are apparently committed to programs that invite community input and reflect family values, many ethnic and minority parents are intimidated by the large, institutional structure of the school. For some, this feeling may be based on unhappy memories of their own schooling experiences. Others may be intimidated because they are brusquely received, spoken to in a language that they do not understand, or confused by expectations that they do not think they can meet (Finders & Lewis 1994; Lott 2001).

Many educators are now recognizing that these traditional ways of thinking about their role with students and their families do not work for today's students. As educators learn more about the disparities between children's home worlds and culture and the world and culture of school, they are discovering that the traditional ways of "delivering" instruction actually undermine the sense of identity and efficacy of many children (McCaleb 1994; Trumbull, Rothstein-Fisch, Greenfield & Quiroz 2001).

Building on Students' and Families' Funds of Knowledge

〜〜〜〜〜〜〜
〜〜〜〜〜〜〜

When researchers began to look more closely at the educational disparities that exist among middle-class suburban and working-class and poor children, they discovered that children from different home, community, and economic backgrounds learned different "funds of knowledge" (Velez-Ibanez & Greenberg 1992), and that these funds of knowledge are not treated equally in school. We use this phrase, *funds of knowledge*, to mean the various social and linguistic practices and the historically accumulated bodies of knowledge that are essential to students' homes and communities (Moll & Gonzalez 1993). For example, in her influential study, *Ways with Words*, Heath (1983) described the language practices of three communities in the rural Piedmont Carolinas. One was a working-class, predominantly White community; one was a working-class, predominantly Black community; and one was a middle-class community with a history of formal schooling. Heath found that, although the people in these communities lived within a few miles of one another, they socialized their children into talking, reading, and writing in profoundly different ways.

As she followed the children into school, Heath discovered that the differences in language practices among these three groups had significant implications for the children's academic success. To varying degrees, the children from the working-class families, both Black and White, found that they did not know how to show their teachers what they knew in ways the teacher could recognize. Further, these children were often asked to engage in activities that they did not fully understand and found that their teacher talked in ways that were unfamiliar and confusing. Thus, from the start, the culturally diverse, low-income, or working-class children often found school to be a confusing and sometimes uncomfortable place because their ways of knowing were not culturally compatible with the schooling environment (i.e., curriculum, teaching practices, structure, content, materials, organization). In contrast, children from the middle-class homes, where the funds of knowledge corresponded nicely to those that were valued at the school, experienced much less discontinuity. They knew what the teacher was talking about most of the time, and, if they did not, they knew how to ask for help in ways that the teacher recognized. In addition, they were likely to know how to tell stories in ways that the teacher understood. As a result, school failure was a much less likely outcome for the middle-class than for the working-class children. The children from the working-class families, both Black and White, fell behind in school—some early on, others more gradually—and, eventually, dropped out of school. In contrast, the children from the middle-class families, although not all top scholars, ultimately graduated from high school.

Building on Heath's work, other researchers have also described the discontinuities that children from diverse economic and cultural backgrounds can experience between the world that they know at home and the world of school. Moll et al. (1992) and Valdes (1996) examined how schools ignore the Hispanic language and culture of its students. Researchers (Delpit 1995; Foster & Peele 2001) who examined African American students also demonstrated the inadvertent effect of schooling in undermining students' cultural ways of knowing. These researchers (McCaleb 1994; Moll & Gonzalez 1993) discovered that, when the "ways of knowing" of the home and community were discounted or rejected (i.e., when the student felt that people at school did not value the ways of knowing that they brought with them to school), a student's sense of competence and identity was threatened. When the values and teaching of the home were devalued by the school, students often felt forced to choose between allegiance and respect for their teacher(s) and loyalties to their family and home community and to accept one set of ways of knowing and talking and reject the other. Other children reported that they felt ashamed of the language and culture of their parents and other family members. Some children believed that if they took on one identity, they had to give up the other.

Influenced by these findings, many educators (McIntyre, Roseberry & Gonzalez 2001) began to see teaching and learning in a new way. They began to realize that if they could focus on what students' households and communities actually do, they could bring multiple dimensions of students' lived experiences to life in the classroom. Further, these funds of knowledge could become the foundation for student learning of school-based funds of knowledge. For example, Moll and Gonzalez (1993) and McIntyre, Roseberry, and Gonzalez (2001) described how teachers first interviewed families to learn about their distinctive "funds of knowledge" and then used that knowledge to contextualize their instruction and curriculum. In a similar vein, Gay (2000) reported how culturally responsive teachers wove students' cultural knowledge into their classroom conversations. Heath (1983) coached teachers to pay attention to students' different ways of knowing and talking and to not view these abilities as deficits in need of remediation. As a result, teachers were able to help their students use their own ways of knowing and talking as a foundation for learning the language system of the school. Rather than attempting to destroy or replace the language or knowledge that the students brought to school, teachers encouraged students to identify the differences between their familiar world and the unfamiliar world of the classroom. "They became researchers into the reality of their dual language and knowledge worlds, and they gained a new sense of self awareness as they reconstructed a social and cognitive system of meanings" (Heath 1983, 202). By inviting students to articulate how the knowledge that they had gained from their homes and communities related to what the school wanted them to know, they became more successful learners.

The latest research that assesses the effects of various bilingual education approaches mirrors these new ways of thinking about teaching and learning. Many of these programs that build on the home language of non-English-speaking children through a dual-language immersion approach (in which there is a dual emphasis on speaking and reading in the primary or home language and culture and in the secondary language of English) have resulted in stronger academic gains than those resulting from traditional monolingual instructional methods (CREDE

2005). In the dual-language immersion approach, the goal is student bilingualism. The students start off in their primary language, but, over time, the secondary language is introduced during a portion of the day so that, gradually, the primary and secondary languages of instruction are balanced out across the school day. Parents are closely involved in this instructional effort, both in agreeing to this dual language focus and in reinforcing the home/primary language skills and the secondary language skills.

Sharing the Role of Expert with Families

Discovering the value in using children's home and community *funds of knowledge* to contextualize new, school-based knowledge has resulted in many educators rethinking how they might develop their relations with students' families. Rather than relegating family members to an invisible role or only calling upon them when a student has difficulties, these educators are creating strong, ongoing working relationships with students and their families, centered on sharing the role of expert with families. This means working with and learning from families instead of doing to or for families.

To effectively build such relationships, educators need to examine their own beliefs and expectations about how roles should be structured and power shared. Many traditional parent involvement efforts are based on the belief that something is wrong or lacking in families when their children struggle in school, and that, because educators know what parents should be doing, the educator's job is to help parents change their ways of relating to their children and to have parents teach their children the skills that schools deem are important (and in the same manner as the school.) As a result, educators often devise practices, such as (a) giving parents guidelines, materials, and training to carry out school-like activities in the home, (b) training parents in effective parenting, (c) teaching parents about the culture of American schooling, and (d) developing parents' language and literacy skills. These practices inadvertently convey the message that the schools' and educators' knowledge and "ways of knowing" are all important and that the families' knowledge is not important or valued.

However, a growing body of research evidence indicates that families successfully use a wide range of "non-school-like" experiences to teach their children. For example, Taylor and Dorsey-Gaines (1988) studied the literacy practices and experiences of children in poverty-level families and found that, although direct parental instruction in school-like literacy tasks did not occur, families used significant experiences that occurred on a regular basis—such as family outings, a visit to the clinic, or a game of cards—to enhance their children's literacy. The most important aspect in determining whether these were successful literacy experiences seemed to be that children were engaged on a regular basis in activities that were integrated into their lives in meaningful ways.

As a result of these findings, teachers are inviting parents to become significant participants in their children's learning by contributing their oral or written words, ideas, and experiences as part of the text of schooling. For example, McCaleb (1994) developed a project in which Spanish-speaking parents and their first-graders are invited to coauthor books that depict their life and values. These books then become the texts that are used to teach reading and writing in the children's first-grade classrooms.

Practicing No-fault Problem Solving

Teachers are also inviting parents to participate in new ways in resolving children's academic and behavioral difficulties. Traditionally, teachers have met with parents, usually the mother, when children are experiencing difficulties at school (Christenson & Hirsch 1998). Parents usually dread these encounters with the school for fear of being blamed for their children's difficulties. Students are usually left out of these conversations or only included as a punitive measure. Because these are the most common, and the most anxiety-producing encounters that teachers have with parents, a number of educators (Amatea, Daniels, Bringman & Vandiver 2004; Weiss & Edwards 1992) have put considerable effort into redesigning these meetings to change the pattern of fault-finding endemic to them. Amatea et al. (2004), for example, introduced a "no-fault" parent–teacher conference format in which both parents and students are invited to play an active, co-expert role with teachers, and renamed these meetings *family*–school problem-solving conferences. The message is that the student/child can be helped only when everyone—including the student—works together. The school staff developed a concrete action plan with the family (student and parents) in which everyone (family and school) has a task to do to help the child. This action plan is written down and a copy is made for the family and the school. Unique features of this conference format are its task focus, blocking of blame, and involvement of all members of the family as persons who can contribute to resolving the child's problems. Although the development and implementation of a concrete action plan usually helps a child significantly, the more important outcome is the change in the relationships among the students, school staff, and family members. Data from parents and students reveal that they like this new format because it provides a specific approach for the student, teacher, counselor, and family to work together in a *nonblaming context* to develop solutions to students' behavioral or learning problems. Data from teachers reveal that what they most value in this new format is having time to think through possible ways of solving a student's problem together with families and other staff while keeping the blaming between parents and teachers at a low level so that people can remain calm and level-headed while solving problems.

Creating Opportunities for Meaningful, Nonproblematic Interaction

Educators are recognizing that to develop more collaborative relations with students and their families, they need opportunities to have positive, nonproblematic contacts in which the student and family can play meaningful roles. Rather than assign parents to the usual passive roles of audience member or supporter, educators are creating opportunities for parents and students to demonstrate their interest in their child and interact more directly with them. One illustration of this shift to more meaningful roles is the student-led parent conference, in which students are given an opportunity talk about their goals and share their academic work with their parents (Austin 1994; Benson & Barnett 1999; Davies, Cameron, Politano & Gregory 1999). Not only do students share their school progress (academic and behavioral) and develop a plan together with their parents for how to move forward, but also they learn an approach to cooperative planning and problem solving that gives them ways of communicating with their parents in a respectful and cooperative manner (Amatea et al. 2004).

Discovering the Benefits of Connecting with Families

Powerful benefits result from these new ways that educators are connecting with families. First, researchers report positive changes in student grades, homework completion, and student attitudes toward school and teachers when educators work with families at the preschool, elementary, middle school, and high school levels. For example, researchers reported that elementary students' reading literacy improved significantly when their families were involved with their children at home in specific learning activities around reading (Epstein, Herrick & Coates 1996; McCarthy 2000). Homework completion, report card grades, and attitudes about school and teachers were also positively affected by particular activities educators introduced to families of middle and high school students (Epstein & Van Hoorhis 2001; Payan, Jayanthi & Polloway 2001; Scott-Jones 1995). Lee (1994) revealed that educators' efforts to enhance families' involvement in monitoring and interacting with their high school age children about homework, and, particularly, family discussions about schoolwork, courses, grades, and the future, had strong positive effects on high school students' report card grades and attitudes about school and teachers.

Second, parents reap benefits from participating in their child's schooling. Not only do parents develop a greater appreciation for their important role in their child's learning, but also family–school connections impact parents' sense of adequacy and self-worth, strengthen their social network, motivate them to resume their own education, and enhance their view of their child's teacher and school (Dauber & Epstein 1993; Hoover-Dempsey, Walker, Sandler, Whetsel, Green, Wilkins & Closson 2005). For example, a study of parent involvement in elementary schools found that parents' confidence in their ability to help their children with school tasks was increased when teachers coached them on how to help their children with schoolwork (Dauber & Epstein 1993). Moreover, teachers' practices in reaching out to students' families strongly influenced what families did to support their children's learning and schooling (Epstein 2001.) In fact, what teachers do to connect with the families of their students appears to be a much stronger predictor of family involvement in their children's school progress than family background variables, such as race, ethnicity, social class, marital status, or mother's work status (Walker, Sandler, Whetsel, Green, Wilkins & Closson 2005).

Third, many teachers report significant benefits from collaborating with parents, such as (a) strengthened school programs through expansion of teaching resources, (b) improved student academic achievement, (c) improved student behavior and reduced student discipline problems, (d) greater retention of student skills over the summer because of work conducted at home during the vacation, (e) more favorable perceptions of families, and (f) reduction in their feelings of isolation and nonsupport (Hoover-Dempsey & Sandler 2005; Sheldon & Epstein 2002). For example, a study of parent involvement in elementary schools found that parents and principals rated teachers higher in overall teaching ability and interpersonal skills if the teachers frequently used practices of parent involvement (Dauber & Epstein 1993; Epstein 1991). Furthermore, a large scale study of elementary teachers, parents, and students, revealed that teachers who were "leaders" in the frequent use of parent involvement did not prejudge less-educated, poor, or single parents (Dauber & Epstein 1991). Those teachers who frequently involved families in their children's education rated single and married parents and more and less formally educated parents equally in helpfulness and follow-through with their children at home. By contrast, teachers who did not frequently involve families gave more stereotypical ratings to single parents and to those with less formal education, marking them lower in helpfulness and follow-through than other parents.

Identifying the Barriers

The ways of working that we describe in this book take time, reflection, and an openness to change. We know that many teachers and administrators say they would like to interact more with their students' families but have neither the time nor the "know how" to go about building such positive and productive relationships and, consequently, are fearful of trying (Epstein 1995). Some teachers do not believe that encouraging parent involvement is a part of their professional role and see it as interfering with the teaching tasks that have been entrusted to them (Christenson & Sheridan 2001).

The culture and work norms of many schools present significant barriers to developing these ways of thinking and working with students and their families. Swap (1993) noted that many teachers expect to be self-sufficient in their teaching practice and to operate independently from their colleagues and from students and parents. "Adult collaboration in any form is relatively rare in schools. . . . The traditional approach to managing schools emphasizes hierarchy, individualism, and technology rather than dialogue, relationship and reciprocity" (17). Moreover, traditional family–school interactions are often designed to avoid conflict by minimizing opportunities for personal contact and expression of differences. Teachers expect to channel parents into passive roles as audience members or supporters at family–school events. Students are often expected to be either absent from such encounters or passive participants.

As a result, few opportunities exist for educators, students, and families to develop skills in working together to enhance student learning, resolve conflicts, develop educational plans, or solve student problems. Krasnow (1990) contends that schools are characteristically structured to withhold negative information to avoid conflict, and neither interpersonal nor intergroup conflict is discussable at school. Because schools have failed to learn how to deal constructively with conflict, they have failed to improve as organizations that represent a broad-based constituency.

In addition, many teachers feel overburdened by expectations to teach in new ways, to develop new curriculum, and to help all students learn and perform well in high-stakes testing. Collaborating with families may not seem possible. Because we know that time is in scarce supply in the lives of educators, we have found that these ways of working can be time-efficient in the long run. We are proposing that teachers not add to what they do but change their existing ways of doing things. Showing educators how to work differently, not add on more work, is our goal in writing this book. Thus, you will see examples of how both individual teachers and entire school staffs have changed how they involve families in their children's school life. Clearly, this new way of working is more impactful when it can extend across the whole school. However, a teacher's influence may not span the entire school. Hence, we showcase individual teacher's experiences with these changes in practices.

The Philosophy That Underlies Our Approach

This book is based upon our experiences working in schools with educators, students and families, and in teaching pre-service courses on family–school involvement to elementary and middle school teachers, counselors, and administrators. As a result of our "front-line" experiences, **we believe that developing strong working relationships with the families of students is not only a nice activity, but also a necessary step for developing effective ways of reaching and teaching all students**. In this book, we describe various ways of learning from students and families and how to use that knowledge to build instructional activities that foster children's learning and development. We believe that interacting with families is a means toward the end of improving students' learning and school achievement, not simply an end in itself. In addition, we do not offer one approach that we assume will work for everyone. Hence, you will see many different ideas showcased about how you might change your teaching practices.

Because these ways of working with students and their families are a radical departure from traditional practices and beliefs, information about these new teaching practices, the research on their effectiveness, and the theory that underlies their development have not been a standard part of teacher preparation programs. Consequently, most beginning education professionals continue to have an exceedingly narrow conception of the role that families might play in their children's schooling—conceptions that all too often keep families in a marginalized, disempowered position.

This book is designed to acquaint you with these new ideas and practices in the field of family–school relationship building and to highlight the changes in thinking that underlies these new educational practices. In this book, we hope to describe

- The changing context of schooling in the United States and the challenges to traditional beliefs and practices about how we, as educators, should interact with students, their families, and their communities
- What practitioners and researchers are learning about how families' beliefs, values, and interactions contribute to children's success in school
- A new approach to family–school relations, the family–school collaboration approach, and the distinctive beliefs and practices that characterize it
- Everyday instructional and noninstructional routines that individual teachers use to communicate, build collaborative partnerships, and forge a sense of co-ownership and connection with students' families and the larger community
- How school staffs are changing the school-wide norms and routines to support a more collaborative way of working with students, their families, and their communities.

Summary

In this chapter we discussed the changing context of schooling in the United States, the research evidence that examines the influence of families on children's school success, and the evidence on the influence of schools on families. Next, we highlighted the revolutionary changes in teacher beliefs and practices that undergird educators' current efforts to build more culturally responsive relationships with students and their families. These new practices require educators to (a) build on students' and families' funds of knowledge, (b) share the role of expert with families, (c) practice no-fault problem solving, and (d) create opportunities for nonproblematic family–school interaction. We then describe the benefits and barriers to be derived from these new ways of interacting with families. Finally, we discuss the philosophy and goals that underlie the development of this book.

Resources

ChildStats.gov,
www.childstats.gov
ChildStats.gov provides information on key national indicators of U.S. children's well-being on an annual basis.

Children 's Defense Fund,
www.childrensdefense.org
The Children's Defense Fund provides effective advocacy for all children in the United States, with a particular attention to the needs of impoverished children from culturally and linguistically diverse backgrounds. This organization offers current data related to trends in children's well-being and highly relevant publications.

Chapter 2

From Separation to Collaboration: The Changing Paradigms of Family–School Relations

Ellen S. Amatea

Learning Objectives

After reading this chapter, you will be able to:

- Explain what is meant by a mental model or paradigm.
- Describe how educators' mental models/paradigms of family–school relationships have changed over time as a result of changes in theory, research, and legislation.

■ Summarize the distinctive assumptions of the separation, remediation, and collaboration paradigms and their influence on educational practice.

■ Describe the benefits and drawbacks of each paradigm of family–school relations.

■ Explain your current mental/model or paradigm of family–school relations and how you may wish to modify it.

> *How are you planning to interact with the families of your students? Would you prefer to have parents come to school only when their child has a problem, or will you encourage them to drop in at will to observe your classroom activities? Do you hope to invite parents to share their expertise and knowledge about their children and their family's culture or do you believe that information is unnecessary? Do you expect to have "the final say" on decisions that you make about your students, or will you share your decision-making power with their parents?*

Each of us—whether educator or parent—operates from a particular "mental model or map" that consists of certain beliefs as to how roles and relations between educators and families should be structured and responsibilities allocated. These beliefs are socially constructed, shaped through our interaction with others and their ideas. As we move through the world we build up our beliefs about what the world is like by means of our conversation with other people. The beliefs we hold about how we should interact with students, their families, our colleagues, and our superiors grow out of responding to the (a) specific implicit or explicit expectations and norms of members of our key reference groups (e.g., our work associates at school, our students and their families, our professional organizations); (b) larger cultural stories or beliefs that shape our own personal conceptions about how we should behave; and (c) actual role experiences and behaviors that we learn to perform (Harrison & Minor 1978).

Our mental model is like a window pane, both clarifying and distorting what we see. For example, as clearly and objectively as we think we see things, we may discover that other people may see the same set of circumstances quite differently based upon their own apparently valid and objective point of view. Sometimes, we may find that our mental model of family–school relations is not supported by the policy (written or unwritten), customs, and culture of the school in which we work. For example, one teacher who wanted to design her classroom's "back to school night" event to include children as well as their parents was met by the response: "We just don't do that around here." In another case, a principal who wanted her teachers to learn more about their students' lives reported that she got raised eyebrows when she suggested that the school staff put on a parent workshop in one of the housing projects where many of the school's students lived. Often, however, our mental models are so widely shared by others in our world, that they are difficult to see. Only when a new mental model or paradigm emerges can we see more clearly the features and assumptions of the old paradigm. This "news of a difference" in our mental model or paradigm is the result, and we are able to compare the features of our old mental model, or way of thinking, with a new way of thinking.

Over the past three decades, three different mental models or paradigms of family–school relations have emerged in the field that prescribe how roles should be structured between home and school. Each of these paradigms is based on distinctly different assumptions about the purposes of family–school interactions, the responsibilities of each role participant, the structure of power relations, and the preferred styles and methods of interaction. As a result, educators may construct widely differing "mental models" about how adults at school and at home should relate with one another. Similarly, parents can hold quite different beliefs about the requirements and expectations of the educator and parent roles.

Before you interact with your students' families, you need to become aware of your current mental model of family–school relations, and discover what other options you have for how you might structure your relations with students and their families. In this chapter we describe three different paradigms/mental models for how educators *should* work with parents: (a) the separation paradigm, (b) the remediation paradigm, and (c) the collaboration paradigm. Each of these paradigms represents a consistent pattern of assumptions, goals, attitudes, behaviors, and strategies that help us understand how people believe that families and school staff should behave with one another. You will find educators who operate from each of these paradigms in today's schools. In this book we hope to encourage you to move toward a more collaborative paradigm in working with the families of your students. But first, let us explain what we mean by a paradigm.

Understanding Paradigms

The word *paradigm* comes from the Greek. It was originally a scientific term and is more commonly used today to mean a model, theory, perception, assumption, or frame of reference. In the more general sense, it is the way we "see" the world—not in terms of our visual sense of sight, but in terms of how we perceive, understand, and interpret the world. A paradigm depicts distinctive ways of "ordering experience" or of "constructing reality" (Bruner 1996, 11). For our purposes, a simple way to understand family–school paradigms is to think of them as "mental maps of relationships." Of course, we all know that the map is not the territory. That is, a map is simply a depiction/explanation about certain aspects of a territory. That is exactly what a paradigm is. It is a theory, a system of explanation or model of something, a larger cultural story or *discourse* that describes how our particular social world operates, how you and others should behave, and how we should "see" reality.

Why might you want to examine your paradigm? Suppose you wanted to arrive at a specific location in central Miami. A street map of the city would be a great help to you in reaching your destination. But suppose you were given the wrong map. Through a printing error, the map labeled "Miami" was actually a map of "Orlando." Can you imagine the frustration, the ineffectiveness of trying to reach your destination? You might decide to work on your *behavior*—you could try harder, be more diligent, or double your speed. But if you were using the wrong map, your efforts to find your way to your destination in Miami would only succeed in your getting yourself to the wrong place faster.

Or you might decide to work on your *attitude*—you could think more positively. However, you still would not get to the right place using the mislabeled map as your guide, but perhaps you would not care. Your attitude would be positive, so that you would be happy wherever you were. Our point is, with the wrong map, you would still be lost. The fundamental problem has nothing to do with your behavior or your attitude. It has everything to do with having a wrong map. If you have the correct map of Miami, then diligence becomes important, and when you encounter frustrating obstacles along the way, then attitude can make a real difference. But the first and most important requirement is the accuracy of the map.

Each of us has many mental models or maps in our heads about a variety of aspects of our social worlds. We interpret everything that we experience through these mental maps. Yet we seldom question their accuracy. We simply *assume* that the way we see things is the way they really are or the way they should be. For example, we may assume that inclusion of students with disabilities into regular classrooms or tracking students by ability levels is the ideal way to organize schooling and instruction. As a result, we will see the evidence to support these assumptions much more readily than evidence that does not support them.

More important, although each of us tends to think that we see things as they are, that we are objective, in fact we see the world not as *it is* but as *we are*—or as we are taught to see it by others in our social world. Consequently, when we open our mouths to describe what we see (in our classroom, our school, our community), in effect, we describe our perceptions and mental models. When other people disagree with us, we immediately think that something is wrong with them. However, sincere, clearheaded people can see things quite differently because they are following their own mental map.

This does not mean that no facts exist. However, the more aware we are of our basic mental models or paradigms and the extent to which we have been influenced by our experience, the more we can take responsibility for them, examine them, test them against reality, listen to others and be open to their perceptions, and thereby get a larger picture and far richer view.

The Power of a Paradigm Shift

Perhaps the most important insight to be gained from studying the different ways that people look at their social world is in the area of paradigm shifting—what we might call the *Aha!* experience when someone finally "sees" a certain situation in another way. The more bound people are by their initial perception, the more powerful the *Aha!* experience. The experience is as if a light were suddenly turned on inside our heads. The term *paradigm shift* was introduced by Thomas Kuhn (1970) in his highly influential book, *The Structure of Scientific Revolutions.* Kuhn showed how almost every significant breakthrough in various scientific fields is first a break with tradition, with old ways of thinking, with old paradigms. For Ptolemy, the great Egyptian astronomer, Earth was the center of the universe. But Copernicus created a paradigm shift, and a great deal of resistance and persecution as well, by placing the sun at the center. Suddenly, everything took on a different interpretation. The Newtonian model of physics was a clockwork paradigm that is still the basis of modern engineering. But it was a partial, incomplete view of the world. The scientific world was revolutionized by the paradigm proposed by Einstein, the relativity paradigm, which had much higher predictive and explanatory value. According to Kuhn (1970), when a paradigm becomes established and dominates public discourse, it becomes difficult for other systems of explanation to emerge and to become institutionalized. When one paradigm replaces another, Kuhn states, a scientific revolution takes place. However, in education and the social sciences, rarely does one paradigm replace another. More typically, new paradigms compete with established ones, and they coexist. So the educational world is characterized by competing paradigms and explanations.

The educational world has experienced two significant paradigm shifts regarding family–school relations in the United States. The first paradigm shift involves a shift from educators who assume that they can operate successfully on their own in educating students despite what students experience at home to believing that they need to educate and remediate families to support the school's efforts to educate their children. For example, the *separation paradigm* was depicted by educators and policymakers in the 1960s who made no provision for interaction with parents and believed that educators alone could minimize the impact of low-income conditions by offering compensatory education to remediate children from low-income families. This paradigm of separation was represented in the Elementary and Secondary Education Act of 1965, the federal compensatory education initiative, in which assumption was made that the school environment could mitigate the poor or negative experiences provided by the home and compensate for the disadvantaged background of certain students. By the late 1970s, however, educators and policymakers had shifted to a *remediation paradigm* in which educational programs that served economically disadvantaged children were required to involve parents in their children's education. This remediation paradigm is illustrated by the Education Amendments of 1978 that made explicit reference to the requirement of parent participation in programs designed for economically disadvantaged children.

We are now experiencing another paradigm shift in family–school relations as the educational world is revolutionized by the *paradigm of collaboration*. With this shift in thinking, school staffs embrace the idea of seeing students and their families as collaborators in the effort to educate children. Instead of assuming the role of expert and believing that the school staff know best about how to "fix" students or families, educators are reaching out to students' families, viewing them as co-experts and sharing power with them, and identifying *together* those resources that exist in the family and school for taking action to enhance children's learning or resolve their difficulties.

Several factors have contributed to this second paradigm shift toward family–school collaboration. First, theories of child development, such as Bronfenbrenner's ecological systems theory (1979; 1986a), shifted the focus from exclusively emphasizing how the family influences the child's development to underscoring how the broader sociopolitical context influences the attitudes and resources that shape how schools and communities interact with students' families. Hence, rather than just looking at family life, educators began to see how a child's family, school, and community *collectively influence* a child's development by means of their interactions. In addition, theorists, such as Vygotsky (1978), a Soviet psychologist, who studied how children learn, revolutionized how educators think about the teaching and learning of children from low-income, culturally diverse families (McIntyre, Roseberry & Gonzalez 2001).

Second, research has consistently shown that students' home environments and out-of-school time contribute powerfully to their learning (Hoover-Dempsey, Walker, Sandler, Whetsel & Green 2007; Weiss, Mayer, Kreider, Vaughan, Dearing & Hencke 2003). Researchers who study what families do to support children's learning and development have repeatedly documented the powerful influence that families have on the in-school and out-of-school socialization of children. For example, whether through home-based modeling, instruction, and reinforcement or school-based activities or parent-teacher communication, family influence and involvement have been repeatedly documented to be positively linked to indicators of student achievement, including teacher ratings of student competence, student grades, and achievement test scores (e.g., Deslandes, Royer, Potvin & Leclerc 1999; Epstein & Van Voorhis 2001; Fan & Chen 1999; Hill & Craft 2003). Family involvement and influence have also been strongly associated with other indicators of school success, including lower rates of retention in grade, lower drop-out rates, higher on-time high school graduation rates, and higher participation in advanced courses (Barnard 2004; Ma 1999; Marcon 1999; Trusty 1999). Family involvement has also been linked to important psychological processes and cognitive, social, and behavioral attributes that support student achievement, such as students' sense of personal competence or efficacy for learning ("I *can* do this work"; e.g., Frome & Eccles 1998); their mastery orientation (Gonzales, Holbin & Quilter 2002); their perceptions of personal control over school outcomes (Glasgow, Dornbush, Troyer, Steinberg & Ritter 1997); their self-regulatory knowledge and skills ("I know *how* to do this work"; e.g., Brody, Flor & Gibson 1999); as well as their beliefs about the importance of education ("I *want* to do this work"; e.g., Grolnick, Ryan & Deci 1991; Sheldon & Epstein 2002).

Third, federal policies for family involvement established in various laws began to explicitly link families and schools and encouraged educators to consider how school policies and practices influence their relationships with families. For example, the Improving America's Schools Act of 1994 (Pub. L. 103–382) includes detailed parental involvement components designed to empower parents to be a part of their child's educational program, while charging Title I- (formerly Chapter I of the Education Consolidation Improvement Act of 1981) funded schools to provide avenues for them to do so. In addition, National Education Goals 1 and 8, which are presented in Table 2.1, lay out the expectation that every child will start school ready to learn, and that every school will promote partnerships that increase parent participation in facilitating the social, emotional, and academic growth of children (National Education Goals Panel 1999).

These ideas were further explicated in other legislation, such as the Individuals with Disabilities Education Act (IDEA; U.S. Congress 1999; 2004), the IASA

Table 2.1   National Educational Goals 1 and 8

Goal 1: School readiness. "By the year 2000, all children in America will start school ready to learn. The objectives for this goal are that

- All children will have access to high-quality and developmentally appropriate preschool programs that help prepare children for school.
- Every parent in the United States will be a child's first teacher and devote time each day to helping such parent's preschool child learn, and parents will have access to the training and support parents need.
- Children will receive the nutrition, physical activity experiences, and health care needed to arrive at school with healthy minds and bodies and to maintain the mental alertness necessary to be prepared to learn, and the number of low-birth weight babies will be significantly reduced through enhanced prenatal health systems." (8)

Goal 8: Parent participation. "By the year 2000, every school will promote partnerships that will increase parental involvement and participation in promoting the social, emotional, and academic growth of children. The objectives for this goal are that

- Every state will develop policies to assist local schools and local educational agencies to establish programs for increasing partnerships that respond to the varying needs of parents and the home, including parents of children who are disadvantaged or bilingual, or parents of children with disabilities.
- Every school will actively engage parents and families in a partnership that supports the academic work of children at home and shared educational decision-making at school.
- Parents and families will help ensure that schools are adequately supported and will hold schools and teachers to high standards of accountability. (36)

Note: From Goals 2000: Educate America Act, Public Law 103–227.

Title 1 (U.S. Department of Education 1997), and the No Child Left Behind Act of 2001 Title 1 and Title 3 (U.S. Department of Education 2001), all of which underscore the pivotal role that families play in developing children's learning habits and values. The Individuals with Disabilities Education Act (IDEA; U.S. Congress 1999) and its reauthorization (IDEA 2004) require state education agencies and local education agencies to provide every student who has a disability with a free, appropriate public education. One part of the law, Part B, provides for the education of students ages three through twenty-one; another part, Part C, provides for the education of infants and toddlers, from birth to age three. Table 2.2 describes the six key principles of IDEA that have contributed to an awareness of the need for more collaborative relationships between schools and families.

The No Child Left Behind Act of 2001 (Public L. 107–110) embodies six principles of parental involvement that empowers parents to be a part of their children's educational and explicitly commanded Title I-funded (formerly Chapter I of the Education Consolidation Improvement Act of 1981) schools to provide avenues for parents to do so. Not only does this law increase the means for parents to monitor and evaluate the academic progress of their child, but also it requires schools to inform parents about the performance of the whole school and their options if their child's school is not making adequate yearly progress in meeting state-mandated achievement outcomes. Table 2.3 describes NCLB's six principles for school reform.

Table 2.2   Six Principles of IDEA

Zero Reject. Enroll all children and youth, including all those with disabilities.

Nondiscriminatory Evaluation. Determine whether an enrolled student has a disability and, if so, the nature of special education and related services that the student requires.

Appropriate Education. Tailor the student's education to address the student's individualized needs and strengths and ensure that this education benefits the student.

Least Restrictive Environment. To the maximum extent appropriate for the student, ensure that every student receives education in the general education environment, and do not remove the student from regular education unless the nature or severity of the disability is such that education in the general education classes with the use of supplementary aids and services cannot be achieved satisfactorily.

Procedural Due Process. Implement a system of checks and balances so that parents and professionals may hold each other accountable for providing the student with a free and appropriate public education in the least restrictive environment.

Parent Participation. Implement the parent participation rights related to every principle and grant parents an access to educational records and opportunities to serve on state and local special education advisory committees.

Table 2.3   *Six Principles of NCLB*

Accountability for Results. Reward school districts and schools that improve and reform those that do not improve student academic achievement.

School Safety. Acknowledge that all children need a safe environment in which to learn and achieve. Require states to report on school safety to the public and districts to establish a plan for keeping schools safe and drug free.

Parental Choice. Grant parents the right to transfer their child from a "failing" or "unsafe" school to a better and safer one.

Teacher Quality. Recognize that learning depends on teaching; students achieve when they have good teachers. Hence, federal aid is made conditional upon states' agreement to hire "highly qualified" teachers.

Scientifically Based Methods of Teaching. Assumes that teaching and learning depend not only on highly qualified teachers but also on teachers' use of scientifically based methods of teaching. Hence, federal funds are to be granted to states and school districts that use only those methods.

Local Flexibility. Encourages local solutions for local problems and does not hold schools accountable for student outcomes unless the schools can also use federal funds to respond to local problems in unique local ways.

A Typology of Family–School Paradigms

How might we make sense of these changing ideas about family–school relations? At first glance, the term *family–school collaboration* may be easily confused with the term *parent involvement*. Yet these terms represent significantly different paradigms about the nature of the family–school relationship. Whereas parent involvement depicts a one-way flow of information between schools and parents, family–school collaboration involves a two-way exchange of information (Christenson & Sheridan 2001). In addition, while parent involvement focuses on parents becoming involved in their children's education, family–school collaboration focuses on the joint involvement of parents/caregivers and school staff in children's education.

Let us look more closely at how researchers have depicted these varying beliefs about how family–school relations should be structured. Swap (1993) described four distinctive philosophies of family–school relations held by educators: (a) protective philosophy, (b) school-to-home transmission philosophy, (c) curriculum philosophy, and (d) partnership philosophy. Henderson, Jones, and Raimondo (1999) identified four philosophies that characterize a school's relations with families: (a) fortress mentality, (b) "come when called" mentality, (c) "open door" mentality, and (d) partnership mentality. In contrast, Lewis and Forman (2002) identified three distinctive "narratives" about parents depicted in the conversations of school staffs: (a) in loco parentis narrative, (b) deficit narrative, and (c) relational narrative. Although each of these typologies emphasizes different aspects of family–school relations, they consistently point to the importance of two basic dimensions. The first dimension depicts variations in the structure of power relations between parents and educators (i.e., the extent to which one role participant has more social power than the other). The second dimension concerns the extent to which educators and parents view their roles and responsibilities as shared and overlapping or as specialized and separate. We have integrated the thinking of Swap (1993); Henderson, Jones, and Raimondo (1999); and Lewis and Forman (2002) into a typology of three different family–school paradigms. In the following sections we describe each of these paradigms and identify the expectations as to the roles and responsibilities that educators, students, and parents should play; the purposes and styles of communication and decision-making; the structure of power relations; and the specific practices in which educators engage.

The Separation Paradigm

Some educators believe that home and school should be separate "spheres," each having separate goals and responsibilities and providing different inputs to the education and socialization of children (Coleman 1987; Epstein 2001). These educators might say: "The school's job is to help children learn; the parents' job is to inculcate values which prepare their children for learning and schooling. If parents have any role at all in the school sphere, it is that of encouraging children's compliance with the school's socializing and academic demands" (Weiss & Edwards 1992, 219). According to Swap (1993), this philosophy is driven by three assumptions: (a) that parents delegate to the school the responsibility of educating their children, (b) that parents hold the school personnel accountable for the results, and (c) that educators accept this delegation of responsibility.

Educators who operate from this paradigm assume that parents rely upon their expertise, and that direction and discussion with parents (or with students) to do their job are not needed. They believe that the teacher's job is to provide an academic, and often social and emotional, education with very limited or no participation from students' families. Parent involvement in decision-making or problem solving is seen as an inappropriate interference with the educator's job. Instead, educators believe that their decisions (whether about classroom instruction or individual children's class placement) do not require negotiation and hence can be made independently of interaction with students' families. Educators who embrace the separation mindset consider this arrangement ideal for minimizing conflict and for maintaining their professional autonomy. These educators assume that, because parents delegate children's learning to the school, conversations with parents are necessary only when there are problems. As a result, communication between parents and educators is implicit, limited, indirect, and based on tacit agreement and presumed mutual goals.

The origin of this philosophy that home and school are separate spheres has been attributed to the school management theory that developed in the late nineteenth and early twentieth centuries, when many schools faced the challenge of inducting large numbers of children of immigrants into the American culture (Reich 1983). In this bureaucratic management theory, educators viewed their purpose as educating students to be American citizens. They saw schools as giant "factories" organized to educate children for their role in society on a high volume, large batch basis. There was often a rigid boundary constructed between the school and the home so as to reduce the cultural impact of the home and increase the school's socializing influence in producing American citizens. Schools were managed in a top-down, hierarchical fashion with the *separate* operation of each part, or component, determined by a grand design developed by the organizational layer above it. For example, teachers were individually responsible for designing and delivering to their batch of students an educational experience in a specific, separate domain whose content was determined by standards set at higher organizational levels (e.g., district and state level curriculum mandates/standards for first grade level or for eleventh grade English).

Educators who embrace this philosophy *assume* that interaction between educators and families is inherently conflictual and should be kept to a minimum to minimize the inherent/inevitable conflict between these two parties. This should be done primarily through the separation of parents' and educators' functions. Second, this clear separation of functions should also be based on the idea that schools clearly have more competence at teaching, have been delegated responsibility for teaching the child, and see families as deficient in educating their children. Thus, the role of expert is not shared. Swap (1993) labeled this mental model as the protective model because its aim is to protect the school/teacher from conflict and interference by parents. The following teacher's comment illustrates the expectations for desirable parent behavior held by teachers operating in this paradigm:

> Parents should adhere to the rules and trust teachers to do what is right by their children. They should trust the fact that the teachers are following the program. (Swap 1993, 29)

As a result, in this paradigm the preferred style of interaction between educators and families is a very distant, impersonal one. Events are impersonal and highly ritualized (such as the traditional open house in which educators tell parents about their program), communication is one-way (from educator to families), and opportunities for authentic dialogue are greatly restricted. One of the consequences of using this philosophy is that it is generally very effective at achieving its goal of protecting teachers against parental intrusion in most circumstances. However, it assumes that teachers are familiar enough with each child's context to be able to function effectively in place of the parent, knowing what each child needs. Unfortunately, as Swap (1993) describes, the negative consequences of operating from this paradigm are that "this approach to family–school relations often (a) exacerbates the conflicts between home and school by creating no structures or predictable opportunities for preventive problem solving, (b) ignores the potential of home–school collaboration for improving student achievement, and (c) rejects the rich resources for enrichment and school support available from families and other members of the community that could be available to the school" (29). For example, when a student experiences academic or emotional difficulties, school staff often do not call upon a student's parents until all other avenues within the school have been exhausted. When they do meet with parents, educators often delegate responsibility to the family to "fix" the child and assume that the parents will think like them regarding their child's difficulties. Viewed this way, educators often see that the solution to children's learning problems is to "take over the job of educating and socializing children and put it in the hands of real experts since the parents obviously are not equipped to prepare their children" (Swap, 1993, 30).

Educators who operate from this paradigm assume that working-class and poor parents generally are not capable of contributing in significant positive ways to their children's education and development. Lewis and Forman (2002) captured the essence of this thinking in their observation: "Many urban schools have taken the posture of educating students in spite of their families rather than in concert with them" (82). As a result, educators have high expectations for students but limited or low expectations for their parents.

Evidence of this paradigm can be found in several recent reform initiatives that exhort educators to raise their expectations for the potential of their working-class and low-income students and to work to narrow the achievement gap among students of different classes and races, yet do not articulate a significant or visible role for parents in accomplishing these objectives. For example, in the popular Success for All reading initiative, parents are not mentioned in any particular area of work but are identified only in terms of supporting them in getting their child to school or being the recipient of social or psychological resources. Although the role of parents may be evolving in this project, it would appear from the written materials that the relationship between parents and educators is one of separate spheres. As a result, the nature of family–school relations in the separation paradigm might be depicted as a tall fortress with a deep moat around it (Figure 2.1). Why is a fortress an appropriate illustration of this philosophy of interacting with families? The reason is not only does it depict educators structuring their roles with families so as to have a great deal of protective distance from them, but also it shows the lack of a permanent structure for interacting with them.

The Remediation Paradigm

In the 1950s educators began to recognize that the impact of family life strongly influences children's school success and that to succeed in educating students, educators need students' families to support the school's efforts. Fueled by the growing interest in looking at the social context of the developing child and the discrepan-

Figure 2.1   The Fortress Mentality of the Separation Paradigm of Family–School Relations

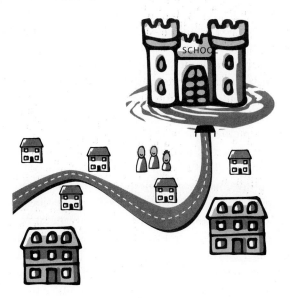

cies in academic achievement observed between students from affluent and those from economically deprived backgrounds, educators began to shift their thinking from believing that they could educate children in spite of their families to believing that their efforts at educating students were undermined by the problems and pathologies of their families. Embracing the deficit view of family life promoted by social scientists and mental health professionals of that era, educators believe that some families are flawed by problems or deficiencies and that these parents need to be remediated by showing them how to create environments that support their children's school success. As a result, unlike the "hands off" philosophy depicted in the separation paradigm, educators who embrace the remediation paradigm expect to be very involved with parents in encouraging them to actively adopt and support the values and "ways of being" that have traditionally led to children's success in school.

In the remediation paradigm, educators believe that their views of what students need to learn to succeed should be dominant, that they know best. Consequently, educators who operate from this philosophy are focused on enlisting the parent to support the objectives of the school. Swap (1993), who termed this *family-to-school transmission* philosophy, asserted that this paradigm is "based on the assumptions that (a) children's achievement is fostered by a continuity of expectations between home and school, (b) educators know which values and practices outside the school contribute to school success, and (c) parents should endorse educators' ideas regarding the importance of schooling, reinforce school expectations at home, provide conditions at home that nurture development and support school success, and ensure that the child meets minimum academic and social requirements" (30).

Many current parent involvement efforts are based on this philosophy. In contrast to the separation paradigm, the remediation paradigm acknowledges that there is (and should be) a continuous interchange between the home and school, and that parents have an important role in enhancing children's educational achievement. Epstein (1987) illustrates this viewpoint by the following statement: "The evidence is clear that parental encouragement, activities, and interest at home and participation in schools and classrooms affect children's achievements, attitudes and aspirations, even after student ability, and family socio-economic status are taken into account. Students gain in personal and academic development if their families emphasize schooling, let the children know they do, and do so continually over the school years" (120).

In her early work, Epstein (1987) proposed four ways that parents might support their children's schooling: (a) providing the basic necessities to their children, such as food, clothing, and shelter; (b) communicating with the school; (c) involving themselves at school; and (d) involving themselves in learning activities in the home. More recently, Epstein (1995; 2001) has expanded this typology by proposing six types of school-related opportunities for parent involvement in their children's learning: (a) assisting parents in child-rearing skills, (b) communicating school information to parents, (c) involving parents in school volunteer opportunities, (d) involving parents in home-based learning, (e) involving parents in school decision-making, and (f) involving parents in school–community activities.

As a result of these role expectations, educators who embrace the remediation paradigm perceive that their job is to tell parents what they need to do at home to support their children's learning. Henderson, Jones, and Raimondo (1999) referred to this philosophy of family–school relations as the "come when called" model. Educators expect that parents will fulfill two very important roles. First, parents are expected to endorse the importance of schooling with their child, ensure that the child meets the minimum academic and behavioral requirements (e.g., attending school on time, making sure child completes homework), reinforce the educators' expectations for desirable social and academic behavior, and follow through in changing any home conditions that educators deem necessary. Second, educators expect parents to spend enough time with their children to transfer to them what has come to be known as *cultural capital,* that is, the ways of being, knowing, writing, talking, and thinking that characterize those who succeed in this culture (Delpit 1995). A minimum version of this hope/expectation is that parents will read to their children and listen to their children read to them. Ideally, by spending time with their parents, children will extend and enrich what they learn at school.

In contrast to the separation paradigm, the family remediation paradigm explicitly assumes that there should be an interchange between home and school. However, the home is to take a subordinate role to the expertise of educators. In this paradigm, the parents are assumed to have the significant responsibility of helping their children succeed within the guidelines specified by the school culture. According to Swap (1993): "The parent role includes preparing their children to begin school, encouraging them to succeed in school, and transmitting values, attitudes, and skills that characterize those who succeed" (30). Students do not have an active role in the interaction between home and schools in this paradigm. The educator's role is to define the goals, values, and programs in which parents are to participate. Neither two-way communication with parents nor student inclusion is viewed as necessary or sought out, because the goal is for the parents to understand and support the school's objectives. Figure 2.2 illustrates the nature of the remediation paradigm of family–school relations as a drawbridge. The control of the drawbridge connecting the worlds of school is exclusively in the hands of the school staff. This perspective is clearly depicted in the words of a teacher working in an urban school who explained her concept of desirable parent involvement:

> Parents should be *trained to parent,* talk to their kids more—interact with children and take them places. (By desirable parent involvement, I mean) parents cooperating with homework, looking at it, reading notices, coming to school when called, taking an interest in their child's education. (Swap 1993, 31)

In this perspective, if educators invite parents into the school, they are asking parents to support the teacher's plan and routine, not to contribute to it. Parents may be asked to perform a myriad of tasks at the school or for the school (e.g., helping in the library, preparing food for school parties, building playgrounds, raising money, serving on advisory boards or in parent–teacher associations), but in each of these they are expected to play a subordinate role.

Figure 2.2 The One-way Drawbridge of the Remediation Paradigm of Family–School Relations

Many parent involvement programs now being developed in school are based on this philosophy. One advantage of the remediation paradigm of family–school relations is that parents receive a very clear message from the school about the social and academic skills that children need to succeed in school and about their role in helping their children succeed. A second advantage noted by Swap (1993) is that, because this paradigm maintains educators' control over parent involvement, it can provide a framework for a transition from an isolating "separate spheres" mentality of the separation paradigm to a co-expert/collaborative paradigm. If the teacher and parents begin to develop trust and comfort with each other it might lead to a more comfortable and mutual exchange of ideas and joint planning between adults at home and at school.

However, Swap (1993) noted some distinct hazards that are inherent in the use of this paradigm. First, because this paradigm is organized around developing the parents' expertise, it is grounded in a mindset of perceived parental deficits. Educators often describe parents or caregivers—especially members of immigrant, low-income, or culturally diverse families—in terms of their deficiencies. For example, describing their conversations with the principal and other school staff as they prepared to set up interviews with parents in an elementary school in Northern California, Smrekar and Cohen-Vogel (2001) wrote:

> These officials suggested that most of the parents in the school were lazy, irresponsible, and apathetic when it came to school involvement and that these attitudes were inextricably linked to the low performance of their children. . . . School officials warned that it was unsafe and unwise to enter the school neighborhood and conduct interviews at parents' homes. Teachers warned that we would be lucky to get one-third of the initially contacted parents to participate. . . . Contrary to expectations of the school staff, all but one of the 15 parents we contacted were willing to participate in their interviews, and the parents welcomed us warmly and politely into their homes. (85)

As a result, strategies built on this paradigm often reveal an inherent resistance to considering the parent on an equal footing with educators. For example, parents may receive a contract from the school about what the school considers are their obligations with little to no appreciation of the parents' constraints. Workshops or activities may be designed to make parents more effective in their role, implying that parents are deficient and that educators know more than parents about how to parent.

Second, all parents may not be able to devote sufficient time and energy to the level of parent involvement expected by the educators if faced with certain life conditions that command their attention (e.g., hazardous living conditions, unstable employment, chronic illness). Moreover, parents may be asked to teach children certain skills despite the emotional and financial costs to the family and then blamed if these interventions fail. However, if educators could recognize these constraints and provide a link to resources that would address them, they might be able to build community and school programs that would be stronger safety nets for families.

Third, a danger exists of demeaning the value and importance of the family's culture in an effort to transmit the values and culture of the school. This becomes increasingly important as we think about the growing diversity of the student body and growing homogeneity of the teaching profession. Teachers who operate from the remediation paradigm think in terms of identifying the needs or deficits of parents and develop an experience to direct/train them to be better parents. Parents are told how they are expected to carry out their role; they are expected to cooperate with educators and follow directions. Many parents do just that. Some reluctantly go along with these mandates. However, many parents resist these directives, are labeled *unmotivated* or *resistant,* and judged as minimizing their deficiencies and refusing to own up to their problems.

The Collaboration Paradigm

In the 1980s, a third paradigm shift began to emerge in the thinking of many educators and social scientists. Educators began to realize that their own beliefs about children's development and learning not only influence how they teach students and structure their relationships with students' families; these beliefs had a reciprocal influence on how students' families responded to them. This realization contributed to a shift in philosophy of jointly working toward a common goal with families and sharing power.

Two theories—Bronfenbrenner's (1979; 1997) ecological systems theory of child development and Vygotsky's theory of learning and teaching—strongly influenced the development of this paradigm. According to the ecological systems theory (Bronfenbrenner 1979; 1997), a child's development is influenced either directly (e.g., through daily routines and interactions that occur in the child's immediate context) or indirectly (i.e., through more distant factors that impact those routines and interactions). A primary idea of ecological systems theory is that every level of the ecological system (e.g., the child's home or classroom, the caregiver's workplace, and the family's and school's neighborhood) is interconnected and thus can influence all other levels of the system. Thus, persons across each system level reciprocally influence persons at other levels. For example, the way that teachers and other school staff structure their classroom routines and interactions and school routines and interactions with family members affects what happens in the child's home, and vice versa. Moreover, larger social and economic policies and resources (considered distant from a child's everyday experience) also influence the routines and interactions that occur in the child's immediate contexts of the home and classroom.

Thus, rather than focus only on how families influence their children, educators who embrace this theory began to "hold a mirror up" to examine the ways that their interactions with families may affect how families interact with them or with children. This led many researchers to examine what school staffs believe about teaching and learning and interaction with low-income/low-status families and how that influences educators' behavior with students' families. For example,

Davies (1988) interviewed 150 teachers and administrators who worked with poor children in Boston, Massachusetts; Liverpool, England; and Portugal and who "thought of low-income/low-status families as being deficient and dwelled on family problems while ignoring family strengths" (53). Interestingly, the educators' convictions about the apathy of "hard-to-reach" parents were not supported by data from the parents. Davies (1988) found that despite teachers' negative attitudes toward parents, parents in all three cultures expressed active interest in their child's progress at school and in getting involved in school; they admitted that they just did not know how to get involved. Lott (2001) examined the research literature to determine whether educators held stereotypes about low-income adults that influenced their responses to poor parents. She reported that, in numerous research studies, researchers discovered that the beliefs about low-income children and adults held by many teachers and administrators are negative, discouraging, and exclusionary and are communicated to parents in myriad ways. Low-income and working-class parents, as compared to middle-class parents, receive fewer warm welcomes in their children's schools; their interventions and suggestions are less respected and attended to; and they are less able to influence the education of their children. Epstein's (1987) research adds another interesting wrinkle to this discovery of the educators' influence on parents. In her survey of 3,700 teachers in Maryland, she discovered that: "Teachers who used parent involvement frequently rated all parents higher in helpfulness and follow-through with learning activities at home, including parents with more or less education and single and married parents" (128).

Second, Vygtosky's (1978) work provided an additional theoretical tool that allowed educators to recognize that many of their current instructional practices were based exclusively on transmitting middle-class funds of knowledge and ignoring the existing funds of knowledge that low-income children bring to school. Vygotsky devoted his career to studying how children learn and describing learning as a process that involves social as well as cognitive transformations. His writings emphasized how interactions between people are central to the ways in which individual learning and development occur. He argued that children internalize the kind of help they receive from others and eventually come to use it independently to direct their own problem solving. For Vygotsky, the shift from needing help to accomplish a task to accomplishing it independently constitutes learning. Central to his theory is the belief that children learn best when parents and teacher create instructional activities that use what children already know as resources for learning new knowledge and practices.

These two theoretical traditions—Ecological System Theory and Vygotsky's learning theory—influenced the thinking of many educators who recognized that they needed to work in a *different* fashion with all students' families and, particularly, those families who were culturally and economically diverse. Envisioning that the goals of educating all children could only occur if families and community members were involved as equals, these educators proposed a fundamental restructuring of educators' attitudes and roles. Rather than involve parents only when there was a crisis or problem to be solved, or telling them how to parent their

children, these educators created opportunities to *collaborate* with families on a regular basis.

But what exactly is collaboration? According to Merriam-Webster's (1985)
definition, it means "to work jointly with others or together . . . to cooperate with
an agency or instrumentality with which one is not immediately connected" (259).
This definition seems simple and straightforward, yet most individuals believe collaboration is difficult to define. Seeley (1985) offered an elegantly simple definition:
"Collaboration is a common effort toward a common goal by participants who
share power" (65). Describing how collaboration would look in a family–school
context, Weiss and Edwards (1992) defined it "as a cooperative process of planning
and problem solving that involves school staff, parents, children, and significant
others so as to maximize resources for students' academic achievement and social-
emotional development" (215).

Implicit in all of these definitions is not only the recognition of common
goals, but also the assumption that power—the ability and intention to use authority, influence, or control over others—and responsibility for children's school
success should be *shared*. Moles (1993), for example, in a U.S. Department of Education publication, proposed that family–school roles should be conceptualized as a
shared responsibility and specified five distinctive roles shared by families and school
personnel: co-communicators, co-supporters, co-learners, co-teachers, and co-
decision makers.

Christenson and Sheridan (2001) illustrated the specific actions that characterize each of these five co-roles. The shared role of family and school as *co-
communicators* can be implemented as both family and school address the need to
exchange information to assist children's learning. A variety of techniques, including written, face-to-face, telephone, and formal and informal meetings can be used
to increase the shared meaning and understanding about students' performance.
The shared role of family and school as *co-supporters* addresses not only the needs of
the partners to support the child but also to support each other. Families can show
support to children by providing positive encouragement for learning, and to
schools by attending back-to-school nights and student performances. Schools can
support families by being responsive to their questions and providing a welcoming
climate. Teachers can support families by calling at the first sign of concern and
inviting them to visit the classroom or school. The role of families and schools as
co-learners entails providing opportunities for educators (e.g., administrators, teachers,
support personnel) and families to learn about each other and how to work together
to support student learning. For example, families may want information about
school policies and practices, whereas school staff may need opportunities to learn
about the cultural knowledge in the home and community so as to enhance
instructional effectiveness. The shared role of family and school as *co-teachers* recognizes the formal teaching of students in school settings and the ways families teach,
support, and encourage learning at home and in the community. Finally, the shared
role of home and school as *co-decision makers, advocates, and advisors* focuses on participation in formal organizations and committees.

Viewing parents and families as co-experts challenges the established ways in which power has been distributed in most schools in the past. As you will recall, in the separation and remediation models, educators are placed at the top of the relationship and families at the bottom. The use of hierarchies and professional dominance represents how power is distributed within these relationships. Educators (and parents) in this sense hold very narrow conceptions about the roles that parents can play in the school or in their child's learning. More often than not, parents are relegated to the passive roles of audience members or supporters, and teachers are the isolated, overburdened experts who are expected to have all the answers.

Collaborative educators view these traditional role conceptions as unnecessarily limited. As a result, these educators are now designing family–school activities in which parents have meaningful, active roles. They are also routinely involving families in planning and decision-making about their children's educational experience. These more meaningful role expectations fit with the role that researchers report parents are preferring to have with their children's school. For example, in a major review of the research on low-income parents' preferences for involvement with their children's schools, Lott (2001) reported that low-income parents describe their involvement with the school as meaningful when (a) they have opportunities for informal communications with school staff and feel "invited in," (b) they have a meaningful role in school activities other than that of consent-giver or signing of notes, (c) they can rely upon teachers and administrators to bridge the gap between themselves and school staff, (d) they can sense that teachers and administrators value their role in their child's learning, and (e) they believe that their involvement makes a difference in their child's educational experience and can see the direct benefits of their involvement for their children.

Hence, rather than assume that families are deficient, educators who operate within the collaboration paradigm assume that families may already have their own ways of teaching their children important social and cognitive skills (such as how to set a goal or define a problem, how to set priorities for action, and how to design solutions). Consequently, these educators believe that they share common goals and roles with parents, have a reason to work together with them, and draw the boundaries of their role with families quite differently from those who view their roles as separate or as needing to educate or remediate families. Rather than exclude families or control all communication and interactions to protect their autonomy, collaborative educators look for ways to include families to maximize resources for children's learning. Hence, communication between educators and parents is explicit, regular, and directive. Decision-making about children is based upon negotiation, open communication and consensus, when group problem solving is actively promoted, and when students are included in problem solving. Lewis and Forman (2002) described the parent conferences in an elementary school guided by such a collaborative paradigm:

> Parent conferences were not viewed as a time for teachers to report to parents about a child's academic progress, but as a way for the important adults in a child's life to share not only academic information but also social and emo-

tional information. Expert status was understood not as the sole purview of school staff but as something shared with and encouraged in parents.... Parents were rarely called upon to be fundraisers, bakers, or room moms. Instead, they were involved as members of a community as educational collaborators with important information about their children and as comrades in struggles related to keeping the school functioning. (77, 78)

As a result of such new ways of working, parents and students come to view themselves as co-experts with the school (Hoover-Dempsey, Walker, Sandler, Whetsel, Green, Wilkins & Closson 2005; Lareau & Horvat 1999). They see themselves as having an integral role together with the school in educating their children. Parents pride themselves on using their own home learning activities (e.g., cooking together, attending church events) to facilitate their children's academic and social learning, and to monitor their child's progress. They expect to be informed about their child's progress by the school, and might say: "I really need to know what is happening in school to help my child." They also expect to be involved in decisions that the school makes concerning their children's educational progress and to exert control over those decisions.

The collaborative paradigm of family–school relations can be contrasted with the separation and remediation paradigms in which the authority (e.g., teacher) identifies the concern or problem that merits attention, decides what type of solution is necessary, and decides how the clients (i.e., student and family) should be involved with a philosophy of "doing to" or "doing for" the client. In both the separation and remediation paradigms, educators assume unilateral or dominant roles in educational decision-making and action. In contrast, in the collaborative paradigm, educators interact with students and their families to identify *together* those resources that exist in the family and school for taking action to solve children's problems or to celebrate their learning. Many other differences exist between the remediation and the collaboration paradigms (see Table 2.4).

These differences are significant and have to do with the focus of the relationship; the roles of the educator, student, and parents/caregivers; the nature of the relationship, including the goal toward which it is directed; the nature of the activities and the expected outcome; the assumptions about the roles and responsibilities of educator, student, and parent; the purposes and styles of communication and decision-making; and the structure of power relations.

Figure 2.3 illustrates the nature of family–school relations in the collaboration paradigm as a stationary bridge. Why is a bridge an appropriate illustration of the ways of interacting between educators and families? The answer lies in the purpose that the bridge serves. On one side of the bridge is the child's life at school; on the other side of the bridge is the child's life at home and in their community. The purpose of the bridge is to form a stable, connecting path between the worlds of home and school that students traverse each day.

The bridge denotes the quality of the home–school relationship. In a solid bridge that parents trusts to have their child cross, the family–school relationship is

∿∿∿∿∿∿∿∿∿∿∿∿∿∿∿∿∿∿∿∿∿∿∿∿∿∿∿∿∿∿∿∿∿∿

Table 2.4   Comparison of Role Expectations and Power Relations in the Remediation and Collaboration Paradigms

Remediation Paradigm	Collaboration Paradigm
Focus	
Diagnose and treat the academic/social problem of the student	Foster a process of cooperative planning and problem-solving between the family and school to maximize the resources for children's learning and social-emotional development
Educator's Role	
Expert who does "to" or "with" the family; serving as the central decision-maker or problem solver	Professional working "with," not doing "to"; resource person who shares leadership and power with family
Student's Role	
Often is excluded from family–school interaction or has a passive role; assumed not to know their own needs	Has active role in all family–school activities in determining own progress, problems, and solutions
Parent/Caregiver's Role	
Often passive recipient of "service/activity" that is defined by school professional	Has active role in all family–school activities; seen as capable and competent in deciding how to contribute to student's learning or to solving student problems
Nature of the Relationship	
Distant, sometimes adversarial; frequently characterized by overt or covert blaming by each party. Roles are set. Educator is to lead; parent to follow.	Cooperative, nonblaming atmosphere created to promote problem-solving. Roles are flexible and change according to situational demands; educators and parents defer to each other in their respective domains; reciprocity is valued.
Goal	
To only have contact between the two parties when there is a problem to be resolved and need information from parents that would help educator solve the problem	To design opportunities to get to know one another and establish a partnership to prepare the child for learning and success in school.
Nature of the Activities	
School staff only communicate with parents when they need to assess a problem and prescribe the necessary cure. Parents are expected to be compliant with the school's decisions.	Parents and students are seen as important resources for problem-solving and learning so there is a regular communication between home and schools to routinely share information on issues of mutual concern.
Expected Outcomes	
Crisis or problem is resolved.	Increased family involvement in the student's school experience; improved academic performance; fewer "insoluble" discipline problems

〰〰〰〰〰〰〰〰〰〰〰〰〰〰〰〰〰〰〰〰〰〰〰〰〰

Table 2.4   Continued

Remediation Paradigm	Collaboration Paradigm
Assumptions Regarding Power and Politics	
Schools know best what a child needs. Do not need to consider possible differences between home and school.	Adults at school and at home have different kinds of information useful in helping a child learn and succeed, which are shared openly and directly.
Contact is limited to very structured, ritualized events; each expects to be blamed or manipulated by the other.	Time is taken to build trust and engage in regular communication. Educator and caregiver share information and communicate openly about concerns, expectations for child, and so on.
Therefore, educators and caregivers adopt blaming, deficit-labeling attitude with each other, focusing on who caused the problem	Educators and caregivers adopt a trouble-shooting attitude, looking for what might solve the problem, assuming responsibility for discovering possible solutions without being blamed for causing the problem.
Emphasis is placed on protecting the autonomy of the educator by not giving caregivers too much information or control. "Either/or thinking"—either preserve autonomy or submit to control by family; either school has responsibility or home.	A shared belief that teacher autonomy and family interests are interdependent, and reciprocal; both individual teacher & family interests can be met.
Problem-solving is imposed by the educator	Problem-solving grows out of a consensus facilitated by the educator.
Power for others or against them	Power with others
Win/lose orientation	Win/win orientation
Differential power. Aggressive educators, passive family members.	Shared power. Educator does not express superiority of expertise or knowledge, views family and school as being in a reciprocal relationship, each affecting the other.
Preserving the family–school relationship is sacrificed in the service of the school's own interests. Only do as much as other does.	Initiate and engage in behaviors to build the relationship and advance the interests of both parties.

strong, predictable, and positive. If the family–school relationship is weak, the bridge offers no predictable support to the child traversing the path between home and school. Hence, the child cannot depend upon it as a trustworthy resource.

How are schools translating the collaborative paradigm into practice? One set of principles, developed by the staff at Ackerman Institute's Family School Collaboration Project (Weiss & Edwards 1992) provides a clear template for changing family–school relations. Successfully tested in schools in the United States and Canada over a fifteen-year period, this set of principles helps school faculties successfully transform their current family–school activities to "connect the two key

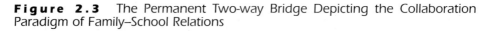

Figure 2.3 The Permanent Two-way Bridge Depicting the Collaboration Paradigm of Family–School Relations

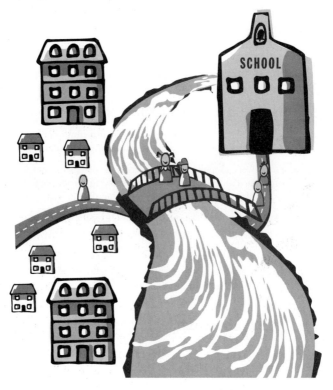

systems in a child's life—the home and the school—in ways which create a shared commitment to children's learning" (Weiss & Edwards 1992, 215).

The first principle is that the school commits to building relationships with all parents whether the parents can come to school. To do this, educators must make clear to parents how their active participation in their children's educational experience will directly enhance their children's achievement and development. In addition, the educator must look for ways to communicate a genuine interest in connecting with the parents of all of the students to ensure these outcomes. Consequently, if some parents are not able to come to the school because of work or family demands, the school staff signals their belief that these parents still care deeply about their child's learning by providing them with the means to understand and keep up with what is happening in school (e.g., through use of summary letters describing an event they missed, regular newsletters, and homework assignments).

A second principle is that all family–school activities are planned to maximize student learning. Rather than simply trying to get parents involved, school staff use the family–school relationship to meet specific educational goals, solve problems, and celebrate the children and their achievements. Rather than be organized only around discussion of problems, the school maintains a dialogue about learning and about the school's interest in each child. Consequently, the school staff look for opportunities for parents, students, and staff to interact with one another in ways that emphasize family involvement in children's planning, decision-making, problem solving, and learning. To do this, the staff examines the various aspects of the school experience (curriculum, administrative and communication procedures, special programs, after-school activities, assessment and evaluation programs, health programs, etc.) to design opportunities for families and school staff to experience each other differently.

In keeping with this emphasis on maximizing student learning, the third principle is that the child is included as an active participant in virtually all family–school interactions. To do this, children of all ages are taught to function as active participants in family–teacher (i.e., the old parent–teacher) conferences. Because it is their life at school that is to be discussed, they come to such meetings as "experts on themselves" who must be there to describe their own experience, thoughts, and feelings. As the children contribute to the solution of their problems and the improvement of their own school experience, they gain confidence and a sense of efficacy. Family–school interactions that involve the children are embedded in orientations, classroom instruction, homework routines, celebrations, presentations of new curriculum, transitions to new grade levels and programs, procedures for home–school communication, and for resolving difficulties. (See Reflective Exercise 2.1 for an illustration of one parent's account of how a routine school orientation was redesigned with these principles in mind.)

Reflective Exercise 2.1

A Parent's View of a "Collaborative" Fall Orientation

Below is one parent's reaction to a fall orientation designed in terms of the collaborative principles described.

Dear Sis:

Do I have news for you! After years of dutifully attending school "open house" events at Tim and Stephen's schools, I thought I had them all figured out. Was I ever surprised by the "back to school" night put on by Stephen's teacher and school! I had expected for this fall orientation to be like every other one I had attended. I would sit in a large auditorium, listen to a parade of speakers talk to a huge audience of parents and a few wiggly children (whose parents had not been able to get baby-sitters), and then "race" to each teacher's classroom in which I had a child. My purpose for going was to, at least, "show my face" and let these teachers know that I was interested in meeting them.

This orientation night was far different. First, Stephen was invited to come with me (as a matter of fact, he invited me to accompany him to the orientation.) Second, Stephen and I spent the evening just with his teacher, classmates, and their parents. (The school had organized a schedule in which the grade levels met on different evenings so that parents would not feel rushed to get to every child's room in the same evening!) Third, his teacher had organized an activity in which, after greeting us and giving us a preview of the evening's activities, she asked each parent and child to talk together privately for a few minutes about what their goals were for the student's learning this year, and what the parent might do to help their child accomplish these goals. After Stephen and I talked we had a chance to share our ideas, and to hear the ideas of his classmates and their parents. The teacher listed all these ideas up on the board and then talked about how our ideas fit with her goals and plans for the year. It was obvious, when all those ideas got written on the board, that we shared many of the same goals and concerns about the new school year!

Not only was this activity useful for showing us as parents what we have in common, but also it provided me with an experience interacting with my child at school which I had never had before. Usually, parents expect to come to these types of events and be quiet and listen; if a parent has to bring his or her child (due to not getting baby-sitting), the parent is expected to be quiet and entertain the child. This time it was different; we were asked to talk with each other during a school event. I was surprised by how seriously Stephen took what I had to say to heart about him doing his homework without me having to nag him to get down to work. (Of course, we'll have to see just how much he follows through on this!) I think that he liked being treated and talked to as a grown-up. I certainly liked my opinion being asked for too!

More importantly, this activity gave me an opportunity to see "up close" how Stephen's teacher relates to him and to the other children. It is obvious that she cares about each one of them. It showed in the way she solicited their participation in the discussion and took their answers seriously. So, I'm relieved that he's got such a caring teacher. What's more, I'm amazed that with just this one orientation night, I've gotten a very different view of what this year may have in store for me as well as for Stephen!
Love,
Anne

A fourth principle is that parents should be actively involved in all family–school events, not as an audience but as full participants. Rather than unnecessarily restrict the role that parents can play to that of classroom volunteer, instructional support person, or audience member, family–school events are designed to underscore the role of parents as active co-decision-makers and illustrate the belief that everyone—parents, teachers, and students—has a job to do to ensure the students' educational success.

Another major effort to create more collaborative partnerships between schools and families is Comer's School Development Program (SDP). Created by James Comer (1980; 1991; 1996), this program illustrates how some schools are changing their social psychological climate so as to be more inviting to low-income and culturally diverse families. Comer et al. (1991) developed an approach in which teachers, administrators, and other school personnel make decisions about the school. Parents also participate in this decision-making process. The end goal of this process is "the creation of a sense of community and direction for parents, school staff, and students alike" (Comer 1991, 271). A recent description about the Comer process emphasizes the importance of all adults working together to improve the schools:

> The key to the Comer process is that schools must make adjustments to bring all adults in the community together in a supportive way—to create an ethos, tone, feeling—that is supportive of children. . . . An additional key aspect of the Comer process is the inclusion of parents in all levels of school activities: SPMT, volunteers, conferencing, "make and takes," PTA, PTO, special programs, subcommittee, etc. Parents are truly welcome and home–school relationships are fostered. (Comer, Haynes, Joyner & Ben-Avie 1996, 45)

The SDP is designed for whole-school implementation, with the goal of improving the ecology of the school by improving the school governance system, the functioning of the mental health team, and the development of a parent program that allows parental participation in school governance and school activities. Started in New Haven, Connecticut, Comer's program is now being implemented in a number of other U. S. cities.

These types of collaborative interactions transform the way families and schools experience each other. As parents learn they can make a difference in their child's learning, they invest in school. As staff learns to build on the strengths of children and families and to block blaming from undermining the collaborative process, they create a shared vested interest in the child that brings the family and school closer together. When each person feels known, understood, and cared about by the other parties, a sense of community and common purpose unites the classroom and school with the families of school-aged children.

Implications for Your Professional Practice

As in any change effort, it is important to recognize that personal change does not happen overnight. Instead, for change to be lasting, we often go through a series of stages. The first stage is that of recognizing an area of your life in which you wish to change, while a second stage consists of assessing where you are, where you want to be, and what will be the costs and benefits of getting from where you are to where you want to be. A third stage emphasizes preparing yourself for the change effort by getting concrete ideas about how you might change, whereas the fourth stage involves trying out these ideas, gathering feedback to learn how they work, and then deciding what to modify or continue doing.

Identifying the distinctive paradigms of family–school relationships allows you to discern both your current and your preferred ideas about relationships between parents/families and educators (i.e., where you are and where you want to be). Although you may be tempted to first look outward at what you see and hear as the expectations for how parents and educators should relate in your professional training context or in the school with which you are familiar, it is critical to first look inward to consider which paradigm is most prominent in your thinking about relationships with parents and their children. What do you notice in your own thinking about the kinds of relationships and style of contact you expect to have with the parents of your students? (See Reflective Exercise 2.2 for questions to guide you in this self-assessment process.)

Reflective Exercise 2.2

Assessing Your Thinking about Family–School Relations

What do you notice in your own thinking about the kinds of relationships and style of contact you expect to have with the parents/caregivers of your students?

1. Which paradigm is most prominent in your thinking about the relationships you expect to have with parents/caregivers?
2. As you think back on your first exercise in Chapter 1 in which we asked you to describe your future vision of yourself teaching, which of the three mental models/paradigms seems to most closely reflect the thinking about relationships with families that you depicted in your vision?
3. What influences do you think have led to your development of your current mental model/paradigm of family–school relations?
4. Given that our first paradigms are very influential, what evidence or experience would you need to decide to shift your mental model/paradigm? What do you think would be the hardest shift for you? Why would this be the hardest shift for you?

Once you have some clarity about your own paradigm, you may want to listen to the language and observe the everyday interactions of educators in your training program or at the schools in which you work to discern in which paradigm(s) they seem to be operating. To assist you in this task, you may want to consider the following questions:

- What language is used by the professors in your training program or by the principals and teachers in the schools you visit or work in when they talk about parents? Does their language reflect high or low expectations for parents' positive influence on their children's academic success?
- Are there different expectations for parents marginalized by poverty or language differences?
- Is an adversarial or a collaborative style of interaction anticipated in contacts with parents?
- What kinds of implicit and explicit cues do educators give parents about their "proper" role in the school? Do they expect parents to be passive recipients of knowledge from them, the experts? Or do they expect parents to have knowledge about their children and their children's worlds that would facilitate the learning process?
- Do the staff expect that they alone will define the priorities of the school, or do they expect parents to help define the priorities and issues the school needs to address to improve?
- Do teachers and other staff members regularly collaborate by making joint decisions and plans, or do they operate separately from one another?
- Are there times and places during the workday where school staff talk with each other about their hopes and concerns for the school as a whole as well as for their classrooms? Is there time for conversation with parents not only about their children but also about the school as a whole?

Obviously, the paradigm shift from separation or remediation to one of collaboration represents a change in power dynamics between parents and educators. The usual power arrangement in most public schools (particularly those that serve the urban poor) excludes parents from knowledge about the school's functioning and from important decision-making about their children much less about the school as a whole. As a result, educators may have strong reactions to requests to treat parents as co-experts on their children. Instead, some teachers will view parents as needing instruction or guidance in parenting and believe that their role as teachers is to provide expert guidance or advice. Other teachers will view their role with parents as an expert/advice-giving role and see it as an additional burden to an already over-demanding instructional role with students. Still others who view that their role should be a parent educator or advice-giver will feel inadequately prepared to function as parenting experts with parents and thus avoid interaction with them. (See Reflective Exercise 2.3 for samples of the varying attitudes and styles that teachers may demonstrate as they interact with their students' families.)

Reflective Exercise 2.3

Assessing Other Educators' Attitudes Toward Students' Families

What do you notice in the thinking of the school staff depicted below about the kinds of relationships and style of contact they expect to have with their students' parents or caregivers? Given the paradigm they are operating under, what could you expect from this teacher if you were a parent of a student in their class?

Teacher 1: Why should I worry about making connections with my students' parents? It's not my responsibility to teach parents how to raise their children or help them figure out how to help their child. They need to learn how to raise their children on their own. I think we do too much for parents as it is, like providing public housing and welfare for many of these parents. How will parents learn to be responsible, with us doing for them every step of the way? My parents raised four children without any teacher working with them and telling them how to do it.

Teacher 2: I've been teaching elementary students for twelve years now, and, believe me, the majority of parents don't seem to care. I've knocked myself out planning meetings to teach them the things they should do with their children. Most of them never show up, and those that do don't change. You tell them what they should do and they keep on doing what they were doing before. I find myself saying: "Why bother? I have better things to do with my time!"

Teacher 3: I already spend a lot of my free time trying to figure out how to teach my students and run my classroom. Now you want me to think up things to do with parents. I have enough to do as it is. Besides, I wasn't trained to work with parents. I am really much more comfortable working with children than talking with their parents. I don't know what I would tell parents to do, and I'm not sure what I have to offer them. What's more, I don't want parents asking a lot of questions about what I am doing or why I am doing it.

Teacher 4: I have discovered that if I ask parents, they can give me a real head start in getting to know their children. I used to think that I was the one who had to "have it all together" and that I shouldn't contact them until I could show them that I knew their child and knew what to do to help their child. But I am learning that parents/families can teach me a lot not only about their particular children, but also they can help me be more effective in solving children's problems and making my teaching more relevant.

Teacher 5: Over the years, I have come to realize that I not only depend upon students' families to deliver their children to school, fed and cared for, but also I depend on them to help their children want to learn and succeed in school. So I now think of them as vital working partners in my job of educating children. Without them I cannot succeed.

Once you develop a sense of your current mental model/paradigm, you can decide whether and how to work toward changing both your beliefs and your professional practice. Obviously, having concrete examples of different ways of relating to parents and students is an important resource in this change effort. Recognizing that these ways of thinking and working take time, persistence, and the cooperation of others is another important step. In the following chapters, you will see a chronology of stories by educators who decided to change their ways of working with students and their families and made the change. In each of these stories, you will hear showcased the thoughts and feelings of the educators as they experimented with making these changes, their specific changes in practice, and the thoughts and reactions of parents and students as they experienced these different ways of working.

Summary

In this chapter we describe a typology of mental models/paradigms of family–school relationships. This typology can provide a framework that can be used to reflect on the nature of your own beliefs as well as to locate in which paradigm other educators operate. Two out of the three paradigms—the separation/separate spheres paradigm and the remediation paradigm—locate parents in more limited and passive roles, whereas the other, the collaboration paradigm, offers opportunities for both parents and educators to take on active roles in which all parties can bring their knowledge and strengths to improving students' academic achievement and social and emotional competence. We end this chapter with a discussion of the change process you may experience as you experiment with ways of thinking and working with families that may be new to you.

Resources

U.S. Department of Education,
www.ed.gov/nclb
This Web site provides information on NCLB's key principles. It also has a Teachers' Toolkit and Parents' Guide, as well as an opportunity to sign up to receive e-mail updates.

Family and Advocates Partnership for Education Project,
www.fape.org
The FAPE project provides information to parents and advocates related to IDEA information. Information is also provided on the statues, regulations, resource organizations, and best practices. Some of this information is available in Spanish and Hmong translations.

Chapter 3

Building Culturally Responsive Family–School Partnerships: Essential Beliefs, Strategies, and Skills

Ellen S. Amatea

Learning Objectives

After reading this chapter, you will be able to:

- Summarize the essential beliefs about family–school partnerships that guide educators' professional practice
- Describe specific dyadic strategies that enable you to develop more collaborative family–school partnerships
- Summarize the specific aspects of a school's social climate that might be altered to create a more collaborative family–school environment

- Describe specific core routines that can be redesigned to enhance the climate of family–school relations in a classroom or school
- Discuss the structural supports needed to create family–school partnerships
- Summarize the research evidence about the effectiveness of family–school collaboration
- Outline the essential attitudes and skills needed by educators committed to building collaborative family–school partnerships

I was surprised to learn how many of the messages we send to parents from schools have been about the school telling parents what to do. We need to make our family–school communication more two-way so we can learn from families as well as they can learn from us.

I never thought about how intimidating the school and teachers are to some parents, particularly those who did not have good experiences in their own schooling. I need to recognize that parents/families may have very different perspectives on my invitations from the school.

I am recognizing that if we only contact parents when there is a problem, they will continue to dread interacting with schools and teachers.

Like the educators depicted in the previous comments, many educators are realizing that the traditional ways that schools have interacted with caregivers can often put them on the defensive. To send a different message to families—especially those who are culturally diverse—these educators are redesigning both how they think and how they act with the families of their students. Rather than having a one-sided focus on getting parents involved, these educators are using a variety of ways to come together with families to enhance children's school performance and development. How are they doing this? What theories and ways of working with families do they rely on? How are their new ways of working responsive to the widely varying cultural backgrounds of today's students and families? In this chapter, we discuss the distinctive beliefs that underlie a culturally responsive approach to family–school collaboration and the theories on which it is based. We then illustrate how these ways of thinking and working have been translated into action by showcasing the experiences of educators who use either a dyadic or group approach to developing these types of family–school relations. Finally, we discuss the skills required to create such partnerships and describe how we will examine them in this book.

Thinking and Working as Partners

The word *partnership* refers to a relationship that involves close cooperation between people who have joint rights and responsibilities (Merriam-Webster OnLine 2006). As early as 1989, Seeley proposed that educators move from thinking of their relationship with students' families in terms of service delivery—provider and client or of professionals and target populations—to one of partnership characterized by common goals and complementary efforts. Illustrative of this shift from viewing families as clients to viewing them as partners was the work of Swap (1993), who spoke to the need for a "true partnership" between families and educators characterized by a *mutuality of interaction*. She stated: "A true partnership is a transforming vision of school life based on collegiality, experimentation, mutual support, and joint problem solving. It is based on the assumption that parents and educators are members of a partnership who have a common goal: generally improving the school and supporting the success of all children in the school" (56).

Although thinking of families and educators as partners does not refer to a specific approach or set of activities, it is characterized by a common set of beliefs and expectations:

1. *A belief that all families are knowledgeable experts who powerfully influence their children in school and out of school learning.* Educators who partner with families are aware of the many forms that families may take and the many ways that families may influence children's learning, both in school and out of school. As a result, these educators define families as including two or more people who regard themselves as a family and who carry out the functions that families typically perform. These people may or may not be related by blood or marriage and may or may not usually live together. In addition, these educators believe that it is important to build on, rather than ignore, the strengths and ways of knowing of these families. This requires that educators learn from families about how they uniquely function and the challenges they face in rearing their children, seek to understand their diverse strengths and perspectives, and utilize the skills, experiences, and wisdom that families can share with them.

2. *An expectation that educators will seek ways to reach out, listen to, and understand the unique needs, perspectives, and strengths of families and to use that information to enhance children's learning.* Some families have no difficulty in initiating contact with the school and expressing their perspectives and concerns. Other families, particularly those who have had negative experiences with schools or come from cultures that differ markedly from the middle-class culture of most schools, are intimidated by schools and teachers and avoid contact with the school. Many families expect the school to only contact them when their child has a problem. Educators committed to building collaborative relationships with families are aware of the differences in power and resources that can block caregivers from interacting with school staff. Rather than expect parents to bridge the economic and cultural gap, these educators assume that it is their responsibility to develop ways to interact with and involve all families in their children's learning, not only those families who are easy to talk with or easy to reach. In addition, these educators seek out ways to learn about and build on families' distinctive cultural values, expectations, and social and economic resources.

3. *A belief that sharing responsibility for educating children can best be fostered by schools developing a school-wide climate characterized by trust, two-way communication, and mutual support in achieving their educational aims for students.* Educators who view parents as partners and co-decision-makers design their family–school routines (e.g., orientations, parent–teacher conferences, school-written communications) so that caregivers have meaningful and active roles. Rather than involve parents only as consent-givers or audience members, these educators actively involve families in the planning and decision-making about their children's educational experiences. To do this, educators invite parents to participate in new ways in resolving children's academic and behavioral difficulties and to practice "no-fault" problem solving. In this approach to problem solving, both parents and students are invited to play an active, co-expert role with teachers in developing concrete action plans, in which everyone (family and school) has a task to do to help the child.

4. *An expectation that educators will develop positive, nonproblematic ways to interact with families in the educational process of their children, recognizing that this may look different for different families.* Many educators are recognizing that investing in building relationships with families and developing trust before a problem emerges can make any problem-focused interaction run more smoothly. Looking at how they might "dig the well, before they are thirsty," these educators are creating opportunities to get to know and become known by their students' families, and to build trust with the caregivers of their students. Rather than communicate with families only when there is a problem, these educators are creating opportunities for ongoing, routine, informal communication between the school and families for the purpose of sharing information, developing educational plans, and solving problems. This requires that teachers learn how to (a) reach out to get acquainted with student's families, (b) design family–school interactions in which all their students' families can participate, and (c) tie family–school contacts to children's learning and development.

5. *A belief that sharing responsibility for educating children can best be fostered by reaching out and engaging members of the larger community in developing their assets and resources to support the development of children and families.* Many educators are recognizing that they need to think about what children and families experience beyond the school walls. This requires educators to learn about what children and families need during out-of-school as well as in-school time and to create community resources to meet those needs. To do this, many educators are working to make their schools a vital hub for community support of children and their families, either by helping community members develop a stronger network of community resources and social ties or by offering to function as a school-based health center that provides referral or direct community social services to families.

Translating Beliefs into Action: Dyadic or Group-focused Strategies

How are educators translating these beliefs into action? Educators use a variety of different approaches and strategies to create culturally responsive family–school partnerships. These approaches differ in terms of their focus and the level of influence given to the family. The focus may be on either (a) creating a collaborative dyadic (i.e., one-to-one) relationship between an educator and a family member or (b) developing a collaborative relational climate among a group of families in a classroom or school and an educator or group of educators. The level of family influence ranges along a continuum from (a) activities/strategies designed to reach out, include, and elicit the caregivers' perspective to (b) activities that both elicit and apply the caregiver's perspective in the development of decisions or instructional activities. These variations in focus and influence are depicted in Table 3.1.

The dyadic, one-to-one relationship focus is illustrated in the family literacy development practices depicted in the work of McCaleb (1994); Shockley, Michalove, and Allen (1995); and Kyle, McIntyre, Miller, and Moore (2002). In this approach, not only do teachers build positive relationships with students' families, but also they may invite families to become significant participants in their children's learning by contributing their oral or written words, ideas, and experiences as part of the text of schooling.

The collaborative group focus in a classroom or school is well illustrated in the works of the Family–School Collaboration Project of the Ackerman Institute (Weiss & Edwards 1992); Amatea, Daniels, Brigman, and Vandiver (2004); and Christianson and Sheridan (2001). Strategies that utilize a group focus typically involve educators in redesigning their existing parent–school activities so that they contribute to

Table 3.1   Focus and Depth of Influence of Family–School Collaboration Strategies

Dyadic Focus	Group Focus
Limited Influence of Family on Educator Decision-making	
Welcome letters home	Back-to-school orientation
Family interviews	Teacher story books
Family visits	School letters/newsletters
Substantive Influence of Family on Educator Decision-making	
Family–school problem solving	Student-led parent conferences
Special education planning meeting	Family story books
	Family funds of knowledge lesson/unit

building a more collaborative family–school climate characterized by trust, two-way communication, and mutual support in achieving their educational aims for students.

Both dyadic and group approaches to developing family–school partnerships have been presented in the professional literature and implemented in a wide variety of schools, serving culturally diverse student populations. Because each approach provides a set of explicit strategies for rethinking and redesigning family–school interactions and addresses the need for educators to design practices that are responsive to culturally diverse students and families, we now describe the assumptions and strategies illustrative of each approach.

Creating Collaborative Dyadic Relationships

Many educators are committed to developing positive, trusting relationships with their students' families so that students can become more confident and competent learners. Three types of relationship-building strategies are emphasized: (a) reaching out and sharing oneself with families, (b) valuing and affirming family expertise and ways of knowing, and (c) involving parents as significant participants in children's learning.

Reaching Out and Sharing Oneself

Many educators emphasize the need to establish personal relationships with their students' families characterized by trust and understanding. One strategy for creating such relationships is to reach out and share oneself with students' families. A teacher might reach out and become known to students' families in a number of different ways. First, a teacher might make immediate personal contact in the first weeks of school when the parents bring their children to school. Or teachers might send home letters that express their pleasure in having the child in their class, meeting the parents, and inviting the parent into the classroom to see how their children are learning. Not only is it important to ensure that the letter is written in the home language of the child, but also that the tone of the letter is friendly and inviting. (This may require the teacher to establish relationships with someone whom they can rely upon to translate their letter into the home language of the child.) Figure 3.1 depicts an example of a letter that one first-grade teacher wrote and sent home.

To make parents feel more comfortable with them, teachers also look for ways to share information about who they are and what they are like. As described in her Building Community of Learners Program, McCaleb (1994) reported one creative way that a teacher described herself and her curriculum to parents by creating and sharing a storybook that she had created about her own family.

∿∿∿∿∿∿∿∿∿∿∿∿∿∿∿∿∿∿∿∿∿∿∿∿∿∿∿∿∿∿

Figure 3.1   Teacher's Introductory Letter to Family

Dear Ms. Nogales,

It has been a pleasure to begin to get to know Alberto during this first week of school. All of the children are so bright-eyed and seem so ready to learn. I know we are going to have an exciting year together.

As Alberto's first teacher, I know that you have taught him a great deal. I hope that we can talk soon and that you can share with me some of the ways in which you have taught him at home. I'm sure that you will have good suggestions about what you want him to learn at school and how I, as his new teacher, can help him to learn better.

We have a bulletin board in our classroom that we have saved for pictures of our students and their families. We would like for each student to bring a picture or drawing of the special adults in his or her life. In that way, the students will feel your presence and know that your support is there while they are learning at school.

Thank you very much.

Sincerely,
Ann Tannen

The teacher explained that all of the children in the class would become authors that year by writing and illustrating their own books and that with many of these books they would be seeking their family's participation or asking for their help. The teacher then confessed that she had written a short book about herself that she was soon planning to read to the students, but that she would first like to read it to the parents. It began with an old black-and-white baby snapshot from her family album and talked about where she was born. A beautiful picture of her parent's wedding was also included, alongside a picture of herself when she was three, wearing her favorite bathrobe. Another picture of the teacher was included as a youngster being lovingly carried by her parents and another with a baby goat named Schwenley, whose mother had gone away. The teacher also had included some pictures of her travels to Latin America before she became a teacher and mother. Finally, she had pictures of her husband, her children, and other children she had taught. When the story was finished, the parents applauded. In the parents' eyes, the teacher was becoming a real human being. (35)

Other teachers talk about sharing pictures of themselves and their own families during back-to-school nights as a way to have their students' caregivers learn information about who they are and what they are like. In Reflective Exercise 3.1 we ask you to think about how you might create a family storybook by which you might share some of your own family background with your future students and their families.

Valuing and Affirming Family Expertise

An effective strategy for building trusting relationships with families that can directly influence how teachers develop their instruction is to routinely invite families to share their perspective and expertise about their child. Rather than assume that the educator is the sole expert, these educators look for ways to learn from and use the parents' perspective. For example, in the previous back-to-school night, after the teacher read her story, she asked the parents to help her make a list of what they thought would be important for their children to learn during that year (McCaleb 1994). Another way that educators use parents' expertise and knowledge is through requesting information about their children.

> One teacher issued an open-ended invitation to parents at the beginning of the year. She wrote: "Welcome to third grade! It's always exciting to start a new school year with a new group of students. I am looking forward to working with your child. Would you please take a few moments and tell me about your child?" Every parent wrote back. They shared how very special their child was in their family. They shared tips and talents, information about illnesses and family situations, and, most of all, the love they have for these special children. (Shockley, Michalove & Allen 1995, 19)

> Another group of teachers (Kyle, McIntyre, Miller & Moore 2002), who felt that their culturally diverse parents might be intimidated by the task of writing about their child, initiated a routine of making family visits in which they visited children's homes and invited parents to talk with them about their children's strengths and interests. They differentiated these visits from the traditional home visit conducted when professionals believed there was something wrong in the home. Instead, these family visits were a way to gain information about a family's educational and cultural practices that the teachers could use to improve what they

did in school. Not only could a teacher learn more about a child, but also about the unique circumstances of the family. These authors reported the following:

> Through our family visits we learned of the schedules and circumstances of our families' lives and gained a deeper understanding of the relationship between home and school from the parents' perspectives. We learned how much time the families have to read to their children or help with homework projects and during what part of the day this gets done. We learned about who works and when they work and who is without work. We learned of family problems that interfere with the child's sleep and homework. We learned about who cooks dinner and whether they use recipes or read off packages to prepare food. We learned which parents struggle with literacy and how they try to compensate. We also learned who teaches their children and how they do it. (65)

Involving Families as Significant Participants in Children's Learning

Teachers' assumptions about the family environment of their students can either build links between home and school or sever them. In the separation and remediation paradigms, the diverse social, economic, linguistic, and cultural practices of some families are represented as serious problems rather than as valued knowledge. Yet the belief that these kids don't live in a good environment can destroy the very relationship a teacher is trying to create. In the collaboration paradigm, rather than ignoring families' ways of knowing, educators seek to build on culturally diverse students' and families' experiences and knowledge by first focusing on learning about what students already know from their home and community and then designing instructional activities that are meaningful to students in terms of this locally constructed knowledge.

McCaleb (1994) described one teacher's application of this teaching philosophy. It involved first-grade children and their non-English-speaking families developing individual storybooks. The teacher chose themes for the books based on the participants' common interest in improving their children's literacy. The goals of the book development project were to (a) create a tool to give voice to parents and encourage their participation in the school, (b) offer them an opportunity through dialogue to nurture their children's literacy by engaging in literacy development activities with their children, and (c) celebrate and validate their home culture and family concerns and aspirations. McCaleb reports the following:

> In the first book development session that involved both parents and children, I explained to the participants how to make a simple bound book with masking tape, needle, thread, and glue. At the end of the session, they had completed a book with blank pages, ready for words and illustrations. I then asked them to try to write a story in which their children and other family members appear as the principal characters. I suggested that the parent could write

the words and that the child could do the illustrations, or that the whole effort could be collaborative. I encouraged them to include photographs and collage materials (which they had in their supply box). Encouraging students and their families to write stories about themselves gives them the opportunity to be the main characters in a story that the child reads and other children will read in class. Not only are the children excited, but also parents feel that their experiences are heard. (114–116)

These activities underscore the importance of empowering parents to contribute *intellectually* to the development of lessons by using the *funds of knowledge* of the family. If you recall, we defined a family's funds of knowledge as the various social and linguistic practices and the historically accumulated bodies of knowledge that are essential to students' homes and communities (Moll & Gonzalez 1993). Moll and Gonzalez (1992) recommend assessing the funds of knowledge in the family and community and then using this knowledge to teach academic concepts. For example, they describe how a teacher discovered that many parents in a Latin community where she taught had expertise in building construction. As a result, she developed a unit on construction, which included reading, writing, speaking, and building all with the help of responsive community experts—the children's parents. Another teacher (Moll, Amanti, Neff & Gonzalez 1992) assessed the funds of knowledge of one of her students through a home visit. She discovered that one of her students was quite the little merchant, selling candy that the family brought back from their numerous trips to Mexico to children in his neighborhood. As she talked with the family and learned of the mother's candy-making abilities, the teacher decided to develop a curriculum unit around the use of mathematics and culture in candy making and invited the mother to help her develop some of the learning activities and to demonstrate candy making in the classroom.

As you can see, a variety of ways exist to build positive, trusting relationships with students' families that place families in a more influential role in helping teachers develop and implement effective learning experiences for children. As children's caregivers feel respected and comfortable with their child's teacher, they are more willing to share their family world with educators who can then develop instructional strategies that more directly include families in their children's learning. We describe these strategies in more depth in Chapters 8 and 9.

Focusing on Group Climate-building

In contrast to the one-on-one approach to building family–school partnerships, many educators focus on building a more collaborative family–school climate across an entire group of families and educators in a classroom or school. These educators focus on assessing the current ways that families and staff interact in a school and designing (or redesigning) school activities so as to create a more collaborative social climate between school staff and families characterized by trust, two-way communication, and mutual support in achieving their educational aims for students. The work of Weiss and Edwards (1992); Amatea, Daniels, Brigman, and Vandiver (2004); and Christiansen and Sheridan (2001) are illustrative of this focus.

Why focus on improving the family–school climate? First, individual educators always operate within the larger organization of the school, an organization that gives distinctive messages about the appropriate role of parents and educators. Hence, if the message that parents receive is consistent across educators, it will have a more powerful impact. Second, because educators work with multiple students, they need time-efficient ways to build relationships with families in a group rather than one by one. Third, many parents cannot attend school events, volunteer at the school, or participate in school decision-making bodies on a regular basis. Therefore, it is especially important to be thoughtful about the choice of events and how they are conducted to give the message that families, students, and school staff need to work together to support and enhance the education of the students.

How does one change the climate of interaction of an entire group or school? Where does one start? Two steps are needed to help a staff change the climate of family–school relations in a school: (a) examining current staff attitudes about school–family relationships and existing school norms and practices, and (b) redesigning current core routines and practices or developing new elective activities that address needs emerging in their classroom or school.

Examining Existing School Norms and Practices

Before making changes in family–school practices, the staff of a school often need to become more aware of the current organizational context and norms of their school, how this social context organizes their interactions with and beliefs about students' families, the consequences of these interactional patterns and beliefs, and what alternative ways of relating might be developed. For example, staff may find that many activities at their school are based upon the assumption that the parent is the cause for the student's misbehavior or poor academic performance and hence must assume responsibility for improving it. Weiss and Edwards (1992) recommend that staff look at how they are now interacting with families with an eye toward determining whether these practices address the goals they wish to meet and provide the messages they want to send to caregivers/family members and students (see Table 3.2 for illustrative goals).

To do this, Weiss and Edwards (1992) encouraged staff to determine the level of social connectedness they wished to create through their existing school activities and routines. Building on the work of Durkheim and of Seaman on social alienation, Weiss formulated a set of five dimensions by which to evaluate the degree of social connectedness that individuals might experience through particular school

∿∿∿∿∿∿∿∿∿∿∿∿∿∿∿∿∿∿∿∿∿∿∿∿∿∿∿∿∿∿∿∿∿∿∿

Table 3.2   *General Goals for Creating Collaborative Family–School Relations*

Blocking Blame. Actively work to block the inherent blaming that exists in many of the current parent–school problem-solving routines by restructuring the nature of the routine problem-solving efforts that go on at school so that the major focus of these efforts shifts to addressing what solutions and people are available to help solve a problem rather than assigning blame (i.e., determining who caused the problem).

Building in Routine Opportunities for Positive Nonproblematic Interaction. Create opportunities for interaction with parents that are driven more by a desire to build positive alliances with them rather than to respond to problems only. This can be accomplished by communicating with parents about the positives as well as the negatives of their children's school life and making current school activities (e.g., parent orientation meetings, letters to parents) more positive and engaging.

Redesigning Core Routines to Give Students and Parents Active, Co-Decision-Making Roles. Look for opportunities to create more equal relationships with parents in which they treat them as co-decision-makers about their children's learning rather than only recipients of educators' expertise. Involve parents (and students) in decision-making about their child (e.g., asking them what they would like to see their child learn, what they are worried about, what they know about their child that the school or test does not know).

---

activities. He proposed that participants' social connectedness would be fostered to the extent that the following aspects of participants' experience were enhanced: (a) their sense of inclusion, (b) their self-relatedness, (c) their sense of power, (d) the clarity of communication about expected roles and routines, and (e) the clarity of social norms.

In addition, staff could use the specific aspects of a school's organizational climate to assess how effectively school routines were having these desired effects. Using Taguiri's (1968) definition of organizational climate as a relatively enduring quality of the internal environment of an organization that (a) is experienced by its members, (b) influences their behavior and shapes how they relate to one another, and (c) can be described in terms of the values of a particular set of characteristics (or attributes) of the organization (27), Weiss and Edwards delineate four aspects of the environment that contribute to the climate of a school. The first aspect of school climate, the *culture*, is defined as the belief systems, values, general cognitive structure, and meanings that characterize the social environment. A school's culture comprises beliefs associated with how children learn; with the value of education in one's life; with specific ideas about how teaching and learning should occur or be evaluated; with the conception of children's problems and how to solve them; or with the meanings attributed to the language used in schools (e.g., the "English only" debate).

The second aspect of climate, the *milieu* of the organization, refers to the characteristics of persons and groups involved with the organization. A school's milieu captures the characteristics of the specific persons and groups that make up the family–school community, such as the morale of the school staff, student, and parents; their racial and ethnic backgrounds; their socioeconomic status; their level of education; their age and experience as parents; their previous experiences with schools; and their specific role expectations for how families and educators should interact. In many schools the families and school staff comprise a wide range of ethnic heritages, socioeconomic statuses, role expectations, and previous experiences with schools. In other schools, the milieu may be more homogenous. Being aware of and respecting the diversity of cultural heritages and resources represented by families is a necessary precondition to developing enriching family–school activities and relationships.

The third aspect, the *social system*, consists of the patterned ways in which school staff, family members, and students relate with one another. These relationship patterns might range from being hierarchical to collaborative, from shared leadership to solitary leadership, from adversarial to allied, from alienated to close, and from task-focused to emotionally focused. The ways of interacting among these persons might be face-to-face, on the telephone, or by written letters or notes.

The fourth aspect, the *ecology*, is composed of the physical and material aspects of the organizational environment. In a school this might encompass the (a) design and condition of classrooms and other space designated for particular purposes, (b) design and condition of school buildings, (c) signs and bulletin boards, (d) letters and messages, (e) condition of telephone and intercom systems, (f) computer system, (g) money; (h) time; (i) quality of educational materials; (j) allocation of resources, such as the scheduling of classes; and (k) nature of the surrounding neighborhood and transportation systems.

These four aspects of organizational climate are used by Weiss and Edwards (1992) to guide a school staff in the design (or redesign) of family–school activities by serving as an assessment checklist. For example, do the aspects of the school ecology send messages of collaboration and partnership or messages of domination and disconnection? Do signs at points of entry to the school welcome parents and invite their involvement, or do they emphasize the school's position of power and control? Is the central school office organized in a way that it separates the staff from family members by a high physical barrier behind which one must wait to be recognized, or is the office open and accessible? Does the condition of the classrooms or building have an inviting, yet purposeful quality? Will the planned activity increase a sense of shared power for both family and school? Does the activity take into account the attributes of the specific persons and groups who are to be involved? Will it promote interactions in which families, students, and school staff share information, make plans, and solve problems together? Although all four aspects of a school's climate are attended to, Weiss and Edwards (1992) emphasize that the nature of the social interactions (i.e., social system) and the physical characteristics of the environment (i.e., ecology) are often the most useful entry points for change. In Reflective Exercise 3.2, you will find guidelines for conducting a climate audit or assessment of a school core routine with which you are familiar. As an alternative, you may wish to assess the back-to-school night described by Stephen's mother in the previous chapter.

Reflective Exercise 3.2

Conducting a School Climate Audit

Instructions: Reflect either on the way a school core routine you have experienced was conducted or assess the back-to-school night/orientation described by Stephen's parent in the previous chapter. Use the following five questions to assess the message intended, the elements of the schools' climate carrying that message, and the climate of family–school relations depicted in this orientation activity.

Message: What was the purpose or educational goal of the activity?

Elements of the Climate

Culture: What messages were being conveyed regarding values, norms, and beliefs of the school and teacher?

Milieu: Who was involved and in what capacities?

Social System: How were interactions structured between persons and groups to reach the goal and convey the message?

Ecology: What physical and material aspects of the environment conveyed the message?

Adaptation of materials developed by Weiss, H. *The family-school collaboration project,* Ackerman Institute for the Family. New York.

Redesigning Core Routines and Practices

As a second step, a school staff needs to consider how they might redesign their current core routines and practices (e.g., school orientations, parent–teacher conferences, and problem-solving meetings) to enhance the opportunities for collaboration and parity between themselves and students' families. To redesign core school routines and practices, Weiss and Edwards (1992) encourage staff to use a collaborative group problem-solving approach to assess and redesign family–school activities. This entails inviting important stakeholders/constituencies to work with the staff in (a) identifying the primary concerns experienced in the classroom or school, (b) determining the priorities among these concerns, (c) deciding who will be involved (the target group), (d) selecting a goal, (e) planning an activity and follow-up, and (f) implementing the activity and conducting a follow-up.

In this section we briefly describe several of the core routines that have been redesigned by school staffs. Because they focus on creating a school-wide or classroom-wide activity applicable across a group of students' families in classroom or school, these are considered group climate-building activities.

Redesigning School or Program Orientations

Many educators hold meetings at the beginning of the school year to introduce parents or students to the school and its staff. Traditionally, these back-to-school programs are designed for either parents or students. Typically, they consist of one-way communication from the school to parents (or to children) about the curriculum, rules and routines, and typical procedures in the school. Although the information conveyed is important, the traditional way in which these meetings are structured often sets up a hierarchical rather than a collaborative relationship between families and schools. Weiss and Edwards (1992) describe a more collaborative format for an orientation meeting designed to send the message from the school that they need the parents as partners in educating their children.

> The goal of this type of orientation is for the teacher, parents, and students to get to know one another and to send a message that 'we need to work as partners to achieve quality education for our children.' To do this, the orientation includes the students, as well as the teacher and parents, and gives each an active role and an opportunity for meaningful discussion. One teacher invited participants to first discuss their goals for the school year together in family dyads and then report them to the rest of the group. The teacher listed the family's goals on the board, identified commonalities, and then linked the family's goals to the teacher's goals for the year. Another teacher invited parents and students to first discuss students' strengths and ways they could make progress, then pooled these ideas, and linked them to the teacher's goals and planned activities. Because the orientation occurs at the beginning of the school year, the effects on culture can be powerful. The teacher has an opportunity to demonstrate group problem solving (obtaining information, checking for consensus, and developing joint plans) and to establish the norm of collaboration around educational goals early. (232, 233)

Sometimes there are special programs in the school (e.g., special education, English as a Second Language, or a remedial reading program) that may require a separate orientation. Groups may also exist that are isolated from the rest of the school and may require their own orientation. In Figure 3.2, Weiss and Edwards (1992) describe one such orientation meeting for parents of students in an English as a Second Language program.

Orientations such as this can affect the social system by reducing the isolation of parents. Parents can get to know the parents of other children and can see the children with whom their child will be in school. Parents might also decide to set up their own network to organize volunteer projects for the school or to pass on communications from the school. A meeting of this type can also allow the teacher to get to know the different parents and children in the class, and vice versa, thus addressing the milieu of the classroom. Attention to the ecology is also important. Letters sent to parents communicate the expectation of a family–school partnership

〜〜〜〜〜〜〜〜〜〜〜〜〜〜〜〜〜〜〜〜〜〜〜〜〜〜〜〜〜〜〜〜〜〜〜

Figure 3.2   *Sharing the Meanings of School: A Special Orientation*

In one particular school where 150 children speak 26 different languages, a special orientation was designed and attended by 125 parents. In preparation for this special orientation, the *milieu* factor of having parents speaking several different languages was addressed by having a parent who speaks both English and one of the five main language groups (Spanish, Urdu, Chinese, Haitian Creole, and Russian) serve as an interpreter and main recruiter for the parents. These volunteers created communication networks among parents who speak the same language and thereby encouraged each other to come to the orientation at the school. This greatly decreased the isolation of parents who had been segregated from the school community by virtue of language and cultural differences. The orientation was scheduled in the morning as a breakfast so that parents who dropped their children off at school could stay for an extra hour and half and not miss too much work. After a general welcome in the cafeteria by the principal, along with breakfast foods and coffee, the parents broke into the five smaller language groups. The purpose of the discussion in these groups was to get to know each other. The discussion was stimulated with questions, such as: "What was school like in your home country?" and "How is that different from what you've encountered in this country?" Some parents explained that in their country, parents were discouraged from being involved in their child's school experience—from helping with homework, from even coming into the school building. They assumed that it was the same in this country. Other parents expressed concern over the things in the school they observed (e.g., that some children did not have the same dress for performing in concerts). They thought that the children should all be dressed the same way and volunteered to sew uniforms. From this came a host of proposed volunteer contributions—to each other and to the classroom. By the end of the meeting, the blackboard was full of names and ways in which parents were willing to contribute to the school.

Source: Weiss, H., & Edwards, M. (1992). The family–school collaboration project: Systemic interventions for school improvement. In S. Christenson & J. Conoley (Eds.), *Home–school collaboration: Enhancing children's academic and social competence* (234). Silver Springs, MD: National Association of School Psychologists.

and welcome questions from parents. Engaging the students in the preparation of the invitations for the meeting, and in verbally inviting their parents to attend, is a strong physical channel that invites participation. Table 3.3 depicts some of the key differences between these types of collaborative orientations and the more traditional style orientation. We describe this collaborative style orientation in more detail in Chapter 8.

‹‹

Table 3.3   Comparison of Traditional and Collaborative Family–School Core Activities

Traditional	Collaborative
Orientations	
Goal is to provide information to parents.	Goal is to get to know one another and establish partnership.
Parents are passive recipients of information.	Parents are active participants.
Child is left out.	Child is included.
Family–School Conferences	
Teacher is central.	Teacher is part of team with parents and child.
Child is left out or is passive audience.	Child is active participant and prepared beforehand.
Family–School Problem-Solving Meetings	
Calling in parents is often used as a threat.	Parents are seen as an important resource for solving problems.
Child is left out of process.	Child is central to process.
Parents hear one of two messages: (1) Fix your child or (2) here is what we are going to do to fix child.	Parents, school staff, and child work together to arrive at a joint solution.
Parent, teacher, or child feel blamed for the problem.	Blame is blocked.

Source: Weiss, H. *The family–school collaboration project,* Ackerman Institute for the Family. New York.

Restructuring Family–Teacher Conferences as Student Progress Conferences

Another activity that many educators have undertaken is to restructure the traditional parent–teacher conference to enhance the collaborative climate. Because parent–teacher conferences are a common mode for parents and teachers to have face-to-face interaction, they can be powerful vehicles for reshaping the family–school relationship. In the traditional parent–teacher conference, the teacher is central, parents have a passive role, and students are typically not included. Although teachers are expected to offer parents regular opportunities to confer about their child's progress in the elementary grades and in the middle and high school grades, conferences are usually scheduled only when a student is experiencing problems. Often communication at these meetings is one-way, from teacher to parent. As a result, many parents are unsure what they can do to influence their children's learning or achievement. In contrast, collaborative educators are redesigning these conferences as *family–teacher–student progress conferences*, in which the teacher, parent, and student meet together. In these meetings, each of the participants has an opportunity to talk about what is going well and not so well, and then through consensus a plan is developed that helps the child improve. Table 3.3 depicts some of the key differences between this collaborative style family–teacher conference and the more traditional style conference.

To make their parent–teacher conferences more collaborative, one group of educators (Amatea, Daniels, Bringman & Vandiver 2004) introduced a student-led parent conference format. Drawing from the work of Austin (1994), they set as their goal the development of a new conference format, in which students would share their school progress (academic and behavioral) and develop a plan together with their parents for how to move forward. In this new format, students prepared a portfolio of their work during class time, presented it to their parent(s), and together with their parent(s) assessed their current strengths and weaknesses and brainstormed necessary steps they could take to move forward. These student-led conferences occurred in a large group meeting, in which, after the teacher introduced the conference format and provided ideas for the parents' role in the conference, student and parent dyads met simultaneously together to review their portfolio and plan. We describe this strategy in more detail in Chapter 10.

Although a variety of ways exist in which student-led parent conferences might be formatted (e.g., involving the individual teacher, student, and parents in a meeting, or having the student and parent meet with the teacher merely starting the event), each format can have a powerful effect on the climate between the school and family. The milieu changes by including the child because, in any activity, it is important for all relevant constituents to be present. This new approach enhances students' skills in self-reflection, cooperative planning and problem solving, and communicating with their parents in a respectful and cooperative manner. The changes also affect the school culture by building the norm that a collaborative approach to education is more effective and reinforcing the belief that children ought to be involved in the discussions and planning around their own education.

Rethinking Problem-Solving Meetings

Educators have a long tradition of meeting with parents, usually the mother, when children are experiencing difficulties at school (Christenson & Hirsch 1998). Students are usually left out of these conversations or only included as a punitive measure. Typically, these are conversations in which the teacher tells parents the nature of their child's problem and recommends a particular solution (such as telling parents how they need to fix their child or how the school plans to fix the child).

Educators interested in collaboration have developed a very different format for such problem-focused meetings, in which parents and students are invited to play active, co-expert roles with teachers and have renamed these meetings *family*–school problem-solving meetings. In these meetings, teachers first solicit everyone's perspective regarding their concerns, then the participants prioritize the concerns and select a target concern. Next, the participants together develop a concrete action plan to address the concern with the family (student and parents), in which everyone (family and school) has a task to do to help the child. This action plan is written down, and a copy is made for the family and teacher(s). What is unique about this family–school problem-solving format is its task focus, blocking of blame, and involvement of all members of the family as persons who could contribute to resolving the child's problems. The message of this meeting format to parents is that the student/child can be helped only when everyone—including the student—works together. Table 3.3 depicts some of the key differences between this collaborative style family–school problem-solving meeting and the more traditional style, problem-focused meeting.

The idea of including the child in an active, problem-solving role in such a meeting, along with the parents and teachers, was first proposed by Weiss and Edwards (1992) of the Ackerman Family Institute, who initiated this meeting format fifteen years ago in their work with the New York City public schools. We describe this problem-solving meeting format in Chapter 11. Using this group problem-solving meeting format with students and their families across an entire school, Amatea et al. (2004) reported the following benefits:

> First, the children had an opportunity to observe their parents and teachers cooperating. In addition, they heard the same message coming from both parents and teachers and had an opportunity to clarify the expectations that adults had for them, as well as those that parents and teachers had for each other. Another benefit derived from students being invited to come to such meetings was that they could be "experts on themselves" because they were the best suited to describe their own experience. Including the student as an active participant also increased the student's ownership of the plans and solutions that the teachers developed in the meeting. Finally, including the children gave the teachers an opportunity to teach them how to function as active participants in conferences organized to address their problems. (402)

Revising Written Communications

Another type of climate-building intervention involves the written communications sent from the school to the parents. The way in which school memos or letters are written always sends a powerful message to parents about the relationships that the school wants to have with them. An underlying goal of written communications of educators interested in collaboration is to provide consistent messages to families that the school will work with them in a collaborative way to promote the educational success of the student. Weiss and Edwards (1992) emphasize that a school staff must examine the messages they send to parents. If the school staff want to send consistent, positive messages to parents about collaboration, they may need to examine and possibly revise existing letters, so that they send messages such as (a) "We want to build a working partnership with you/families"; (b) "We know that your input is essential for the educational success of your child"; and (c) "If there is a problem, we can and will work together with you to find a solution." These messages are quite different from the authoritarian tone conveyed by letters that contain phrases such as: "We regret to inform you that your son/daughter may not be promoted to the next grade" or "You are required to attend a meeting to discuss your son's/daughter's academic progress" or "Please come to a meeting where the team will present their assessment findings to you and make recommendations for your child's placement." Rather than emphasizing the power of the school, a collaborative message needs to convey the notion that all of the resources of the school, parents, and students (i.e., shared power) are needed to help students do as well as they can in school. Hence, a different message about the same types of situations might be: "We share your concern for your child's education. We are holding a group meeting for parents, children, and teachers to discuss ideas and suggestions about how to help children improve their school performance. Teachers will also be available for individual family conferences following the meeting."

Structural Supports for Family–School Collaboration

Although a school or district policy that supports efforts to develop family–school collaboration is an essential element in the change process, this way of thinking and working cannot be mandated. With respect to the change process, Fullan (1996) cautions: "If you try to mandate certain things—such as skills, attitudes, behaviors, and beliefs—your attempt to achieve change starts to break down. Where change is mandated, policies at best are likely to achieve only superficial compliance" (496).

Most educators involved in family–school collaboration recommend that the principal be committed to family–school collaboration as central to academic and social school activities and must communicate this commitment to staff, parents, and students. In addition, a coordinating committee of school staff (and, ultimately, family members) should be established at the school to initiate efforts to assess current family–school relationships and identify areas of need, to plan key family–school activities, and to obtain feedback from parents and students about these activities. Finally, a family–school coordinator should be designated at the school site to organize and facilitate activities to enhance family–school relationships.

With these supports, educators can implement a philosophy of collaboration that pervades everything that happens in the school. In these ways, individuals who may initially seem different because of diverse educational background, culture, ethnicity, and/or socioeconomic status can get to know one another. They can develop an alliance based on their shared vested interest that the family and school have in each child's educational progress and social/emotional development. As a result, they can begin to communicate regularly and reciprocally, develop trust in one another, and find ways to cooperate in educating the children. In the final chapter of this book, we describe the school-wide efforts of school staffs to change their ways of interacting with their students' caregivers.

Evidence of Effectiveness

Although considerable research has been made on the parent involvement practices driven by the remediation paradigm, the effect of the collaborative relationships between parents, teachers, and schools on children's school outcomes is a recent area of study. Three of the programs we discuss in this book—McCaleb's (1994) Building Community of Learners Program, Comer's School Development Program (Comer & Hayes 1991), Weiss and Edwards' (1992) Family–School Collaboration Project—have reported successful outcomes. Parents in McCaleb's program increased their involvement in their children's school and became more empowered in communicating with school staff. Research studies (Comer 1980; Comer, Haynes, Joyner & Ben-Avie 1996; Cook, Murphy & Hunt 2000) on Comer's program demonstrate that SDP schools have been very successful in increasing the academic achievement of low-income, inner-city students with improvement in attendance, overall academic achievement, behavioral problems, parent–teacher communication, and parent participation in school activities. Research conducted on the Family–School Collaboration Project reported that project schools significantly increased parent–teacher communication and parent attendance in parent–teacher conferences and other school activities (Weiss & Edwards 1996).

Developing Your Skills in Family–School Collaboration

As you can see, collaborating with families may take many forms. Underlying these various educational practices are some important skills. In Chapter 2 we illustrated the nature of collaborative family–school relations as a stationary bridge that forms a connecting path between the worlds of home and school that students traverse each day. If you recall, the bridge symbolizes the nature and quality of the family–school relationship. In a solid bridge that one trusts to have their child cross, the family–school relationship is strong, predictable, and positive. If the family–school relationship is weak, the bridge does not offer reliable support to the child who traverses the path between home and school. Hence, the child cannot depend upon it as a trustworthy resource. In Figure 3.3, we have added six pillars

Figure 3.3 The Foundational Pillars/Supports for the Bridge Between Home and School

that support the bridge to denote six foundational skills needed to build strong working relationships with your students' families. Let us describe these six skills.

Skill 1   Understanding Oneself, One's Personal Reactions, and Attitudes

Why take the time to develop relationships with your students' families? After all, don't you have enough to do just working with their children? Why can't you just follow the traditional way of relating to parents, of calling them in only when a problem arises and otherwise leaving them alone? Teachers may have this common reaction to the idea of reaching out and learning from families. It may be fueled by the anxiety of not knowing how to relate to parents who look and act far differently from themselves, or the concern that the teacher may "lose control" of their classroom if they invite in parents who become overintrusive and demanding. Obviously, your emotional reactions and attitudes are important to understand as you undertake this new role. The more you are aware of and understand your own emotional reactions and attitudes toward change and difference, the more you can decide how to proceed in trying out new behaviors. This personal understanding can also help you understand and appreciate the attitudes and emotional reactions of others. We believe that to work effectively with students and their families, you need to be willing to explore and examine your own emotional reactions and thoughts and to reflect on how they affect your relationships with students, their families, and other school staff. Throughout this book, we will invite you to reflect on your attitudes about specific families and their situations and your beliefs and expectations as to how you should structure your interactions with families. We find this to be an important first step toward working effectively with others.

Skill 2   Understanding and Valuing Family and Community Strengths

How do families contribute to their children's academic development? Do they differ in how they rear their children? What life-cycle experiences do families go through that affect their resources and their abilities to foster their children's learning? Just as it is important for you to understand yourself to function as a competent and compassionate educator, you also need to understand families. Traditionally, many educators viewed nontraditional family forms, families with limited incomes, those from minority groups, and those with children born out of wedlock as being deficient or defective. As a result, those educators thought such families needed remediation and parent education. But the collaborative approach to working with families requires that you recognize and appreciate the unique ways that families influence children's learning, both in school and out of school, and build on, rather than ignore, those strengths and ways of knowing. This requires that you learn how to look for family strengths and build on them. To do this, you need to learn from families about how they function, appreciate the challenges that families face in rearing children, and seek to understand their diverse strengths and perspectives. In addition, you must learn about the distinctive cultural values, expectations, and social and economic resources that families possess and build on those resources and strengths. Part II, the next section of this book, is devoted to (a) understanding more fully how families function to influence children's learning, (b) appreciating the unique challenges and stresses they experience, and (c) recognizing the impact of diversity of family cultural backgrounds and of their socioeconomic circumstances. The section will introduce you to ways of looking at family life and assessing family strengths, whereas Part III will introduce you to specific strategies you can use to reach out and learn from families.

Skill 3   Reaching Out and Communicating

Communication has always existed between school staff and students' families. How-ever, in the past, schools and families rarely established ongoing, routine vehicles or opportunities for sharing information in a two-way dialogue. One reason for this is that school staff often lacked the skills needed to elicit input from parents and stu-dents or to constructively use that input. When parents and teachers talked, they often talked *at* each other not *with* each other. In addition, the interactions that occurred between the family and school were triggered exclusively by problems. As a result, most communication that parents had with the school was negative and problem-focused and was typically authoritarian and one-way (from the school to the home). School staff told families what to do, and families generally expected interactions to be negative. School staff did not place much value in interacting with students' fam-ilies, believing it would take too much valuable time away from teaching. Families were only contacted when educators had a problem they could not solve.

As you read in this chapter, collaborative educators are moving away from the "no news is good news" mentality (i.e., contacting parents only when there is a prob-lem). They are recognizing that investing in building relationships with families and developing trust before a problem emerges can make any problem-focused interac-tion run more smoothly. Looking at how they might "dig the well, before they are thirsty," they are creating opportunities to get to know and become known by their students' families and to build trust in the parents of their students. Hence, they are creating opportunities for ongoing, routine communication between the school and families for the purpose of sharing information, developing educational plans, and solving problems. This requires that you learn how to (a) reach out and communi-cate with students' families, (b) design family–school interactions for all students' fam-ilies, and (c) tie family–school contact to children's learning. In Part III of this book, we describe in detail the skills and practices that you will need to engage in collabo-ration and introduce you to specific skills for developing family–school activities that allow you to create regular vehicles for communicating with your students' families.

Skill 4   Understanding and Appreciating Family Diversity

Family diversity refers to the different elements that shape family members' sense of identity, such as the family's composition, culture, economic circumstances, and reli-gious beliefs. We assume that each of the social groups to which a family belongs contributes to the construction of their identity as a family as well as to the identity of individual family members. Many factors shape our cultural identity and family group identity, such as race, ethnicity, immigration status, gender, religion, geo-graphical location, income status, sexual orientation, disability status, and occupa-tion. Appreciating/honoring family cultural diversity means (a) reaching out to people with cultural identities different from your own by learning about the assumptions, belief systems, role perceptions, and prejudices that may affect how families rear their children and interact with the school and larger community; (b) developing opportunities to incorporate the unique skills of families from different cultural contexts into their children's learning; (c) creating comfortable, respectful relationships with them; and (d) tailoring family–school activities to the constraints and capacities of individual families. In Part II, the next section of this book, we look at the diversity of family cultural backgrounds and social and economic circumstances and the unique strengths and stresses of these families. In Part III, we introduce strategies for tailoring family–school activities to the diverse cultural backgrounds of your students' families.

Skill 5   Building in Opportunities for Positive Nonproblematic Family-School Interaction

Collaborative educators are creating opportunities for interaction with parents that are driven more by a desire to build positive alliances with them rather than to respond only to problems. By making current school activities (e.g., parent orientation night, letters to parents) more positive and engaging, and by communicating with parents about the positives as well as negatives of their children's school life, educators are creating opportunities for interaction that are not problem-driven only. To do this, you need to know how to (a) carefully assess the current family–school activities and communication you engage in and (b) redesign these activities so as to create more positive, meaningful roles for parents and students. In Chapters 8, 9, and 10 we describe specific skills and practices for designing nonproblematic opportunities for families to participate in their children's learning and schooling.

Skill 6   Creating Active, Co-Decision-Making Roles in Planning and Problem Solving and Accessing Needed Services

To develop strong, collaborative relationships with students and their families you will want to create active, co-decision-making roles for them in matters concerning their child. For example, to solve a child's problems it will be important to restructure the nature of your problem-solving efforts with students' families so that the major focus of these efforts shifts from assigning blame (i.e., determining who caused the problem) to addressing what solutions and people are available to help solve a problem. To do this, you will want to develop skills in conducting meetings to which both parents and students are invited to play an active, co-expert role with you in developing a concrete action plan in which everyone (family and school) has a task to do to help the child. Chapters 11, 12, and 13 are devoted to showcasing the skills for conducting group problem-solving meetings with families in the context of resolving children's academic and behavioral problems, of individualizing educational plans for students with special learning needs, and of accessing community resources to meet family needs.

Discussion

As you can see, the process of moving from a separation or remediation paradigm to a collaborative one is a developmental process that occurs over time and involves a multitude of skills. Even when you are committed to a philosophy of partnership, learning how you might restructure your typical ways of interacting with families can be a challenging experience. Discovering how you might invite families into their children's educational process—learning how to invite their input, how to seek consensus, and how to develop joint plans and decisions—involves new types of learning for most educators. Hence, it is important as you learn of these possibilities, to be patient with yourself as your try out these ways of working with families from your own classroom or school.

Summary

In this chapter we looked at how educators are redesigning the nature of their relationships with culturally diverse families to be more collaborative. We looked at the typical ways of thinking and working with families that these educators have developed. We then described how these ways of thinking and working to develop collaborative relations have been translated into both dyadic and group-focused strategies. The dyadic strategies include (a) reaching out and sharing oneself with families, (b) valuing and affirming family expertise and ways of knowing, and (c) involving parents as significant participants in children's learning. In contrast, group climate-building approaches typically focus on (a) redesigning existing school routines, such as orientations or parent–teacher conferences, to be more collaborative; (b) creating more positive, nonproblematic family–school interactions and communication; and/or (c) redesigning family–school problem solving and blocking blame. These group climate-building efforts are based on examining the specific message of social connectedness to be sent by a school via four aspects of its organizational climate: (a) culture, (b) milieu, (c) social system, and (d) ecology.

Finally, we describe six skills needed to develop such family–school partnerships that are showcased in this book: (a) understanding oneself, one's personal beliefs, and attitudes; (b) understanding families and communities and valuing their strengths; (c) reaching out and communicating; (d) understanding and appreciating family diversity; (e) building in opportunities for positive nonproblematic family–school interaction; and (f) creating active, co-decision-making roles for families.

Resources

Family Involvement Network of Educators (FINE),
www.gse.harvard.edu/~hfrp/

FINE is a national network of over 2,000 people who are committed to promoting strong partnerships between children's educators, their families, and their communities. No cost is required to join. Members receive free monthly announcements through e-mail of resources related to partnerships. Information online includes research, training tools, model programs, and other topics of interest.

Part II

Understanding Families in Their Sociocultural Context

Families vary significantly from one another, not only in terms of their surface characteristics, but also in terms of their ways of interacting, their cultural traditions, and their economic and social resources. Using family systems theory and ecological systems theory as frameworks, Part II explores how family members may interact with one another and with schools and the impact of cultural and community conditions on these interactions. In Chapter 4 we will look at how families interact with one another and the functions that they perform together as families. Chapter 5 explores the varying family forms and how they move through various stages of their lives. Diverse cultural and socioeconomic backgrounds of families are examined in Chapter 6. Chapter 7 explores how families' neighborhood and community conditions influence the day-to-day lives of families and schools.

Chapter 4

From Family Deficit to Family Strength: Examining How Families Influence Children's Development and School Success

Ellen S. Amatea

Learning Objectives

After reading this chapter, you will be able to:

- Explain the changes in thinking of researchers who investigate how families influence their children's learning and social adjustment.
- Describe the assumptions of family systems theorists and ecological systems theorists regarding the influences on children's development of the family and larger social systems.

■ Know the research that describes the specific family processes used by families varying in structure and social background to rear children to be academically successful.

■ Describe strategies for assessing and strengthening how families foster their children's learning.

> *The summer that I turned thirteen my father sat my 12-year-old sister and me down and showed us how to make a weekly schedule in which we laid out our week's activities of chores, swimming at the community center, and trips to the library. Every Sunday night he would ask us how our schedule had helped us keep track of what we did with our time. He would then have us make up a new schedule for the coming week. That habit of thinking purposefully about how I spend my time has stood me in good stead for the past forty years as I tackled the multiple responsibilities of running a household, raising children, and having a demanding career.*

Like this successful professional woman in her late fifties, every one of us can tell a story about the lessons our families have taught us about managing our lives. Through one's family, children learn who they are, where they fit into society, what kinds of futures they are likely to experience, and how to plan for those futures. Although families have frequently been blamed for children's academic difficulties, particularly when families are poor and not consistently involved with the school, most educators are not exactly sure how families, particularly those of oppressed minorities, shape their children's future. How do families prepare their children to be successful academically? What do families, especially families who are very poor or are headed by a single parent or a grandparent, do at home to groom children for school success?

A considerable body of research is now available that describes how families who vary in structure and social background rear children who are academically successful and socially adjusted. The purpose of this chapter is to examine what we have learned about such families. We will first look at how, over the past fifty years, family researchers have changed their research perspective and moved from looking only at the surface characteristics and deficits of families to looking at the internal lives of families. Next, we discuss family system theory and ecological systems theory and how these two theories have become the major theoretical frameworks that organize how researchers have studied the lives of children and families. Finally, we describe the key ways that researchers are reporting that families organize their lives to effectively rear their children. We believe that this information can be of value to you as an educator for several reasons. First, it can counter many of the stereotyped descriptions of family lifestyles and customs depicted in the mass media that may influence your efforts to reach out to students' families. Second, it can help you understand what families actually do at home to teach their children to be successful in school. Thus, it can counter the belief that some educators hold that only those families who show up at school are effectively rearing their children. Third, it can guide you in deciding how to help families further strengthen their capacity to rear children who are successful in school and in life.

Moving Beyond Stereotypes: Changing Research Perspectives

Can children from "broken homes" be successful in school? What about children of welfare mothers, children with absent fathers, or "latch-key" children whose mothers work and cannot supervise them after school? During the 1950s, 1960s, and 1970s most social scientists who study the family's influence on children's school performance embraced the popular stereotype that nontraditionally structured families (e.g., the family with one parent or the family with an employed mother) had a negative effect on children's school performance. (Even the language of "broken homes," "absent fathers," and "latch-key children" has a pejorative ring, does it not?) These early family researchers, who took a *family structure* research perspective, assumed that only one type of family structure—the idealized 1950s intact nuclear family headed by a breadwinner father and supported by a stay-at-home mother—was "normal" and had a positive effect on children. Like many social scientists of that era, these researchers believed that the major source of youth's needs and academic problems was their *location* in particular family groups with one or more of the following characteristics: (a) divorced parents, (b) working mothers, (c) missing or absent fathers, (d) young mothers, (e) poorly educated mothers, (f) recently migrated to American cities, (g) racial or ethnic minority, (h) living on limited incomes, or (i) residing in depressed, inner-city neighborhoods. Illustrative of this approach were studies that examined the effect of the presence or absence of fathers from the family on children's school performance (Herzog & Sudia 1973; Kriesberg 1967; Moynihan 1965).

Until the early 1980s, practically all empirical research that studied the influence of family on children's school achievement used this family structure perspective in which they compared the adjustment or achievement of children from two different types of family structures (e.g., single-parent versus two-parent families). Although this family structure research is voluminous, efforts to predict students' academic achievement, based on family socioeconomic status or family structure configuration alone, have not been too successful. White (1982), for example, analyzed 101 different studies and found that only 25 percent of the variance in student school achievement could be accounted for by family socioeconomic status or family structure configuration. Despite this modest success, the family structure research perspective continues to be used to confirm many of the stereotypes and misconceptions that appear in the popular media about the negative influence on children of being in low-income, non-White, or single-parent family structures.

In the 1980s, however, a number of social scientists (Clark 1983; Dornbush, Ritter, Leiderman, Roberts & Fraleigh 1987) began to challenge this deficit-oriented perspective. Noting that little attention had been paid to studying how the surface characteristics of family structure or income (e.g., two-parent or one-parent) might be shaping the actual behaviors and daily lives of family members, these researchers observed that family structure researchers had no means to explain the differences in student achievement within a social group. This criticism was eloquently expressed by Clark: "Of the many studies that have shown a statistical correlation between background, life chances, and life achievement, few seem to explain adequately the fact that many youngsters with disadvantaged backgrounds perform very well in school and in later life" (Clark 1983, 18).

Rejecting the idea that family structure and/or socioeconomic status alone were reasons for students not succeeding in school, these researchers (Clark 1983; Dornbush, Ritter, Leiderman, Roberts & Fraleigh 1987) proposed a *family process* perspective. They insisted that only by *looking inside the family* at the particular ways in which family members behaved with each other could one understand how families influenced children's school achievement. Moreover, they believed that under no conditions should it be inferred that family background characteristics alone were the reason why students did not succeed. Instead, these researchers sought to show how the beliefs, activities, and overall style of interaction of the entire family, not only the surface characteristics of family composition or social status, produced the necessary mental structures for children's successful school performance. Using *family systems theory*, these researchers studied how family members organized themselves to carry out important family tasks, such as establishing rules for children's behavior, getting children to school on time, monitoring children's whereabouts, organizing who would prepare meals or keep clothes washed, or fostering children's cognitive or social development.

Over the past two decades, many family researchers (Bugental, Blue & Cruzcosa 1989; Edin & Lein 1997; Furstenburg, Cook, Eccles, Elder & Sameroff 1999; Murry, Brody, Brown, Wisenbaker, Cutrona & Simons 2002; Xu & Corno 2003) have begun to draw the circle more broadly by looking at a family's larger system of environmental and institutional contexts and assessing how these contexts influence family life. Using Bronfenbrenner's *ecological systems theory*, these researchers examined how the various systems in which a family was engaged (such as schools, work settings, or community agencies), affected children and families. Many of these researchers were particularly interested in how families who face adverse environmental circumstances carried out their functions. Noting that the same adversity appeared to result in different outcomes in different families, these researchers adopted *a family resilience* perspective. They explored what happened inside families as a result of adverse external events and circumstances and studied how families withstood, adapted, and rebounded from adversity. Edin and Lein (1997), for example, in their interviews with 379 low-income single mothers, uncovered families who lived in extreme poverty and deprivation and who demonstrated surprising resilience and creativity in building strategies to help their children overcome poor life conditions. Even with low incomes and the struggles of getting and keeping public assistance, a high proportion of these economically disadvantaged families were able to keep their children in school, live in their own homes, and engage their children in developmentally appropriate activities. A basic assumption of family resilience researchers and practitioners is that, although stressful crises and persistent economic, physical, and social challenges influence the whole family and their capacity to successfully rear their children, key family processes can mediate the impact of these crises and facilitate the development of resilience in individual members and in the family unit as a whole (Walsh 2003).

A volume of research that uses either a family process or family resilience perspective has now been conducted (Bempechat 1998; Collignon, Men & Tan 2001; Crouter, McDermid, McHale & Perry-Jenkins 1990; Dornbush & Ritter 1992; Eccles & Harold 1996; Garcia Coll, Akiba, Pacio, Bailey, Silve, DiMartino & Chin 2002; Kellaghan, Sloane, Alvarez & Bloom 1993; Lam 1997; Snow, Barnes, Chandler, Goodman & Hemphill 1991), generating a rich picture of how families of varying socioeconomic backgrounds influence their children's school lives. We now know that, although lower-SES parents' work often involves inflexible schedules and long or unpredictable hours, these circumstances are not predictive of less involvement in their children's education. As Hoover-Dempsey et al. (2005) state:

> Socioeconomic status does not generally explain why and how parents become involved in their children's schooling, nor does it explain why parents in similar or identical SES categories vary substantially in their effectiveness in raising educationally successful children. (114)

Instead, researchers (Desdimone 1999; Fan & Chen 1999; Horvat, Weininger & Lareau 2003) have found that the particular ways that family members interact with their children are much more powerful predictors of children's school achievement. For example, Fan and Chen (2001) reported that parent's aspirations and expectations for their children's educational achievement were much more strongly predictive of their children's academic achievement than their socioeconomic class. Furthermore, Walberg (1984) reported that 60 percent of the variance in reading achievement was explained by the particular interactions that family members engaged in with their children, whereas only 25 percent of the variance in student reading achievement was explained by social class or family structure configuration (e.g., intact or divorced family).

Using Systems Theory to Understand Family Life
〰〰〰〰〰〰
〰〰〰〰〰〰

Families have always been recognized as a central influence on children's emotional well-being and school learning. However, the traditional training of most educators has not given them systematic ways of assessing and working with families (Christenson & Sheridan 2001). Lacking an explicit conceptual framework for understanding how families influence their children, educators often fall back into using common stereotypes to describe students' families, such as "overly involved mother," "neglectful parents," or "broken home." Such thinking can result in simplistic explanations for children's performance and moralistic parent blaming. To correct this situation, many educators are beginning to use family systems theory and ecological systems theory to understand students' families and their larger life contexts. The central advantage of these theories is that they provide educators with a more explicit, nonblaming lens by which to understand the complex ways that families rear their children and the complex forces that shape their interactions with schools.

Family Systems Theory

Family systems theory, developed initially by family therapists who work with troubled families and then expanded to assess healthy family functioning and strengths, is now the major theoretical model used by clinicians and researchers to understand how families function together. It provides a different way of looking at students and their families that moves us beyond describing them exclusively in terms of individual characteristics, such as low-income or two-parent households, toward viewing that person as positioned within a context of relationships and interactions with others. Very simply stated, a family is seen as a system that is defined as "any perceived whole whose elements hang together because they continually affect each other over time and operate toward some common purpose" (Minuchin, Nichols & Lee 2007, 4). Inherent in this definition are the ideas of wholeness, interdependence, adaptability, and purposefulness.

By *wholeness* we mean that any system—whether it be a family, a work organization, or an athletic team—is made up of parts (e.g., family members), but it may be seen as an organic whole that "hangs together." This sense of wholeness or unity is created by the way that family members talk about themselves and their life together and define themselves in relationship to others. A family may describe itself as religious, close-knit, supportive, or strong—adjectives that might not necessarily apply to every member. Moreover, a family often defines itself by describing who is in the family group and who is not. As a result, family systems theorists tend to describe families in terms of the quality of the boundary that families establish defining themselves as a group. Do people know who is in or out of the family and who is to be included in family discussions and decision-making?

A positive consequence of this sense of wholeness is the experience of unity of purpose and synergy that may develop as family members work together. Have you ever had the experience of working with someone else and realizing that the two of you together can accomplish more than can each of you working individually? When you consider a human system like a family, the parts or people have importance, but once these parts become interrelated they may take on a life greater than their individual existence. In other words, the whole is greater than the sum of its parts. For example, history has often documented the collective power of immigrant families to accomplish dramatic improvements in their social position and income through their members' joint efforts. Think about the accomplishments of your own family or other families you know and try to imagine how differently they would have to act if it were assumed that these accomplishments could only occur if each person acted as an isolated individual. In most cases you will probably conclude that the group spirit can be a positive force that contributes to your family's accomplishments.

By *interdependence*, we mean that the parts of the system are interconnected or interrelated so as to be dependent upon each other for proper functioning. The actions of one member trigger reactions in another member, and, over time, patterns of interconnections are developed. For example, think of your own family. How do you greet family members in the morning? How do you show affection to family members? How do you resolve family disputes? The patterns you develop for living together reveal the degree of connectedness or interrelatedness that you have established among yourselves as a group. All human systems, such as families, develop predictable ways of interacting. Although you may not be aware of it, you have learned to live within a relatively predictable pattern of interaction that characterizes how your family members affect each other over time. Moreover, changes in one part (i.e., a member) of the family will result in changes in other parts. Satir (1972), a noted family therapist, said it well when she described a family as a mobile. Picture the mobile that hangs above a child's crib as having family members instead of animals on it. As events touch one family member, other family members reverberate in relationship to the change in the affected member. Thus, if a member of your family were to flunk out of school, lose their job, marry, or become ill, each of these events would affect the surrounding group of family members to a greater or lesser extent, depending on each person's current relationship with the specific individual. Each of you may be able to pinpoint major or minor events in your own families that influenced all members of your family in some ways. In the next chapter, we will examine the types of changes that families experience and the impact that these changes can have on the lives of family members.

All families need some regularity and predictability to streamline their functioning. Through a system of feedback, family members develop and then maintain their patterns of relating with each other within a defined range. Yet families also *adapt* by changing their ways of relating as they face internal and external demands for change. By means of feedback, healthy families change their roles and ways of relating and organizing themselves in response to demands from inside the family or from the environment. Parenting, for example, involves continually adjusting as children change developmentally. Hence, a parent's style of monitoring their young children would be inappropriate for monitoring their teenager. Moreover, in the face of illness or other family crises, some families are able to adapt their roles and routines, whereas other families become stuck in patterns of operating and relating that no longer work.

Finally, human systems, such as families, live together and jointly organize their efforts for specific *purposes*. Families serve a variety of purposes, whether it is to rear and socialize children; to provide food, clothing, and shelter for their members; to provide daily care for their members by means of a well-run home; to be a source of emotional support and affection for one another; to share recreational activities and interests; to provide educational and vocational skills to its members; to provide a sense of personal identity and meaning; and to provide spiritual support.

Ecological Systems Theory

Ecological systems theory applies the idea of systems to interactions among different levels of a system and across different systems. Bronfenbrenner (1979; 1997) hypothesized that developing individuals are active participants located within a variety of systems. These systems, ever changing, constitute the different settings with potential to impact the developing child. According to the ecological systems theory (Bronfenbrenner 1979; 1997), a child's development is influenced either directly (i.e., through daily routines and interactions that occur in the child's immediate context) or indirectly (i.e., through more distant factors that impact those routines and interactions). You will recall from our brief discussion of this theory in Chapter 2, that a primary idea of ecological systems theory is that every level of the ecological system (e.g., the child's home or classroom, the caregiver's workplace, and the family's and school's neighborhood) is interdependent and interconnected and thus can influence all other levels of the system. Thus, persons across each system level reciprocally influence persons at other levels. For example, the way that teachers and other school staff structure their educator–student classroom routines and interactions and their family–school routines and interactions affect what happens in the child's home, and vice versa. Moreover, larger social and economic policies and resources (considered distant from a child's everyday experience) also influence the routines and interactions that occur in the child's immediate contexts of the home and classroom.

Ecological systems theory can be represented visually as a set of concentric circles surrounding the child (see Figure 4.1). The immediate interpersonal contexts in which the child interacts (e.g., parent–child, teacher–child, sibling–sibling) compose the microsystem. Adults who nurture and teach children, peers and siblings who play and socialize with them, and settings, such as day care, home, and school, constitute the *microsystem*. One of the most salient points that Bronfenbrenner makes is that a child's learning and development are facilitated when the child participates in complex patterns of reciprocal activities with someone with whom the child has a strong and enduring emotional attachment. According to Bronfenbrenner (1979), for the child to have the greatest opportunities to develop: "Somebody has got to be crazy about that kid" (174). However, not only does the

Figure 4.1   Bronfenbrenner's Ecological Systems Theory

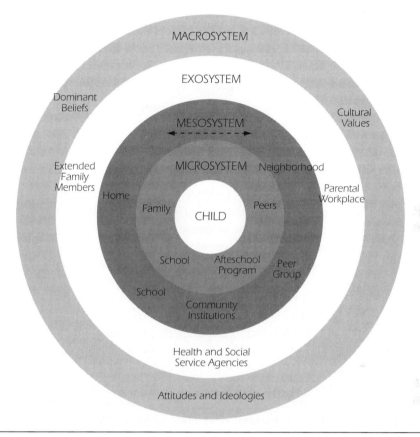

Source: D. Bukatko & M. Daehler (1995). Child Development: A Thematic Approach, Boston, MA: Houghton Mifflin, p. 62

caregiver influence the child, but also the child and his or her characteristics influence the nature of the interaction.

The *mesosystem* is the next level of ecological systems theory and involves interactions and social relationships between and among individuals and settings. For example, mesosystem interactions include those between specific individuals (e.g., a parent and a teacher) and microsystem settings/institutions (e.g., an after-school program and a school). Hence, the social relations in the mesosystem may be at the institutional level (general messages sent out by the school to all families) or individual level (e.g., when a parent and a teacher meet in a conference or talk on the phone). In this way, the mesosystem represents the degree of connection, coordination, and continuity across the child's microsystem settings.

The *exosystem* of ecological systems theory provides the context in which events occur that affect the individual child's immediate environment (e.g., child's microsystem) and do so indirectly. Settings within the exosystem may include work, church, neighborhood, extended family, and/or the quality and availability of community health, recreational, or social services. Thus, the exosystem exerts its influence on the child via its impact on individuals and institutions in the child's microsystem. For example, parents' workplaces may institute new work schedules that interfere with parents' ability to read to their child each night, which then affects the child's literacy achievement.

The *macrosystem* operates at the broadest level of influence and determines, to a great extent, the resources, opportunities, and constraints present in the lives of children and families. The macrosystem comprises the cultural beliefs, values, and attitudes that surround family life and children's development embodied in political systems, social policy, culture, economic trends, and so on. Bronfenbrenner (1979) defines this context as the generalized patterns, overarching ideology, and organization of social institutions common to a particular culture or subculture. Rather than referring to specific ecological contexts, the macrosystem refers to the general patterns of values and beliefs that exist in any culture or subculture. These patterns influence the structure and activities that occur in a particular culture or subculture and include the institutional patterns in which the microsystem, mesosystem, and exosystem are embedded. For example, national policies, such as welfare reform, have exerted control over parents' access to economic support and have changed the conditions under which parents receive that support and the ways that they provide and care for their children. Another example are the dominant cultural practices and belief systems around individual achievement that affect what parents and teachers prioritize and value and how they organize their daily routines to achieve their goals. An additional example of macrosystemic influences are the attitudes of educators and the general public regarding providing inclusive educational opportunities for children with disabilities. If a school does not provide inclusive settings, then the child with a disability who attends that school has limited opportunities.

The *chronosystem* represents the element of time, both in the individual's life trajectory (e.g., infancy, childhood, adolescence, adulthood) and historical context (Bronfenbrenner's theory 1997). For example, there has been a dramatic increase in the number of dual-income families in the United States, which, in turn, has affected children's daily routines and experiences through nonparental care. In the next chapter, we will examine how the family's and individual's life trajectory both influences and is influenced by the larger systems context in which they operate (Bronfenbrenner 1979).

Looking at Key Family System Processes

As a result of the influence of family systems and ecological systems theories, a consistent picture is now emerging from research revealing how the families of successful students interact with their children to prepare them to be successful in school (Brody 1999; Bugental, Blue & Cruzcosa 1989: Clark 1983; Crosnoe, Mistry & Elder 2002; Eccles & Harold 1996; Edin & Lein 1997; Fan & Chen 2001; Hoover-Dempsey et al. 2005; Jackson 2000; Murry, Brody, Brown, Wisenbaker, Cutrona & Simons 2002). From this research we now know that, despite multiple adverse conditions (e.g., socioeconomic disadvantages, urban poverty, community violence, chronic illness, and catastrophic life events), effective families demonstrate remarkably similar ways of relating to each other that contribute to their children's academic success. We have organized these ways of interacting into a framework that consists of four domains: (a) family beliefs and expectations, (b) family patterns of emotional connectedness, (c) family organizational patterns, and (d) family patterns around learning. These patterns of relating, outlined in detail in Table 4.1 on page 92, appear to operate in an interrelated fashion, with all working to positively influence student learning.

Family Beliefs and Expectations

Family members of academically successful students demonstrate a distinctive pattern of beliefs and expectations characterized by a (a) strong sense of purpose, (b) positive outlook, and (c) high level of personal efficacy (Brody 1999; Bugental, Blue & Cruzcosa 1989; Clark 1983; Edin & Lein 1997; Jackson 2000; Mandara 2006; Murry, Brody, Brown, Wisenbaker, Cutrona & Simons 2002).

Sense of Purpose

Researchers report that the parents/caregivers of successful students have a strong sense of purpose and demonstrate in their own lives the necessity of setting goals, committing themselves to meet these goals, and persisting at difficult tasks (Clark 1983; Edin & Lein 1997; Furstenburg et al. 1999; Jackson 2000.) For example, a review by Fan and Chen (2001) of 25 studies that examined the influence of specific aspects of parent involvement on children's achievement indicated that parents' expectations and aspirations for their child's educational achievement were very strongly correlated with their child's academic achievement.

Parents also expect their children to set goals for themselves and to work hard to achieve those goals (Clark 1983; Crosnoe, Mistry & Elder 2002; Eccles & Harold 1996; Snow, Barnes, Chandler, Goodman & Hemphill 1991). This expectation for purposeful action is delivered several ways. First, parents frequently talk with their children about future life goals and the necessary steps to getting there, and they encourage their children to dream, to make plans for the future, and to seek "a better life." As one mother of a high school student interviewed by Clark (1983) stated:

〜〜

Table 4.1   Key Family Interactional Processes Contributing to Children's Academic Success

I. Family Beliefs

   A. Sense of Purpose
- Focus on setting goals, taking concrete steps, building on successes, and learning from failures
- Demonstrate sense of purpose through commitment to family life and parenting role
- Encourage children to lead purposive lives

   B. Positive Outlook
- Hopeful, optimistic view, confidence in overcoming odds
- Courage and encouragement; focus on strengths and potential
- Master the possible; accept what cannot be changed

   C. Sense of Efficacy
- Active initiative and perseverance (can-do spirit)
- Confidence in one's ability to learn, persevere, and overcome odds
- Appraisal of adversity as normal and an opportunity to learn

II. Family Emotional Connectedness

   A. Emotional warmth and belonging
- Provide emotional warmth and caring
- Demonstrate mutual support, collaboration, and commitment
- Respect individual needs, differences and boundaries of family members
- Enjoy each other; have pleasurable, humor-filled interactions

   B. Open, emotional sharing
- Share range of feelings rather than repress or avoid expressing feelings
- Demonstrate empathy for each other
- Take responsibility for own feelings and behavior rather than blame others

   C. Clear communication
- Have consistency in words and actions
- Clarify meanings and intentions if information is ambiguous

   D. Collaborative problem solving
- Share decision-making and conflict resolution
- Focus on mutuality, fairness, and reciprocity

III. Family Organizational Patterns

   A. Strong Leadership and Clear Expectations
- Clear leadership hierarchy of roles and responsibilities
- Strong caregiver leadership alliance
- Sets clear and realistic guidelines and expectations for children's behavior

   B. Firm But Friendly Management Style
- Actively monitor children's activities and performance at home and at school
- Maintain dependable family routines and responsibilities
- Adapt and reorganize to fit changing needs and circumstance of children

   C. Developed Social Network
- Mobilize extended kin and social support
- Find and develop community resources
- Initiate home–school contacts

Table 4.1 Continued

IV. Family Learning Opportunities

  A. Development of Family Routines that Support Achievement
   ■ Monitor homework and child's school performance
   ■ Engage in enriching learning activities
   ■ Engage in frequent parent–child conversation about current school performance and long-term goals
  B. Explicit Skill Instruction
   ■ Seek knowledge of child's current school performance and strengths and weaknesses in learning
   ■ Orient the child to both academic and social skills learning opportunities
   ■ Give regular, explicit feedback to child about his or her performance in learning activities
   ■ Demonstrate positive affect about learning activities

Source: Amatea, E., Smith-Adcock, S., & Villares, E. (2006). From family deficit to family strength. *Professional School Counseling*. 9(3)180 in 177–189.

I told my son to do whatever interests him. I make no decisions for him. I'd be interested in whatever he is. I know in order for him to get a job, whatever it is, he's gotta be interested in it. I told him I would like for him to go to school but I don't want him to because of me. I want him to be interested in it because you're not really going to be a success at anything unless you have your mind to it. So, it's up to him. (99)

Second, parents frequently use themselves as reference points, repeatedly emphasizing that their children should try to do better in educational and occupational attainment (Brody, Flor & Gibson 1999; Eccles & Harold 1996; Frome & Eccles 1998; Grolnick, Ryan & Deci 2000). One father interviewed depicted this message in his conversations with his teenage son (Clark 1983):

This is what I'm trying to explain to my son; I want him to succeed. The only way he can do this is to be even smarter than I was because things are getting tougher instead, you know every day things is getting out of reach. And there's no way I can get him these things with what I make. So I told him he can get them on his own but he's got to get his schooling finished. So I told him all you can do to survive these days is to have an education. (101)

Third, these parents teach their children how to set goals and act purposefully by systematically stressing that their children commit themselves to purposeful schooling. One mother illustrated this message in her report of her conversations with her teenage children:

I always told my children that you don't go to school for a love affair, you go to school for an education. And it does not matter whether a teacher likes you or not. You don't go there to be liked. You go there to get an education. And if you act like a young lady or gentleman you can get the respect of people whether they like you or not. (Clark, 1983, 105)

A number of studies (Clark 1983; Crosnoe et al. 2002; Eccles & Harold 1996; Frome & Eccles 1998; Gonzalez, Holbein & Quilter 2002) have confirmed this positive relationship between parental expectations of purposeful action and student's goal orientation and school achievement.

Positive Outlook

Families of successful students think optimistically about their life circumstances, and they teach their children to think optimistically—viewing adverse circumstances as providing an opportunity to learn. Parents demonstrate confidence that they can surmount adversity by actively mobilizing their thought and resources, and they teach their children these ways of responding. One student talked about her family's positive response to the birth of a disabled child in the family:

> My parents were very open about my sister having Down syndrome. We were taught to believe we were capable, and that she was capable. She wasn't a special case. People in stores sometimes stared or said stupid things about my sister. But my parents taught us how to be respectful of them and yet be blunt with them in saying what my sister could do. People can change for the better, they'd say. (Turnbull & Turnbull 2001, 211)

Researchers who study the parenting practices of low-income mothers with optimistic outlooks found that these mothers use more supportive and involved parenting practices (Edin & Lein 1997; Furstenberg et al. 1999). Despite severe financial pressures, those mothers who were optimistic about the future had a greater sense of perceived control, reported fewer psychological and physical symptoms, and engaged in more effective parenting practices, including consistent discipline, monitoring, problem solving, and inductive reasoning (Bugental, Blue & Cruzcosa 1989; Murry et al. 2002). Other researchers have also reported that when optimism and collective efficacy are present in low-income families, children perform much better in school and are much more likely to go on to college and improve their life opportunities (Crosnoe et al. 2002).

Such a sense of optimism in parents promotes psychological resilience in children as well. Recent research that explored how parents teach children to be optimistic and how optimism correlates with psychological resilience confirms the power of families to instill psychological resilience (Aspinwall, Richter & Hoffman 2001; Seligman 1991; 1996). Seligman (1991), for example, introduced the concept of *learned optimism* to depict the process by which people learn how to resist the potentially harmful effects of stressful experiences. He reported a strong relationship between the parents' level of optimism and that of their children. In summary, families of academically successful children teach their children firsthand about the personal roadblocks they may confront and strategies for circumventing those roadblocks (Clark 1983; Furstenberg et al. 1999; Jackson 2000; Orthner, Sampei & Williamson 2004).

Sense of Personal Efficacy

Families of high-achieving students demonstrate a proactive stance toward life tasks and challenges. Rather than become discouraged and immobilized by stresses and difficult life challenges, family members "rise to the challenge." They are confident about their ability to succeed. This "can-do" attitude shows itself in several ways. First, parents have positive expectations about their relations with teachers and other members of the community. As a result, parents expect to take an active role in helping their children prepare for schooling. Rather than believe that the school has all of the responsibility for educating children, these parents believe that they should actively work alongside the school in developing their children's talents. Hence, they expect to engage in home learning activities to help their children gain a general fund of knowledge and to assist them in developing literacy skills needed for school (Cooper, Lindsay & Nye 2000; Izzo, Weiss, Shanahan & Rodriguez-Brown 2000). In addition, these parents visit the school and routinely monitor (and are emotionally supportive of) their children's involvement in school assignments and other literacy-producing activities (Mandara 2006).

Second, parents attempt to develop their child's sense of personal efficacy by actively encouraging the child's persistence and performance in the face of difficulty or challenge (Murray & Mandara 2003). This effort is done in two identifiable ways. First, parents frequently enjoin their children to take charge of their life. Typical of these efforts was one teenager's report that his mother always told him: "The world don't owe you anything. You owe something to yourself. You're responsible for your own fate. If you don't do what you're supposed to do, you don't have nobody to blame but yourself." (Amatea, Smith & Villares 2006, 181) Another student from a low-income family reported that his mother always told him: "If you don't get off your butt and go after it, you ain't never gonna have anything" (Snow, et al. 1991, 76). Second, parents actively bolster their child's feelings of self-competence and sense of hope when facing difficult circumstances. As one parent remarked:

> So if you've got enough personal pride, you go as far as you're able to go—and then I tell them to go one step further. And that way, you might get what you want out of life. And then if you don't, at least be big enough to live with what you do have. I used to tell the kids when they were little, if you have to be a bum, then be a good bum. Whatever, you are, be a good one. And then you're satisfied with yourself. (Snow, et al. 1991, 79)

Third, parents in these families routinely take time to teach their children how to persevere in the face of difficulty and how to evaluate their personal responsibility for their own circumstances. They often emphasize how to appraise what is possible to change and what is not. When students fail in a task or goal pursuit, parents offer reassurance and consolation. They try to teach the students to place failure in the appropriate context so that self-blame is avoided. Parents routinely reaffirm the student's self-regard and sense of adequacy (ability) by verbally stressing their self-worth and importance to the family and repeatedly telling them they are deeply cared for. For example, one high school student reported how her mother's comment, "Don't ever let anybody tell you they're better than you, always remember that," had influenced her. Another student recounted how, when he was complaining about how difficult school was, his parents had told him: "Do your best, and that's all you can do."

One mother stated:

> We try to teach the kids everyone is not good in everything. Where one is good in math and the other in reading or one may be good in history or the other may draw well. Just like Janice and Marie can draw very well. Carla couldn't even draw a stick doll. She used to say I gave her a "bad" pencil, and the other two had to show her it wasn't the pencil; it was her ability, you know, but they can't be good in everything. (Snow et al. 1991, 83)

As a result of these practices, students learn how to calm themselves and to tell themselves: "You are all right." With this orientation children are able to bounce back from failures and inadequacies and avoid using others as scapegoats for their personal shortcomings. Bempechat's (1998) research underscores this pivotal role that parents play in encouraging children's persistence and performance in the face of difficulty and challenge. Investigating parents' influence on low-income fifth and sixth graders' attributions for success and failure in mathematics, Bempechat (1998) discovered that not only were poor, minority parents involved in their children's education, but also high achievers, regardless of their ethnic background, credited success to their innate ability and effort and tended not to blame failure on lack of ability. Hence, we can conclude that parents' motivational support for children's learning is crucially important, particularly the subtle messages parents convey about children's abilities to persevere, in the face of stress or failure, in learning and mastering new skills. Now reflect upon how your own family encouraged you to succeed in school by examining Reflective Exercise 4.1.

Reflective Exercise 4.1

My Family's Beliefs and Expectations

How did your family interact with you to encourage you to succeed in school? What might be an example of a time they conveyed their belief in your ability to succeed and to make something of yourself when you were struggling at something? Did they teach you to be optimistic or pessimistic in looking at a challenging situation? How might these experiences impact you as a teacher?

Family Emotional Climate

The families of academically successful students view their family as a source of mutual emotional support and connectedness. Family members value spending time with each other both to celebrate good times and to provide emotional support, guidance, approval, and reassurance in bad times (Orthner et al. 2004; Wiley, Warren & Montanelli 2002), and they engage in open, emotional sharing (Conger & Conger 2002), clear communication, and collaborative problem solving (Cox & Davis 1999). As a result, children in these families are taught how to express themselves emotionally, how to calm themselves when stressed, how to resolve conflicts and engage in collaborative problem solving, and how to take responsibility for their own feelings and behavior rather than blame others when experiencing personally demanding situations. Although a more firm, authoritarian parenting style is reported to be more characteristic of many low-income African American families, and more effective in rearing children living in low SES communities for school success (Murry, Kotchcik, Wallace, Ketchen, Eddings, Heller & Collier 2004), the style is combined with affection. Harsh arbitrary control by parents is negatively related to children's school performance across income and ethnic groups (Scott-Jones 1995).

Providing Emotional Warmth and Belonging

Families of successful students demonstrate high levels of warmth, affection, and emotional support for one another. These families sustain emotional connections with each other through promotion of shared family rituals, family celebrations, spiritual connections and traditions (Clark 1983; Crosnoe et al. 2002; McCubbin & McCubbin 1996; Orthner et al. 2004). Various researchers have described how the simple family rituals of hair grooming and styling, nail cutting and polishing, bathing and massaging, dancing and singing, storytelling, television watching, grocery shopping and cooking favorite foods, serving and eating meals, and joking sessions as well as family celebrations served as vehicles for family members to share affection and "good times," and were also excellent situations for (a) verbally validating the child's importance as a person, (b) expressing to the child that he or she is loved, appreciated, and understood, and (c) soothing, reassuring, guiding, and protecting the child (Clark 1983; Wigfield, Eccles & Rodriguez 1998; Wiley et al. 2002). In addition, family members regularly offer practical and emotional support during crises periods and provide a reliable support network. This reliable support network reduces anxiety and assists in the resolution of the normal conflicts that all families face. As one twelfth grader observed:

> My parents don't get tore down when something goes wrong. They stick together. Like if we need something and know we can't get it, but we really need it, we all stick together. Like when my mother's purse got stolen. We all stuck together. We really needed that. We didn't criticize her about what she

should have done. Instead, we gave her understanding and let her know that it was not her fault that her purse got stolen. I like my parents because they stick together in times like that. (Snow et al. 1991, 89)

Open, Emotional Sharing

Families of successful students have frequent nurturing conversations in which children receive affirming messages about their strengths and uniqueness (Conger & Conger 2002). In addition, family members show empathy for each other and make themselves available for emotional support and guidance during crises times (Conger & Elder 1994; Conger & Conger 2002). Moreover, family members view each other as capable, competent, and basically healthy in mind, body, and spirit (Orthner et al. 2004; Wiley et al. 2002). Parents recognize and respect the individual strengths of each child and convey positive verbal and nonverbal (symbolic) evaluations about the child (Clark 1983; Edin & Lein 1997; Seccombe 1999). For example, one mother reported how she attempted to engender feelings of pride in herself and in her children as human beings:

> I'm like Jesse Jackson (nationally known minister). They are somebody. They are people. You don't run a person down if they make a little mistake or they don't get a grade as high as what they think they should. You always just encourage them to try just a little bit harder, and let them know they are people, that whatever they do, it wasn't the worst thing in the world. But if a momma or father is forever telling the kids, "You're no good" or "You're dumb" or "You could have done better," or something like that, they don't believe they're somebody. I make them feel that if they don't do it, they're letting their own self down, not me. But they have to have a certain amount of pride to want things nice themselves, to want to know a little more than the next person because, you know yourself, you feel good if you think that you are a little smarter than somebody else. (Clark 1983, 34)

As illustrated in this quote, there are a variety of family evaluations that form the self-image that a child perceives, internalizes, and, ultimately, identifies with. This parent conveyed that her child was capable, competent, and basically healthy in mind, body, and spirit.

Clear Communication

These families use clear communication in their interactions with each other. Consistency is evident between what is said and what is done. In addition, family members discuss personal fears, stresses, criticisms, complaints, and other feelings with each other rather than censoring such topics from conversation. Moreover, adults attempt to clarify ambiguous situations to children, explaining their own expectations or feelings in terms that children can understand, and encouraging children to express their own fears and feelings and to have a voice in family decision-making and problem-solving (Conger & Conger 2002). One middle school student from a low-income family described how this operated in her family:

> In sixth grade I felt I was kind of left out because it was a new school and everything. I didn't know anybody. I felt scared; it was an altogether new environment, and I just didn't know how to cope with it. So my parents started asking me about how I felt and really pushing and encouraging me to go. I might or might not have gone to school and they knew this, so they pushed me about going. . . . My mom helped me get my head together. She said, "Oh, it's gonna be all right. Don't be afraid." So then I went and found that most of the people on this block went to school there, and I got over it. (Snow et al. 1991, 132)

Collaborative Problem-Solving

A spirit of family togetherness and support is nurtured in the families of successful students through positive communication and shared problem-solving and conflict management (Clark 1990; Conger & Conger 2002; Cox & Davis 1999). Even when facing difficult financial circumstances, such families exhibit confidence in their ability to solve problems and to pull together and depend on each other (Edin & Lein 1997; Orthner et al. 2000; Seccombe 1999.) Family relationships are not highly conflictual. Instead, parents keep a degree of control and maintain a reasonably cooperative, consensus-based relationship with their children by encouraging a generally pleasant mood in the home, by showing patience, by providing plenty of opportunity for communication, and by sharing decision-making while continuing to seek voluntary compliance and avoidance of a direct conflict of wills with their children. One single parent of three teenage girls described this style of family communication and problem-solving as follows:

> At least twice a month we sit around the kitchen table. I encourage each of my girls to speak about anything or anyone in the household. I let them know that anything they say—positive or negative—is okay. I believe that they need to be able to bring up what they are upset about and not worry about getting punished for it. They need to say whatever is truly on their minds. We try and work it out then and there. (Amatea, Smith & Villares 2006, 182)

Such parents are able to get voluntary compliance with their authority-derived demands by encouraging a generally pleasant mood in the home and never allowing the parent–child bond to deteriorate into irreparable discord and hate. Engaging the child in regular communication rituals and traditions that involve verbal comforting, praising, hugging, kissing, smiling, showing, helping, instructing, questioning, and responsive behaviors will accomplish this. In summary, the emotional connectedness that some families—despite poverty, slum environments, or natural tragedies—can provide for their children turns up again and again in studies carried out in various parts of the world as a factor linked to the development of a successful, competent child (Garmezy 1983). Now reflect upon how your own family expressed affection and support by examining Reflective Exercise 4.2.

Reflective Exercise 4.2

My Family's Affectional Expression and Support

How did your family show affection and support? What types of activities did your family enjoy together? How did your family support each other during stressful times? How did they teach you to deal with conflict and difference of opinion? How might these experiences impact you as a teacher?

Family Organizational Patterns

Academically successful children tend to have families that are clearly organized and in which role relationships of family members are appropriate and well defined. Parents assume an active leadership role in forging a strong caregiver alliance with adults inside and outside the family, in developing cooperative sibling relationships among the children, and in developing a strong social support network with extended family and community members (Conger & Conger 2002; Edin & Lein 1997; Furstenberg et al. 1997).

Strong Leadership and Clear Expectations

Distinctly different role expectations and power differentials exist for parents and for children in the families of academically successful children (Baldwin, Baldwin & Cole 1990; Clark 1983; Conger & Conger 2002; Edin & Lein 1997; Furstenberg et al. 1997). Parents define themselves as having the primary right and responsibility to guide and protect their children's academic and social development. In addition, a strong alliance is present among those family members who comprise the caregiver alliance as to who is in charge and with what responsibilities. Adults in both the family and outside it communicate regularly and consistently about their expectations concerning children's behavior (McCubbin & McCubbin 1996). A low level of conflict exists between caregivers and between children and caregivers. Instead, children accept their caregivers' decision-making authority across a diverse array of activity contexts. Researchers (Clarke 1983; Mandara 2006) who intensively study the home life of low-income African American families with high-achieving and low-achieving students reported that, regardless of whether the family was headed by one or two parents, parents in the families of successful students assert their "legitimate right" to set house rules, delegate role responsibilities for each child, and consistently supervise and monitor the children in the performance of these activities. Moreover, parents do this in a way that enlists their children's voluntary and enthusiastic adherence to the parents' rules, standards, and expectations for responsible behavior.

In addition, in the families of academically successful children, caregivers delegate responsibility to children. Children may be asked to assume leadership while engaged in home academic tasks, leisure tasks, or household maintenance tasks. However, when asking their child to assume a leadership role, parents carefully organize and clearly explain the children's roles and functions for particular activities in ways that the child perceives as legitimate, and then provide evaluations about how a role is to be performed. As a result, children feel responsible for their siblings, as depicted by a high school senior who talked about her responsibilities for caring for her younger sister:

> My little sister is kind of hard-headed. I have to fuss at her to make her study. I want her to do more than what I'm gonna do. I always want us to get ahead. (Clark 1983, 32)

As a result of sharing leadership roles, children experience the benefits of having older siblings as well as parents serve as mentors and guides in their lives. A high school senior interviewed by Snow et al. (1991) depicted the central role that siblings can play in shaping her academic aspirations and providing her with moral support:

> My brother is more than a brother. He's also a friend and a confidant. If I have a problem it becomes his problem. He's really helped me get through some rough times in high school. (189)

These opportunities for taking on family leadership responsibilities enable the child to develop greater skill in accepting and meeting adult expectations, while learning to adjust to a more expansive variety of role responsibilities.

Using a Firm but Friendly Parenting Style

One of the most striking features in the families of successful students is the parents' supervisory strategy. Parents know where their children are and take a strong hand in structuring the child's time. They set definite and consistent time and space limits on children's behavior while in school and outside of school (Clark 1983; Crouter et al. 1990; Mandara & Murray 2002; Steinberg, Lamborn, Dornbush & Darling 1992). Children have a routine daily and weekly schedule—that includes certain before-school activities, after-school activities, evening activities, and weekend activities—through the childhood and teenage years. Parents carefully set rules defining "socially acceptable" out-of-home environments and activities for their children based on their perceptions of the quality of the out-of-home environment and their assessment of the child's level of development or maturity. As one high school senior noted:

> My mother is the undisputed boss on the issue of curfew. She simply but firmly insists on a reasonable time I am to be back home. Even now when I am a high school senior, although she gives me more of a voice in negotiating when I can be in at night, she gives final approval to whatever I propose. (Amatea, Smith & Villares 2006, 183)

As their children become older, parents of teenage children adjust their expectations by carefully setting rules defining socially acceptable out-of-home environments and activities for their children. For example, one low-income parent who lives in a Chicago housing project who was interviewed by Clark (1983) spoke about the managerial role over her teenage daughter's activities which she continued to perform:

> There are certain limitations you put on children. You don't put them out there to be tempted to do anything wrong. It's stupid for anybody to say, "OK, I trust my child so it can go anywhere it wants to go." You wouldn't send a kid, because you trusted him, into a dope den. If you have no guidelines for a child, then you're not raising the child. You have to have a certain amount of rules and then let the child live within those rules. They're going to stray from them a certain amount because they're not gods. They're not perfect. But they don't go so far as to make it bad. (37)

Parents' enforcement of these rules is based on their own perceptions of the quality of the out-of-home environment (e.g., Is it acceptable to my standards? Is there adult supervision?) and their perception of the child's level of development or maturity (e.g., You're too old for that kind of thing). Parents expect their children to act in a responsible, self-reliant, and honorable manner when participating in school-related activities, athletic and sport projects, shopping, certain dance parties, and church activities. Sometimes parents believed a child would behave maturely in a questionable setting (e.g., a party with neighborhood punks) but would still refuse permission to go. In these situations, parents were censoring how much of the "bad elements" the child would be exposed to. Hence, a student's friends, buddies, girlfriends, and associates are also observed and questioned by parents to screen out the "problem children" and "troublemakers" who might have a negative influence on their child. The home environment and parents of these friends are also evaluated, and decisions are made whether or not to support a continuance of a friendship between the children. Objections by the child were often met with parents' forceful assertions: "I don't care if every parent on this block lets their kids do that, you are not going to do it."

Yet parents also attempt to make these expectations reasonable to their children rather than merely announce them and demand obedience (Brody, Flor & Gibson 1999; Clark 1983; Dornbush & Ritter 1992; Mandara & Murray 2002.) They do this by first explaining how their decisions can be justified by fundamentally good ethical standards and by labeling children's conformity with these decisions as the "good and right" thing to do. Second, when the child is being tutored on certain moral and ethical standards that define correct behavior, parents shower their child with verbal and physical signs of affection, praising the child's personal worth to the family and providing liberal emotional support. This typically results in the children accepting the ways of the household and committing themselves to behaving in a trustworthy, responsible manner (Clark 1983; Dornbush & Ritter 1992; Mandara & Murray 2002).

Disputes and conflicts among siblings or parents and children are usually given due process so as to resolve them in a fair and loving way. Parents attempt to "get to the bottom" of conflicts and trace the source of the conflict to the children's needs.

On those times when enforcement of rules is needed to get the children "back into line" with their role responsibilities, parents typically warn the child of impending punishment before they actually mete out the punishment. The two types of warnings that parents use are (a) verbal, such as "If you keep it up, I'm going to spank you," and (b) nonverbal, such as using distraction techniques to draw the child away from undesirable experiences, or quietly staring at the child with disapproving looks or "the evil eye," which the child has come to understand as being the precursor of a more direct form of parental confrontation. When parents do use more corrective feedback sanctions, they consist of a temporary withdrawal of privileges, spanking, and face-to-face talks with the child about the behavior in question.

This firm but friendly style of parenting characterized by clear and consistent expectations implemented in a warm, inclusionary style is reported to be associated with high levels of social and academic achievement in children by a variety of different researchers. Labeled authoritative by Baumrind (1989), who investigated how preschool children's school and home adjustment are related to parental management style, this parenting style is characterized by a high level of warmth and responsiveness to children and a high level of demandingness. The authoritative style is exemplified by (a) expectation of mature behavior from the child and a clear setting of standards by the parents, (b) firm enforcement of rules and standards, (c) use of commands and sanctions when necessary, (d) encouragement of the child's independence and individuality, (e) open communication between parents and their children with encouragement of verbal give-and-take, and (f) recognition of the rights of both parents and children. Baumrind (1989) reported that preschool-age children of authoritative parents tend to be more socially responsible, more independent than other children, and higher in social and cognitive competence.

In contrast, three other parenting styles are known that differ in their degree of demandingness and warmth demonstrated. The second pattern, authoritarian parenting style, is characterized by a high degree of demandingness by the parent coupled with a low level of responsiveness and warmth toward the child. According to Baumrind (1989; 1991), authoritarian parents attempt to shape, control, and evaluate the behavior and attitudes of their children in accordance with an absolute set of standards. These parents emphasize obedience, respect for authority, work tradition, and the preservation of order. Verbal give-and-take between parent and child is discouraged. Baumrind's studies found that such a coercive mode of family interaction was associated with low levels of independence and social responsibility in children.

Baumrind (1989; 1991) described a third pattern, the permissive parenting style, in which parents demonstrate a high level of warmth and responsiveness to their child, but a low level of demandingness. According to Baumrind, permissive parents are tolerant and accepting toward their child's impulses, use as little punishment as possible, make few demands for mature behavior, and allow considerable self-regulation by the child. She reported that preschool children of permissive parents were immature, lacked impulse control and self-reliance, and evidenced a lack of social responsibility and independence. Neglectful parenting, the fourth style of parenting, was added to Baumrind's typology by Dornbush & Ritter (1992). A neglectful parenting style is characterized by low levels of parental warmth and responsiveness to children and low levels of parental demandingness. Neglectful parents do not routinely "take charge" or manage their children's activities and are not consistently responsive to their children's needs and demands. Few predictable role expectations are evident in these families as to how parents and children are to interact with one another. Instead, family patterns of decision-making and communication are chaotic and inconsistent.

Using data collected from 7,836 students ages fourteen to seventeen and 2,996 parents, Dornbush and Ritter (1992) examined how these four parenting styles related to student academic performance in adolescents from diverse ethnic and economic groups. These researchers discovered that low grades were associated with neglectful and, to a lesser extent, permissive and authoritarian parenting styles. In contrast, authoritative parenting was associated with high grades. These patterns were consistent across gender, diverse family structure (i.e., biological two-parent, single-parent, or stepfamily structure), ethnic groups, student age, and family social class.

Although a more firm, "no-nonsense" parenting style is reported to be more characteristic of many African American families, and more effective in rearing children living in low SES communities for school success, some authors (Murry, Kotchcik, Wallace, Ketchen, Eddings, Heller & Collier 2004) have noted that harsh arbitrary control by parents is negatively related to children's school performance (Scott-Jones 1995). In fact, Young (1970) observed in her ethnographic study of Southern African American families that the use of very firm and vigilant parenting practices was used within affectively positive relationships. This form of parenting has been associated positively with African American children and adolescents' self-regulation, academic achievement, and psychological adjustment (Brody & Flor 1998; Mandara & Murray 2003; Murry & Brody 1999).

In summary, parental expectations of their children's behavior and their style of enforcing those expectations appear to strongly influence children's academic success. Parents who assume authority over their children and clearly and regularly delineate their standards and rules for their child's conduct, while also attempting to make these standards reasonable to their child, tend to raise children who not only understand what to do at home but also find it easier to understand and follow the instructions and requirements of adults at school. Now reflect upon your parents' managerial style by examining Reflective Exercise 4.3.

Reflective Exercise 4.3

My Parents' Managerial Style

Which parenting management style did your parents use with you? What would be an example of your parents' disciplinary/management behavior that would support your selection? If you are a parent, which parenting management style do you use and why? As an educator, which classroom management style paralleling the parenting style will you use with your students?

Creating a Strong Social Network

The families of successful students intentionally develop relationships with staff at their children's school and show great concern about the school's effectiveness/success in educating their children (Eccles & Harold 1996). They visit the school, even when not invited by the school, ostensibly to check on their child's progress. They actively advocate for assessment of their children's needs and provision of necessary educational opportunities for their child. These families also work to build strong social support networks in their extended family and in their community to help them in rearing their children. In these social networks, other siblings, neighbors, and friends are actively solicited by parents to keep an eye out for their child (Barber & Eccles 1992; Ensminger & Slusarcick 1992). Obviously, the effectiveness of this strategy depends on clear, consistent communication between the parents and these surrogate authority figures (Salem, Zimmerman & Notaro 1998). Yet these perceptions of community social support appear to be a powerful source of strength, particularly for low-income families. When the interpersonal connections in a neighborhood are strong, parents are more likely to get their children into organized programs and, in general, to feel safe being part of the community (Conger & Conger 2002; Furstenburg et al. 1999). Moreover, this sense of safety and belonging significantly enhances parents' perceptions of efficacy and, in turn, their parenting practices (Jackson 2000).

Family Learning Opportunities

The influence of family functioning on academic achievement is most apparent in looking at how families develop particular in-home routines to support their children's learning. Not only do parents engage in frequent conversations with their children about their current school performance and monitor their children's performance, but also they organize and delegate tasks and duties in the home to teach specific academic and interpersonal skills (Clark 1983; 1990; Eccles & Harold 1996; Sui-Chu & Willms 1996; Wigfield et al. 1998). These activities may range from parents' deliberate instruction of their children through games, through monitoring homework and their children's use of free time, through reading and storytelling, or other literacy-enhancing activities. In addition, these parents often engage their children in household maintenance and leisure time activities from which the children learn diligence, independence, and commitment. In each of these types of home learning activities, parents create a positive, affective experience for their children by providing them with frequent, verbal support and praise and giving them regular, explicit feedback.

Developing Family Routines that Support Achievement

The families of successful students expect to be actively involved in their children's learning (Eccles & Harold 1996; Sui-Chu & Willms 1996; Wigfield et al. 1998). With younger children, parents often use learning activities that involve sensory simulation, learning by rote, sorting, classifying, and memorizing. To prepare their children for school, parents use specific strategies during home conversations, study encounters, and other activities to help their child learn to speak, read, spell, and solve challenging problems. For example, one parent described the learning activities that she engaged in during her children's early years:

> I played games with them to build their number recognition. For example, I would play cards or dominoes with them to teach them the difference between a 6 and a 4. My daughter learned to just look at a 6 and know it was a 6. She'd look at a 4 and would not have to count. She knew the difference. It helped her catch on to numbers.

Another parent recounted her expectations about engaging in learning activities at home during her child's early years:

> It was just something I always did with my kids. The first step was training them for the toilet; the next step was teaching them the alphabet. I was always trying to teach them something; and it was just a habit. But I made it a game we enjoyed together rather than serious teaching.

During their children's older years, parents instead try to discover their interest, encourage learning by doing, and systematically help their children to draw on their past experience to solve current problems (Clark 1983; Eccles & Harold 1996; Mandara & Murray 2003). They expose their children to a wide array of instruction in academic and social skills through a process of discussion, modeling, and feedback. Parents encourage their older children to explore their own intellectual interests and ideas and to explore resources that might expand their learning. For example, parents often talk about showing their upper elementary-age children how to use the dictionary and encyclopedia to find answers to homework questions. These home lessons usually occur spontaneously as children demonstrate a readiness for more complex home learning tasks. Parents also encourage their children to engage in outside activities to expand their vocabulary through listening, speaking, and reading.

In addition, these families offer explicit social skills training to their children in behaving responsibly both in the classroom and the wider community. Parents specifically impart information to the child about how to prepare for the teacher–peer–pupil relationships in the school environment and how to handle themselves in socially complicated situations. Parents also consciously train children in interpersonal diplomacy. Such lessons are often transmitted in a matter of fact fashion through dialogues, study sessions, routine verbal labeling of events, and observation of selected television programs with the child. Examples include statements, such as "Look at people and speak your mind when you talk to them," "Don't look down or away," and "Don't be afraid." These parents expect their children to interact positively and fairly with others, and they coach them actively in developing these skills.

Finally, in the families of high-achieving students, homework and study are regularly performed, almost ritualistically, and are generally done in the early evening hours (Clark 1983; Snow et al. 1991). In these families, the student is expected to accept responsibility for completing homework assignments and to devote sufficient time and energy to successfully complete school assignments. Yet the parents believe that it is their responsibility to see that homework gets done and to guide their child's study efforts until they see that children can operate self-sufficiently. Routine family dialogues are used for parents to not only stress how schooling is important, but also to praise the child's efforts at homework performance.

Explicit Skill Instruction

Parents of high-achieving students are very conscious of how they design learning opportunities for their children by the way they delegate tasks and duties in the home (Clark 1983; Conger & Conger 2002; Crosnoe et al. 2002; Taylor & Dorsey-Gaines 1988). Obviously, those home activities that have the greatest instructional power are those that become routine and ritualized into the frequent, everyday practice of the family. Such home activities might be divided into two general categories: (a) deliberate activities believed to lead to specific information, knowledge, or academic skills, and (b) activities that family members engage in for enjoyment yet are an occasion for indirect educational instruction. Of course, families differ in terms of which home activities they engage in and with what frequency. They also differ in the degree to which they establish strict, specific rules about when and how such activities should occur. For example, parents in one family may insist that beds be made without a wrinkle each morning, whereas another family may only check up on bed-making on Saturday when bedsheets are to be changed. One family may carefully monitor the amount of time spent watching television as well as the nature of the programs their child views, whereas another family may allow their child to determine when and what television programs they watch. Such home tasks provide opportunities for children to practice problem solving and enable children to develop skills for solving challenging classroom problems. The more implicit forms of instruction offered by home maintenance activities and leisure activities are also occasions in which parents teach their children leadership skills, time management, money management and budgeting techniques, reading skills, and troubleshooting and problem solving.

What are your memories of your family's role in your education and schooling? By means of Reflective Exercise 4.4, consider how your family and other members of the community influenced your learning and schooling.

Reflective Exercise 4.4

Reflections on Me and My Learning

Reflect upon your own memories of your education and schooling. Use the questions below to recollect the role of your family in your education and/or your siblings' education.

1. Who was in your family as you were growing up?
2. What are some of your earliest memories of learning in your family? Think of a time you learned something that was important to you. Who taught you and how?
3. In the opening of this chapter, one woman commented upon an important self-management skill that her father taught her and her sister. What were some important skills that your family taught you? How did your family teach you this skill? As an educator, how do you teach such self-management skills?
4. What important things do you think your caregivers felt they should teach you? How did they teach these things?
5. Who were other members of your family or community that were considered wise? How did they share their knowledge with others?
6. What did you know about reading before you entered school? How did you learn about it? How do you think you learned to read?
7. What are your earliest memories of school? Did school learning seem similar to or different from the kinds of learning you participated in before with your family?
8. How would you describe yourself as a student? What were some of your experiences in school?
9. What do you recall about your family's involvement in your school experiences? What type of school functions or activities did they participate in? What do you think were the school's expectations in this regard? Looking back, what do you think about the match between the school's expectations and your family's involvement?
10. How were your experiences in school different from those of your sibling(s) and those of your parents or caregivers? If you have spent any time volunteering in a classroom, how do the students' school experiences differ from your own?

Strengthening Families' Capacities to Help Their Children Succeed

But what of those families who do not demonstrate these ways of interacting with their children? Often teachers are quick to say, "These are not the parents we worry about. How can I get the parents who do not even come to school or seem to care about their children's learning, to act differently?" An important first step in strengthening these families' efforts to rear children who will be successful in school is to become conscious of the biases and expectations that we and others in our school may bring to understanding how families influence children and how schools influence families. Often we as educators have been guilty of making sweeping generalizations about family functioning based on family structure or status explanations. For example, a strong line of research depicts how teachers differentially explain children's classroom behavior or academic performance based on whether they live in a single-parent or two-parent family (Santrock & Tracy 1978). Moreover, we often overhear colleagues not only justify a child's school difficulties based on a structural status that is unalterable (such as being poor or belonging to a divorced family or a single-parent family) but also dismiss a family as hopeless and beyond repair (e.g., they just don't care; they never come to school; they don't spend time with their child). A family strengths perspective fundamentally alters this deficit-based perspective. Rather than looking at families as damaged and children as in need of rescuing from hopelessly dysfunctional families, we see children's families as competent but challenged by life's adversities and as having strengths that may be hidden from our view and theirs.

Benefits of a Family Strengths Perspective

Use of a family strengths framework has several benefits. First, it can help you think more positively about the role that families play in their children's schooling and, as a result, help you fortify your relationships with students' families. Second, it can help you when you are involved in problem solving with families to engage families with respect and compassion for their struggles, to affirm their strengths, and to strengthen those key family processes that contribute to student success. However, using a family strengths perspective is not without its challenges. Schools have not had a history of soliciting families' involvement for positive reasons. Instead, parents have usually been contacted by the school only at times when their children were experiencing difficulty. As a result, parents across the socioeconomic spectrum expect that any invitation from the school will be bad news about their child. Moreover, parents often view the school problems that their children experience as negative reflections on their parenting skills or as signs of future difficulty for their children, over which they have little or no control. Parents may also be experiencing stress in other areas of their life, and already feel like a failure, to which their child's difficulty in school represents yet another failure. In addition, some parents may have had bad school experiences themselves and may have mixed feelings about interactions with school officials. As a result, parents often respond defensively to the school's invitation or demonstrate reluctance about coming to school or seeking special services out of the belief that they will be judged by the school as disturbed or deficient and blamed for their children's problems.

Scanning for Strengths

This book is designed to help you overcome these perceptual barriers and change your existing patterns of family–school interaction. You will learn about many educators (Amatea, Daniels, Bringman & Vandiver 2004; Delgado-Gaitan 1991; Weiss

& Edwards 1992) who are redesigning their common family–school routines so as to both recognize families' contribution to their children's learning and increase families' opportunities to foster such learning. These educators, rather than simply trying to get parents involved, actively search for opportunities for parents and students to interact with them in ways that emphasize family involvement in children's planning, decision-making, problem-solving, and learning. As a result, these educators embed a collaborative focus into a variety of different school events (e.g., orientations, classroom instruction, homework routines, celebrations, presentations of new curriculum, transitions to new grade levels and programs, procedures for home–school communication and for resolving difficulties). For example, in one school, students are taught to conduct student-led parent conferences in lieu of the traditional parent–teacher conference in that the teacher is central and the student is usually not in attendance. In this student-led conference format, students share their school progress (academic and behavioral) and develop a plan together with their parents for how they can move forward. This new format demonstrates an approach to cooperative planning and problem-solving, in which students and parents are encouraged to communicate in a respectful and cooperative manner (Amatea et al. 2004).

Such non-problem-oriented interactions can also aid in the identification of those families whose children are struggling in school or dealing with other problems that negatively impact their children's learning. In interacting with these families, educators should first focus on identifying those strengths, resources, and abilities the family is already demonstrating and guide the family in using the resources for change in resolving a student's problem and then help the family develop additional strengths, resources, and abilities to apply to the problem situation (Amatea 1989; Bemak & Cornely 2002; Kraus 1998; Lyons, Uziel-Miller, Reyes & Sokol 2000). In the following section, strategies that educators might use to further strengthen particular family processes are described.

Family Beliefs. Rather than judge some families effective and others flawed and deficient in their manner of parenting their children, it is more useful to attempt to understand families in terms of the stressful life conditions they operate in, the style of parenting and family–school interaction which they have learned from their own family, and the ways of handling stress that they develop. Family members need to be viewed as intending to do their best for their children and for one another and as doing the best they know how to do. Parents also need to be viewed as experts on their children. To counter parents' fears that they are being summoned to the school to be told what they are doing wrong, Nicoll (1997) recommends educators carefully shape the tone of parent–school interaction so that a "no-fault" perspective is conveyed in which staff operate with the assumption that "no one is to blame but everyone is responsible."

One way to foster parents' sense of efficacy in rearing their children is by helping them make sense out of stressful, challenging situations involving their child or their larger life context. To eliminate helplessness around these stressful events and to build mutual support and empathy, an educator should first encourage families to share these stories of adversity openly and without judgment. To facilitate a positive outlook and provide a sense of purpose or value, teachers might choose to reframe these difficult situations as shared challenges that are comprehensible, manageable, and adaptable. For example, when a family is experiencing divorce, children may act out at school. The custodial parent may be unsure how to manage their children's emotional reactions and behavior and ashamed of their divorce. Often it is helpful to hear what the parent is experiencing, and to affirm the parent's concerns and commitment to their children and to acknowledge the strengths they do have before discussing new ways to respond to their child's increased emotionality.

Drawing out and affirming family strengths in the midst of difficulties helps to counter a sense of helplessness, failure, and despair and reinforces parental pride, confidence and a "can-do" spirit. Furthermore, contextualizing family members' distress as natural or understandable in a crisis/stressful situation can soften family members' reactions and reduce blame, shame, and guilt. In evaluating family strengths, parents' ideas and theories about child rearing and child management are of particular interest to educators. Examining parents' beliefs allows us to understand the motivation underlying their behavior. These ongoing conversations may reveal how the parent interacts with their child and whether a parent believes that she or he is an important and capable facilitator for her/his children's school success. If parents report low parenting efficacy, the teacher can identify strengths unseen by parents and suggest ways that parents already help their children. By ascertaining the parent's beliefs about their own efficacy, a teacher can redirect or highlight parenting behaviors that promote children learning at home. In addition, teachers can bolster families' efforts to persevere in their efforts to overcome barriers and to focus their efforts on setting goals and accepting that which is beyond their control. Seefeldt, Denton, Galaper and Younoszai (1998) reported that parents' beliefs about their perceived control over their child's learning was an important mediator between participating in Head Start transition demonstration projects and parents' involvement during the kindergarten year. In this ethnically diverse sample, parental beliefs about perceived control were more strongly correlated with increases in parents' active involvement in their children' classrooms than participation in a transition program.

Family Emotional Connectedness. How might teachers create opportunities for enhancing the emotional connections among students and their families as well as between themselves and families? At first glance, this family intervention focus is not usually considered the domain of the school. However, more effective family communication and problem-solving can be fostered through using existing classroom based programs which model effective communication and problem-solving, provide opportunities for students and parents to work together toward educational and social goals for their child, and encourage parents to share their hopes and fears concerning their child's education. Prevention programs such as those designed to educate parents about how to approach and discuss difficult topics (e.g., sexual activity or tobacco, drugs, and alcohol use) with their children can give parents opportunities to be involved and share their own personal views, hopes and desires with their children. Student-led conferences (Amatea et al., 2004) are another means for promoting such family connectedness and communication if they are approached as opportunities for caregivers and children to share feelings toward schooling, engage in joint decision-making, and to set clear goals and priorities for achieving their goals.

Exploration of the feelings that parents have for their children's education might be one of the greatest untapped strategies which teachers might use. Teachers can "join" with parents; help them to share their dreams with their children, and then help them garner the resources needed to meet their educational expectations. Some specific questions that showcase a family's strengths include: "What are some of the most successful experiences your family has had in school? Does your family talk about (your child's) future? How do you get through difficulties in (your child's) schooling? What would you like your family to be like in 5 years or 10 years? (see Echeverria-Doan, 2001). Walsh (1998) emphasized the need to examine what families do well, what works for them, and what their "healthy intentions" are. When parents are given an opportunity to explore their connections to their children and positive expectations for their future, a valuable resource emerges for intervening with them.

Family Organizational Patterns. Most parents learn how to parent from their own families, and may unthinkingly use the same style of parenting with their own children to which they were subjected as children. For example, many parents use an authoritarian parenting style—characterized by a high level of demandingness and a low level of warmth—because that is what their parents used with them. They may be unaware of the consistent research finding that an authoritative style—depicting both high levels of demandingness and high levels of warmth—is more effective in preparing children to be successful in school than other styles of parenting. To help authoritarian parents move toward a more authoritative style, teachers might acknowledge that while their parenting style has the strength of predictable and consistent standards, for children to internalize those standards (such that they follow them even when parents are not around) it helps to explain one's standards/demands in a way that is reasonable to children (rather than just arbitrarily announcing and enforcing a standard/expectation). In this manner, teachers affirm authoritarian parents as having strengths in terms of the degree of demandingness they demonstrate in their current style while also encouraging these parents to strengthen the warmth aspect of their parenting.

By means of helping parents learn how to develop more flexible family structures, share leadership, and foster mutual support and team work, parents can be assisted in navigating many challenges, including structural changes as with the loss of a parent or with post divorce and stepfamily reconfiguration. Myths of the ideal family can compound families' sense of deficiency and make their transition more difficult. When families experience instability, these disorienting changes can be counterbalanced by coaching parents to develop organizational strategies and behaviors that reflect strong leadership, security, and dependability. Such organizational strategies can reassure children when the family is undergoing change.

Reflective Exercise 4.5

Exploring Families' Strengths

As we begin to explore the specific qualities, characteristics, and diversity of families, reflect on your personal experiences with families. Answer the following questions.

1. Some educators assert that all families have strengths. What are/were some of your family's strengths? How did these strengths affect or benefit you growing up in your family unit?
2. Think for a moment about your family as a system. As you were growing up, do you recall an event or occurrence within your family unit, either positive or negative, that seemed to have a ripple effect on the entire family or several members? Examples would be a divorce, death, loss of job, moving, and so on. How did different members of the family react/respond to this event or occurrence? How did this affect you?
3. Thinking about diverse family forms and compositions, have you ever heard anyone make a negative comment about a particular family form or family structure? If so, what was it? How did it affect you?
4. Considering your responses to the previous questions, how will your experiences affect, both positively and/or negatively, the way you interact with your students' families? What assets/experiences do you view yourself as having that will enhance familial interaction? What stereotypes/barriers do you foresee hindering your interactions?

Families can also become more resourceful when interventions shift to a proactive stance of anticipating and preparing for the future. Efforts that are future-focused, and that help families "bounce forward" (Walsh 1998), help families learn how to be proactive, to envision a better future and take concrete steps toward their hopes and dreams. Helping families to maximize their control over the amount, timing, and methods of support, resources and services can be an important first step in reaching their goals. It is always useful to include families in decisions versus make decisions for them. Some families are capable of "struggling well," that is, even when faced with difficult choices and decisions; they find a way to success (Walsh 1998). One of the goals of a family resilience approach is to help a family identify what their resources are and how they currently use them. While some families do this naturally and effectively without intervention, many families can adapt and begin to "struggle well" and become more able to recognize and capitalize on their available resources through recommendation of seeking out family counseling.

Family Learning Opportunities. Creating family learning opportunities may be one of the most time-consuming tasks for parents and thus, represents a challenge for educators. However, this is also the family process that is most structured and task-oriented. Teachers can provide families with information about what they can do at home to foster their children's academic development. These may be ideas about how to help their child successfully complete homework and avoid procrastination, or how to help their child resolve conflicts. However the way such information is framed is crucial to its utilization. These suggestions should not be intended to make the home like a replica of the school. For example, in many low-income families, if parents are working long hours, it may be difficult for them to spend a lot of time supervising the homework activities of their children. However, from a resilience approach, limited time for homework activities is not necessarily a liability. Each family can structure activities according to their own strengths and resources. In addition, not only must families be recognized and responded to as experts on their own children but as a source of knowledge about strategies and resources for helping their children. Developing parent information networks, which capitalize on what other families know, formally acknowledging the expertise of families, and soliciting feedback from families about their reactions to school events are important conditions for building a families' capacity to develop learning opportunities for their children. Think for a moment about your own family. What were some of your family's strengths? How do you view families who have limited resources to care for their children? Consider these questions as you engage in Reflective Exercise 4.5

Summary

The shift in family research perspectives to looking at the internal processes of family life refocuses a long-standing overemphasis on deficits inherent in much of the early family–school research and practice. This family process perspective challenges the outdated assumption that the family is the exclusive cause of a child's educational or mental health problems. As a result, educators are now being invited to shift their attention from looking at family status and deficits (i.e., what families are not doing correctly) to looking for family strengths and resiliencies that can be utilized to facilitate children's learning. Four aspects of family life are described that have been strongly tied to student academic achievement, and they are (a) family beliefs and expectations, (b) family patterns of emotional connectedness, (c) family organizational patterns, and (d) family patterns around learning.

To understand how these aspects of family life influence students' academic achievement, we describe how teachers might use this family strengths framework to first assess their own family's functioning and then to apply it to all families regardless of their economic and social resources. Finally, we offer suggestions for how educators might help families further develop their ways of supporting their children's learning.

Chapter 5

Understanding Family Stress and Change

Silvia Echevarria-Doan and Heather L. Hanney

Learning Objectives

After reading this chapter, you will be able to:

- Describe the diverse forms or structures in which families might organize themselves.
- Explain what is meant by family life-cycle stages and transitions.
- Describe important nonnormative transitions that families might experience.
- Explain how families are impacted by normative or nonnormative family transitions.
- Describe how families might respond to stress and crises and the role educators might take so as not to increase the stress felt by families who experience transition and change.

In today's world, the modern family may consist of multiple forms, gener-ations, races, cultures, and religions. A family may be headed by two parents, grandparents, or by a single parent. It may have the luxury of financial freedom or may be struggling to make ends meet. Although the typical 1950s style fam-ily with a breadwinner father and a stay-at-home mother was once considered the norm, this family type reflects the living arrangements for only 43 percent of two-parent households in the United States (U.S. Department of Labor 2007). Moreover, two-parent households represent only 67 percent of all U.S. families raising children (Centers for Disease Control and Prevention 2006). Whatever the family structure and circumstances, each family goes through times of stress and change that include both normative and nonnormative events. The ways in which families confront these events are indicative of their resiliency and, in turn, suggest how each individual family member's emotional stability is impacted.

Acknowledgment of a student's family situation gains even greater significance when teachers look toward greater family involvement in their students' education. Although numerous studies have documented the positive outcomes of active partic-ipation by family members in children's education, many educators are recognizing that expecting caregivers to demonstrate greater involvement than they are able may have negative effects on both the student and the family (Fieldler, Simpson & Clark 2007). We believe that deciding to collaborate with families requires that we commit ourselves to learning more about the families of our students—their values, daily demands, stressful circumstances, and resources—and how these impact their chil-dren's lives. Only by doing so can we appreciate what our students and their families are dealing with, support them in their efforts to function effectively, and foster a level of educational participation that is both realistic and comfortable for a given family.

In this chapter, we first examine the diversity of family forms and structures depicted by today's families. We then use the lens of the family life-cycle theory to describe two types of family changes that most families experience: (a) developmental, normative changes and (b) unpredictable, nonnormative changes. We explore how these changes affect family relationships and functioning which, in turn, affect student performance in the classroom. We then examine the various resources that families use to interpret and cope with these stressful events. Finally, we consider the role that edu-cators might play in helping families who experience such stressful life changes.

Diverse Family Forms

Throughout history there have been a multiplicity of ways that families have struc-tured themselves, including traditional nuclear families, single-parent families, gay and lesbian families, blended families, multigenerational families, and adoptive fam-ilies. In contemporary U.S. society it is not the configurations of the family that are new but the changes in the number of such family configurations. For example, although single-parent households are not new, the number of such families has doubled during the last thirty years. Another change is the increased incidence of mothers in two-parent families who are working while their children are young. Another change is the increased age of first-time parents, and the increased role of fathers in parenting. Hence, in 2005, according to the National Center for Health Statistics (2006), 67 percent of U.S. children lived with two parents, 23 percent lived with single mothers, and 5 percent lived with single fathers. These numbers do not include children who lived in unmarried partner households, those who lived with grandparents, or those who lived with gay, lesbian, or transgendered (GLBT) parents. Let us look more closely at the characteristics of the possible family forms or structures in which children may live.

Blended Families

In 2000, it was estimated that for every two marriages, there is one divorce. At least 70 percent of divorced people remarry within five years of their divorce, and many of these remarried couples bring children from previous marriages into their new union to form a *blended* family (a term preferred to the older one of *step-family*). As a result, some 6.4 million children, representing a tenth of the nation's children, live with one stepparent and one birth parent (U.S. Census Bureau 2006). The successful adaptation of children to blended family relationships can be quite challenging due especially to the quality of the stepparent–child relationship. In addition, issues of jealousy can be a major source of tension in these families that can spill over into school. Furthermore, school staff must often interact with a wider variety of adults who may have differing levels of power to make decisions about the child's welfare. For example, a parent–teacher conference might involve a mother, a father, and a stepmother—each committed to developing strategies to help their child.

Single-Parent Families

Single-parent families include children and an adult who is divorced, never married, or one who has experienced the death of a spouse. Although there are a growing number of such families headed by men, women most often head single-parent families. Between 1970 and the late 1990s, the number of women who raised children alone increased from 3.4 million to approximately 10 million (Tutwiler 2005). In the past, children from single-parent families were described as coming from "broken homes." Single parents continue to be evaluated as less capable in meeting the needs of their children compared to two-parent families. In fact, living in a single-parent home has often been identified as a key characteristic of children at risk for failure in school settings. A growing body of research suggests, however, that the impact of limited economic opportunities, not the characteristics, of the parent or family determines the ability of single parents to run their household and raise their children. In 2006, 36 percent of all families who lived below the poverty level were single families headed by women (American's Children in Brief 2006). According to Tutwiler (2005): "Nearly half of female-headed families live below the poverty line, making them disadvantaged in terms of housing, health, and other family support resources many two-parent families are able to purchase" (40). As a result, being a single parent can be quite stressful because the lack of financial resources influences the parent's ability to purchase adequate housing, health insurance, child care, food, and clothing for the children.

Gay and Lesbian Families

An estimated 10 percent of the total population is lesbian, gay, or transgendered (LBBT), and four million gay, lesbian, or transgendered parents are raising approximately ten million children (Lamme & Lamme 2001). Children enter gay families in many different ways; some may be adopted or born to a heterosexual union before a divorce. In some cases, lesbians may choose to become parents through surrogate parenting, foster parenting, or through artificial insemination with an unknown or known donor.

Opinions vary about the impact of gay and lesbian parenting on children. Yet two comprehensive reviews of research conducted over the past two decades came to the same conclusion that children raised by gay and lesbian parents do not differ significantly from children raised by heterosexual parents, with respect to their gender roles and social and emotional development (Fitzgerald 1999; Tasker 1999). Although acceptance of gay, lesbian, and transgendered lifestyles has increased, prejudice and discrimination persist. Same-sex couples continue to be stigmatized and often face legal and moral challenges in their desire to become parents.

Many gay and lesbian parents worry about the reaction of school personnel to them and their children. Two research reports point to the great likelihood that these children will experience stigma, bullying, and societal discrimination. Australian researchers interviewed more than 100 gay and lesbian parents and 48 children and youth with gay or lesbian parents (Ray & Gregory 2001). Their findings document the societal discrimination that these parents and students faced; 73 percent of the parents said their most common concern was whether their children would be teased and bullied. In addition, 62 percent were concerned that there would be no discussion in the preschool or school curriculum about gay and lesbian families, and slightly more than half of the parents worried that their children would have to answer difficult questions. The actual experiences reported by children in this study were particularly worrisome. Bullying was a major problem reported by almost half of the students in third grade through sixth. In addition, the bullying that usually started around third grade became progressively harsher as students moved into middle school and high school. Educators need to be aware of their personal views and how they may hinder their ability to establish strong working relationships with these families or to create respectful school environments for students who have gay and lesbian parents (Lamme & Lamme 2003).

Intergenerational and Multigenerational Families

An increasing number of grandparents are raising children in their homes. This family structure may be intergenerational and consist of grandparents and grandchildren or a multigenerational family that includes grandparents, adult children, and grandchildren. In 1998, there were over 2.5 million grandparent-headed families, with or without parents present. Together these families cared for over 3.9 million children, or 5.6 percent, of all U.S. children (U.S. Census Bureau 1998). Today, the number of such families has increased 44 percent, with approximately 5.4 million children who live in homes where grandparents are the primary caretakers (www.childstats.gov 2007).

Grandparents may become the primary caretakers due to the death of a parent, divorce, parental drug abuse, or when children are abandoned. Grandparents may also assume the role of parents for children born to young, teenage parents, as well as for children born to parents who are chronically ill, incarcerated, are substance abusers, or who engage in child neglect or abuse. Although grandparents may be willing to take on this responsibility, the financial and psychological demands may exceed their existing resources. Researchers have reported that children in the care of grandparents are often exceptionally needy, due to a combination of congenital and environmental factors. Many grandparented children have experienced abuse and neglect as a result of living with a drug-involved or otherwise poorly functioning parent (Smith, Dannison & Vacha-Haase 1998). As a result, grandparented children deal with many troubling emotions. Feelings common to grandparented children include grief and loss, guilt, fear, embarrassment, and anger (Smith, Dannison & Vacha-Haase 1998).

Grandparents who are raising grandchildren span all ethnic groups and all social and economic levels. In addition, over half of custodial grandparents are caring for two or more young children, and approximately half are grandmothers without partners. Thirty percent of children in grandparent-headed homes are living with grandparents who have not received a high school diploma, whereas only 12 percent of children who live with parents have parents without a high school diploma (Smith & Dannison 2007). As a result, teachers need to be sensitive to the possible vulnerability of these children and needs for additional family supports.

Adoptive and Foster Families

Some couples or single adults create families with children through adoption or foster care. Adoptive or foster care families occur in a number of forms, ranging from single female or male-headed families to those headed by a heterosexual or a gay or lesbian couple. Disagreement exists over whether adopted children suffer more psychological and nonpsychological problems as compared to nonadopted children. In a review of literature that examines the emotional health of adopted children, Miller, Fan, Christensen, Grotevant, and van Dulmen (2000) reported that adopted children do receive more mental health services than nonadopted children. However, in a study of two nationally based matched groups of adoptive and biological parents, Borders, Black, and Pasley (1998) found no significant differences between the two groups in parental well-being, attitudes toward family life, discipline practices, and at-risk status of the children.

Adoption is generally viewed as a more preferable living situation for children than foster care (with the exception of foster placements in which the children are placed in the homes of relatives who have been approved as foster parents). Foster parents have the permanent or temporary custody of children who are in the care or custody of a state's children protection agency because they have been abused, neglected, or otherwise maltreated by their natural parents. The foster parents do not have the same legal status as the children's natural parents or of parents who legally adopt a child. Approximately 600,000 children are in foster care in the United States (Emerson & Lovitt 2003). Approximately one-fourth of the children and youth in foster care are placed with relatives, and approximately half are placed with nonrelatives. Others are usually placed in group homes or institutions (Behrman 2004), spending an average of approximately thirty-three months in foster care. According to Turnbull, Turnbull, Erwin, and Soodak (2006, 32), "The longer children stay in foster care, the greater the likelihood that they will experience many different foster care placements (i.e., foster care drift)." As a result, children in foster care have high rates of school absenteeism, midyear changes from one school to another, discipline suspensions from school, and a need to repeat one or more grades (Emerson & Lovitt 2003). Hence, as Tutwiler (2005) notes, educators need to have a plan for enrolling and integrating foster children into their school on short notice. They need to also become accustomed to working with both the foster parents and the child's caseworker. Finally, because the attention and resources of the foster parent may be divided among several unrelated foster children living in the same home, educators may have to take a more active role in ensuring that these parents understand how to assist the child who may be below grade level or in need of special services.

Using Family Life-Cycle Theory to Understand Family Stress

Whatever their form, all families constantly change as time and events alter their lives. Some events are developmental and predictable, such as when family members are born, grow up, leave home, bring in new members through marriage or other permanent relationships, retire, or die. Other events occur that are unpre-dictable and out of sync with usual expectations, such as divorce, unexpected death, immigration, unemployment, or natural catastrophes. Families experience varying degrees of stress in responding to these events, depending on the resources that they possess and their interpretation of the events.

Think about your own family. What have been some key family events and changes that your family has experienced, and how has your family marked these changes? Some families emphasize *marker events,* or the transition points of human development, more than others do. A child's first steps or entry into school, a con-firmation or bar/bat mitzvah, a teenager's driver's license, or a wedding may serve to mark major changes in the family. Other families emphasize unpredictable events as significant symbols of family change. For example, the premature death of a new baby, a divorce, or a parent's heart surgery may symbolize the greatest moment of change for some families. Whether the event is expected or unexpected, the fam-ily is forced to respond by changing its ways of relating and functioning. How a family responds to a stressful event depends on the organizational structure of the family prior to the stress, its available resources, and its guiding values and beliefs.

Meet the Families

Within the typical classroom, children behave very differently from one another. Sometimes a teacher's natural reaction is to categorize each child based on that behavior. For example, a child who often disobeys the class rules or does not turn in work on time may be labeled as "disruptive," "uncooperative," or "difficult." In contrast, a child who is always quiet and earns high grades may be labeled as "suc-cessful," "well behaved," or "good." We create these labels without truly examin-ing what the behavior might reflect. Rather than taking a child's behavior in the classroom at face value, teachers can benefit from looking deeper into each child's situation to discover the impact that family circumstances and other related matters have on their behavior. Consider the following family situations.

The Robertson Family

Callie Robertson is a student in your second grade class and has just moved to your school from a school in Orlando, Florida. She is seven years old and is one of three children in her family. Her parents, Bill and Laura, have been married for twelve years. Bill is the manager of a local department store, and Laura is a stay-at-home mother. Callie has an older sister, Lisa, age ten, and a younger brother, William II, age four. Bill and Laura both graduated from the University of Central Florida, where they met. Before becoming parents, Laura worked for a public relations firm in Orlando. You have become acquainted with this family through several after-school conversations with Callie's mother.

The Reynolds Family

Ella Reynolds is also a student in your second grade class. She has lived in the same town for most of her life and has been a student in your school since kindergarten. She has an older brother Michael, who is eleven years old and a fifth grader at the school, and a younger brother Brian, who is three and enrolled in the school's pre-K program. Ella's mother Kim is a single mother whom you have not had an opportunity to speak to, but Ella has told you that her mother is often working. Ella's grandmother Nancy occasionally picks up all three children from school and seems to help out a great deal with child care. She has been very pleasant in the few interactions you have had with her, and it is apparent that she cares very much for her grandchildren.

The Castillo Family

Adrian Castillo is another student in your second grade class. Adrian has lived in this town since he was born, but he has told you that his parents moved to this country when his mother was pregnant with him. He is an only child and lives with his mother Lucy. Another teacher in the school has told you that Adrian's father died about 18 months ago. Adrian is very quiet in class and keeps to himself. His mother drops him off and picks him up from school each day, and she always greets you with a pleasant smile, but you have never had an opportunity to talk with her.

Now reflect on your initial expectations about these families by means of Reflective Exercise 5.1.

Reflective Exercise 5.1

My Assumptions and Expectations About Families

What are your initial reactions to the descriptions of the families? Although it has not yet been revealed, what cultures and races do you imagine each family to be a part of? Which family would you expect to provide the most assistance in your classroom? Which family would you expect to not attend a "back to school" parent night? How do you think your expectations of these families will affect your interactions with them throughout the year?

Family Life-Cycle Theory

Relationships with parents, siblings, and other family members shift in response to expected developmental changes in the family (Carter & McGoldrick 2005). We are born or adopted into families, then grow and develop, and perhaps raise our own families, in which case, we may watch our children and grandchildren do the same. A family's life cycle is made up of these normative transitions through time that are rather expected and somewhat predictable but also include nonnormative transitions that consist of unexpected life events that uniquely affect families through time (e.g., untimely deaths, disaster, illness, unemployment). As a moving system through time, families are constantly dealing with change while also needing to remain stable. Therein lies the challenge of balance that keeps families full of activity throughout their lifespan (see Table 5.1 on page 124; Carter & McGoldrick 2005).

Family Life-Cycle Stages

Table 5.1 depicts the normative developmental changes that are more typically consistent with two-parent, middle-class American families. Keep in mind the importance that different family forms (e.g., remarried or blended families), cultural factors (e.g., associated with multiple generations in the home), or societal trends (e.g., marrying or having children later in life) tend to shift a family's developmental transitions throughout their life cycle.

As the table shows, each stage requires family members to go through key emotional processes to proceed developmentally. To accommodate needed developmental changes, families also need to be flexible enough to shift their family rules that dictate how they behave with one another. For instance, the Reynolds family we introduced earlier is a three-generation family that can be characterized as a family with young children. In that case, they would be faced with the life-cycle demands associated with adjusting the marital system to accommodate the children as well as the decision-making and management of child rearing, finances, and household tasks that are part of this stage. However, with the grandmother as a live-in member of the family, they are also faced with the impact of role negotiations between the mother and grandmother as well as older generation issues typically associated with later stages of family development. This means that besides the tasks and organizational changes that families with young children need to attend to, the Reynolds family may also find themselves dealing with changes that are usually associated with families with adolescents or families launching children. These needed adjustments impact each family member, including Ella, your student.

~~~~~~

Table 5.1   The Stages of the Family Life Cycle

Family Life-Cycle Stage	Emotional Process of Transition: Key Principles	Second-Order Changes in Family Status Required to Proceed Developmentally
Leaving home: single young adults	Accepting emotional and financial responsibility for self	a. Differentiation of self in relation to family b. Development of intimate peer relationship c. Establishment of self in respect to work and financial independence
The joining of families through marriage: the new couple	Commitment to new system	a. Formation of marital system b. Realignment of relationships with extended families and friends to include spouse
Families with young children	Accepting new members into the system	a. Adjusting marital system to make space for children b. Joining in child rearing, financial and household tasks c. Realignment of relationships with extended family to include parenting and grandparenting roles
Families with adolescents	Increasing flexibility of family boundaries to permit children's independence and grandparents' frailties	a. Shifting of parent/child relationships to permit adolescent to move into and out of system b. Refocus on midlife marital and career issues c. Beginning shift toward caring for older generation
Launching children and moving on	Accepting a multitude of exits from and entries into the family system	a. Renegotiation of marital system as a dyad b. Development of adult-to-adult relationships between grown children and their parents c. Realignment of relationships to include in-laws and grandchildren d. Dealing with disabilities and death of parents (grandparents)

〰〰〰〰〰〰〰〰〰〰〰〰〰〰〰〰〰〰〰〰〰〰〰〰〰〰〰〰〰〰〰〰〰〰〰

Table 5.1   Continued

Family Life-Cycle Stage	Emotional Process of Transition: Key Principles	Second-Order Changes in Family Status Required to Proceed Developmentally
Families in later life	Accepting the shifting generational roles	a. Maintaining own and/or couple functioning interests in face of physiological decline: exploration of new familial and social roles
		b. Support for more central role of middle generation
		c. Making room in the system for the wisdom and experience of the elderly, supporting the older generation without over-functioning for them
		d. Dealing with loss of spouse, siblings, and peers and preparation for death

Source: Carter, E. & McGoldrick, M. (1999) The expanded family life cycle: individual, family and social perspectives. Allyn & Bacon, p. 2.

Given the high rates of divorce and remarriage, you may very well encounter students whose parents have remarried and are living in blended family households. Remarried families with older children from first marriages and younger children from the current marriage will also find themselves dealing with several family life-cycle stages simultaneously. Societal trends related to marrying and having children later in life can also have families who experience several family stages at once as families deal with tasks associated with young children in the home, midlife career issues, and older parents.

This stage-oriented family life-cycle framework serves as a way of understanding family changes over time. Even though it may not account for different values and beliefs associated with diverse cultural groups and family forms, it offers unifying principles that define stages and tasks in general developmental terms. McGoldrick and Carter (2003) acknowledge that "most descriptions of the typical family life cycle, including our own, fail to convey the considerable effects of culture, ethnicity, race, religion, and sexual orientation on all aspects of how, when, and in what way a family experiences various phases and transitions" (395). These authors further explain that, although these variables are left out for the sake of theoretical clarity, in practice it is important to help families develop rituals that correspond to their life choices and transitions, especially in cases in which they are not validated (e.g., life-cycle patterns of multiproblem, poor as well as gay families). For instance, even though certain ethnic groups strongly emphasize close extended families and may not place great importance on the need for adults to leave the parental home, they will need to deal with the separation and redefinition of the parent–child relationship as children move into adulthood.

In the following section each of the stages of family development over time will be discussed. Despite that certain stages refer to individuals and families you may not work with, presenting all of the stages of the family life-cycle framework is important to give you a holistic view of a family's developmental process through time. The first stage of becoming an adult is a unique feature in this framework because others tend to begin with couplehood.

Leaving Home

According to Carter and McGoldrick's (2005) family life-cycle stages, young, single adults must deal with separation and leaving home to form their own relationships and future families. Emotionally, they are faced with the need to tolerate independence while remaining connected. Young adults may struggle with uncertainty often associated with career choices. They also contend with a range of emotions associated with developing intimate relationships and making lifestyle choices outside of their family. Leaving home is a time of separately defining yourself from your family while also remaining a part of the fold. During this time, young adults establish peer networks, complete school, make career choices, and find close friends and intimate partners. The aim is for healthy interdependence to develop between the young adult and his or her parents or caregivers.

The Couple

The family life-cycle stage framework purports that successful completion of tasks associated with young adulthood prepares individuals for couplehood. Gaining a greater sense of self, exercising individual choice and self-reliance, and independent management of your life adds to your readiness for coupling and marriage. A great deal of negotiation is required when a couple first comes together. In marriage, coming together also requires negotiations with extended family members on both sides. In marriage or domestic partnerships, partners/spouses face major decisions related to commitment, power, and closeness (Galvin, Byland & Brommel 2004). Commitment requires that each one become the other's primary partner, implying that ties with others are lessened. Another task the couple must deal with is exercising self-determination and influence in the relationship, while also yielding power for the enhancement of the relationship. Third, the couple must decide what is mutually satisfying for both of them as they balance the need for individual self-determination and attachment as a couple.

Becoming Parents

The key emotional process associated with parenthood is the acceptance of new members into the family system. This requires that the couple adjust their marital system to make space for the children. They will also need to realign relationships with extended family members in terms of roles and find ways to join in child rearing and household and financial tasks. Two-paycheck, dual-worker couples will need to sort through significant work–family dilemmas as they try to juggle their new parental roles, keep up with employers' demands, and attempt to fit in time for individual and relational needs.

Typically, with young children, parents contend with sleep deprivation, endless chores, changing schedules, and the constant care that the baby demands. This can put an enormous amount of stress on any individual or couple "since no amount of doing ever seems enough to get the job done before it needs to be done again" (Carter 2005, 249). The threat of divorce is high during this family life-cycle stage, given the serious role conflicts and socioeconomic strains that couples go through at this time. From a gender-based perspective, the stress associated with issues of money, time, isolation, chores, and sexual dissatisfaction can often lead to a shift in power from previously "equitable" ways before having children, to more traditional ways after children come along. This perspective is usually based on the strong assumption by the workplace, and by couples themselves, that juggling work and family is a dilemma for mothers not fathers.

In the families that were presented earlier, some of these factors could have entered into the Robertson family's decision to have Mrs. Robertson resign from her full-time public relations position to become a stay-at-home mom. How we view and judge these decisions and circumstances based on our own career-oriented perspectives and family-oriented values can have a significant impact on how we view our students and their families (e.g., mothers who decide to stay home as opposed to those who do not, or fathers who stay at home as opposed to the mother doing so).

For students who reside in single-parent households, different stressors are considered during this life-cycle stage that may be associated with lack of available resources and supportive networks. However, assuming that all single-parent families are deficient or lacking, based on structure alone, is problematic. Being a single-parent family is not the problem; to view them as such is. Like any other two-parent/caregiver-headed family, they can range from highly functional to very dysfunctional. As you read in the previous chapter, factors associated with a family's beliefs, their organization, and their communication and emotional connectedness with each other and with their community make the difference.

Families with Adolescents

The key process that families with children in this phase of development find themselves focused on is how to successfully prepare them for the responsibilities and commitments associated with the outside world. Obviously, it goes without saying that the family's handling of previous stages throughout the earlier years has a bearing on this stage as well. The challenge for most families lies in the profound shifts that need to be made in terms of relationship patterns across generations. In other words, families will define this stage of development based on their view of adolescence as a life stage and the acceptable roles and behaviors that are expected in this stage (Garcia-Preto 2005). Therefore, cultural and socioeconomic factors weigh heavily in this process. For instance, socioeconomic status can dictate the difference between a thirteen-year-old from a middle-class environment that can lead a more typical, school-oriented, care-free adolescent lifestyle, as opposed to a thirteen-year-old from a poorer or more marginalized background, who may be required to work instead of attend school.

For the most part, after some degree of chaos and disruption, families manage to reorganize themselves in ways that accommodate new rules to allow the adolescent some autonomy and independence. For others who end up struggling with the renegotiation of relationships, roles, rules, and limits, family counseling can help strengthen emotional bonds between family members and facilitate a way for them to sort through their differences. For example, Michael Reynolds is eleven years old. Soon, Michael will encounter his own developmental transition to puberty. This represents a shift between childhood and adulthood and brings with it an array of issues, such as sexuality, independence, and self-concept. Much of what happens during puberty and adolescence will have a strong impact on the development of Michael's personality (Bozhovich 2001). Despite that Michael will experience his own individual development, the way his family responds to and deals with this transition will have an impact on how it all turns out for Michael. He will not be able to make the necessary adjustments entirely on his own, and he will require the support and assistance of his family. Michael's mother Kim will be faced with the need for increased flexibility in rules associated with Michael's desire for greater independence, while also needing to stay connected as a trusted parent. This may also be a time when the absence of his father may be strongly felt by him and Kim when the presence and support of a male or father is so valuable.

Oftentimes, the parents' own unresolved emotional issues with their parents can resurface in their struggle to redefine relationships in the family. Family issues may also get complicated with other developmental demands experienced by individual family members (e.g., the adolescent's own bodily/physical changes and peer influence, parents dealing with midlife issues related to marriage or career, as well as older family members' ailing health). Adolescent risk factors to be considered during this life-cycle stage are associated with drug and alcohol use, early and unprotected sexual activity, delinquency, depression, and eating disorders (Garcia-Preto 2005). Staying emotionally connected in a culture that pulls parents away from their adolescents is a challenge. Yet teenagers who feel close to their parents and feel trusted and heard are less likely to resort to risky behaviors.

The Launching Phase

From a family perspective, by midlife, most parents are faced with numerous tasks and experiences of exits and entries into their family systems. This includes the launching of grown children and the entry of significant others, spouses, and children. As children exit the family home, the marital couple is faced with the task of renegotiating their relationship (without the children) and realigning boundaries to include in-laws and grandchildren. Grown children and their parents must forge new adult-to-adult relationships. As elder members of the family age, illness can bring up significant issues related to caregiving (with major emotional, financial, and role-related implications) and, eventually, death.

On a more individual level, this stage may be viewed as a time to explore new opportunities and roles, which is especially true for women who cared for others most of their lives and can move on to focus on friendships, educational and employment opportunities, and other leisurely activities. Men, on the other hand, may yearn for greater intimacy with their wives and closeness with their children when they reevaluate what they missed out on because of their focus on achievement, productivity, and work. So, while women with limited opportunities outside the home may not be as sorry to see childrearing come to an end, in contrast, men may find themselves wanting to "do it better" (McGoldrick & Carter 2003).

Those who may still be dealing with childrearing in midlife will need to contend with the tasks and demands associated with the stages of family members (e.g., young children and elderly parents), the so-called sandwich generation. This can place a great deal of pressure on individual family members and significantly strain relationships, especially when elders live in the home. Yet this multigenerational arrangement can present children with opportunities for closeness and learning from grandparents that may not otherwise happen.

Families in Later Life

A key transition for families in later life is the shifting that occurs in terms of generational roles and status for elder members of a family. Most often, this is associated with their acceptance of lessening powers (e.g., ability to drive or live by themselves), the views of the younger generations in the family toward them, and the role reversals that may occur in terms of dependency and competence. In most cases, individuals will need to adjust to retirement at this stage of development.

Walsh (1999) points out: "Our culture generally presents a rather pessimistic view of old age based on myths that prevail—such as most elderly have no family, or they have minimal interactions with family members, or are institutionalized" (392). Yet she reports that the majority of adults over age 65 either live with another family member or live within an hour from at least one of their children (80 percent), and that most between ages 65 and 80 are in good health and lead active lives.

In our classroom, we often encourage students to reflect on their family of origin. These reflections not only assist in understanding our own family and the influences they have had on us, but also it can help us to be more sensitive to the changing dynamics of other families. In Reflective Exercise 5.2, we ask you to describe key characteristics of your own family. Let these questions serve as a basis for understanding the concepts presented in the rest of this chapter. Reflect on what life has been like for you and your family of origin.

Reflective Exercise 5.2

Key Characteristics of My Family

Who are the members of your family? Which of those members live together now?

Where has your family lived? Where did you go to school?

What kinds of work do you and other family members do?

What types of schooling have you and your family members had?

What were these school experiences like?

How might these experiences of schooling compare to the experiences of your parent(s) or caregivers?

Understanding Family Stressors

To account for the unexpected events and unique challenges that families face through time, Carter and McGoldrick (1999) also developed a model depicting the types of stressors that affect a family's well-being and functioning (see Figure 5.1). This figure mirrors Bronfenbrenner's ecological systems theory that we discussed in the previous chapter because it depicts the levels of system influences on children and families' development operating over time. However, the figure is more specific in describing the nature of the predictable, developmental and unpredictable, non-developmental stressors that may impact a family. As you can see depicted in this figure, within the same family, individual members may experience and react differently to these stressors as a function of both the age of the family member and their position in their life cycle. We suggest that educators use this model to more fully understand their students' lives within the context of their families and the larger cultural contexts in which they are embedded.

The model depicts the sources of family stress that families may experience over time. The vertical dimension depicts stressors that encompass biological, familial, and behavioral characteristics based on given temperament, physical nature, or genetic makeup. In terms of history, these factors also include unique family patterns of relating and functioning that are "handed down" across generations, including family attitudes, values, expectations, secrets, rules, and societal pressures. Many of these stressors are the myths, rules, boundaries, and expectations of how people are to relate with each other in the family and with persons outside of the family. Think of it in terms of what we inherit and bring into experiences and relationships.

Figure 5.1   Flow of Stress through the Family

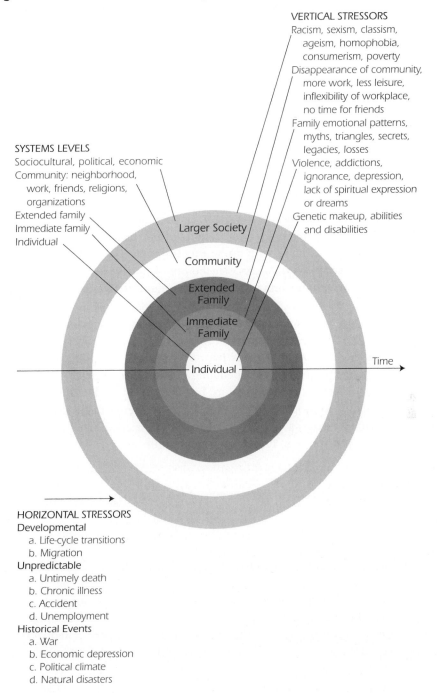

VERTICAL STRESSORS
Racism, sexism, classism,
   ageism, homophobia,
   consumerism, poverty
Disappearance of community,
   more work, less leisure,
   inflexibility of workplace,
   no time for friends
Family emotional patterns,
   myths, triangles, secrets,
   legacies, losses
Violence, addictions,
   ignorance, depression,
   lack of spiritual expression
   or dreams
Genetic makeup, abilities
   and disabilities

SYSTEMS LEVELS
Sociocultural, political, economic
Community: neighborhood,
   work, friends, religions,
   organizations
Extended family
Immediate family
Individual

Larger Society

Community

Extended
Family

Immediate
Family

Individual

Time

HORIZONTAL STRESSORS
Developmental
   a. Life-cycle transitions
   b. Migration
Unpredictable
   a. Untimely death
   b. Chronic illness
   c. Accident
   d. Unemployment
Historical Events
   a. War
   b. Economic depression
   c. Political climate
   d. Natural disasters

Source: Carter, E. & McGoldrick, M. (1999) The expanded family life cycle: individual, family and social per-spectives. Allyn & Bacon, p. 6.

The horizontal dimension depicts stressors, including the individual family member's development (emotional, cognitive, physical, and interpersonal) over time within a given historical context. By acknowledging system levels of influence, Carter and McGoldrick (2005) suggest that, "Certain individual stages may be more difficult to master, depending on one's innate characteristics and the influence of the environment" (5). The horizontal flow of stress in a family through time is associated with its developmental demands on the system, the unpredictable nature of family life events (such as death, chronic illness, accidents, or unemployment) and significant historical events we live through (such as war, political climate, economic changes, and natural disasters).

In the Castillo family, for example, several stressors are considered besides the normative developmental demands on this family as a system. Horizontal stressors related to family migration can affect families throughout several generations beyond the point of actual migration. Also, the death of Adrian's father a year and a half ago has required significant adjustment and coping by family members. Additionally, as a recent Hispanic immigrant to the United States, Mrs. Castillo is fluent in Spanish but is only familiar with a few English phrases. When she has an issue she would like to discuss with Adrian's teacher, her language barrier creates a great deal of anxiety for her. She anticipates poor communication between herself and the teacher and feels that it would only create a bigger problem if she were to schedule a meeting. She finds herself making a decision not to involve herself with it and "just see what happens." In at least three or four cases, these problems have grown with time and her son's grades have declined. At this point in the school year, she does not know whether scheduling a teacher conference will give him enough time to improve his grades before his next report card. She still feels as if she may not be able to properly articulate what she is seeing and is slowly separating herself further. Her brief polite contacts with Michael's teacher will not reveal her ambivalence and concern, unless it is explored further.

Unpredictable Stressors and Family Coping

Crisis and stress are often grouped together and can be easily confused. At various points in life, we all experience different levels of stress. Sometimes, the stress is easily manageable and requires little effort to balance it and move forward. At other times, major adjustments are necessary to maintain healthy functioning. When these stressors exceed the control of the individual or family, the potential for crisis is high. In other words, stress precedes crisis, and crisis does not occur without the onset of stressors. Major stresses can throw a family off balance. Crises and persistent challenges have an impact on the entire family. Although some may be shattered by crisis or persistent hardship, remarkably, others emerge stronger and more resourceful. Key family processes that enable family members to rally together through hard times can mediate the recovery of family members and their relationships, making relational transformation and growth possible through adversity. Resilience is the ability to withstand and rebound from disruptive life challenges (Walsh 1998).

In the previous chapter you learned about the specific family processes that contribute to children's school success. You will recognize that these are the same internal family strengths and resources that enable individuals and families to recover and grow from experiences associated with difficult and challenging stressors. This process involves the family's ability to "bounce forward" and "struggle well," effectively working through and learning from adversity and identifying and fortifying key resilient processes (Walsh, 1998).

Family Crisis

To understand and address crisis and stress in children and their families, we must first generate a clear definition of what it means to be in crisis. Crisis can be defined in many different ways. What may be a crisis for one individual or family may not be viewed as a crisis for another individual or family. The experience of stress and crisis is truly individual. However, more generalized definitions of crisis would categorize it as a state in which a complication arises that impedes an individual or family in some way. In general terms, "A crisis is a challenge to the previous structure of the family in the sense that in order for the family to remain functional, the structure must change" (Becvar & Becvar 2000). Although normative in nature, the transitions that families must go through as part of the family life cycle can also be thought of as crisis states. The typical ways of reacting to past circumstances are not effective when faced with the crisis, and, as a result, a sense of disorganization and immobilization may ensue (James & Gilliland 2001).

From a developmental perspective, some crises are considered to be normal steps in the progression of life. With each step, an individual is required to draw upon his or her repertoire of concepts and skills to master that step before moving onto the next one (Blackburn & Erickson 1986). Successful completion of that step adequately prepares the individual for the next developmental challenge. Within the system of the family, each individual who encounters a developmental challenge often requires the support of the entire family to successfully overcome the crisis.

A stressor is an event "that causes a change in the family system" (Turner & West 2002). Stressors within a family may show their "faces" in many different ways. They may serve as an opportunity for growth or may become debilitating to the family. In this book, stressors are divided into two categories, *developmental stressors* and *nonnormative stressors*. Note the importance of recognizing the differences between the two and understand not only how a child may react to each, but also how his or her family may react as well.

Other crises are not so common and expected. Although they can be broken down into more specific categories, for the purpose of this book, they are grouped as nonnormative crises (discussed earlier as horizontal stressors). A nonnormative crisis can occur with the onset of unforeseen stressors. According to James and Gilliland (2001), these crises may be situational, existential, or environmental. Situational crises occur unexpectedly and often result in feelings of shock or fright, and a lack of preparedness, in contrast to developmental crises (or vertical stressors), which may leave those affected by them in a state of distress.

To gain a clearer understanding, let us think of the Castillo family. Upon moving to the United States eight years ago, Lucy Castillo felt tremendous isolation. She was pregnant with her first child Adrian and was often left alone and confused. Her husband worked most of the day while she was at home, her mother was still in her home of Venezuela, and she had no friends or family nearby. Lucy's husband Jose met another Venezuelan man at work and was able to introduce their wives. Through this one connection, Lucy was able to form a friendship and meet other women who had recently immigrated to the country. It provided a support system that offered her answers to questions she had about the area and allowed her to discuss her concerns. Although it never made the transition from one culture to another easy, it certainly helped.

Family researchers and theorists have examined stressors and crises in families for the past fifty years. A noteworthy contribution is Hill's (1949) classic family stress model from which current stress models have evolved. Hill was one of the first to classify family disruptions that cause crises in a family. They included the loss of members (e.g., death), the addition or return of family members (e.g., birth or reunification), a sense of disgrace (e.g., resulting from infidelity, alcoholism, or nonsupport), and a combination of all of these factors for particular types of losses (e.g., suicide, homicide, imprisonment, or mental illness). Bain (1978) associated a family's coping capacity to the following factors: the number of previous stressors faced by family members in recent years, the degree of role change in coping, and available social and institutional support for family members. The original stress model developed by Hill (1949), referred to as the *ABCX Model*, proposed that *A* (the stressor event) interacted with *B* (the family's resources to cope with the stress), which interacted with *C* (the family's definition of the event), that produced *X* (the crisis). Based on Hill's work, McCubbin and Patterson (1983) developed a Double ABCX Model that extended the model to include postcrisis variables (i.e., the family's efforts to recover over time).

Stages of a Family Crisis

Walsh (1998) reminds us that a crisis can serve as a wake-up call, offering family members an opportunity to reassess priorities and stimulate greater investment in meaningful relationships and life pursuits. Patterson (2002) also suggests that "A crisis is very often a turning point for a family, leading to major change in their structure and/or functioning pattern"(p. 307). Crisis can occur in countless ways and will undoubtedly impact the entire family system. The family's response to the crisis will determine the severity of the impact and the family's resiliency in the aftermath.

In the aftermath of crisis, a significant breakdown in the family's organizational structure can occur. Communication patterns can be altered, boundaries broken, and the power hierarchy shifted, potentially leading to role confusion, limited support, and a downward shift in family functioning. Depending on how this is handled, this shift could bring on a long future of vulnerability to crisis that could prevent a family's full recovery.

Individually, people react to crisis with intense emotions. Fear, shock, distress, and insecurity are typical emotions experienced during crisis, among others. Families can react to stress with these same emotions. In addition, the potential for more severe reactions, such as anxiety or maladjustment, are also present (Jackson, Sifers, Warren & Velasquez 2003). The stages usually associated with an individual or family's response to crisis are shock, recoil, depression, and reorganization (Galvin et al. 2004, 320).

Shock

The initial response to a crisis is most often associated with disbelief and denial of the actual event or the minimization of its severity. Eventually, as reality sets in, the numbness wears off, and the feelings and reactions more closely linked with the experience will come. For example, in the case of death or loss, feelings of pain, grief, withdrawal, or quietness may be noted. Wanting to recapture what was lost, or reexperience what previously existed before the crisis event, may occur as well (e.g., expecting a loved one who died to walk in the room).

Recoil

At this stage, individuals and families may find themselves blaming, bargaining, or expressing anger directed at the event or persons most directly involved or close to the situation (e.g., oneself, doctors, family members, and God). Anger is often associated with a sense of injustice. Bargaining efforts are aimed at trying to restore things to normalcy (e.g., "If mom makes it, I will quit smoking").

Depression

Gradually, anger turns into depression and sadness. The feelings that were directed outward are directed inward as individuals take in all that has happened. Coming to terms with daily life and the future implications of the crisis event can be overwhelming. Rather than avoiding discussion about your feelings and experiences, sharing your story with others (whether they are directly involved in or outside of the situation) is best. In some cases, sharing with outsiders may actually offer the greatest source of support, and, therefore, it is important for those less directly involved to remain available and open in their supportive roles.

Reorganization

As individuals and families recover from stressful crisis events, they come to a point where gradual progress is made, which is often associated with a decision related to a turning event that signals they are moving on (e.g., getting rid of mementos or daily reminders, joining a group, or dating). Your ability to communicate about the loss or experience of the critical event facilitates reorganization. In terms of time, moving through all of these stages can take days, months, or years, depending on the level of loss, trauma, severity, and impact of the event. No one frame of time is to be prescribed or expected.

Crisis presents both threat and opportunity in that it can potentially impair the individual family member or family to the point of pathology or can serve as a strengthening learning experience, through which new coping skills and resources are developed and defined. It presents a challenge for families to find a way to "balance family demands with family capabilities" (Patterson 2002, p. 234) to reach successful acceptance and adaptation as part of their reorganization.

As teachers, we must recognize that we cannot adequately handle every crisis that we encounter among our students. By means of Reflective Exercise 5.3, think about the developmental and nonnormative crises discussed in this chapter.

Reflective Exercise 5.3

Comfort Level with Type of Stress Experienced

What might be a type of crisis or stress that you might experience that would exceed your comfort level?

What might be the underlying factors behind this discomfort?

What resources would be useful to have if you observed a student or a student's family experiencing this type of crisis or stress?

Family Resources for Responding to Crisis and Stress

Family worldviews affect a family's perceptions of the stresses that enter its world. If one family perceives the world as chaotic, disorganized, and frequently dangerous, any change may be upsetting. If another sees the world as predictable, ordered, and controllable, change may be perceived as manageable. How a family responds to stress depends upon the organizational structure of the family prior to the stress and the values it upholds. The family's first response to stress may be to try to maintain organizational continuity and emotional balance, but this may fail if the shock to the family is too great.

Family Resilience Theory

As families move from the initial shock and denial of a crisis event to reorganization and healing, key family processes exist that mediate the recovery of all family members and their relationships. If families are able to tap into these key processes for resilience, they can emerge stronger and more resourceful in meeting future challenges (Walsh 1998). Walsh developed a framework that describes key family processes that are useful in overcoming hardship and difficulties. Her family resilience framework serves as a conceptual map to identify family processes that can help families reduce stress and foster healing and growth when faced with crisis and adversity.

The key processes of family resilience proposed in Walsh's framework are divided into three primary areas: belief systems, organizational patterns, and communication/problem-solving. Belief systems can significantly influence how families think about a crisis or suffering. Beliefs are also instrumental in decision-making that can lead toward reorganization and recovery. Within this framework, the meaning that family members make out of a crisis situation, their outlook, and their level of transcendence and spirituality can make a difference in their process of adaptation. If, for instance, a family has a strong sense of affiliation with each other that allows them to feel supported by each other in approaching adversity (e.g., "We shall overcome this together"), then there is a stronger chance that they can buffer the stress toward more optimal adaptation.

In terms of outlook, families that are more likely to bolster themselves out of challenges and crisis events are those who hold a more optimistic outlook, have hope, share a sense of confidence in their abilities to overcome situations, and focus their energies on making the best out of their options. Transcendent beliefs and spirituality provide meaning and purpose beyond our own experience. When families are able to tap into the strength, comfort, and guidance that cultural or religious traditions offer them, they are more likely to emerge from adversity as a stronger family.

Another key process in Walsh's framework is based on the family's organizational patterns, or their structure. Resilience is sustained in families whose organization is flexible (in terms of structure) and connected (in terms of relationships). The availability and use of social and economic resources also have an impact on their sense of organizational structure (e.g., kin, community, financial, and social networks).

Finally, in terms of communication and problem-solving, families will benefit most from clarity, emotional expression that leads to open communication, trust, empathy, tolerance, and collaborative efforts to manage conflict and solve problems. Families must find their own culturally relevant ways through adversity that facilitate personal strengths and resources. In some cases, they may simply need to be heard or allowed to explore their own set of possibilities. The first author has developed a method of interviewing families in counseling that helps them elicit, discover, and utilize internal strengths and resources as part of their own therapeutic process. Although we are not proposing that teachers take on the role of a therapist, the method does illustrate how listening and strength-based conversation can be instrumental in getting families to trust you and, most important, believe in themselves.

Resource-Based Reflective Consultation

Resource-based reflective consultation is a consultative method that encourages therapy professionals to invite their client families to inform them of their family resources and strengths. Family resources and strengths are conceptualized as "those individual and systemic characteristics among family members that promote coping and survival, limit destructive patterns, and enrich daily life" (Karpel 1986).

By its very nature, the consultant's request that the families come up with this information about themselves and their family, rather than expecting their counselor to do so, affirms a family's voice and level of expertise (Echevarria-Doan 2001; Rafuls 1994). This interviewing method has been implemented and used with seriously troubled, multistressed, ethnically diverse families of lower socioeconomic means, indicating that strength-based practice can bring out the best in families regardless of their status, level of hardship, or culture. Some family resources identified by these families were *Family Formation* (associated with related and extended family forms); *Family Service* (associated with age- and gender-related family functions); *Family Adaptability* (which revealed strengths associated with temporal dimensions); *Shared Past* (associated with transgenerational links and lessons learned); *Shared Present* (brought up in terms of humor, togetherness, preservation of family, perception of hardship); *Shared Future* (with focus on hope for children's future); *Family Connectedness* (referring to time spent together, shared interests and experiences, and passing down traditions); and *Ethnic Affiliation* (associated with traditions and rituals that held them together).

The family's identification of their own strengths and resources allowed families (and their therapists) to challenge their own deficit-based views that can be constraining and detrimental to change and recovery. We believe that this interviewing method might also be applied by educators who might invite the families they work with to talk about their own resources and strengths.

As a teacher, you need to be familiar with the various types of stressors that can precipitate a crisis for both students and families. This knowledge will allow you to recognize a potential crisis, either in its early stages or before it arises, so that you might provide the support and resources necessary for the student and his or her family. As you gain knowledge about the stressful events in your students' lives, you may find yourself challenging your own belief systems and thoughts that get in the way of staying engaged and supportive, which is especially true when we think that only certain families who look a certain way, or are formed a certain way, are functional. Remember family form does not equal family function (Walsh 1998). Think for a moment about the characteristics of your own family by means of Reflective Exercise 5.4.

Reflective Exercise 5.4

Strengths in My Family

Think about a time when your family experienced stress or crisis.

What are some of the strengths or coping skills that helped your family through that difficult period?

What cues might you have given your teacher(s) during that time to let her or him know that your family was experiencing stress or was in crisis?

The Importance of Teacher Advocacy for Families

One of the wonderful aspects of being a teacher is that you have an opportunity to get to know your students. Particularly in elementary school, children spend a great deal of time with one teacher. As their teacher, you often have time to learn about them, predict their behaviors, and watch them grow throughout the year. You are in a unique position to recognize when a student is making dramatic improvements and reward them when they do. Unfortunately, you may also be one of the first to notice problem behaviors. Children may act out and become disruptive, or they may internalize their feelings and become more withdrawn. When these changes are apparent, the child may be at risk for experiencing crisis.

When future teachers are asked what they might do once they have encountered a child or family under stress or in crisis, a common response might be to send the child to the school counselor. The school counselor can be an excellent resource for talking with the child; however, the counselor may not always be available. Because the problem might require immediate attention and an ongoing relationship with the student's family, teachers may be in a better position to share their concerns about a child with his or her family. As we know, teachers spend a great deal of time with their students and often know them quite well. During this time, students may form a relationship with their teacher in which they feel comfortable and secure. It may cause students additional distress to leave that comfort zone and be referred to the school counselor, whom they may not know. This certainly does not mean that teachers should take on all responsibility, but it does suggest that teachers should be knowledgeable about the resources that their students or students' families might need. (In Chapter 13, we discuss the types of resources and process by which you might link a family to outside support services.)

The key idea for teachers is to maintain a sense of teamwork. Building relationships with other faculty and staff and learning from one another can make a big difference in your efforts to make things happen. This extends beyond the bounds of the school into the community, where you can also tap into resources that can provide specialized assistance and care for your students and their families.

Schools and Stress

When most of us think of a typical school, we might imagine a place where children come together each morning, learn from their teachers, and return home in the afternoon. We may even think about the social interactions between students and how they learn from one another. What we usually do not think about are some of the negative effects that schools can unknowingly have on their students and their families. In this section, you will be given a brief review of the three paradigms of family–school relations that we discussed in Chapter 2. Through this discussion, you will note that some of the patterns of interactions that school staff may have with families can have an adverse effect on families and can result in less family participation in school activities.

The three paradigms of family–school relations discussed earlier in this book include the separation, remediation, and collaborative paradigms. As you can probably guess, the purpose of this book is aimed at creating a more collaborative paradigm within schools, where families are considered a powerful ally in educating each child. In shifting our thinking toward this direction, we are moving away from the separation paradigm. Note, however, to not only move ahead, but also to look back and recognize how these assumptions about learning may have contributed to both individual stress on each student in the classroom, as well as stress on the family.

For decades, the separation and remediation paradigms held by educators and families shaped the ways in which family–school relations were structured within schools. Students and their families functioned under the assumption that schools provided education in its entirety, and that learning did not actually occur in other arenas. Teachers and administrators were considered the experts and their methods and presented content generally went unquestioned (Senge et al. 2000). Most parents of today's children were educated in settings guided by either of these paradigms. For example, this was Mr. Robertson's experience with school: His parents sent him off each morning, he spent the day learning the fundamentals of education from his teachers, came home in the evening and finished his homework, and prepared for the next day. His parents, and the parents of his peers, were rarely seen on the school's campus, unless there was some sort of problem. Hence, the separation style of family–school relating is very familiar to him and it has taken major adjustments, on his part, to become more involved in his children's education.

Some parents welcome the change in thinking from separation to collaboration and enjoy playing a vital role in their children's education. For other parents, the memories they have of their own school experiences can create a sense of anxiety and inferiority before even setting foot in their children's classroom. They often remember that their own parents were only called to school if there was a problem and, in turn, come to negative conclusions about their children before a meeting or school event occurs. They may have also experienced times in which their attendance at school or teacher meetings resulted in a message of their inadequacy as parent educators (Finders & Lewis 1994). These negative incidences result in lesser involvement by parents, thereby making it more difficult for them to reach out to teachers.

In many cases, the culture of a family may also have an impact on their involvement in their child's schooling. It can potentially heighten the amount of anxiety and inferiority discussed previously. Many students and their families feel that cultural boundaries prevent them from succeeding in school and becoming involved, respectively (Senge et al. 2000). Research has shown that African American students, particularly males, show consistent underachievement in school. One factor that contributes to this problem lies in low teacher expectations (Mandara 2006). Very often, negative, general assumptions by educators about the culture and/or race of their students may actually contribute to the student's underachievement in the classroom. It may also be assumed that providing extra attention to this student will not be successful because the environment in which he is raised will not be conducive to retaining the material taught in school. This mentality prolongs a cycle in education, which may likely have been present when this child's parent was in school. For example, Mrs. Reynolds, a Caucasian woman, does not recall many positive memories during her education. Her public elementary school was located in a rural community that valued women working on the family farm rather than excelling in school. Hence, Mrs. Reynolds did not receive much academic assistance at home and was often falling behind in classes. Her initial underachievement in science and grammar increased as time went on. She was placed in remedial classes and, eventually, dropped out of school in the eleventh grade, after coming to the conclusion that she would never excel academically. As a result, Mrs. Reynolds does not feel prepared to assist her daughter Ella with her homework and worries that she will be judged negatively as a "typical high school dropout" by Ella's teacher.

As you can see, teachers and schools can unwittingly create stress for individual students and their families without even being aware that such stress is being created. The social climate of a school, although planned to be conducive to a child's learning, may actually serve as a source of anxiety for the parents of students. Over time, invisible boundaries may develop, separating families from schools regardless of the efforts made by the school staff to integrate families into their children's education. In the end, the students are the victims, missing out on opportunities to enrich their learning experiences because of the lack of communication between the school and the families. Teachers and school administration need to recognize this as a potentially hazardous problem and take the appropriate preventative steps. Now that you understand the importance of recognizing these potential problems, you can be equipped with the tools to prevent and cope with them. But first, by means of Reflective Exercise 5.5, think back to your own experiences in school and note how some schools may either have unwittingly created stressful conditions for families or have found ways to counteract these conditions.

Reflective Exercise 5.5

Thinking Back to My Elementary School Days

How did your school encourage parental/family involvement in your education?

What are two examples of your family's involvement in your schooling then?

Supportive Schools

As we have discussed, every family is different and every family will undoubtedly experience times of stress or crisis. In the educational system, we have the opportunity to use our positions to provide assistance to families to create a positive learning environment for our students. To do this, we must move away from the traditional paradigms of education, in which a clear separation exists between family and school. Teachers must work together with the caregivers of their students to have a greater understanding of each student and to design a classroom in which students benefit to their individual maximum potential. Teachers must welcome the involvement of their students' families and celebrate the diversity present within the classroom.

Diversity within the classroom not only exists as a result of differences in race or religion of the students in your classroom, but also in family composition and family culture. Although two children may appear to be of a similar race, their family experiences may vary greatly. The diversity among students is sometimes considered a hindrance in the classroom, requiring extended efforts from teachers to find a common ground among the students. Within the collaboration paradigm, diversity is celebrated among students. Each student is encouraged to educate peers about their culture, creating an environment of acceptance and appreciation. In the next chapter, you will learn more about the divergent values of families from different cultural backgrounds and be introduced to several of the strategies that teachers are using to create more culturally sensitive classroom environments.

In Chapters 2 and 3, you were presented with the family–school collaboration paradigm. This paradigm will serve as the foundation for developing strong relationships with the families of your students. Using the concepts presented within the paradigm, you will begin to see the benefit of incorporating families into the classroom, resulting in an enriched educational experience for each student. In the following chapters, you will be presented with techniques, such as student-led conferences and family–school problem-solving meetings. These techniques embrace the collaboration paradigm and can be used throughout the school year to promote this approach to education.

Summary

Students' experience within the classroom is strongly influenced by their families' social world. Today's families come in many different forms that strongly influence the nature of their social worlds. Moreover, from a developmental perspective, families evolve and change through time in response to individual and systemic demands placed on the family system. Normative, developmental changes and unpredictable, nonnormative changes in the lifespan of a family were discussed in this chapter, using a family life-cycle framework. This framework provides a useful perspective on change within a family from young adulthood to later life stages. Normative and nonnormative changes impact family relationships and functioning. The stressors and critical events associated with these changes can have an effect on student performance in the classroom. Families and individuals respond to stress and crises in very unique ways, based on factors associated with belief systems, organizational patterns, and communication/problem-solving skills. School-based examples of family situations have been used throughout the chapter to illustrate theoretical concepts. Reflective exercises have also been introduced for teachers to gain self-awareness and perspective, as they prepare to deal with family-related situations in their schools.

The importance of a strength-based perspective was highlighted as a way of supporting students going through stressful family events and changes. Methods that challenge deficit-based assumptions and practices were introduced as a way of engaging families and students in need of your support and understanding. Utilizing a collaborative paradigm, we considered the role that educators might play in helping students' families during stressful life changes. Situational stressors within schools were addressed as were aspects of supportive schools that promote teacher advocacy for families.

Chapter 6

Equal Access, Unequal Resources: Appreciating Cultural, Social, and Economic Diversity in Families

Cirecie A. West-Olatunji

Learning Objectives

After reading this chapter, you will be able to:

- Explain the various meanings of the term *culture*.
- Describe the diverse economic, cultural, and social contexts that influence an individual or a family's worldview.
- Explain the differences in individualistic and collectivistic worldviews of families.
- Discuss the impact of worldviews on student learning and educators' interactions with students' families.

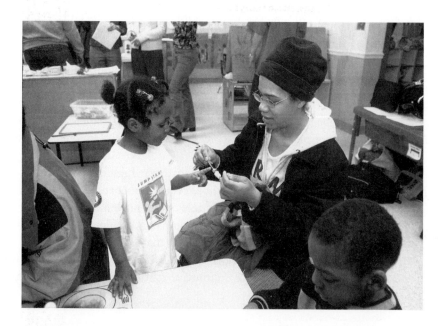

What is culture? What is poverty? How do culture and poverty affect children's and families' experiences of schools and educators? How can educators recognize and appreciate the social, cultural, and economic diversity of their students' families? In this chapter we describe the varying worldviews that characterize families from diverse cultural, social, and economic groups, and examine the impact of these worldviews on student learning and educators' interactions with students' families.

If you recall, in the first chapter of this book, we asked you to visualize what your classroom of students would look like and how you envision interacting with them and the key adults in their lives. When we ask our students to do this, we notice that they usually envision working with children who look very much like themselves and come from families very much like their own—European American (White), middle-class families who have had at least a high school, if not college, education. Moreover, their ideas about how they expect to structure their interactions with their students and their students' families reflect the *middle-class, monocultural* orientation of most schools in which a single, homogenous dominant culture is depicted in teaching and learning practices, with little attention being given to varying multicultural perspectives (Derman-Sparks, Ramsey, Edwards & Brunson-Day 2006; Tutwiler 2005).

However, as you are learning, a strong probability exists that you will be teaching children who come from far different economic and cultural backgrounds. In addition, a high probability exists that school staff with whom you work will be "educentric" in their perspective about family–school relations, viewing family or community involvement in children's education from a perspective that reflects only the school staff's values, goals, and priorities rather than the perspectives of the families served by the school (Dunlap & Alva 1999; Lawson 1999). Yet, as you are learning, this perspective can limit the ability of educators to work productively with children's families.

A variety of different approaches have been taken to understanding the influence of culture and class on children's learning and family–school interactions. One approach has emphasized learning about the specific histories and traditions of different ethno-linguistic groups and how to change instruction to reflect them. For example, in an effort to make curriculum more inclusive, teachers have developed specific lessons on African American history or American Indian history, as part of their social studies instruction. Other educators have thoroughly revised curriculum and textbooks to be more representative of the histories and traditions of groups that make up U.S. society (Ladson-Billings 1991).

Another approach has emphasized raising educators' awareness of school and community institutional practices that unwittingly promote racism (Derman-Sparks & Brunson-Phillips 1997) and working to transform these institutional practices. This approach requires educators to first examine the power relations between the school (representing the dominant community) and groups that have traditionally wielded less power. Second, specific cultural values and perspectives of diverse families are examined to determine how they differ from those of the dominant European American White, middle-class culture. Third, learning activities and family involvement methods are designed to be more in keeping with these values (Trumbull, Rothstein-Fisch, Greenfield & Quiroz 2001). This approach is what we highlight in the chapter.

We believe that educators need to understand how families in diverse economic circumstances and cultural contexts view their role interacting with the school and how families' participation in their children's learning may take different forms from those expected within European American, middle-class standards and mores. In this chapter, we first explore the diverse economic, cultural, and social contexts that influence family life and shape families' worldview and their children's learning. We then introduce the concept of *cultural reciprocity* as a means of considering how these diverse contexts influence family–school relationships and describe several educational innovations that can support the learning of children from diverse cultural and economic contexts.

But first take a moment to consider what might be your specific expectations and assumptions about the goals of schooling and the roles that you think educators and families should play in their children's learning and schooling. To gain a greater understanding of our own "taken-for-granted" cultural assumptions about school roles and goals, we have found that stepping outside of our familiar world is often useful. Hence, we ask you to imagine in Case Study 6.1 that you are a parent attending a parent–teacher conference at a school situated in a culture that differs from your own. What conclusions might you draw from this exercise about the ways that cultural beliefs shape our ideas about the goals of schooling and the roles that teachers and parents should play in student learning? Second, how do you see the decision-making power being distributed in this parent–teacher interaction? Did the parent, for example, have the power to change how the teacher interacted with her daughter?

CASE STUDY 6.1

Differences of Cultural Beliefs that Affect Parent–Teacher Interaction

Imagine that you are a parent of a fifth grade girl from Midland, a community that, like some Western cultures, values independence, and that you have moved with your family to the Far East into a fictitious culture that values interdependence and reliance on immediate and extended family, as do some Eastern cultures. As a parent you notice that your child is not faring well in her new school. You prepare for the first parent–teacher conference by drawing up a list of questions designed to find out why your child is not doing well in subjects she previously excelled in, such as creative writing. You have been actively involved in her education and you expect to continue to be and are willing to help at home.

At the meeting, you find the teacher, female, to be polite but distant. A young man who is majoring in languages at the local university is there to interpret for you, but you are unsure of his ability to accurately convey your message; his English seems sketchy. When you bring out the last writing assignment that your daughter completed and ask why it received such a low grade, the teacher looks puzzled. After some back and forth dialogue between the teacher and the interpreter, the interpreter relays the information. The teacher is perplexed that you are questioning her grading at all. Again, some dialogue is exchanged, then she seems embarrassed as she painfully describes through the young man that your daughter wrote the composition about herself. She explains that her intent is to not have her students "self-cherish" in their schoolwork. The aim of all education is to transcend self-worship and become part of the whole. To do this, students must not dwell on themselves. She looks embarrassed to have to explain this to you. As the conversation continues, you mention that you have provided everything, including a computer and book resources in your daughter's bedroom that she has had since she was four, to help her advance her education. Again, the teacher looks embarrassed. The young man lets you know that the teacher has politely suggested that maybe part of your daughter's problems in school could be due to her early and unnatural separation from her parents or the family bed, and that she is subtly trying to curb your daughter of emotion. The teacher also tells you that your daughter's unhealthy need to express her feelings makes the other children uncomfortable. As you leave the conference, the teacher closes by saying that she hopes for your daughter to be surrounded by blessed family members during her whole life.

Questions to Consider

In this scenario, the teacher did not try to understand your family, your culture, or your background. Instead the teacher appeared to see your daughter's cultural differences as deficiencies.

What impact do you think this might have on your daughter?

What are the conflicting perceptions of the teacher and the parent about—

Their expectations and goals for students?

The role of the teacher?

The role of the parent?

How "good" people behave?

How the daughter can be successful?

Source: Cowdery, J., Ingling, L., Morrow, L., Wilson, V. (2007). Building on student diversity: Profiles and activities (178–180). Thousand Oaks, CA: Sage.

Understanding Differences in Class and Culture

〰〰〰〰〰〰
〰〰〰〰〰〰

Just as in the previous simulated case, when an educator and parent with differing worldviews and life perspectives meet, their first encounter will more likely be confusing or negative. However, if their perspectives and worldviews are similar, their reactions to each other are more likely to be positive. Our life perspectives and worldviews emerge out of our cultural identities and differing life experiences. Examples of cultural identity categories include ethnic identification, race, socioeconomic status, gender (i.e., male or female), gender identity (masculine or feminine), sexual orientation, regionality, religious affiliation, family structure, and disability status. Think about the identity categories by which you define yourself. By means of Reflective Exercise 6.1 depict yourself in relation to each category.

Reflective Exercise 6.1

My Identity Web

Educational Experiences

Race   Regionality
Socioeconomic Status   Ethnicity

YOU

Sexual Orientation   Gender
Religion   Family Membership

Age   Disability Status

How does each of your identity categories shape your attitudes and perspectives? For example, does your ethnicity or religious background hold specific expectations for gender identification? Are men and women expected to act in specific roles? How do your hobbies, dress, interests, and friendships align with such gender expectations? These are some of the different ways that our distinctive identities can influence our interaction with families.

Because schools and educators frequently represent the dominant European American (White) culture, understanding how certain categories of identities (culture, race, and class) affect the nature of interactions between school professionals and families is important. The following terms are frequently used in discussions of diverse identities: *culture, race, ethnicity, nationality*, and *class*. Often used interchangeably, these terms actually connote different meanings. Hence, prior to looking at specific differences in class and cultural identity, let us clarify these terms.

Culture

According to Murry et al. (2004), "*Culture* encompasses macro-level processes and deals specifically with the values and norms that govern and organize a group of people defining characteristics and behaviors that are deemed appropriate or in-appropriate for an organized group. Culture also specifies the context of human behavior, and its transmission occurs in an environment that includes a specific place, time and stimuli in which skills, knowledge and attitudes are learned" (83). Culture might also be defined as influencing how a person perceives and interprets what is happening and determines how the person behaves, initiates, and reacts to various situations (Gollnick & Chinn 2002). According to Turnbull, Turnbull, Shank, and Smith (2004), culture "influences our rituals, determines our language, shapes our emotions; and is the basis for what we determine is right or wrong about ourselves, others, and society" (93). Gollnick and Chinn (2002) present a listing of characteristics that merge to form one's cultural identity and that include one's gender, ethnicity, race, social class, geography, age, exceptionality, religion, and language.

Race

Race refers to a system of biological taxonomy developed to classify plants and ani-mals. When applied to humans, it represents an assumption of shared genetic her-itage based on external physical characteristics, such as facial features, skin color, and hair texture. Rather than using biology alone to study humans, some social sci-entists advocate the use of the more inclusive concept of *ethnicity* that encompasses not only physical characteristics but also culture. Although the terms *ethnicity* and *race* are often used interchangeably, the concepts they represent have different con-ceptual meanings and operational definitions. More important, definitions of eth-nicity include socially constructed elements, such as the language, beliefs, norms, behaviors, and institutions that members of a group share. Moreover, although some social scientists use the term *ethnicity* interchangeably with *culture*, because the concepts share a similar emphasis on delineating how people think, behave, make decisions, and define events and experiences, these are also distinctive concepts. *Nationality*, although commonly used to inquire about an individual's ethnicity or cultural background, is more narrowly defined as one's citizenship.

Social Class

Social class connotes the socioeconomic standing of an individual or, in the case of children, their families. Curiously, in studying the poor, social class is rarely defined consistently. Conceived, at times, as a group's norms and values or, at other times, as its attitudes toward work and family or as patterns of behavior, social class in the poverty literature has been studied with neither the depth nor precision of analyses of specific ethnic groups. Yet, however defined, it remains a subtext of distinctions between the "deserving" and "undeserving" poor (Lamont & Small 2006).

In conceptualizing social class, researchers have embraced two very different perspectives that are closely tied to families' participation in society (Tutwiler 2005). The first perspective focuses on cultural explanations for a family's poverty (and social class position). Cultural explanations emphasize that each social class has distinctive sets of attitudes, values, and behaviors that comprise a culture shared by others at their economic level. This *culture of poverty* theory characterizes the poor in terms of deficits by assuming that the poor have certain attitudes, values, and behaviors that keep them at the bottom of the economic or social hierarchy, and that they pass on these traits to their children (Payne 1998; Tutwiler 2005).

Yet many contemporary researchers offer a different theoretical perspective that focuses on structural explanations for social class differences. This perspective, often referred to as a theory of *cultural capital,* emphasizes that the difference in resources available to families influences their daily living situations. In other words, the differences in economic and social resources, rather than a family's attitudes and values, shape the nature of a family's relationships with other groups and institutions and result in certain levels of class privilege (i.e., opportunities and advantages) for their children (Baca-Zinn & Eitzen 1996). According to this framework, children of poor and working-class families are handicapped by a schooling system that systematically uses criteria for evaluation that are biased in favor of middle-class culture.

Moderating Influences

Despite common challenges faced by children from culturally and ethnically diverse backgrounds, two important moderators have been found to significantly impact their resilience and coping, especially within the realm of education. Research has shown that an individual's level of acculturation can influence their self-esteem, social competencies, and academic performance. Additionally, assessing children's ethno-cultural worldviews without considering their families' socioeconomic status (SES) can yield conflicting outcomes.

For many culturally diverse schoolchildren, navigating within a culturally foreign environment can cause anxiety and fear and can impact their ability to interact with their peers and perform academically. Confronted with new expectations and assumptions by their teachers and other school personnel, children will develop coping mechanisms to decrease their discomfort level. One way in which they may respond is to *assimilate* into the social mainstream by conforming to the Eurocentric values and beliefs of the school community.

Helms and Cook (1999) define assimilation as "the process by which the person is accepted and or incorporated into a group" (37). Cultural assimilation takes into account the impact of the sociopolitical context for the absorption and integration of the new culture (Ivey 2000). For culturally diverse individuals in the United States, cultural assimilation refers to the expectation that culturally diverse children must embrace the norms (values, beliefs, language, family patterns, and behavioral style) of the dominant culture. Contemporary scholars have asserted that this absorption into mainstream values and beliefs comes at a significant personal price in that it causes stressful experiences in relation to one's ethnic identity (Helms & Cook). This narrow cultural lens is known as *ethnocentric monoculturalism,* in which not only are the values, assumptions, beliefs, and practices of only one segment of the society valued (e.g., monoculturalism), but also they are structured in such a manner as to enhance the position of only that narrow segment of the population (Sue & Sue 2003).

Acculturation differs from assimilation in that it allows for the retention of one's own beliefs and practices while assuming the cultural norms of a new and different culture. Acculturation is a significant challenge to immigrants coming to the United States (Roysircar-Sodowsky & Maestas 2000). Moreover, current research on acculturation suggests that individuals who arrive at younger ages, such as twelve years and under, who attend elementary school in the United States, tend to be more assimilated than those who immigrated at older developmental periods, such as adolescence or adulthood (Phan, Rivera & Roberts-Wilbur 2005; Zhou & Bankston 1998). Although acculturation is commonly discussed regarding immigrant families, this process can occur for migrant individuals as well, especially within highly diverse societies, such as the United States (Roysircar 2004). For instance, individuals who move from the South to the Northeast often express feelings of culture shock as they seek to adjust to regional norms for behaviors and expectations.

In addition to the issues of assimilation or acculturation, SES has an impact on culturally diverse children and their families. Low-income parents experience a host of environmental concerns that academically influence their children's behavior and performance. In addition to financial difficulties that affect their food supply, educational resources, and parental stress, these families often experience inadequate housing and thus are frequently relocating. Moreover, families who experience stress often have problems in their familial relationships, causing secondary problems, such as marital conflicts, domestic violence, and substance abuse (Evans & Carter 1997). Within this context, children from high poverty communities are coming to school.

Children from families and communities that are culturally, linguistically, and socially divergent from the schools that they attend often experience low academic achievement, significant emotional anguish, and psychological distress (Phillips 1993). Common responses to this lack of congruence between home and school in young children are significant changes in behavioral patterns, bed-wetting, fretfulness, and developmentally regressive behaviors. Children who may be talkative and precocious at home may be shy and unresponsive in the classroom. Similarly, children who are even-tempered and compliant in the home environment may exhibit a lack of control in the school setting in response to a culturally unresponsive classroom. Without considering the effect of cultural continuity on children's behaviors, teachers may misinterpret their behavior.

Sociocultural Stressors

Children from high poverty communities and culturally diverse students have a multilayered set of obstacles to overcome to succeed in the school environment (Olatunji 2000). Primarily, prevailing sociopolitical conditions exist that predispose teacher dispositions and expectations about the students. These conditions also influence the quality of the physical environment and accessibility to educational resources. Moreover, conflicts occur between the students' socially constructed knowledge and that of the school (Gordon 1997).

If you recall from our previous discussion of the ecological systems theory, Bronfenbrenner posited that macrosystemic factors influence family life and family–school interactions. Nowhere is this more readily observed than in families who experience poverty. Macrosystemic factors heavily influence low-income families' parental practices and expectations, family stressors, unique characteristics, and dynamics. Factors, such as family stress, parent–child interactions, family conflict, and marital functioning have all been found to impact children's adjustment and development of externalizing behaviors (Papp, Goeke-Morey & Cummings 2004). Current research suggests that marital functioning and parental distress are significant predictors of children's behavioral problems (Papp et al. 2004). Family risk factors (e.g., family stress, family conflict, and low SES) and poor parenting practices are highly predictive of both externalizing behaviors and poor emotional adaptation (Prevatt 2003). Low-income single caregivers, who often encounter a great deal of family stress, may limit their involvement within schools if they are experiencing difficulties in family functioning (Unger, Jones, Park & Tressell 2001). Thus, family stressors can influence parental involvement as well as children's adjustment to school and their overall academic and behavioral functioning.

Exploring the Cultural Worldviews of Families

One of the major causes of the discontinuity between culturally and economically diverse families and the culture of school communities is a lack of shared values and expectations. This discontinuity influences how educators view the aims and objectives of the learning experience. This may not be readily evident to socially privileged, dominant culture teachers who often have limited interactions and experiences with culturally and economically diverse individuals. Moreover, because teachers often share the cultural assumptions of the school culture, they may unwittingly uphold the hidden curriculum of the dominant culture. In defining the goals of multicultural education, Banks (1994) stated that the traditional curriculum presents a narrow, Eurocentric perspective on content, delivery, and assessment. Without strong multicultural teaching competencies, teachers are likely to devalue children's home culture. This is problematic in that the home culture informs children's patterns of language, behavior, and cognition (Hale-Benson 1986; Neal, McCray, Webb-Johnson & Bridgest 2003).

Researchers have distinguished between different cultural groups on the basis of individualistic versus collectivistic worldviews that then shape their behavior, thinking, and beliefs (e.g., role expectations vis-à-vis how parents and children or educators and families should interact). Dominant culture families define their family unit as nuclear, emphasize individualism in human interactions and development, and have specific role definitions for family members (Tutwiler 2005). This stands in contrast to nondominant cultures, such as African American, Asian/Pacific Islander, Latino/Hispanic, and Native American/Indian cultures, which are often collectivistic in their value orientation. For example, rather than defining the family unit by immediate family members (i.e., mother, father, and children), families who hold these culturally diverse worldviews emphasize extended family units that include not only related family members but also unrelated members, known as *fictive kin*. This notion of fictive kinship is especially evident within the African American community in which intergenerational family units provide collective economic, social, and emotional resources that have historically aided them in coping with systemic oppression (Nobles 1997; Sudarkasa 1997).

As with other culturally diverse groups, Asian American families tend to focus on collectivism rather than independence and autonomy (West-Olatunji et al. 2006). Family offspring may choose, in adulthood, to live in close proximity to their parents, frequently interact with other family members, and share economic and social resources. Moreover, Asian American families tend to emphasize interpersonal harmony and reciprocity in their interactions (Atkinson 2004). Note that, although Asian Americans are viewed as the model minority because of their emphasis on educational attainment, this view is an overgeneralization for the group as a whole. Not all ethnic groups within the Asian American culture share high levels of academic achievement and occupational success. Students of Southeast Asian and Pacific Island ethnic backgrounds have high poverty rates and low educational attainment that often relegate them to low-wage jobs in the workforce. Although considerable variation exists within the Latino[1] culture, shared values among Latino families center around an extended family network that emphasizes the primacy of family and around interpersonal dynamics that promote pleasant social situations and personal respect (Baca Zinn & Wells 2000; Casas & Pytluk 1995). Particularly relevant for Mexican American families is the emphasis on the

---

[1]The term *Latino* is used here rather than *Hispanic*, a widely used term by governmental agencies, as a more historically, geographically, and culturally inclusive identifier. However, individuals of varying experiences, such as age, immigration status, and socioeconomic background may choose a variety of self-referent terms that relate to ethnic identity or country of origin.

family, or *familismo*. This value is significant when contrasting the Latino family characteristics with those of mainstream or dominant group families. Characterized by a strong sense of loyalty and unified solidarity, *familismo* emphasizes prioritizing family needs over those of the individual. In interpersonal dynamics, Latino family members place value on harmonious interactions. This *simpatica* often results in sacrificing their individuals needs to avoid appearing rude (Santiago-Rivera, Arredondo, Gallardo-Cooper 2002). Finally, Latino families promote personal respect, or *respeto*, to offer deference to individuals based upon age, socioeconomic status, or gender. Other family values include an emphasis on personal interactions *(personalismo)*, affectionate expression *(cariño)*, and the development of familiarity *(confianza)*.

Similar to other culturally diverse families, the Native American/Indian family unit is an extended family system (Atkinson 2004). Moreover, the family system can include extended family, clan, and nation leaders who may determine child-rearing responsibilities and provide guidance and counsel to children (Joe & Malach 1998). This interlocking family system can pose challenges to mainstream outsiders who are culturally encapsulated in dominant group family structures and dynamics that define the standard in U. S. society. Native American families emphasize humility, harmony, relation, and patience. In traditional families, Native American individuals are inculcated with a sense of modesty and humility to foster harmony within the group rather than emphasize the worthiness of one person over another. "No one is worthy of staring into the eyes of an elder or looking into the spirit of that honored person" (Atkinson 2004). In fostering harmonious interactions, Native Americans with traditional values often practice patience and humility through silence. The verbal expressiveness and assertiveness rewarded in the dominant culture are often viewed as disrespectful and inconsistent with Native American family values.

As depicted in Table 6.1, the collectivistic values of culturally diverse families often differ drastically from the individualistic values of the dominant culture that are reflected in the school environment and shared by the majority of teachers. When we consider that home is where children learn knowledge and skills (Nieto 1999), this value discontinuity between home and school can be a significant barrier both to facilitating children's learning and to developing effective teacher–parent partnerships. Moreover, without an awareness of the role that culture plays in student learning, teachers are apt to misinterpret student behaviors, deportment, and achievement, and these misinterpretations can lead to diminished teacher expectations.

Researchers are discovering that teacher expectations are very powerful aspects of the teaching–learning environment, particularly with respect to gender, class, and ethnicity. For instance, research on elementary school teachers' gender beliefs and how those beliefs affect what occurs in their classrooms revealed that observations of teachers' instructional methods reflected a differential treatment of boys and girls and imposed gender expectations, despite the teachers' reporting gender-blind self-perceptions (Garrahy 2001).

~~~~~~

Table 6.1   Contrasting Values of Collectivistic and Individualistic Worldviews

Collectivistic	Individualistic
Child as part of group	Child as individual
Family–group–community emphasis	Individual emphasis, privacy
Extended family	Nuclear/blended family
Interdependence & helpfulness	Independence
Social skills	Cognitive skills
Cooperation	Competition
Patience, modesty	Assertiveness
Tradition	Change
Hierarchy, rank, status	Egalitarianism
Listening to authority	Oral skills
Stable family member roles	Flexible family member roles
Indirectness	Directness/openness
Build relationship before task completion	Build relationship as complete task
Suppression of emotions	Expression of emotions
Personal disclosure inappropriate	Personal disclosure appropriate
Decision-making delegated to authority	Personal decision-making valued
Harmony, conflict avoided	Conflict accepted
Personal relationship dominates	Time dominates

Source: Adapted from Trumbull, et al. (2001) and LeBaron, Michelle. *Bridging Cultural Conflicts. A New Approach for a Changing World*. San Francisco: Jossey Bass, 2003.

Teacher beliefs and expectations for students also have a large impact on the level of achievement students attain. Research demonstrates that teachers who focus on higher-level thinking contribute more positively to students' reading growth. Also, teaching methods that positively correlate with students' literacy growth are characterized by (a) high student engagement rather than passive responding, (b) coaching or modeling rather than telling, and (c) active involvement (Taylor, Pearson, Peterson & Rodriguez 2003). Unfortunately, high-performing and gifted teachers are least likely to be found in schools populated by low-income and culturally diverse learners (National Collaborative on Diversity in the Teaching Force 2004).

Without instruction that considers alternate worldviews, school failure for low-income and culturally diverse students can be a likely outcome. Yet teachers can acquire the skills to enhance the academic engagement and academic performance of low-income and culturally diverse students (Brown & Jones 2004; Schinke, Cole & Poulin 2000; Skinner, Pappas & Davis 2005). Failure to engage in school has been attributed to a lack of emotional attachment or feelings of relatedness to the school (Sirin & Rogers-Sirin 2004). By means of Reflective Exercise 6.2, think about what you know about the varying expectations for involvement of the culturally diverse families of students at a school with which you are familiar.

Reflective Exercise 6.2

Assessing the Values and Expectations of Families

Think about the families of various cultural and economic backgrounds at a school with which you are familiar. By whom do parents/caregivers expect the following responsibilities to be implemented?

- Communicating expectations to children about their educational success and future life goals
- Initiating contact and maintaining communication between adults at home and school
- Teaching academic skills to children
- Teaching children positive work habits and attitudes
- Making decisions about children's educational program
- Developing children's social and emotional skills

Do parents/caregivers from various sociocultural backgrounds differ in terms of their perceptions of their roles and responsibilities for their children's schooling? Do some groups expect to have more influence than others in interacting with school staff?

Practicing Culturally Responsive Teaching

As you are learning, many children are socialized to communicate and learn based on cultural and communication patterns that are not practiced in their schools. In fact, the values honored in their homes and families may be disparaged at school in ways that negatively affect their motivation and performance (Nieto 1999). However, a significant body of research has now analyzed the impact on diverse, at-risk students of classroom practices that reduce this discontinuity between home and school (Dalton 1998). Defined as culturally responsive teaching by several different educators (Gay 2000; Weinstein, Curran & Tomlinson-Clark 2003), this approach to teaching develops methods that validate students and allow them to co-construct knowledge in school settings.

Culturally responsive educators have now developed five explicit standards for pedagogy that are applicable across grade levels, student populations, and content areas. Emerging from practices that have proven successful with mainstream, diverse, and at-risk students, these standards provide specific guidance to teachers about how to teach (Dalton 1998). They specify "how to introduce a content topic, how to encourage students' questions and comments, how to involve students in content activities, and how to assess student progress continually" (Dalton 1998, 8). The five standards are as follows: (a) joint productive activity; facilitating learning through joint product activity among teacher and students; (b) developing language and literacy competence through instruction across the curriculum; (c) making meaning by connecting teaching and curriculum content with experiences and skills of students' home and community; (d) teaching complex thinking by challenging students toward greater cognitive complexity; and (e) teaching through conversation by engaging students through dialogue and instructional conversation.

Involving parents as key stakeholders in school communities and moving toward including them in curriculum and program planning creates a true teaching–learning environment. Such a model for school communities incorporates an acknowledgment of families' funds of knowledge and an appreciation of diverse forms of knowledge construction. In Chapter 9, we showcase contextualized teaching methods that are informed by parents and other key stakeholders in the child's ecological system.

Culturally responsive teachers actively connect what and how they teach to the cultural and linguistic backgrounds that exist in the homes and communities of their students. Thus, students are able to use what they already know to construct new academic knowledge. To do this, teachers assume that all children and families have "funds of knowledge" (Gonzalez 1994; Moll & Gonzalez 1993). These funds of knowledge are the historically developed and accumulated skills, abilities, practices, and knowledge that are essential to household functioning and well-being. (Ironically, information about the funds of knowledge of European American middle-class families is so commonly known and taken for granted that its influence in shaping the instructional activities and social organization of the classroom is almost invisible.) Teachers actively seek to understand the specific funds of knowledge possessed by children from particular cultural and linguistic minority homes. They do this by learning from students and their families about the families' social and labor histories, how they develop social networks both within and outside of the home, and, for some, how the exchange of resources between families occurs.

Given the cultural diversity within classrooms, it is prohibitive for teachers to acquire extensive knowledge about each of the students in their classroom. However, through collaborative learning and reflective teaching, teachers can enhance their instructional efficacy with culturally diverse children. Collaborative learning commonly involves the arrangement of a small cluster of teachers who perform a team project. Collaboration is used in educational settings in many parts of the world (Tsaparlis & Gorezi 2005). Collaborative learning is practiced in preschool classrooms

(Vermette, Harper & DiMillo 2004) as well as in elementary, secondary, and higher education and has been shown to help groups improve their problem-solving abilities (Fawcett & Garton 2005). Moreover, collaboration has been shown to (a) help groups enhance their problem-solving abilities, (b) facilitate conflict resolution (Stevahn, Johnson, Johnson, Oberle & Wahl 2000), (c) aid teacher–student comprehension and rapport building (Davis & Blanchard 2004; Webre 2005), and (d) augment student motivation (Shindler 2004).

Opportunities for reflective teaching can be gained through forms of teacher inquiry, such as action research or lesson study. Action research in education involves teachers who engage in inquiry and use data to make informed decisions and plan intelligent interventions so as to improve the quality of their performance. Lesson study is a professional development process that teachers engage in to systematically examine their practice, with the goal of becoming more effective. This examination centers on teachers who work collaboratively to plan, teach, observe, and critique a number of study lessons (Lewis & Tsuchida 1988).

To provide focus and direction to this work, the teachers select an overarching goal and related research question that they want to explore. This research question then serves to guide their work on all study lessons As a team, the teachers create a research question and formulate a detailed lesson plan for a specific subject that they have selected for investigation at the onset of the project. Next, the group observes the lesson as it is taught, then re-evaluates the plan and makes revisions. Teachers repeat this cycle as often as is needed during the period of inquiry. Based upon the results of their study, teachers generate a report on lessons learned then distribute it to the school community.

The focal point of this lesson study inquiry can be dispositions (i.e., intervening with a culturally diverse child who is socially isolated) or skills (for instance, a bilingual student may be lacking basic skills or knowledge). The lesson study can target all students at the school or just one grade level or content area. The number of teachers on a lesson study team is not a set number, and the focus of the group's interaction can be regional or statewide in scope, a particular school, or a classroom (Fernandez 2002). The illustration depicted in Case Study 6.2 describes how one kindergarten teacher used a lesson study to change her teaching practice to respond to the needs of her students.

Family–School Collaboration as Cultural Reciprocity

As you learned in Chapter 2, much of the communication that occurs between teachers and parents has focused on parent–teacher conferences, home visits, telephone contact, written communication, and other informal exchanges (Barbour,

CASE STUDY 6.2

Illustration of "Betty"

Betty is a white, middle-class kindergarten teacher who is teaching at a culturally diverse university lab school. In her class this year, she has 22 students. Approximately one third of her students are African American (the majority of whom are children of working-class parents) or Latino American (mostly children of local migrant workers), and a few of her students are Vietnamese American children. Although Betty has participated in several professional development workshops on multicultural teacher education, she is interested in advancing her ability to incorporate nonmainstream values in her instruction. When the opportunity came around to participate in a semester-long (15 weeks) research study with a professor from the local community, Betty volunteered to engage in teacher inquiry with a group of other teachers with similar interests from her school. After reading the literature on effective teaching practices for culturally diverse children, Betty decided to focus her investigation on integrating a sense of caring and *personalismo* into her interactions with students that emphasized the collectivistic values of helpfulness and social ability rather than emphasize the values of independence and cognitive ability that are reflective of the current *monocultural* environment of schools (Tutwiler, 2005). Each week, Betty developed a collectivistic lesson plan, implemented her lesson with an observer present, and then discussed the outcomes of her intervention in a weekly seminar with the other teacher/researchers at her school. At the end of the semester, Betty developed a presentation for her school in which she shared the results of her study. In reflection, she stated that, *"When I initially embarked on this assignment, my students' cultural identity was simply not part of the equation. I simply thought about teaching children basic academic skills. The Lesson Study templates have helped me to infuse more culturally appropriate materials into the curriculum.... Many of these findings need to be shared with the public schools system because their curriculums offer little to no culturally appropriate approaches."*

Questions to Consider

In this scenario, what impact do you think this teacher's efforts might have on the students, their families, or other staff at her school?

Barbour & Scully 2005). These traditional forms of engaging with parents have frequently been prescriptive in nature and have operated from the assumption that the school knows what is best for children (and parents, in some cases). Traditionally, parent–teacher conferences have involved teachers as the primary expert and active agent in making contact, preparing materials, providing input, and facilitating a productive exchange. This hierarchical relationship between teachers and parents has traditionally been evident in home visits, telephone calls, and written communiqués to parents, in which the relationship is usually unidirectional (i.e., one way from school to home). Moreover, as discussed previously, the traditional forms of working with parents have not incorporated an understanding and appreciation for cultural differences that reflect diverse expectations and concerns. As a result, many of the efforts by school staff to reach out to culturally diverse, economically disadvantaged, and other socially marginalized families, have not been very successful.

Current research on parent involvement suggests that, in general, parents' participation in their children's schooling experiences has positive outcomes for students' educational achievement (Hoover-Dempsey, Walker, Sandler, Whetsel, Green, Wilkins & Closson 2005). Scholars differ, however, on what should be the nature of that involvement, especially when considering culturally diverse families. Central to this discussion is an understanding of the diverse parenting practices amongst various cultural groups and how those practices affect parents' (a) sense of self-efficacy, (b) role expectations in their interactions with teachers, (c) expectations for their children's behavior and dispositions, and (d) interpretation of invitations from teachers to be involved.

Teachers often have a set of expectations regarding parent involvement that are shaped by the norms of the dominant culture. Parent self-efficacy, for example, is often understood to imply parents' demonstration of a belief in their own ability to positively influence their children's learning outcomes (Hoover-Dempsey & Sandler 1997). However, immigrant parents and other parents from culturally diverse families may have differing expectations regarding parent and teacher interactions. In the Latino culture, for example, Latinos who exert their own power in interpersonal interactions may be viewed as disrespectful, especially when engaged with representatives of authority, such as teachers (Trumbull, Rothstein-Fisch, Greenfield & Quiroz 2001). Unfortunately, traditional responses of teachers who lack an understanding of cultural diversity are to interpret such parental responses as signs of disinterest or incompetence (Goodnow & Collins 1990). These attitudes toward families from low-income and culturally diverse communities can significantly impede efforts for successful collaboration between home and school. Although teachers may perceive these parents as not wanting to be involved, research suggests that parents from these diverse backgrounds seek more involvement with schools (Cassanova 1996; Delgado-Gaitan 1992).

Parents can also have conflicting role expectations that create challenges during parent–teacher interactions. Parental roles are culturally embedded and, as such, are linked to parents' hopes and dreams of what and whom they wish their children to become. Some culturally diverse families, who value collectivism, desire that their children become well mannered and respectful. In fact, some cultural group members believe that these behaviors are correlated with academic success and educational attainment. In contrast, Vietnamese American parents often do not view moral development as part of their role in contributing to their children's education (Collignon, Men & Tan 2001). Moreover, Vietnamese American parents often do not participate in school programs and are often reluctant to share their concerns and voice opinions with teachers and other school personnel. These behaviors can be confusing and sometimes frustrating for teachers who are culturally encapsulated and maintain a narrow view of what parents' roles should be in partnering with schools.

Another challenge to parent involvement in schools are parents' expectations for their children's behavior. Parents serve as their children's first teacher and provide the context for their learning. Thus, children's learning is naturally linked to their cultural and family norms for behavioral and interpersonal styles. Whereas the school culture, as a reflection of the dominant culture, values and rewards autonomy and creativity, many culturally diverse families emphasize interdependence and conformity to external standards. Teachers are not always aware of the multiple explanations for parents' hesitancy to engage in communication or to participate in school events. Oftentimes, teachers fall prey to misinterpretation of parents' lack of involvement and lack the necessary cross-cultural interaction skills to create bridges between the home and school cultures.

Finally, parents' interpretation of invitations from teachers is an important factor when considering the challenges to parent involvement. Low-income parents often cite feeling intimidated when entering into school structures and are often disinclined to respond positively to invitations from teachers to engage in communication regarding their children's educational experiences (Lott 2001). Additionally, parents may not trust school staff because of historical or systemic contexts that are unique to a particular cultural group's sociocultural context. Moreover, schools may have a social climate that is impersonal or bureaucratic.

These challenges have led educators to construct very different kinds of family–school relations that move away from teacher-dominated approaches toward approaches that emphasize collaboration and cultural reciprocity. Many educators have noted that a first step in moving toward more cultural reciprocal practices is to recognize and understand your own cultural group membership. Understanding your own culture and how it differs from the cultures of families with whom you work will greatly facilitate your ability to develop collaborative relations with them. Without such an understanding of your own culture, to recognize and understand the unique needs that result from other cultural and linguistic backgrounds is very difficult. Reflective Exercise 6.3 provides a list of questions that can help you examine your own cultural background.

As a second step, Tutwiler (2005) recommends that school staffs assess the ethnic–cultural and socioeconomic group membership of their own staff and of the families at their school, examine the staff's current beliefs and communication practices in interacting with diverse family groups, and identify particular school practices and routines that might be redesigned so as to be more culturally responsive. This step is depicted in Reflective Exercise 6.4.

Reflective Exercise 6.3

Examining My Thoughts About Culture and My Cultural Group

What is my definition of culture?

Of what cultural group am I a member?

What is the status of my cultural group among other groups?

What are the characteristics of my cultural group?

How do I meet the general characteristics of my cultural group?

What are stereotypes about my cultural group?

How do I meet the stereotypes of/about my cultural group?

How fair are these stereotypes?

Which stereotypes of my cultural group do I agree with, and which ones do I disagree with?

Which stereotypes of my cultural group would I change if I could?

If I were not a member of my cultural group, to which cultural group(s) would I want to belong and why? To which cultural group would I not like to belong and why?

Of all cultural groups I encounter on a regular basis, which ones have fair stereotypes and which ones do not have fair stereotypes?

What are the cultural groups represented in my class/school?

Reflective Exercise 6.4

Developing a Profile of Family–School Relations for a School that I Might Visit or Work in

What family structures are represented in the school population?

What ethnic, cultural, language, and socioeconomic groups are represented in the school population?

What ethnic, cultural, language, and socioeconomic groups are represented in the school staff?

How do staff members at the school view students' families and their contributions to the process of schooling?

How does the school communicate with families?

How does the school address varying cultural and language patterns among the families?

New Roles for Teachers When Partnering With Parents

A variety of innovative strategies and roles have recently been developed to create more culturally responsive family–school interaction. Such interactions include the opportunity for parents and teachers to conjointly prepare for conferences, in which the child is a contributor as well (Amatea, Daniels, Brigman & Vandiver 2004). Teachers can conduct family/home visits in which they encourage families to voice their concerns and ask questions regarding the schooling process. In general, we have found that parents take on more responsibility and become more active within the school community when teachers acquire culturally responsive skills for assessing parent engagement and facilitating parent participation within a cultural context.

In an earlier section, we discussed the funds of knowledge that exist within families and communities that children bring into the classroom and ways in which teachers can become culturally responsive in their classroom instruction. Embedded in this perspective is a belief that parents are a resource and that they have something to offer that contributes to positive educational outcomes for their children, regardless of their income level, social standing, or cultural background. Teachers can thus build on the "values, structures, languages, and cultures of students' homes" (Nieto 1999, 171).

Developing innovative ways to partner with parents can sometimes involve collaborations with communities. Given the communal nature of many culturally diverse families, working with community structures may assist in building rapport and creating sustainable linkages that positively impact children, families, and schools. Community stakeholders' involvement in education has been an integral part of the history of American education, beginning with the social concerns of Jane Addams[2] (1998) and the settlement house movement. More recently, during the Freedom School Movement (Perlstein 1990), community action spurred a grassroots movement in the Mississippi Delta that focused on the underserved needs of poor African American children by teaching them reading and mathematics. The spirit of community action and schooling continues today in a variety of forms, in which educators take an active role in addressing the achievement gap between socially marginalized students and their more affluent counterparts.

Parents from culturally diverse and low-income communities often lack a sense of ownership in the schooling experiences of their children. Community stakeholders "may also feel that schools do not recognize their voices, traditions, and knowledge within the community" (Tutwiler 2005, p. 200). Beneficial in establishing trust in teacher–parent relationships is visibility in the community. Teachers can send a powerful message of interest and demonstrate cultural reciprocity by

---

[2]At the turn of the 20th century, Jane Addams moved away from elitism in education and sought to bring together poor and working-class families and communities into the educative process during her settlement house activism.

actively becoming visible in the community. Visibility can be in the form of attending a community event, festival, or patronizing municipal services or businesses.

How might you identify the unique attributes and resources that exist within the families and community of the school in which you might work? We will look more closely at community funds of knowledge in the next chapter. However, in Reflective Exercise 6.5, we ask you to begin thinking about what unique family and community resources might be available.

Reflective Exercise 6.5

Assessing Characteristics and Resources to Develop More Culturally Responsive Family–School Practices

How might you learn about the unique attributes and resources that characterize families at your school that might support your teaching and student learning?

What unique resources are you discovering that families at your school might bring to support your teaching and student learning?

What unique resources might exist in the community that your school serves?

Other ways in which teachers are collaborating with communities are by establishing more formal, institutionalized connections through the acquisition of federal grants to develop out-of-school time (OST) programs, such as after-school, weekend, and summer school programs (Pittman, Irby, Yohalem & Wilson-Ahistrom 2004). These programs provide parents with an opportunity to partner in designing developmental programs that meet the social, emotional, and cultural needs of their children. Moreover, such programs allow teachers to increase their knowledge and familiarity with the cultural norms of the community connected to the school.

Another strategy for home–school collaboration is the development of full-service schools in which medical and social services are offered on site within schools in an integrated service delivery model (Dryfoos 1994). For families in high poverty communities, this approach serves the holistic needs of students and their families and is preventive in nature (Harris & Hoover 2003). Moreover, a full-service approach takes into account the interaction between social services and student learning (McMahon, Ward, Pruett, Davidson & Griffith 2000). Children who are experiencing failing or poor health are less apt to stay engaged in the classroom, exhibit sound judgment, or demonstrate keen cognitive abilities. We describe the philosophy behind these programs in greater detail in Chapters 7 and 13.

Some illustrative models of innovative teacher–parent partnerships include the Comer School Development Program, the Child Development Project, and the COPLA (Comite de Padres Latinos) program. These innovative strategies have several features in common. They each view parents from cultural perspectives and understand the role of communication in diminishing barriers between home and schools. Additionally, teachers seek to reduce their biases as they consider multiple realities for culturally diverse families.

Comer School Development Program

Founded by Comer et al. at the Yale Child Study Center in 1968, the Comer School Development Program is an excellent example of home–school–community partnerships. Originally, this program established several major goals: (a) to alter the social and psychological climate of the school, (b) to enhance students' fundamental skills, (c) to elevate students' motivation for learning, (d) to generate a sense of collective responsibility and decision-making among parents and staff, and (e) to join child development and clinical services to the educational plan of the schools (Barbour et al. 2005). The current student development program consists of three guiding principles, three teams, and three operations. The three principles are consensus, collaboration, and no-fault. The three teams consist of the school planning and management team, the student and staff support team, and the parenting team. The three operations involve a comprehensive school plan, program assessment and modification, and staff development. To date this program model has been replicated in over 650 schools across the United States. Environmental changes in one high poverty, urban school have led to "high expectations and where everyone working together . . . has become an attitude, a way of learning and an education for life" (Ramirez-Smith 1995, 19).

Child Development Project

This program is a literature-based moral development program that utilizes family homework activities to connect home culture with school culture by drawing on family experiences (Developmental Studies Center 1995). The program teaches children about personal responsibility, community, and caring that mixes both individualistic and collectivistic values. Using this model, teachers engage students in activities in which they might interview an elder in their extended family to learn about their childhood experiences. Additionally, this model encourages teachers to customize activities to adapt to the various culturally diverse students present in their classrooms. In this manner, teachers acknowledge that families vary within and across cultural dimensions (Trumbull et al. 2001).

Comite de Padres Latinos (COPLA)

Developed by Concha Delgado-Gaitan (1994), this program stresses maintaining Spanish language and Mexican cultural values by opening a cooperative dialogue with parents. The program assists parents in instilling cultural values, such as respect and cooperation, while ensuring that children are able to participate successfully in dominant culture classrooms. The COPLA model of empowerment also merges the collectivism from the home culture with the individualistic orientation expected within the classroom. Students learned how to expand their range of language patterns to include those used in the school. This model has been successful in educating parents about how their involvement can have a positive impact on educational practices. This sense of advocacy and empowerment experienced by culturally diverse parents can help demystify educational practices and expectations in the U. S. school system. However, when teachers and other school personnel are not prepared to include parents as true partners in the decision-making and program planning processes, parents can feel betrayed and mistrustful of school representatives.

Future Considerations and Challenges

Teachers, particularly early career practitioners, often respond subjectively to the challenges of educating culturally diverse students or when encountering classroom management issues. They often express feelings of frustration or shame because of self-perceptions of inadequacy for not having the skills to correct the situation. Additionally, as previously stated, teachers bring their socialized biases about children and their families into the classroom, albeit unintentionally (Derman-Sparks, Ramsey, Edwards & Brunson-Phillips 2006).

Current efforts to incorporate teacher inquiry into classroom practices have been useful in assisting teachers to minimize teacher bias. Reflective teaching encourages teachers to view their classrooms as laboratories in which they investigate the phenomena that occur in that environment. Thus, when teachers experience challenges, they begin to pose questions about why that particular phenomenon is occurring and what interventions they might develop to address the phenomenon observed. Hence, teacher inquiry enhances teacher knowledge and practice through evidence-based methods. When teachers investigate classroom problems by reading empirical and conceptual literature on the problem as well as possible solutions, they then acquire information for problem solving in the classroom (Derman-Sparks & Brunson-Phillips 1997).

One of the most commonly used approaches to reflective teaching is action research. Classroom action research most often involves the application of qualitative, interpretive forms of inquiry and data collection by teachers so that they can make judgments about how to improve their own instructional practices (Kemmis & Taggart 2000). One of the criticisms of classroom action research is that it does not incorporate knowledge of the impact of the larger social system on the development and achievement of students in the classroom. Another approach to reflective teaching is *lesson study*, an approach to teacher inquiry that we discussed earlier in this chapter that utilizes collaborative dialogue to engage teachers in a collective examination of their classroom practices (Lewis & Tsuchida 1988). In lesson study, teachers develop a research question as a team, and craft a detailed lesson plan for a specific subject that they have selected to investigate at the beginning of the project. Next, the team has a representative to observe the lesson when it is being taught, then the team re-evaluates the plan and makes changes. The teachers repeat this cycle as often as needed all the way through the period of inquiry. Based upon the results of their study, teachers create a report on the lessons learned and then share it with the school community. The focus of the investigation can be skills (e.g., a student may be lacking basic math skills or knowledge of the scientific method) or dispositions (e.g., intervening with a child who is socially isolated) for students in an entire school, or it can focus on a specific content area or grade level (Fernandez 2002).

However, these instructional innovations are often challenged by insufficient funding. Other challenges to such efforts include attitudes among education researchers regarding teacher inquiry as a form of legitimate research (Kemmis & Taggart 2000). Moreover, the daily demands within the school community often prohibit time to reflect on instruction, and not all school communities exhibit an interest in instructional innovation.

Despite these obstacles, perspectives on parent and family involvement in schools suggest that schools can benefit by moving to a family-centered (Olsen & Fuller 2003), family-guided (Slentz & Bricker 1992), family-focused (Bailey et al. 1986), or parent-empowerment (Dunst 1985) model. Regardless of the term that is used to describe a more *family-centric* approach to family involvement, all of these terms incorporate an understanding that parents can be equal partners in family–school collaborations. When teachers and other school personnel collaborate with parents, they demonstrate respect and support the family's decision-making role in educational processes, which is particularly helpful when working with culturally diverse families (Olsen & Fuller 2003).

In considering innovative strategies for working with parents, an important consideration is the different types of families in which children are socialized. Moreover, the socioeconomic status of families presents further challenges within contemporary classrooms. Children from high poverty and working-class poor families have a multitude of obstacles to academic achievement. Additionally, children with special needs, diverse religious orientations, and those from gay, lesbian, bisexual, or trans-sexual families have additional needs. Thus, teachers need to consider the multiple contexts in which families operate as they plan their efforts to connect with families.

Summary

This chapter provides teachers with an introduction to key terms that contextualize the experiences of low-income and culturally diverse children and their families. Educators can enhance their teaching practices with a clearer understanding of the disconnections between school norms that reflect the shared expectations of the social mainstream and the values and assumptions that exist among culturally and economically diverse families. This understanding can lead to better academic out-comes for these students. Specifically, educators can seek information about the specific worldviews held by the families of their students. Utilizing an understanding of individualistic and collectivistic worldviews, teachers can enrich classroom experiences and promote parents' active involvement in the school community by learning about their students' families' funds of knowledge. Reflective teaching has potential value as a form of teacher inquiry for educators who work with economically and culturally diverse students. Three models of effective home–school collaborations and partnerships that have aided in the transformation of family–teacher–student interactions with culturally diverse families are the Comer School Development Program, the Child Development Project, and the **Comite de Padres Latinos** (COPLA) program. Future research that investigates cultural, social, and economic diversity and parent–teacher partnerships might consider that teachers bring their own socialized attitudes and beliefs into the classroom. Therefore, training that assists educators in identifying and minimizing their biases toward culturally and socially diverse children and families may be beneficial. Moreover, as parents become more empowered and seek equal partnerships with school person-nel, their active participation may be viewed as intrusive to teachers and adminis-trators who are used to conventional parent attitudes and behaviors. Finally, individuals' backgrounds are not as clearly defined as they have been outlined in this chapter. More realistically, individuals have multiple identities that intersect and sur-face as a result of their dynamic interactions with other human beings. Therefore, teachers may need to acquire flexibility and resilience as they become more com-fortable with culturally and socially diverse families.

Resources

Center for Research on Education, Diversity & Excellence (CREDE),
www.cal.org/crede
CREDE's purpose is to improve communication through better understanding of language and culture. It funds research and develops and disseminates effective guidelines and practices that are responsive to the needs of children and families from culturally and linguistically diverse backgrounds.

National Center for Children in Poverty,
www.nccp.org
NCCP has the mission to conduct policy analysis and academic research to prevent child poverty and improve the quality of life of children and families who experi-ence low income.

Chapter 7

Understanding How Communities Impact Children's Learning

Ellen S. Amatea

Learning Objectives

After reading this chapter, you will be able to:

- Explain the varying meanings of the term *community*.
- Describe the changing physical, economic, and social conditions that impact rural and urban communities in the United States.
- Explain the different need-based and asset-based approaches that school and community members are developing to address the needs of children and families.
- Discuss strategies that individual educators can use to develop stronger links with their communities.

> *I went everywhere with my parents and was under the watchful eye of*
> *members of the congregation and community who were my extended family. They*
> *kept me when my parents went out of town, they reported on me and chided me*
> *when I strayed from the straight and narrow of community expectations, and they*
> *basked in and supported my achievement when I did well. Doing well, they made*
> *clear, meant high academic achievement, playing piano in Sunday school, partic-*
> *ipating in other church activities, being helpful, displaying good manners, and*
> *reading. (Edelman 1992, 4)*

Reminiscing about growing up in the 1940s and 1950s in the community of Ben-nettsville, South Carolina, Edelman describes a large network of persons beyond her family who involved themselves in her growth and development. In contrast, many of today's children and families live in neighborhoods and communities char-acterized by low levels of social organization and community participation. What impact do such neighborhoods and communities have on the children and families who live within them? How are today's educators and community members attempting to change these conditions? What can we learn from their experiences that can enhance our efforts to facilitate children's learning and development?

In this chapter we address these questions by first discussing the meaning of the term *community*. Next, we look at the changing social and economic conditions that U. S. communities are experiencing. We then examine the different community con-ditions that influence the development of children and youth. Afterward, we describe innovative approaches created by school staffs and community members to address the needs of students, their families, and their communities. Finally, we consider how educa-tors might apply these various approaches in their work with students and their families.

Defining Community

What constitutes a community? Who are its participating members? Definitions of com-munity are diverse and complex. The term *community* can have widely varying meanings to its residents, to professionals, such as the educators who work and provide services within them, and to social scientists who study community life. In its broadest sense, community refers to a condition in which people share something with each other (Gold, Simon & Brown 2002a; 2002b). Within this general understanding, however, you can find numerous definitions of what a community may share, such as a geographical place, a common culture, a feeling of belonging, a network of social and emotional ties, or a structure of occupations. A basic distinction offered by many social scientists is to describe a community both spatially and socially. Hence, a school's community can be viewed as the specific, geographical areas or neighborhoods that supply them with stu-dents. However, residents of these neighborhoods may not necessarily share a culture or even a feeling of belonging across what may be defined as the school's community.

Moreover, you may find that in certain neighborhoods, the institutions (such as the school or a social service agency) that operate within them are not actually rooted in the community because they are not staffed by persons who are local residents of that community. Similarly, you often find businesses that operate in a community that are not managed by or employ residents of that community. Instead, these businesses are a part of larger corporations (e.g., Wal-Mart or banking chains) that are run by persons outside that community (Halpern 1995). As a result, although teachers, social workers, or merchants may share space for a portion of their day with community residents, they often do not view themselves as "belonging" to the particular community in which they work.

Not only is it important to learn about the widely varying physical and economic characteristics of the geographical spaces and places served by a school, but also to assess the social organization (i.e., the social networks) constructed by participants of the school's community. Let us first look at the widely varying physical and economic conditions that differentiate communities from one another.

Community as Shared Place

When first asked to describe their community, many people think of their community in terms of its geographical location and population size. The U.S. Bureau of the Census (2002), for example, sorts areas into one of two general categories determined by their population density: (a) metropolitan (i.e., urban) areas and (b) nonmetropolitan (i.e., rural) areas. Metropolitan areas have populations of 200,000 or more people, whereas nonmetropolitan areas have significantly fewer residents. Many non-metropolitan/rural and metropolitan/urban areas have experienced dramatic social, political, and economic changes that have exerted a powerful influence on the life of these communities. Figure 7.1 on page 172 depicts how the U.S. population has grown increasingly urban over the past fifty years, with 80 percent of the U.S. population now living in metropolitan areas of varying population density (U.S. Census Bureau 2002).

As a result, U.S. communities might more effectively be described along a continuum from rural, small-town communities on one end to large urban communities on the other (Tutwiler 2005). Let us look at some of the economic and population changes that have affected the well-being of families and schools in rural, small-town communities and in large, urban communities in the United States.

Rural and Small-Town Communities

Although most Americans now live in urban areas, a number of dramatic changes have been occurring in rural and small-town communities over the past forty years. For instance, drastic changes have occurred in economic opportunities in farming communities that have led to the deterioration of many rural communities (Purdy 1999).

Figure 7.1   Percentage of Total U.S. Population Living in Metropolitan Areas by Size of Metropolitan Area Population: 1950–2000

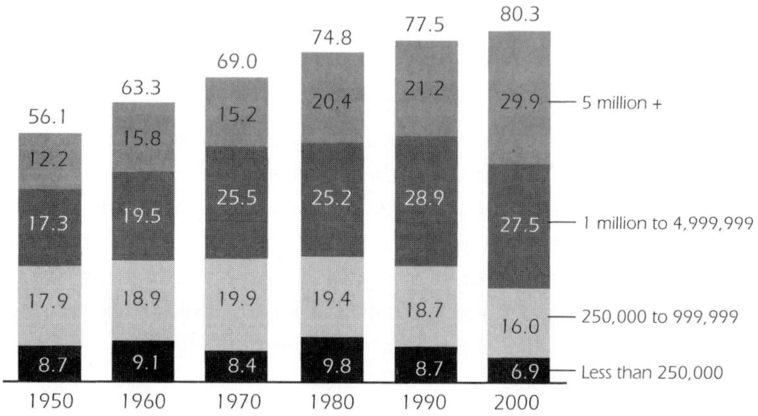

Source: U. S. Census Bureau. (2002). *Census 2000 special report: Demographic trends in the 20th century.* Washington, DC: U.S. Department of Commerce, U.S. Government Printing Office.

During the 1980s and 1990s, corporations began to dominate farming production by increasing agricultural production expenses with their greater use of expensive farm equipment and technology. This made it difficult for individual farmers to compete. As a result, many families abandoned farming as a livelihood, and communities solely reliant on agriculture for employment declined in population. Many young people had to leave their rural communities because of a lack of jobs, resulting in fewer people staying to start families. This population decline had a domino effect because the fewer the students, the greater the reduction in school funding, and the bigger the challenge that school districts faced in offering needed educational programs to the students remaining in the community. In addition, as some corporations chose to employ inexpensive immigrant labor workers for their plants, communities were forced to absorb new residents of varied cultural background. As a result, schools in these areas often faced increased numbers of children and families whose primary language spoken in the home was not English (Purdy 1999).

In contrast, a number of small towns and rural areas in the United States have experienced significant growth as a result of the substantial out-migration of residents from cities to smaller suburbs (Tutwiler 2005). This population change, which began in the 1950s and continues today, is known as *suburbanization.* Whereas some suburban living areas are characterized by segregation by race, class, education, and lifestyle, others may be populated by families that range along a socioeconomic continuum and comprise a mixture of ethnic groups. In addition, a new type of small town living space, the *exburb,* has been emerging in the United States, as a result of corporations locating their headquarters in suburbs (Achs 1992). The exburb is composed of a ring of low-density, automobile-dependent sprawled cities on the edge of metropolitan areas (Urban Dictionary 2006). Located outside of suburbs, these types of low-density communities allow their residents to live greater distances from cities, changing their commute to work away from exburb to the suburb rather than from suburb to city. Exburbs often offer proximity to corporate jobs, tend to have low-density populations, low crime rates, and excellent schools. "In a sense, exburb residents have the best of both worlds. They are able to enjoy the slow pace of a more rural life yet be close to rewarding employment, cultural events, and excellent school and health care facilities" (Tutwiler 2005, 77).

A disadvantage of both exburbs and suburbs noted by many social scientists (Putnam 2000) is that when substantial numbers of residents work outside the community in which they live (thus separating their workplace and residence), the sense of connection and level of social engagement among the residents are often lessened. Not only is the level of community engagement reduced among those who commute out to work, but also among noncommuters whose motivation to be more participatory is lowered by poor attendance at community events (Putnam 2000).

Another recent trend transforming the nature of rural and small-town life is the movement of "baby-boomer" retirees. Demographers are noting that many baby-boomer retirees are not only retiring at a younger age, but also are often more well educated and well off financially than their predecessors. These retirees are often choosing to relocate in states in the Sun Belt with mild climates and smaller, more rural locales (Fetto 1999). This in-migration of retirees to rural and small-town communities has often altered the social, economic, and political landscape of these areas. For example, retirees often expect a greater level of business, social, and community services than the original residents of a rural or small-town locale. In addition, the costs of living and job opportunities in a town may change drastically. New jobs created by retirement in-migration are often low-skill, low-wage service sector jobs, yet, at the same time, the costs for housing, services, and property taxes may escalate, putting the financial stability of the original residents in jeopardy (Tutwiler 2005).

Urban Communities

The high rate of social and economic change experienced by many rural and small-town communities is also occurring in many urban areas in the United States. Because cities are usually centers of economic growth and technological advances, they have historically been attractive to people who seek to improve their economic status. For example, in the late 1800s and early 1900s, a huge influx of immigrants from Europe contributed to the growth of cities. In addition, the migration of African Americans from the South to Northern cities in the 1940s and 1950s swelled the population of urban areas. Although the U.S. population has grown increasingly urban over the past one hundred years with nearly one-third of Americans living in a metropolitan area with five million or more residents, a little more than half of the U.S. population now live in suburban areas rather than central cities (U.S. Census Bureau 2002). Figure 7.2 on page 174 shows the changes in the percentage of Americans who live in the suburbs rather than in the central cities from 1910 to 2000.

Figure 7.2 U.S. Population Density in Metropolitan Areas and in their Central Cities and Suburbs: 1910–2000

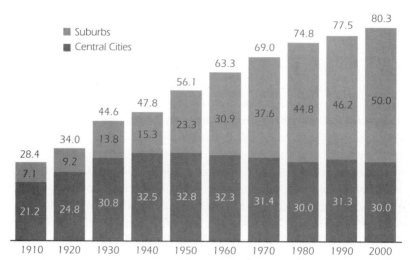

Source: U.S. Census Bureau. (2002). *Census 2000 special report: Demographic trends in the 20th century.* Washington, DC: U.S. Department of Commerce, U.S. Government Printing Office.

As a result, many cities developed a variety of different neighborhoods where residents shared the same ethnic or racial backgrounds. These ethnic neighborhoods provided immigrants with a familiarity of the language and cultural customs, offered a sense of identity and security and economic support, and made adaptation to a new place and life more workable. At the same time, these social enclaves often grew out of segregation policies that restricted where in a city that ethnic minority immigrants were allowed to live. In addition to ethnic minority communities, immigrants from Europe often established segregated White ethnic communities (e.g., Irish, Italian, German, Polish) in large Northern cities in the late 1800s and early 1900s (Alba, Logan & Crowder 1997). People also formed social enclaves based on their religious beliefs. Hence, you will find communities in which the residents are primarily Jewish or Muslim, or some other religious group, each with their own religious institutions, customs, and materials (Livezey 2001).

Although there has been a decline in the number of these communities due to cultural assimilation and out-migration, many of these communities continue to exist. As a result, a number of White ethnic communities (e.g., Little Italy in New York City) or ethnic minority communities (e.g., Chinatown in San Francisco, or Little Cuba in Miami) continue to exist as hubs of cultural activities where the cultural heritage is visible through the use of the native language, and culturally representative shops, restaurants, and other businesses.

In addition to ethnic, cultural, or religious variations, urban neighborhoods range economically from very wealthy exclusive areas to those exhibiting extreme poverty. Despite having many middle-class enclaves in inner cities that are going through processes of gentrification and urban revitalization, many inner-city communities are now sites of extreme poverty, joblessness, welfare dependency, serious crime, drug and alcohol addiction, and violence and homicide.

One factor contributing to the deterioration of many inner-city neighborhoods is the reduction in employment opportunities. Well-paid employment and, in fact, any employment at all has increasingly been relocated outside of cities, isolating inner-city residents from mainstream forms of employment and advancement (Wilson 1997). At the same time, global economic shifts have led to the loss of well-paid jobs for low-skilled workers and falling pay rates for low-skilled positions (Lipman 2002). Furthermore, when inner-city residents found ways to reach these increasingly marginal jobs outside the inner city, they often encountered severe forms of discrimination and harassment (Pager 2003).

These economic changes have resulted in a change in the social class structure of many inner-city neighborhoods. Wilson (1997) pointed out that between the 1940s and 1960s, ethnic communities were places of vertical integration with respect to social class (i.e., middle class, working class, and poor African Americans all lived in the same neighborhoods). With greater economic opportunities, however, the more educated and skilled African Americans moved out of these communities, leaving behind the truly disadvantaged, and thus leading to the growth of areas of extreme poverty. Other ethnic communities are experiencing similar economic and social changes.

Documenting this economic shift, Gutman, McLoyd, and Tokoyama (2005) noted that during the past two decades, poverty has become more spatially concentrated within urban areas, especially among African Americans. "Between 1980 and 1990, concentrated poverty among African Americans grew both in terms of the absolute number of African Americans and the percentage of the African American population living in neighborhoods of concentrated poverty. Poor individuals living in high-poverty communities, as compared with their counterparts residing in communities with lower rates of poverty, are disadvantaged by reduced accessibility to high-quality social services and informal social supports and increased exposure to joblessness, crime, homelessness, violence, drugs and negative role models" (22).

These economic and social changes in a community have a direct impact on the community's schools. School districts receive their funding to deliver education from local, state, and federal sources. Local school funding, which can constitute up to half of a school district's funding, is based on property taxes. State government contributions provide most of the remaining funding, because very limited funding is provided by the federal government. Communities that have substantial numbers of businesses and expensive homes can generate a larger school tax base to support their schools. In contrast, school districts located in communities with deteriorating properties and limited job opportunities receive significantly less local funding to support their schools, to hire teachers, and to purchase materials and equipment. Obviously, there may be great disparities between the schools in the same district in terms of the character of the community, the human and financial resources provided by community members, and the child-serving institutions and services. As a result, schools located in poorly funded districts often have more teacher shortages, a significant number of teachers who are teaching in fields that do not match their preparation, lower levels of student achievement, and higher student dropout rates.

In the next section we examine the impact of community social ties on families and schools. Before we do that, however, think about the current physical and economic conditions that characterize different neighborhoods and the social and economic changes that may have led to these neighborhood conditions. As you drive or walk through a neighborhood, how can you tell whether the neighborhood or community is thriving or deteriorating? Some of the overt signs that you might notice are the types of housing available in the neighborhood, how many families live in that housing, and how the homes are cared for. In addition, communities differ in terms of the range and convenience of shopping, banking, gas stations, and other services available in a community. Some communities have multiple choices for grocery shopping, banking, or entertainment (e.g., movie houses and restaurants), whereas other neighborhoods are characterized by pawn shops and small high-priced grocery stores.

Neighborhoods also differ in terms of the health care (e.g., hospitals) and recreational resources available (e.g., playgrounds), and the relative safety of the neighborhood. In some neighborhoods, people move freely about their community at all hours of the day and night, whereas in other communities they feel unsafe to venture out after dark because of criminal activity in the neighborhood. Conditions, such as community violence and other crimes, can influence both families' and children's feelings of well-being. How have these community conditions been influenced by economic and population changes? Consider how a neighborhood with which you are familiar has changed as a result of economic and population changes, by completing Reflective Exercise 7.1.

Reflective Exercise 7.1

Assessing the Community and Tracking Changes

What is the quality of the neighborhood(s) that are served by your school (i.e., either the school in which you may have conducted field observations or the one you attended as a child)? Where do people live? What is the quality of the living conditions in terms of noise level, population density, and safety? Where do they work? Where do they shop? What is the range of shops and services? Where do they seek health services? What recreational opportunities are available? How safe are these neighborhoods for their residents? How have these neighborhoods changed over time? Have there been economic changes or changes in population that have impacted these families, neighborhoods, and schools? What are the overt signs that these neighborhoods or communities are thriving or deteriorating? You may want to talk with long-term members of the school staff who can tell you about such changes or consult newspaper files about past events.

Communities as Social Networks

In addition to the physical quality of a neighborhood or community, and its economic opportunities and the makeup of its population, communities can also be defined as social networks that provide participants with emotional, social, and economic ties and support. In the following passage, McCaleb (1994) describes a community as a diverse group of people who share the daily realities of life as they support each other:

> The community is the children, the families of the children, people who work in the area and interact in multiple ways with the families, people who create art and make music and keep the neighborhoods vibrating, and the people who live and care and touch the lives of those around them. (42)

McCaleb's (1994) definition of community shares with Putnam (2000) an orientation toward significant people and social ties within a community. Putnam describes a community as a series of formal and informal social networks characterized by norms of reciprocity and trust, and suggests that there exist several types of natural or informal social networks that aid in community identification and maintenance. Extended family, folk healers, religious institutions, merchants, and social clubs are all types of informal social networks that one may find within a particular community. Such networks make a community meaningful as they serve a *bonding* function for its members by reinforcing the exclusiveness of the group and creating a boundary identifying who is in and out of the group.

By contrast, other networks are outward looking and encompass people across diverse social groups. Hence, they serve a *bridging* function in helping members to reach out to others different from themselves. Examples of such bridging social networks include many youth service groups, ecumenical religious organizations, or the civil rights movement (Putnam 2000). Obviously, community groups can serve both functions. For example, a Black church might not only bring people of the same religion and race together, but also bring together people from different social classes.

There continues to be a great deal of diversity in urban areas in terms of how neighborhoods maintain their economic stability and social connectedness. Gonzales (1993) explains that social ties allow individuals and groups to rely on their group cultural values and history to address contemporary issues. For example, Latino cultural characteristics, such as *familism,* and the value placed on owning property, influence the stability and vitality of many poor Latino communities. The existence of integrative ties are so important in Gonzales's view that areas with high concentrations of poverty and few integrative ties may be less stable and have fewer structural resources to support their community members (Tutwiler 2005). By means of Reflective Exercise 7.2 on page 178, describe the nature of the community you lived in as a child and the social ties you and your family developed.

〜〜〜〜〜〜〜〜〜〜〜〜〜〜〜〜〜〜〜〜〜〜〜〜〜〜〜〜〜〜〜〜〜〜

Reflective Exercise 7.2

My Community Social Ties

Describe the community you lived in as a child. Where did you live? How did your family connect with others in your community? In what types of community activities and organizations did you and/or your family participate? What kinds of learning did you gain from members of your community? Who do you remember as wise and helpful people in your community? What kind of learning and support did you receive from them? Which of these social ties served as bridging social networks or as bonding ones?

As we noted in the previous section, larger social, political, and economic factors can exert a powerful influence on a community's social ties from the outside. For example, a significant portion of the difficulties faced by inner-city schools and families is caused by changes in the job opportunity structure created by the larger socioeconomic environment. Moreover, many social analysts (Putnam 2000; Keith 1996) believe that there has been a general weakening of community social bonds throughout the United States, as a result of the following large scale social and economic factors:

1. The scale of institutions that touch our lives makes it harder to make personal connections. The corner grocery store has been replaced by the large supermarket. Neighborhood stores have been supplanted by the regional Wal-Mart. Even our schools are often much larger than those attended by previous generations of students. In the past, each of these domains provided an opportunity for us to be known by others and form bonds with them.

2. Technologies, such as air conditioning, television, and the Internet have made it unnecessary for people to leave the comfort of their home and mingle with others. Rather than interact with neighbors, friends, or children, we entertain ourselves individually by watching television.

3. With increased economic demands, many women have entered the workforce for professional and workplace opportunities rather than volunteering in the community or informally supervising children.

4. Fear of crime or violence has deterred people from gathering informally in public spaces, such as parks or playgrounds. In some neighborhoods, older people are afraid to venture out of their homes. And vigilant parents keep their children—even teenagers—at home to keep them safe.

5. A more typical scenario today is not knowing our neighbors. Advances in transportation and communication, together with the demands of corporate workplaces, have allowed or required people to be more mobile. As a result, Americans move frequently and far from their extended families. With each move, individuals may make less effort to build neighborhood and family ties.

As a result of these factors, many Americans have reported feeling more and more adrift (Bloom 2000). Yet most social scientists did not study the connection

American and Latino male youths. These researchers reported that the youths exposed to community violence who were living in families that functioned well in terms of parenting were less likely to perpetuate violence than were similarly exposed youths who were living in less well-functioning families.

In addition to buffering the negative effects of a dangerous and disorderly neighborhood, many parents seek to overcome negative neighborhood conditions that threaten their children's development by linking children with "mainstream opportunities and institutions" (Jarrett 1999; 2000). This entails a parent seeking out local and extra-local resources to expand their children's skills and linking their children to community resources, such as neighborhood programs. For example, a study of Boston neighborhoods showed that when parents had strong neighborhood ties that extended beyond the family, children's social behaviors and school performance were better. One explanation for this finding is that children who were exposed to more heterogenous social networks had more opportunities to spend time with other adults in socially and cognitively stimulating activities (Marshall, Noonan, McCartney, Marx & Keefe 2001). In contrast, high delinquency rates, educational failure, infant mortality, child abuse, adolescent substance abuse, and gang violence have been found to be related to the absence of neighborhood institutions that promote healthy youth development, including primary supports like Little League, and the number of nonfamily adults who are available and willing to work with youths.

In addition, employment settings can provide opportunities for low-income parents to access resources that enhance their children's learning and development. In a study of low-income mothers' involvement in their elementary school children's education, Weiss et al. (2003) reported how the mothers used their workplaces to call teachers by phone and to gain access to resources, such as computers, educational advice from colleagues or employers, and tutoring or homework help for their children.

Approaches for Linking Schools and Families with Communities

Despite the evidence that indicates that neighborhood circumstances influence how families manage their children, the typical meaning of school–community involvement has emphasized how communities might *support schools.* For example, many schools have created school–community partnerships with businesses to gain additional material and personnel resources to help the school carry out its mission. Only recently have educators actively sought to learn how to connect with neighborhoods and communities *to support families.* As Weiss et al. (2005) observed: "Although much has been written about school practices to involve families in their children's learning, we know less about how such involvement is promoted by the community and, in particular, parents' social networks and organizations other than the school" (51). However, many schools are now beginning to reach out to their communities to increase the available resources for supporting families. These efforts have used two very different approaches. One approach, which we term a *need/deficit-based* approach, is depicted in efforts initiated by members outside of the community to identify family deficits and access needed resources for them. A second approach, that we have termed an *asset-based approach,* is characterized by efforts to engage members of the community in identifying their current assets and mobilizing to develop additional resources to support students, their families, and the community itself. Let us look more closely at these two approaches to forming stronger school, family, and community supports.

Deficit/Need-Based Approach

Many educators have committed themselves to drawing community resources into their schools. In these types of initiatives, the professionals in the school typically decide what the school or community needs (although there may be some token participation by community members in the governance of such activities). Typically, both individual families and neighborhoods served by the schools are viewed in terms of their problems and deficits, with steps being taken to access resources to resolve these deficits.

Drawing in Community Resources

Many educators have looked at how the school might draw community resources into schools. The conventional expectation of many educators is that the community should provide resources for students and schools. These educators tend to present a vision of community either as a resource for schools or as a potential barrier to learning when community values and mores do not fit with those promoted at school. The work of Epstein and Comer, scholars whom we mentioned earlier in this book, epitomize this perspective.

Epstein (2001) conceptualized schools, families, and communities as overlapping circles of influence that affect student achievement and development. Epstein argued that for students to be healthy, these three influences must work together in partnership. Although Epstein's focus on parent–school involvement is broad-based and inclusive, her perspective on the school–community relationship is much narrower. In her discussion of community, Epstein stresses the resources that the community can provide to schools and the ways that communities can either reinforce "school and family goals for student success" or redirect "students away from schools" (76). Hence, in Epstein's view, communities are helpful to schools when they support the school's mission and harmful to schools when they resist or criticize the mission in some way" (Schutz 2006, 704). Much of Epstein's focus appears to be on what the community needs to do for the school.

In contrast, the work of Comer and Haynes (1991) is more inclusive of the community. The initial implementation of Comer's School Development Project (SDP), focused on comprehensive efforts to reform the instruction in schools, is an effort in which family and community involvement is just one element. Until quite recently, these authors did not discuss community engagement much as an issue separate from parent involvement. Instead, for Comer and Haynes (1991): "Parents are a natural link to the communities in which schools are located . . . [because they] bring a community perspective to planning and management activities" (273). One of Comer's key mechanisms for developing initial connections between home and school was to hire parents to work with teachers in classrooms and to participate in leadership positions on the school's collaborative teams. More recently, Comer has begun to address the need for a stronger connection between SDP schools and the larger community. One approach is for the school to integrate itself with a more comprehensive vision of the school as a center for integrated services to the community, including before and after school programs. In his recent book *Waiting for a Miracle: Why Schools Can't Solve Our Problems—And How We Can*, Comer (1998) discusses the importance of arranging for community-focused programs and efforts that might create the conditions for student success in schools. He argues for a "different kind of school that could help put a supportive community together again . . . and envisions a school that, instead of being isolated . . . could be fully incorporated into the larger community. . . . Economic and community development, human services, recreation, and artistic expression programs could be tied to the school setting when possible" (212).

Linking Schools with Community Services

In contrast to Comer's community development focus, many schools are attempting to link to available health and social services in the community to address the complex needs of some children and families. These educators are recognizing that some children live in families and communities that are in such disarray—having insufficient food, health care, or housing—that the children do not have the necessary familial and social supports from home to learn, and that educators alone cannot provide these services. As Schorr (1997) so eloquently described in her book *Common Purpose: Strengthening Families and Neighborhoods to Rebuild America:* "When children come to school tired, hungry, sick, disruptive, unmotivated, undisciplined, disturbed, neglected, or abused, they arrive with problems that interfere with their own or others' learning" (283). To respond to these issues, a number of schools are linking to available health and social services in the community. One such program introduced in New Jersey in the late 1980s is the School-Based Youth Services Program. As suggested in Figure 7.3 on page 184, the school is at the center of a series of partnerships—with local businesses, local educational institutions, service agencies,

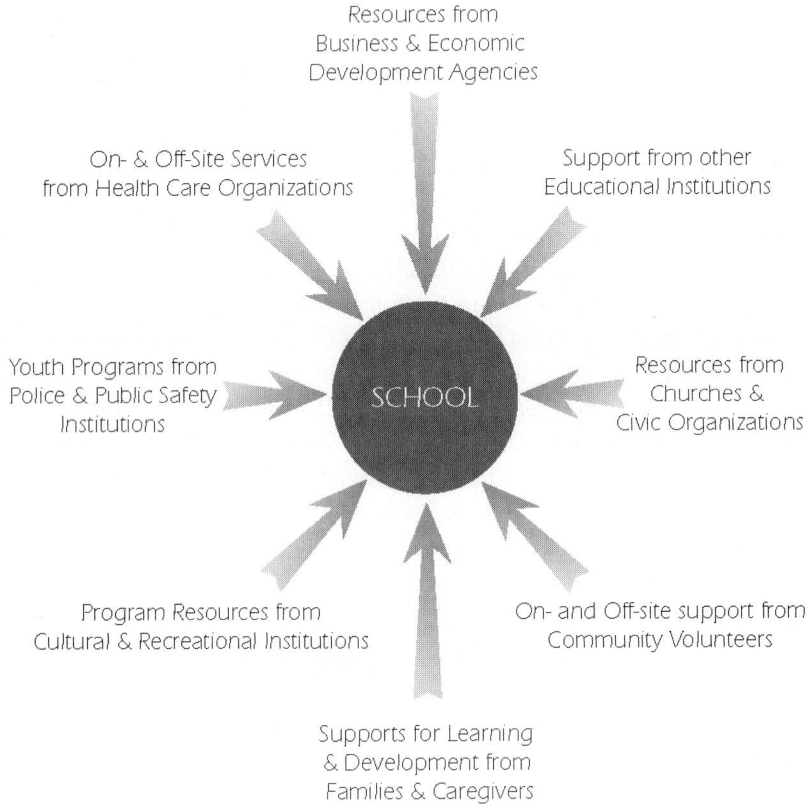

~~~~~~

Figure 7.3 Need-Based Model of School–Community Service Delivery

Resources from
Business & Economic
Development Agencies

On- & Off-Site Services
from Health Care Organizations

Support from other
Educational Institutions

Youth Programs from
Police & Public Safety
Institutions

SCHOOL

Resources from
Churches &
Civic Organizations

Program Resources from
Cultural & Recreational Institutions

On- and Off-site support from
Community Volunteers

Supports for Learning
& Development from
Families & Caregivers

Source: Adapted from Keith, N. Z. (1996). Can urban school reform and community development be joined? *Education and Urban Society, 28(2)*, 243.

and (less so) the local community—to provide families with core services, such as counseling, recreation, and employment assistance at one location.

One of the most successful integrated services programs is that of Hanshaw Middle School in Modesto, California. Showcasing it in their book on full service schools, Dryfoos and Maguire (2002, 108–119) describe:

> This school formed a series of partnerships with local businesses, California State University, service agencies and (less so) the local community. These agreements allowed the school to offer school-based services to students and their families and to connect them with additional resources, including the worlds of higher education and work opportunities beyond the school. For instance, at Hanshaw Middle School, the school is organized into seven "communities," each of which is adopted by a different branch of the university. Students identify with their branch, they wear T-shirts with its name, visit

the campus, and are put in touch with university students. Parents are both the recipients of services (i.e., adult classes, health clinics) and the providers, through volunteer activities. The whole is designed as an integrated approach to improving students' educational environment.

Other programs might involve a different combination of linked services delivered by schools, agencies, and community groups at different locations. We discuss in more detail in Chapter 12 how an educator might access these services for students' families. Unquestionably, educators need effective, high-quality backup services that can be trusted and rapidly mobilized. In addition, there is ample evidence that services that are theoretically available to inner-city residents are often inaccessible in practice, and using local schools as the first point of contact may help improve access. Moreover, providing more coordinated services is certainly more effective than engaging in fragmented efforts. However, one criticism of this approach is that it continues to preserve the hierarchical nature of most professionals in relation to their poor or working-class clients. As Keith (1996) noted, more often than not, the professional community decides the nature of the problem and its possible solutions of the community, "which the relatively unknowledgeable or powerless client is then expected to implement for her or his own good" (244). Schools often have high expectations for how parents will involve themselves in their children's learning and have limited understanding of how the conditions of impoverished families make such involvement difficult. As a result, educators interested in reaching out to low-income families often become frustrated at parents' response to them, begin to view parents exclusively in terms of their deficits (e.g., that they do not come to school or do not help with homework), and expect that the family should change to accommodate the expectations of the school. To counter this school-centric approach, many community-based organizations are using a more asset-based approach to develop needed services for families in which the school is only one of the participants. Let us look more closely at these initiatives in the next section.

Asset-Based Approaches

In contrast to the previous school-centered initiatives that focus exclusively on meeting the purposes and goals of the school, a number of promising initiatives have been developed that focus on how the school might work with community members from a more asset-based perspective. Keith (1996) noted that a key premise of these initiatives is the emphasis on assessing assets as well as needs. It rests on the strong belief that even within the poorest neighborhoods, there exist strengths and capacities to be tapped, not just weaknesses and deficits, and that education is only one feature in a comprehensive effort to restore the economic and social viability of a neighborhood or community. Hence, the focus of these initiatives shifts from an emphasis on matching services and individual needs to a focus on community members joining in mutually enhancing social action to pursue common interests of a neighborhood. In point of fact, Matthews (1996) strongly asserts that "inner-city school reforms need to start in and with the community if they are to have any real hope of long-term success" (11).

To decide what actions need to be taken that reflect the interests and priorities of the community rather than only those of agencies (or schools) requires that networks among different community groups and institutions be created. As a result, these community–school initiatives are asset-based and inner-directed as they rest upon the capacity of community members to decide on common goals and identify existing resources. Figure 7.4 depicts this asset-based approach and shows neighborhood residents and their networks, institutions, and organizations at the center, tasks rather than agencies depicted in the second intermediary tier, and agencies in the outermost tier.

Figure 7.4   Asset-Based Model of School–Community Linkages

Source: Adapted from Keith, N. Z. (1996). Can urban school reform and community development be joined? *Education and Urban Society, 28(2),* 251.

This figure shows the shift in focus away from the service integration model that seeks to match individual needs and agency services to the pursuit of common interests of neighborhood members and outside experts. Let us now look more closely at two examples of such asset-based initiatives: (a) community programs to support students and families that operate parallel rather than in collaboration with schools and preschools, and (b) community schools.

Parallel Community Initiatives

In contrast to the previous section that highlights how schools have attempted to bring community resources into the school, a number of initiatives have been organized to work parallel to rather than in direct collaboration with schools. For example, a growing number of communities offer preschool or after-school programs for children in nonschool settings that not only serve working parents by providing safe places for children to engage in activities, but also engage families in programming. Some parents ensure quality services by participating in surveys and focus groups, although a core group of parents takes on leadership and governance roles. Parents may also participate in children's activities, help raise funds, and find paid positions for coordinators and tutors in these programs (Blank 2001; Caspe, Traub & Little 2002). Through these programs, parents monitor their children's activities and use these programs to expose children to new learning environments.

One community-based social service organization's goal, for instance, was to seek opportunities to help low-income single parents become stronger advocates for improved relationships with the schools (Bloom 2001). This community-based grassroots organization developed an advocacy plan with mothers and school administrators to address the strained relationships between parents and school staff at meetings to discuss a child's academic difficulties (Bloom 2001). The mothers often felt intimidated by these meetings, where they were alone in confronting as many as seven to ten staff members who wielded their professional status in demeaning ways. To address the mothers' concerns, the community volunteers developed an advocacy plan with the mothers, consisting of having the mothers participate in a role-play that involved the mother and several school staff to resolve a fictitious fourth-grade boy's poor performance and then conducting a debriefing session about the role-play. Through the role-play, the mothers could air their concerns in a safe environment and feel empowered. The school staff also gained a different perspective about the parents' behavior in the meetings, that of an impoverished parent wanting her child to succeed. In addition, the mothers have insisted on having a community volunteer attend the meetings with them to serve as an ally.

In other instances, community members may serve as cultural brokers for immigrant families and mainstream institutions and provide resources beyond what families and schools can offer, such as counseling and assistance for college preparation. The Bridging Multiple Worlds Model/Project (Cooper, Chavira, Mikolyski

& Dominguez 2004) is one such university–community partnership designed to increase access to college among low-income, ethnic minority, and immigrant youth. The project model has been used extensively to help Latino youth in California feel confident and safe in their neighborhoods, learn alternatives to violence, and gain bicultural skills needed to succeed in school. Program staff members provide cultural continuity by reinforcing Latino families' beliefs that success in life is measured in both moral and academic terms. Staff also offer youths a view of life opportunities through resources of mainstream institutions, including schools, colleges, and banks (Cooper, Chavira, Mikolyski & Dominguez 2004).

In one community, a church-based nursery school program was developed to serve the needs of inner-city children and their families (Kretzman & McKnight 1993), while in another community a church-based program was developed to serve the needs of Latino children and their families (Nevarez-La Torre 1997). Because many school-based programs and schools geared to Latino and other communities of color have been criticized for their deficit perspective on community and for their lack of meaningful partnerships with community members, this church-based community program attempted to promote increased school participation without accepting a full partnership approach (Delgado-Gaitan 1990; Neito 1996). One of the program staff described the conditions that led to the development of this program:

> There is no good communication among the schools nor between the schools and the community. One reason for the lack of communication is a lack of cultural understanding. . . . The majority of the teachers are Anglo and they do not know what it is to come from a different country to live here, not knowing the language nor the culture. They cannot understand what our children go through, what our families need to confront on a daily basis in order to send the children to school. (67)

Working virtually unnoticed by and parallel to the school system in the city, this program attempted to improve the education of elementary schoolchildren through after-school interventions. In addition, they learned about and utilized the community's funds of knowledge. These funds of knowledge represent what community members knew, what they valued, and what facilitated their daily existence in the larger society. As a result, they sought to influence ways in which the schools could be more responsive to and become part of the Latino community.

In other communities, members who are concerned about the quality of their children's schools recruit parents and other community members to become leaders in addressing parents' concerns about children's safety, after-school activities, school size and school climate (Gold, Simon & Brown 2002a; Shirley 1997). Shirley described how one local community group, Allied Communities of Tarrant (ACT), was invited by the principal of a middle school to work on parent involvement. ACT is an institution rooted in the community but external to the school that is specifically designed to give community members power. The group first met with teachers to discuss their frustrations with parents. Once the teachers were on board, ACT leaders flooded the neighborhood, visiting parents door-to-door, surveying their sentiments about the school, and seeking out potential leaders. In a "slow but cumulative fashion the labor-intensive, face-to-face, relational approach of ACT leaders and teachers began to change the attitude of many parents toward their children's school" (1997, 107). At the same time, the teachers began to learn about the culture of their students and the community. Slowly, through a range of activities, parent and community involvement increased. ACT also became a mechanism through which parents could express their concerns about the school. Later on, these parents became the core of efforts to organize for a range of changes in their community. Ultimately, the project developed into the Alliance Schools Project, and many local groups working together forced the state to provide funding for similar problems elsewhere.

Community Schools

In contrast to these independent community efforts, many school staffs are recognizing that they cannot reform neighborhoods or develop community services for students' families on their own. Hence, they have joined up and become partners with outside community efforts to reform services and build communities (Schutz 2006, 692). As a result, community school initiatives have a distinctive community orientation.

The philosophy of these schools emphasizes transforming the school into a hub for neighborhood activities of many kinds and making the school and its facilities available to the community on evenings and weekends. To do this, the school partners with an outside organization or agency so that they can offer a range of services for children, families, and community members that encompass outreach and prevention, advocacy, mental health counseling, social services referrals, translation and interpretation services, as well as educational, recreational, and avocational activities (Schutz 2006).

Unlike a welfare office or mental health center, schools are a nonstigmatizing setting (especially if parents feel free to come there for reasons other than that their child is in trouble). As a result, many experts, such as Kretzmann and McKnight (1993), argued the crucial need to find ways for schools to contribute to broad community development efforts. Some community schools developed parent centers to cater to families more effectively. Johnson (1993) discovered that the creation of parent centers resulted in organizational changes within schools. In a survey of twenty-eight schools in fourteen cities nationwide that had active parent centers, Johnson (1994) reported that all of the centers provided information, materials, and books that parents could borrow; workshops or seminars to address family needs; referrals to social service providers; and translation services for parents. In addition, Johnson (1994) noted that the centers served a major mediating function in the family–school–community relationship. This function changed the role of parents from "outsiders" to "insiders" within the school community. He noted that community schools that have parent centers undergo structural changes as they strive to accommodate to the daily presence of families in the life of the school.

Many of these programs operate under the assumption that to serve student needs, the family's needs and issues have to be addressed, and that input from the families is essential to the school's decision-making about needed services and activities. One successful example of such a community development effort are the community schools in New York City, known as the Beacon Schools. Innovators of the Beacon Schools not only wanted to collect multiple services in one place and make them more accessible, but also they wanted to make these school-based services part of a community-building venture. Recognizing that substance abuse was deeply tied to the conditions of the community, in 1990, the city commission of New York City identified as a top priority the need for safe havens for children, youths, and families in troubled city neighborhoods. The city targeted nine neighborhoods in which resources would be strengthened and coordinated for the purpose of reducing drug use and providing a vehicle for community organizing. Schorr's (1997) description of one such school depicts the range of services to families and children that are provided to meet many vital nonacademic needs:

> The centerpiece of the Beacon Schools' effort is that schools are transformed into community centers, available to children and adults 365 days a year. We can see this at one such school-based community center, the Countee Cullen Community Center at P.S. 194 in Central Harlem. The center is open seven days a week from 9 A.M. until 11 P.M. or midnight. Youth workers at the center help with homework and conduct after-school sports and recreation programs for about two hundred children from 3 P.M. to 6 P.M. The youngsters are taught conflict resolution and that they have a responsibility to the community. Services for high-risk families are integrated into other Beacon activities. A lot of informal counseling and consultation goes on between staff and both children and their parents. At 7 P.M. one Friday night about forty teenagers showed up to participate in youth leadership activities while parents and children met together in the gym for a joint African dance class. Programs for adults included Alcoholics and Narcotics Anonymous, aerobics, and educational workshops. These activities have brought more and more community adults into the school and allowed the center to take on the values of the larger community and fewer of the values of the adolescents of that community. The staff works hard to alter the traditional, one-sided relationship between neighborhood parents and school personnel. Now parents come to the office and ask for help in meeting with the school staff. Activities for adolescents in the late evenings and on weekends are an important alternative to the streets. Classes include drama, dance, video, community service, job readiness, and computer skills. Boy Scouts meets on Thursday afternoon, and Friday is Teen Movie Night. Canada, the innovator of this program states: "The center looks less like a place where outsiders are coming in to do something for you and more like a place where you are coming together to do something for yourself." (50–52)

These efforts to root schools and school systems more substantively in the local community have been embraced by both rural and inner-city communities that face dramatic social and economic changes. For example, recognizing the power of community revitalization initiatives that can be housed in the school. The New Mexico Rural Revitalization Initiative (Heimerl, 2007) is a school-led movement "dedicated to revitalizing rural districts through unifying schools with their communities" (26). In describing this initiative, Heimerl (2007) noted: "The out-migration of the population from rural to urban areas is resulting in the degeneration, and, in some cases, the death of rural schools and communities" (26).

To address this problem, the New Mexico Rural Education Department, in cooperation with the Rural Education Forum of Australia and the Center for Relational Learning, launched thirteen pilot projects in rural New Mexican communities that were designed to stimulate the economy through developing self-sustaining and profitable projects based on the inherent uniqueness, strengths, and collective ingenuity of these communities. According to Heimerl (2007):

> Since schools serve as the nucleus of rural communities, they are the logical place to initiate rural revitalization. In addition to being the focal point of civic pride, schools are the largest employer in most rural communities, with the most advanced communications infrastructure and brick-and-mortar facilities. Thus, schools are resource factories providing the staff, parent networks, students and facilitators needed to launch a successful community renewal campaign. One of the most valuable assets identified by the NMRRI was the incredible, previously untapped reservoir of youth creativity and energy found in the schools of rural communities. Capitalizing on the students "know-no-limit" mentality and instilling a sense of pride in the community, these groups have created economic development programs in which students have important roles and have resulted in permanent additions to the local school curriculum. (26, 27)

Although a variety of different strategies is used by community schools to serve student needs, all rest on the assumption that families' needs and issues have to be addressed along with student needs and that input from the families is essential to the school and community's decision-making about needed services and activities.

Community Strategies Used by Educators

As you can see, a wide variety of ways exists in which the community can be a resource for educators hoping to support families' efforts to raise their children. However, only recently have educators begun to look at how they might change their connections with community members to support parents and families. We believe that the community and community-based institutions can be an additional resource that contributes to students' school success. Hence, we close the chapter by discussing three general strategies that educators might use initially to link with their school's community: (a) learning about the community and its assets, (b) strengthening parent-to-parent support, and (c) mobilizing communities to develop additional assets for families.

Learning About the Community

First, educators, particularly those who do not live in the community in which they teach but who want to work with families and community organizations, should consider how they might learn about the assets, values, and social norms that characterize interaction among community members. One way to learn about the particular social norms and networks that exist in a community and how they are structured is to interact with members of the community outside of the school day. For example, you might want to use local services and shop in local stores so you can get to know the local merchants. Or you might want to attend important out-of-school events in which your students perform, such as community celebrations (e.g., Kwanzaa celebrations), sporting events, religious activities (e.g., bar/bat mitzvahs, baptisms, or confirmations), or award ceremonies in social organizations (e.g., Boy Scouts or Girl Scouts).

Second, learning about the unique combination of assets available in a particular community is important. Each community boasts a unique combination of individual, associational, and institutional organizations with distinctive assets that might be applied to enhance student success (Kretzmann & McKnight 1993). Four general sources of community assets are described by Kretzmann and McKnight. The first source of community assets are the skills, resources, and talents of individual community residents, including traditionally marginalized groups, such as youth, the elderly, artists, welfare recipients, and the disabled. The second source are citizens' associations that are less formal and much less dependent upon paid staff than formal institutions and are the vehicles through which citizens solve problems or share common interests and activities of a religious, cultural, athletic, or recreational nature. These might include block clubs, religious organizations, community organizations, and cultural groups. The third source are the more formal institutions located in a community: public institutions, such as schools, community colleges, libraries, parks, police and fire stations; and nonprofit institutions, such as hospitals and social service agencies. The fourth source consists of private sector institutions, such as businesses, banks, and corporations. These four different sources of assets provide an array of distinctive community resources and funds of knowledge. For example, what are the unique traditions and cultures represented in a particular community? What unique skills have individuals learned and developed? To effectively discover these assets requires school staff to commit time to building relationships with community members. As a first step to doing this, you might want to examine your school's existing institutional practices and the relationships that staff members have already developed with other community members by means of Reflective Exercise 7.3.

Reflective Exercise 7.3

Assessing My School's Current Relationships with the Community

How does your school staff interact with the neighborhoods/communities served by the school to promote family and student development?

What school activities are supported by the community, and how are they supported? (e.g., sporting events, fundraisers)

What community organizations/activities are supported by the school, and how are they supported? (e.g., Girl Scouts & Boy Scouts)

What community services are available to the students and families? (e.g., after-school programs, church-based parent groups, girls & boys clubs)

With what community-based institutions does the school work (e.g., religious organizations, other schools, junior college/college, businesses/industries) to serve the needs of children and families? What specific services do each of these entities provide to children and families?

What community associations (e.g., Urban League, Latino social organizations) operate in the community, and what services do they provide to children and families? What cultural events occur in the community (e.g., Cinco de Mayo and Kwanzaa celebrations)?

Learning about the norms, values, and assets of a community, as well as the impact of certain economic and social conditions, helps educators more readily identify existing assets and resources that will be useful to students, their families, and the schools.

Strengthening Parent-to-Parent Supports

All families can benefit from increased social support as well as greater knowledge of informal and formal services. By finding out what families self-identify as their needs, educators can help families become more involved in their children's learning. Schools can also use or build on existing parent or family resources through the development of family resource centers. Weiss et al. (2006) describe how some schools have promoted the development of social ties across families by creating opportunities for them to connect with each other and the community. Organizing a social event, providing needed services, or establishing a space for families to meet together are some of the ways that schools have provided structures for community building and social action. For example, one parent resource center, known as the Rainmakers, was operated by parents within an elementary school who took on the role of helping their neighbors successfully fight rent increases that occurred in their low-income community (Turnbull & Turnbull 2005).

Mobilizing Community Assets

How do you mobilize the current assets provided by particular organizations or institutions in the community? For example, how do you find out whether a church is currently operating an after-school program or a parent support program? The Coalition for Community Schools in cooperation with the National Association of Secondary School Principals (NASSP) and the National Association of Elementary School Principals (NAESP) have developed a guide for educators to use for developing stronger ties with the community. This guide, entitled *Community and Family Engagement: Principals Share What Works,* outlines a number of key steps for working effectively with the community (Berg, Melaville & Blank 2006). Kretzmann and McKnight (1993) also state that it is crucial to find ways for schools to contribute to broad community development efforts. They describe the basic features of this community asset development process:

> Focusing on the assets of lower income communities does not imply that these communities do not need additional resources from the outside. Rather, it simply suggests that outside resources will be used more effectively if the local community itself is fully mobilized and invested and if it can define the agendas for which additional resources must be obtained. Second, the discussion of community assets is intended to affirm, and to build upon the work already going on in neighborhoods. (8)

Obviously, the first step starts with identifying what is present in a community—the capacities of its residents, associations, and institutions—rather than on what is absent or what is problematic or what the community needs. This information gathering should lead to the development of the capacities of local residents and organizations in the community. Hence, a basic purpose in gathering such information about a specific community resident (or an organization or institution), is to help him/her (or an organization or institution) contribute to advancing the community's goals as well as to advancing his/her own goals. Will the information help her offer her gifts, contribute her talents, or increase her child's school success? To create investment, and access hope and a sense of control, parents and others from the community need to have a voice with the school staff in developing an agenda and priorities to improve their own and their children's lives. Using the guide appearing in Reflective Exercise 7.4, describe the knowledge, skills and human resources available in the community in which you grew up.

Reflective Activity 7.4

Looking at Community Assets and Funds of Knowledge

Use this guide to think about the skills and knowledge and resources that might be embedded in your community.

People Assets

What are the special gifts, talents, interests, and skills of individual people in the local community?

Artists _____

Elderly Citizens _____

Youth _____

Labeled People (e.g., mentally retarded, disabled, etc,) _____

Citizens' Associations Assets

What particular resources, skills, and activities are possessed by civic associations?

Senior Volunteer and Service Organizations _____

Churches _____

Cultural Groups _____

Block Clubs _____

Civic groups (Kiwanis, Rotary, Alturas, etc.) _____

Formal Community Institutions

What particular assets & resources may exist in the following resources in your community?

Schools_____

Community Colleges _____

Libraries _____

Parks _____

Police and Fire Departments _____

Local and State Government Agencies and Departments _____

Health Care Organizations (hospitals, health departments) _____

Social Service Agencies _____

Private Sector Institutions

Local Businesses _____

National Corporations and Franchises _____

Banks _____

The second step involves building consensus and connections across the various participants by identifying common goals or needs that both community members and school staff prioritize as important. A third step is to inventory the assets and resources of the school and of other community institutions and organizations.

A fourth step entails having community members review this asset inventory and then identify what and how they might choose to build upon their community's assets. For example, Kretzmann and McKnight (1993) described how many churches and synagogues have already begun to utilize their resources within their communities in creative and innovative ways. These religious institutions are recognizing that to remain viable in their communities, they need to contribute to the improvement of their communities. Each of these institutions possesses certain common sets of resources that can be mobilized effectively: (a) their personnel and congregation members who have special skills and interests (e.g., homebuilding, youth development, senior services); (b) their space and facilities; (c) their equipment (e.g., fax machine, computer, telephone, musical equipment, educational supplies, or kitchen equipment); (d) their expertise in promoting greater social and economic justice; and (e) their economic power (e.g., they have the capacity to hire community residents, purchase from community stores, and may have special endowment funds). A variety of different partnerships have emerged between religious organizations and schools, in which these types of resources are used. For example, the Chicago Urban League connects churches with schools through an "adopt-a-school" program, in which churches provide tutoring for neighborhood school children. As a result, the church gains an opportunity to become better connected to the neighborhood. In another community, a church formed a relationship with a local school in which students were allowed to use the church's youth center after school and on the weekend (Kretzmann & McKnight 1993). Although such collective efforts take time and energy to develop in a community, they multiply the resources available to educators for supporting their students and families.

Summary

Communities vary in terms of their location, population size, economic resources, and social ties. Many communities in the United States are being transformed over time as a result of social, economic, and cultural influences. Both rural and urban communities are facing dramatic social and economic changes that are impacting the occupational and educational opportunities for children in those communities. In this chapter, we identified the nature of these changes and examined how neighborhood and community conditions impact children's development. We then looked at two different approaches that schools and communities have developed to counter these negative influences: (a) need/deficit-based approaches and (b) asset-based approaches. Organized around identifying family needs and accessing needed services, need/deficit-based approaches might take the form of (a) schools drawing in community resources or (b) linking schools with community services. In contrast, asset-based approaches emphasize assessing the existing strengths and capacities of communities as well as their needs and then mobilizing community members to identify mutual interests and goals. Illustrative of this type of approach are (a) independent community programs for students and families that parallel the school's efforts and (b) community schools. Finally, we considered how the individual educator might participate in learning about the assets of a community, strengthening parent-to-parent supports, or mobilizing community resources to support children and families' development.

Resources

Coalition for Community Schools,
www.communityschool.org
C/O Institute for Educational Leadership, 1001 Connecticut Avenue, NW, Suite 310, Washington, DC 20036. The Coalition advocates for community schools as the vehicle for strengthening schools, families, and communities so that together they can improve student learning.

Part III

Building Family–School Relationships to Maximize Student Learning

Educators need strategies for building effective partnerships with families, not only for the purpose of solving student problems, but also for maximizing student learning. In the next three chapters, we describe strategies that educators use that focus on creating stronger connections with families to maximize student learning and development. In Chapter 8 we focus on the communication skills and practices that educators can routinely use to build a sense of connection with their students' families. In Chapter 9 we examine the unique challenges faced by second language learners and their families and the instructional and noninstructional strategies that educators can use to build working relationships with families. In Chapter 10 we describe the use of student-led parent conferences as a powerful tool for establishing relationships with students and their families that give students a greater voice in their assessment of their learning.

Chapter 8

Getting Acquainted with Students' Families

Teresa N. Leibforth and Mary Ann Clark

Learning Objectives

After reading this chapter, you will be able to:

- Describe specific attitudes and communication skills needed to develop trusting relationships with students' families.
- Outline cultural differences in communication styles that influence family–school interaction.
- Describe everyday routines by which you can become acquainted with students' families and develop ongoing lines of communication.

> *Educators who take the time to get acquainted with parents, to listen to them, to empathize with their perspective, and to learn from them about their child and their home culture, promote the successful learning of all their students and enhance their own ability to reach and teach each of their students.*

A growing recognition exists that teachers are the key agents for reaching out to parents/caregivers. The teacher's attitude and practices—not the education, socioeconomic status, or marital status of the parent—have the strongest influence on whether parents become involved in their children's schooling (Colbert 1996; Epstein & Sheldon 2002; Erford 2007). Educators, who take the time to get acquainted with parents, to listen to them, to empathize with their perspective, and to learn from them about their child and their home culture, promote the successful learning of all their students and enhance their own ability to reach and teach each of their students. Lawrence-Lightfoot (2003) makes a poignant and powerful point that no dialogue is more important than that between teachers and family members. She states:

> If we think about families and their outside connections to physicians, pediatricians, lawyers, or other professionals, there's absolutely no comparison in quantity and quality to the connections that parents have with teachers. With over 4 million teachers, there are approximately 100 million parent–teacher conferences a year, and that's probably an underestimate. So quantitatively it's just mind-boggling. And we haven't paid much attention to this really important dialogue and to making it meaningful, productive, and informative. (1)

As discussed in the previous chapters, an increasing array of cultural differences exists in our students in today's schools that may appear to present roadblocks to family–school communication. Factors, such as differences in SES and race/ethnicity, speaking English as a second language, and the past educational experiences of parents, can be potential barriers to communication. However, our job as educators is to understand and surmount these differences, find commonalities, and reach out to families in culturally responsive ways. Our experience has been that most families care a great deal about their children and their learning and school success. However, they may need encouragement and invitations from us to help them feel that they are a welcome and vital part of their children's educational experience. Family–school communication needs to become an integral and effective part of our professional practice; it should be second nature for who we are as people and professionals.

Although communication with families should be a school and district-wide initiative, in this chapter we focus on the communication that takes place between classroom teachers and families. Optimally, the strategies that we discuss can also be a part of a school-wide network of communication that takes place among the teachers and students in the classroom, the school as a whole, and families. In this chapter, we first describe the essential skills needed to become an effective communicator when you are interacting on a one-on-one basis with a student's caregiver or family. Next, we discuss some of the differing communication patterns that may influence how you decide to structure your communication with families who differ from you in their cultural background. We then describe everyday routines by which you can become acquainted with students' families as a group and develop ongoing lines of communication. Projecting a personal sense of warmth, welcoming, and caring is important in forging positive relationships. Being a good listener and having positive assumptions about families' intentions and involvement will pay dividends as you develop these important relationships. Being able to offer individual and specific feedback about your students to their family members in a constructive way will assist in establishing and maintaining positive lines of communication. Developing positive connections and building trust that teachers have their students' best interest at heart are essential outcomes of this process.

Initial Considerations

Put yourself in the shoes of the caregivers of your students. What must it feel like to come to the school and meet with a variety of educational experts, particularly if your child is not doing as well as you would hope? What environment would you like to encounter: One that is characterized by one-way communication from teacher to parent, or one that invites shared participation and validates the parents' perspective and issues and concerns? If your child is functioning well and does not have particular problems, do you feel that you, as a parent, should still be given access and opportunities to talk with your child's teacher about your child's learning? Would you like to be invited to participate in your child's learning without being made to feel like you are being intrusive?

Some family members may show reticence in speaking openly with teachers. Lawrence-Lightfoot (2003) points out that when teachers and parents come together, their conversations are often haunted by their own family and school experiences as children, resulting in feelings of vulnerability and insecurity. An important point to remember is that many family members do feel very vulnerable about their children as well as their own educational experiences and may have intense feelings about them. As educators, we need to remember that parents have a much more complex, holistic, and subtle view of their children (Lawrence-Lightfoot 2003). Their knowledge can provide us with greater insight into our students and can be a very useful resource for us.

A first step in developing skills in communicating with family members is to develop and demonstrate empathy with families. Common denominators that help foster family–school communication and involvement are caregivers who feel comfortable in bringing up topics, feel invited, welcomed, and valued for contributions. Caregivers' perceptions not only will influence the way they see you as the teacher, but also how they view the classroom environment for their child. If you gain family support for your teaching efforts, it can assist in creating a more cohesive, caring, and respectful classroom environment, which can result in increased learning and academic achievement. Researchers (Dodd 2000; Elias, Bruene-Butler, Blum & Schuyler 1997; Zins, Bloodworth, Weissberg & Walberg 2004) present evidence that links school success to social and emotional learning and classroom climate.

A concern that most teachers express is that of the amount of time and effort it takes to create the necessary connections with families. Many educators feel that trying to connect is an additional burden to add to the many day-to-day responsibilities required in today's schools. Our experiences have shown us that if we make such communication techniques a part of our teaching practice, many other aspects of teaching and learning fall into place. Conversely, if we do not take the time to nurture relationships, we will find ourselves spending that same amount of time on dealing with problems and attempting to mend fences. The concept of "digging the well before you are thirsty" is most applicable to the idea of establishing relationships from the beginning so that they are in place when most needed. An often unspoken truth is that, as educators, we feel much better about our jobs and students if the communication is going well, students and families are "on board," and we receive support and positive feedback for the work we do. If these essential pieces are not in place, we can become fatigued and feel "burned out."

Using Effective Relationship and Communication Skills

When working with families as well as students, keep in mind the importance to convey that you are interested in, and paying attention to, the information that they relay to you. How do you go about doing this? The ability to show empathy is an essential first ingredient. Being able to put yourself in the shoes of others, and attempting to understand their perspective as mentioned earlier, can give a family member the sense that you understand their concerns, or at least are trying to hear their "story." Also, of course, students are important family members, and we include them here. In fact, teaching and modeling these communication skills for your students and implementing them in the classroom are excellent ways to develop a caring and respectful classroom (Wittmer & Clark 2002a; 2002b). A student's perception of teacher support and school belonging is strongly related to increased academic self-efficacy, positive attitudes about school, and academic achievement (Roeser, Midgley & Urdan 1996).

At teachers' requests, we have helped design communication units on these very same skills for teachers to implement for the purpose of helping their students feel more like a family unit. The message is the same; the majority of students and families want to feel that they are welcome, that they belong, and feel accepted and cared about. The skills we discuss in this chapter include both relationship skills and communication skills. The relationship skills, which provide the base for effective communication, include the demonstration of caring, acceptance, respect, empathy, trust, understanding, and helping. The communication skills, which are the tools by which educators can relate to and connect with their students and families, include attentive listening, using encouragers, asking appropriate questions, paraphrasing, summarizing and clarifying what others have to say, focusing on and reflecting feelings, and giving and receiving feedback (Wittmer & Clark 2002a; 2002b). Furthermore, specific communication skills that are modeled and practiced can be linked with corresponding relationship skills. For example, attentive listening is related to showing respect. Reflecting feelings result in greater empathy. Summarizing, clarifying, and asking appropriate questions demonstrate your understanding and interest in another. Giving and receiving facilitative feedback helps foster trust. Put together, these skills can create both a caring and respectful family–school relationship and a classroom environment that promotes student learning (Wittmer & Clark 2002a; 2002b).

We have mentioned earlier the importance of conveying a caring and welcoming demeanor with families as well as establishing a base of trust. Showing respect, trying to understand others' perspectives and issues by being empathic, and being known as a helper, are all qualities that work well together to encourage trust and open communication. Equally important is for us to be perceived as being consistent and predictable in our relationships with family members; such consistency helps build trust and open up communication. To demonstrate these qualities, we should understand the worldviews of the families with whom we interact without evaluating or judging them. With the increased diversity of our student bodies and their families, being able to enter the frame of reference of a family regarding their culture, creed, or race/ethnicity is a powerful way to show understanding and acceptance. In the next section we discuss the skills of attentive listening, the use of "encouragers," paraphrasing and summarizing, reflecting/focusing on feelings, asking appropriate questions, and using facilitative feedback. Several authors in the fields of education and counseling write about these skills, and you may want to refer to their work for more specific details (see Ivey & Ivey 2006; Wittmer & Clark 2002a; 2002b).

Attentive Listening Skills

Christenson and Hirsch (1998) write: "Effective listening is dependent on the desire to listen, therefore, it is important for educators to create a context for conversation in which parents and educators feel relaxed, comfortable and prepared" (319). In today's busy world, many people feel "dismissed" because others do not take the time to hear their concerns, which is certainly true in many classrooms, because teachers struggle to accomplish many tasks in their tight schedules. Yet being attended to and having an opportunity to talk about an important matter is a very positive experience for most people. It helps them feel that the listener is interested in them, taking the time to listen to them, and is respectful of their point of view.

How can you tell if someone is truly listening to you? Often, the listener's verbal as well as nonverbal behaviors let you know that they are paying attention (Ivey & Ivey 2006; Wittmer & Clark 2000a; 2000b). Some teachers make sure that the first conference of the year is a "listening" conference in which family members do most of the talking. The conference is a great time to ask questions, such as "What is your child good at?" "What does he or she enjoy?" Such questions are not just referring to academic skills but rather to learn more about attributes and gifts that children bring to the classroom (Lawrence-Lightfoot 2003).

Eye Contact

One way that we often recognize when someone else is paying attention to what we say is when the other person gives us eye contact. Making eye contact is a powerful, nonverbal cue that lets others know that we are giving them our attention. Note that looking directly into another's eyes is often perceived differently by people from some cultural backgrounds (Ting-Toomey 1999). As a result, we should be aware that not all people respond to focused eye contact in the same way.

Body Language

The way we present ourselves when speaking with others can also convey nonverbal messages about our interest in what they have to say. Speaking with someone who has an open, relaxed posture (i.e., the person is facing you, perhaps leaning toward you while seated in a chair) tends to be more inviting than speaking with someone who exhibits a "closed" posture (i.e., the person has crossed arms, back toward you, or is leaning back in chair). A person who is fidgety or restless gives the impression that the conversation is not important or that there are "better things to be doing" with his or her time. Interrupting the conversation to take phone calls or to speak with others who may drop in gives a similar impression about the priority of the conversation. Additionally, such interactions are disruptive and do not encourage the flow of communication.

On the other hand, commonly many people "mirror" the speaker. For example, if you, the teacher, lean forward with a smile, the family member may respond in a similar way. If you appear to be relaxed with regard to body language and tone of voice, it helps the other person assume a similar demeanor.

Being a Careful Listener

Four simple steps to attentive listening (Wittmer & Clark 2002a; 2002b) are known:

- Look at the person who is talking, and keep good eye contact.
- Pay attention to the person's words. Tune in carefully to words as well as noting nonverbal cues, such as posture and facial expressions. Tune out other distractions.

- Be aware of the feelings that may accompany the words. Are the words conveying a *pleasant* or an *unpleasant* feeling? Examples of pleasant or positive feelings may include happy, interested, pleased, excited, delighted, accepted, cheerful, relieved, confident, and optimistic. Unpleasant feelings may include angry, sad, troubled, worried, irritated, fearful, offended, suspicious, and threatened. Note that many feeling words may be represented along a continuum representing a depth of feeling. For example, the feeling of anger could also be expressed as "irritation" or "rage," depending on the degree to which that emotion is felt. The listener needs to think about the depth of the emotion being expressed.
- Say something to the speaker to show that you have been listening. Use your own words, and try to restate the message you have heard:

It sounds like you are really enthusiastic about Jared's attitude in school this year.

You're frustrated that Megan is not completing her homework.

You seem irritated that you haven't heard about this assignment until now.

Using Encouragers

Encouragers (Ivey & Ivey 2006) are the brief physical and verbal cues we give people to let them know that we are listening and that we would like them to continue talking. Examples of encouragers may include nodding your head, saying "Yes," "Okay," or "Mm-hmm." These encouragers are often used quite readily during casual conversations. Considering your use of encouragers is important, because using them too frequently may cause the person who is talking to feel rushed. Using an encouraging response acknowledges that you have heard the person and helps them know that you are listening.

Paraphrasing, Clarifying, and Summarizing

Paraphrasing is taking what the person has said to you and reiterating the highlights of what is said. You can shorten and clarify (Ivey & Ivey 2006) what is said. Paraphrasing is using some of your own words as well as the important main words of the speaker. Any response that is an attempt to acknowledge the content of what a person has said, or to identify the most significant points that have been stated, can be termed a *summarizing response* (Wittmer & Clark 2002a; 2002b). Such responses are a way to focus the speaker's words and to "check out" what the person is trying to say. Paraphrasing and clarifying are also ways to show that you are listening and the speaker has been heard. Such acknowledgment helps create a bond between the speaker and the listener, in this case, you and the family member(s). Such statements are attempts to simplify, restate, or focus on the main ideas being expressed. Certain "leads" can be used to make such statements. Following are some examples of such leading statements (Wittmer & Clark 2002a; 2002b):

> *If I hear you correctly, you are telling me . . .*
> *Let me see if I understand what you are saying. You said . . .*
> *If I am following you, you're saying . . .*
> *It sounds to me as if. . . . (112)*

Such responses are conveying that you are trying your best to hear and understand the speaker's message.

Summarizing can be considered an extended paraphrase that is generally used less frequently and to clarify and reiterate larger chunks of information. Ivey and Ivey (2006) point out that summarizing can help organize thinking and is especially useful at the beginning or end of a conversation or conference, at transitions between topics, or to help clarify complex issues. For example, as a conference with family members ends, you will want to summarize the main points of the conversation you have just had. Additionally, you will want to summarize any recommendations that have been made during the conference for future actions to be taken. Putting these summaries in writing as well can be helpful for your record keeping. Most schools provide forms on which you can summarize main points made at a conference. In Chapter 11 we describe a form that we use in family–school problem-solving meetings to summarize the main points and decisions we have made together.

Focusing on and Reflecting Feelings

Earlier in the chapter we discussed the importance of empathy, or putting yourself in the shoes of another person to really understand them and their situation. Focusing on and reflecting their feelings can be a very powerful way to empathize with others. By tuning in and identifying the feelings that others are experiencing, we show empathy. This type of response, which identifies with the speaker's emotions and perceptions, is a way to be sensitive to and understanding of another's situation. It requires that we listen for the feelings that the other person is experiencing and mirror those feelings back so that person feels understood and affirmed (Wittmer & Clark 2002a; 2002b). Timeliness of the use of focusing on feelings is very important. We need to be careful not to rush into naming feelings without hearing the speaker out. Also, as mentioned previously, people from various cultural backgrounds may respond differently to this type of response. Some may believe that delving into feelings is intrusive. However, our experience is that most people really want to be "heard" and affirmed when they are having a conversation with us, and many people are glad to have their feelings validated.

Earlier, we gave examples of feeling words that were categorized as "pleasant" or "unpleasant." Focusing on feelings is what you are doing when you think about what the speaker is feeling and try to identify the feeling. Reflecting the feeling back to them is what we do when we verbalize a word or words that we believe accurately represents their experience. A beginning step is to think about what type of feeling the speaker is conveying through words and nonverbal communication.

The next step is to carefully choose a word that we want to relay to them. Note that many people may express mixed or ambivalent feelings. Also, the possibility exists that a person's words may not "match" their nonverbal behavior or the overall content of what they are trying to say. In other words, there may be discrepancies in what they are telling you. If you are sensing such discrepant messages, sharing those perceptions is okay. The process may sound complex, but it becomes very much a part of who you are as a teacher as you tune in to your students and their families.

Following are some examples of a teacher's focusing on and reflecting feelings of a parent/guardian:

> *It sounds like you are very disappointed in the school's lack of communication with you about Amy's progress in reading . . .*
>
> *It seems that you are angry and frustrated that Garrett was retained this year because of failing the state mandated test . . .*
>
> *On the one hand, you are saying you are unhappy about Joseph's discipline referrals, but at the same time you are laughing about it . . .*
>
> *Despite the hardships you have faced in making a major move this year, you seem to be upbeat and cheerful about being here . . . .*

Focusing on and reflecting feelings can be helpful for several reasons. As we have mentioned, it helps a person feel understood. Such responses can assist in going beyond the superficial to more basic concerns. It can be a relief for family members to talk about a situation with a child that may have been festering over time. In doing so, such responding can open up a conversation and can solicit the support of a teacher for generating ideas about possible solutions and/or resources. We must remember to not evaluate or judge feelings but to accept them as legitimate. Sometimes to "hear" and accept painful feelings is difficult; however, we should not "shrug off" or ignore such feelings. To do so is to dismiss them. Instead of attempting to reassure a person by saying: "You know you don't really feel that way" or "You'll feel better very soon," identify the feeling and let the speaker talk about it. You might say: "It sounds like it has been agonizing for you to get Rico to settle down and do his homework."

Asking Appropriate Questions

Asking appropriate questions helps show interest in others. Often, we would like to know more about family members of our students, and information may exist that is essential to the facilitation of student learning. Research shows that certain types of questions not only encourage the speaker to continue to talk, but also they convey more respect and interest in the speaker than do other types of questions. Also, we need to balance the number of questions we ask with the other types of responses discussed in the chapter. No one wants to be barraged by a stream of questions. Being interrogated feels intrusive and can be difficult to continue to respond. As a teacher, you know that the art and skill of questioning is an essential part of the teaching process. Questions can be used to obtain information, to stimulate conversation, or to query an individual about a specific matter. All of these reasons can be valid in conversations with family members. Effective questions invite the speaker to share thoughts, ideas, and feelings. Open, or inviting, questions start with words such as "*what*" and "*how.*" Closed, or noninviting, questions start with the word *why.* Such questions can also be answered by "yes" or "no." The open or inviting question conveys our interest in the speaker's perspective and hence it encourages the person to continue to expand on a response. The closed or noninviting question tends to shut down a conversation and also may not call for more than a one-word response. Note the difference in the following two questions:

> Closed: **Why** didn't Jacob do his homework?
> Open: **What** was it about the homework that kept Jacob from getting it done?

The first question puts the family member on the defensive, particularly if a lot of "why" questions have been previously asked. The second question sounds more objective, less accusatory, and gives room for explanation and possible help. Here are some other examples:

> **Why** are your children always late to school? (closed, noninviting)
> I'm wondering **what** keeps the children from arriving at school on time? Maybe we can talk about some strategies that may help out. (open, inviting)
> **Didn't** you get the assignment sheet I sent home? (closed, noninviting)
> **How** do Suki and you communicate about school assignments? If you are not receiving the assignment sheets, we can talk about how you can best obtain the information. (open, inviting)

To stimulate a smooth flowing conversation, remember to use a combination of other responses, such as encouragers, paraphrasing, summarizing, and reflection of feelings in between your questions. For example:

> It sounds like Suki isn't checking her homework agenda with you and you're feeling frustrated. (summarizing, feeling focused)

Following up such a conversation with suggestions that are mutually agreeable can be very helpful.

Using Facilitative Feedback

Most people are interested in knowing more about what others think and feel about them. Feedback is an important resource for learning about the impact of one's behavior on another. Thus, a model for giving and receiving feedback can help teachers, family members, and students think more systematically about their relationships and interactions and give them a means by which they can organize their thoughts and verbal messages to others. The components of a feedback message include

- Stating the other person's specific behavior that you want to address;
- Telling how the person's behavior makes you feel when it happens; and
- Saying what these feelings make you want to do. (Wittmer & Clark 2002a; 2002b)

This three-step approach helps you focus on a person's behavior rather than the person, avoiding name-calling and criticism. Feedback messages can be complimentary or confrontive. The first type of feedback is a positive message, whereas the second may focus on a behavior, attitude, or way of operating that is not desirable. The timing of a feedback message is important and should be specific to be most effective. Remember that feedback goes in both directions—from the teacher to the family and from the family to the teacher. It may even be shared from one family member to another within a family–school meeting or conference.

In a meeting with family members, whether requested or routine, feedback is an essential ingredient. Families want to know how their children are doing in school academically as well as socially. Parents and guardians are interested in specific information, such as grades, test scores, skill levels, and how their children are performing in comparison to the rest of the class. They also may want to know about their child's friendships and citizenship. In some cases, they may ask what they can do to help, and, in other cases, they may not know and may not ask. When children are having problems at school, family members may feel intimidated and defensive. You can help them feel as comfortable as possible by assisting in identifying strategies that will help the child and to be receptive to feedback from them about their child's experiences at school. For example, if a child is feeling lonely or intimidated in the classroom setting, we need to know so we can be of assistance in changing the situation. Conversely, if a child is happy and thriving in your classroom, receiving that positive feedback and noting specifically what is contributing to that nurturing learning environment is advantageous. Being able to offer specific feedback in a constructive manner is a valuable skill and can be used to encourage positive behaviors as well as to discourage negative actions and attitudes. The use of constructive feedback, both complimentary and confronting, if done in a genuine and caring way, can help build trust between the teacher and the family. Examples of feedback messages are as follows:

Teacher to parent: *When Greg pays attention in class, and continues to turn in his work, I am encouraged by his change in attitude and it makes me want to congratulate him. (Example of complimentary feedback)*

Teacher to parent: *Mr. Washington, when Sherry failed to show up for the extra tutoring time we had set up after school, I felt ineffective as a teacher, and it made me want to figure out another strategy to get her here. (Example of confrontive, constructive feedback)*

Family members and students can also be taught how to give and receive feedback. Also, as teachers, we must be willing to receive feedback and respond to it in a nondefensive, effective way:

Parent to teacher: *When Aaron leaves the house in the morning, he does not look forward to coming to school. He says he feels discouraged, school is not a friendly place, he doesn't do well on his reading tests, and he would rather be somewhere else. (Example of confrontive feedback)*

Parent to teacher: *When you praise Jackie and her group for their efforts on their science project, the kids feel happy and motivated to work together as a team, and we appreciate your encouragement. (Example of complimentary feedback)*

In the next section, we discuss some of the culturally based communication patterns that can make communication challenging between families and educators.

Communicating Across Cultures

Communicating with students' families is made more complicated by differences in cultural background between teachers and caregivers. These differences are often difficult to evaluate because you may not notice them or recognize that accurate communication has not taken place. For example, cultural patterns often dictate such nonverbal behaviors as the appropriate distance between two persons, the meaning of eye contact, the appropriateness of touch and respectful postures. Cultures may also dictate the structure of verbal exchanges, such as who should initiate conversation, whether interruption is acceptable, the expected time between a question and its answer, and whether and how to bring up problems. If these conversational rhythms are not automatically shared or communicated, participants may feel uncomfortable or alienated but not understand the source of their discomfort (Swap 1993).

Hence, teachers who are able to interpret the verbal and nonverbal communication patterns of parents from diverse cultural backgrounds will be more effective in communicating with them. One way of understanding such communication patterns is to think of communication within the framework of the individualistic or collectivistic value orientations that we discussed in Chapter 6. As a result of research on cross-cultural communication patterns, Ting-Toomey (1999) distinguished between two broad groups that differed in their cultural norms, beliefs, knowledge, and communication patterns. Groups oriented toward individualistic values are characterized by low-context communication patterns, whereas collectivistic-oriented groups lean toward high-context communication. Much less is left to shared assumptions about beliefs, values, and norms within a low-context communication framework. Instead, meaning is expressed through explicit verbal messages. A preference for direct talk, verbal self-enhancement, talkativeness, and person-oriented verbal interaction (i.e., emphasis on unique personal identities, with less attention to formalities and roles or status of those communicating) predominates in low-context communication where individualistic values are the norm. Additionally, speakers are expected to express clear verbal messages.

In contrast, nonverbal communication (e.g., pauses, silences) plays a much larger role in meaning making within a high-context communication framework, as do the respective roles and positions of the communicators during the communication episodes. For example, within high-context communication episodes, the listener is expected to interpret the meaning of the message from what is said as well as what is not said directly. The assumption is that the listener shares the values, norms, and beliefs of the speaker, so the speaker does not have to encode everything in the message itself. Speakers can get by with this because high-context cultures tend to have very clear expectations about how people should behave, what roles they should take, and the meaning of various social rituals. Hence, they do not need to explain everything to each other. As a result, in high-context communication situations in which collectivistic values predominate, a preference often exists for indirect talk, silence, and status-oriented verbal interaction (i.e., status or power associated with individual's roles are important with appropriate languages and nonverbal cues given the respective status of those who are in communication).

Of course, these opposing communication patterns really exist along a continuum of communication preferences, with individuals from both value orientations incorporating some of each (Ting-Toomey 1999). As a result, we believe that becoming alert to such possible communication differences is a part of careful listening by educators. If an educator's background has not included the study of the cultures and communication patterns of the students in his or her classroom and school and their families, then that educator needs to learn more about these patterns either on their own in conjunction with other staff members through reading, consultation, and direct experience with students' families.

In the next section, we describe some practical routines that you can develop to assist you in getting acquainted with the families of your students and in maintaining communication with them once you have established your initial relationship. These ideas are ones that we have tried out, modified when needed, and have been successful for us in our work with families. The routines we present take into consideration the school culture and climate. Having a framework from which to develop relationships and activities helps us become continually mindful of the specific population of families and helps us figure out how best to communicate with them. We encourage you to try out these strategies and adapt them to personally fit you and your students' families.

Everyday Routines for Getting Acquainted with Students' Families

~~~~~~~~~~~
~~~~~~~~~~~

As discussed in previous chapters, family members who have had negative experiences with schools or other institutions and agencies may be reluctant to come to school or communicate with the school staff. They may be wary of school staff and uncomfortable within the school environment (Finders & Lewis 1994; Lott 2001). At the same time, they are often willing, but unsure, of how to be a part of their child's education. Often, it will be up to you as a teacher and a representative of the school, to show family members that you desire to interact with them and that you value their contributions. Rather than crossing your fingers and hoping that families will initiate contact with you, it will benefit you to take the first step and reach out to make a connection with each student's family. Frequently, when discussing the importance of building a collaborative relationship with families, teachers often express that they have the desire to build these relationships but lack the time. The next section describes a way to redesign existing school activities and routines so that they send the message that you wish to get acquainted with students' families.

Rather than add new activities, we encourage you to think about how you might redesign existing school activities based on the approach proposed by Weiss and Edwards (1992) in Chapter 3 of this book. If you recall, Weiss and Edwards adapted Taguiri's four aspects of the social climate of an organization to serve as a guide for designing group family–school activities. These four aspects of the social climate of an organization are its *culture, milieu, social systems,* and *ecology.* Table 8.1 provides definitions and examples of these aspects of the social climate.

Table 8.1   *Weiss and Edwards' (1992) Aspects of School Climate*

	Culture	Milieu	Social System	Ecology
Definition	The belief systems, values, general cognitive structure, and meanings characterizing the school	The characteristics of persons and groups involved with the school	The patterned ways in which school staff, family members, and students relate with one another	The physical and material aspects of the school
Examples	Beliefs on how children learn, the value of education, and theories on children's problems and how to solve them	Racial and ethnic backgrounds, level of education, socioeconomic status, and level of achievement	Hierarchical, collaborative, adversarial, allied, task-focused, and emotionally focused	Design and condition of school building, quality and amount of educational materials, and tone of letters and messages

In this chapter we will use Weiss and Edward's (1992) framework to guide us as we design or redesign specific family–school activities to get acquainted with students' families. You can also use this framework to determine whether your attempts to communicate with families are sending the messages that you intend.

Welcome Letters

Sending letters home is a convenient and popular method used by teachers to communicate with families. A "welcome" letter sent to families at the beginning of the school year can be an effective way to begin to establish a connection with students and their families. Welcome letters can be sent just before the school year begins, or during the first few days of school. However, often letters have been used as a one-way communication vehicle. In addition to using letters to *give* information to families, letters home can be used to *receive* useful information from families.

When writing a letter to send home, especially when it is the first letter you send, considering how it may be received is worthwhile. Remember that a letter sent home at the beginning of the school year sets the tone for your future interactions with families. How do you ensure that it has the desired effect? What is the message you are trying to send, and is it clearly conveyed? Considering factors such as the appearance of the letter, the language used, and the message sent can go a long way in helping you create an effective and inviting letter.

Appearance

Families are often flooded with paperwork during the first few weeks of school. Thus, it is important to think about what you can do to set your letter apart from the others. Consider using colored or patterned paper, or pictures or graphics to make your letter enticing. Sometimes it may be beneficial (or even required) to write letters on your school's letterhead. However, letters received by families on formal or official school stationary may elicit unpleasant feelings, especially for families who have had negative school experiences in the past.

The length of your welcome letter is also an important consideration. It may be best to keep your letter brief; no more than one page. You can always give more detailed information about events, requirements, and assignments at a later time. If your first letter is long and includes several details, families may just scan it rather than read it thoroughly.

Language

As you begin to write your letter, think about the characteristics of the families with whom you will be working. This will help guide you to select the type of information that might be important to include in the letter. For example, a kindergarten teacher may include more information about school routines, the daily schedule, or what to expect during the first few weeks of school—issues that many families may understand more clearly by the time students reach fourth or fifth grade. A teacher who has learned that many of the students come from families with a low literacy level will want to write a letter using less complex language than a teacher who has learned that the majority of the students come from families in which the caregivers hold college degrees.

Try to consider how the language you use may be received by families. Even seemingly minor details, such as the greeting, can influence whether some families feel included or excluded. For example, beginning a letter with the traditional greeting "Dear Parent(s)," subtly excludes families that are headed by other adults, such as grandparents, aunts, or uncles. A greeting such as "Dear Caregiver" or "Dear Family" may be more inclusive.

Try to use clear and simple language to convey your ideas. Consider that your students' families will, in all likelihood, come from a variety of educational and cultural backgrounds. Also remember that, for some families, English is not their native language. If you are aware of a family who is not yet proficient in English, or if you work in an area in which several of your students use English as a second language, it may be beneficial to have your letter translated into their primary language. Not only does this help ease their understanding of the information that you are providing, but also it shows that you are aware of, and appreciate, their particular cultural background.

Avoid using jargon or acronyms without taking the time to explain what they are, because many family members may not be familiar with terms educators take for granted which can create, or reinforce, communication barriers that exist between schools and families.

Style of Relating

The information you choose to include (and not to include) in your welcome letter also contributes to the connection that you are trying to build with families. The welcome letter is an opportunity for you to give families information about and a sense of your teaching style, your priorities, and your desire for family involvement. Think about how you want to structure your relationship with families. Do you want a hierarchical (teacher as expert) relationship or a collaborative partnership? Be sure that the message you send in your letter and your priorities and goals that you have established for your classroom match up. For example, writing that you welcome families in your classroom and value their input, and then stating that families are not to be on campus during school hours sends a mixed message; the first part indicates that you desire a partnership with families, whereas the second part sounds more authoritative and hierarchical.

Additionally, consider the *tone* of your letter. It may be tempting to make your letter sound formal, but it can be challenging to make a formal letter sound enthusiastic and welcoming to families. Often, formal letters send the message that the school is a powerful institution, and that those who work for the school are in control. A letter written in an informal tone, on the other hand, can convey a desire for a partnership or equal relationship between the teacher and the family. For example, although some teachers may feel the need to include extensive information on their education, preparation, and credentials in their welcome letter, such information may be intimidating for some families. They may sense that you are establishing yourself as an "expert" with the expectation that they will follow your advice and direction, rather than share a collaborative relationship with them. This example reiterates the value and importance of learning the characteristics of your students' families so that you can provide the most helpful information and foster the type of relationship you desire with them.

In keeping with the idea that the welcome letter should convey your desire for family involvement, your welcome letter is probably not the best place to make many requests of families before you know much about their particular situation and resources. Together with the language you use, the message you send influences whether families feel included or excluded. If your first letter home is filled with requests for supplies or time commitments, families with limited resources may get the feeling that they are going to be excluded or asked for more than they can provide. You can create other opportunities for these requests to be made at a later time.

In your welcome letter, include information on how you plan to maintain communication with families throughout the school year. Will you be calling home? Sending a class newsletter? Using a school–home notebook or journal? What will be your next step? When and how should they plan to hear from you next?

Additionally, let families know how they can contact you, and keep in mind that not all families have the opportunity to call or visit during school hours.

Although creating your first welcome letter may take thought and time for beginning teachers, remember that once you have successfully created the first letter, you can save and modify it as needed in future years. Ultimately, the time and effort you put into developing methods for communication with families will pay off for you, your students, and their families. In Table 8.2 you will find a brief summary of the important qualities to attend to when writing a welcome letter to families.

Now let us take these key concepts and apply them by looking at two different examples of welcome letters in Reflective Exercise 8.1a and 8.1b.

Table 8.2   Key Aspects to Consider When Creating a Welcome Letter

Milieu	Social System	Ecology
Consider what you know about the characteristics of the families. What information would be the most useful for them?	Consider the kind of relationship you want to establish with families and make sure that your words convey that.	Consider what you can do to set your letter apart from all of the other forms sent home by the school.
Use clear and simple language. Avoid using jargon and acronyms.	Notice the tone of your letter—is it formal or informal?	Keep your letter brief—no more than one page.
	Avoid making too many requests from families before knowing what resources they have.	
	Include information on how you plan to maintain communication throughout the year.	

Reflective Exercise 8.1a

Example 1 Welcome Letter

Imagine that you are the parent of an elementary school child. The new school year has begun, and you receive the following letter from your child's teacher:

To the parent(s) of _____:

Hello and welcome to the new school year! As your child's teacher, I just wanted to take this opportunity to introduce myself and review some of the policies we have in place to make this year successful. Please be aware that your child should be in the classroom by 8:00 A.M., otherwise he or she will be considered tardy. If your child is late, he or she should obtain a pass from the front office before coming to my classroom.

We have an upcoming field trip planned! Our class will be going to the Science and Industry Museum next month. The cost of the field trip is $12.00 per child which will cover transportation, admittance, and lunch. Please be sure to have your child bring in money by this Friday, otherwise he or she will not be allowed to attend.

Finally, I know that many of you may want to speak with me regarding your children and specific concerns you may have. Please schedule an appointment with me, as I am not able to answer your questions if you come to my classroom in the morning. My planning time is from 10:20 to 11:30 on school days, and I am usually available during that time.

I am looking forward to getting to know you and your children. Let's work together to make this a great year!

Sincerely,

Ms. Jones

What is your reaction after reading this letter? What is the tone? Based on the information provided in the letter, how do you think this teacher believes the family–teacher roles should be structured? What paradigm might she be working from?

Reflective Exercise 8.1b

Example 2 Welcome Letter

Compare the first letter with the following one, written by a teacher working from a collaborative paradigm of family involvement:

Dear Families,

Hello and welcome to the new school year! My name is Kelly Jones, and I have the privilege of having your children in my class this year. I would like to take this opportunity to let you know that I value your involvement in your children's education. As you are your children's first teachers, I look forward to learning more about your families as the school year progresses.

I have many exciting things planned for the class this year! Next month we will be going on a field trip to the Science and Industry Museum. Also, during the year, we will be planning a class garden, taking a trip to the Recycling Plant, and preparing for Student-Led Conferences. I will send you more information about these activities in the next few weeks.

Our first event will be Back-to-School Night on September 15 at 6 P.M. Plan on having your children attend, too, as they have an important role! This will be an opportunity for all of us—students, families, and teachers—to share our hopes and goals for the year. There will be child care provided (if you need it for your other children) by some of the high school students. I realize that it may be difficult for some of you to make it to the school at that time due to work or other commitments, so if you are not able to attend I will contact you by phone or letter just to check in with you.

I like to use several ways to keep in touch with families, including newsletters, phone calls, e-mails, and meetings. I will be sending notebooks home with personal messages and reminders at least once a week. Please also feel welcome to contact me with any concerns or questions you may have. My phone number is 222–2222, and there is a voicemail box where you can leave a message at any time. For those of you who have access to the Internet, my e-mail address is kjones@school.edu. You can also contact me to set up an appointment; we can look at our schedules and arrange a time that works for both of us.

Again, I am looking forward to getting to know you and to work with you and your children!

Sincerely,

Kelly Jones

- How are the two welcome letters different with regard to *culture* (the teachers' beliefs)? With regard to *milieu* (the teachers' assumptions about their audiences)? With regard to *social systems* (the teachers' beliefs about how roles are to be structured)? With regard to *ecology* (the tone and language of the letters)?
- What is different about the second letter? How is a feeling of family–school collaboration conveyed?
- What changes might you make to the first letter? What changes might you make to the second letter?

Phone Calls to Families

For many teachers and families, the telephone is an excellent way to maintain ongoing communication and regular contact. Under the separation or remediation paradigms, however, phone calls to caregivers were made when only "bad news" was to be reported. For example, in these paradigms teachers called only when they wanted to report problems with a student's attendance, grades, or behavior. As a result, some families may be wary when you try to reach them by phone. When reaching out to

∿∿∿∿∿∿∿∿∿∿∿∿∿∿∿∿∿∿∿∿∿∿∿∿∿∿∿∿∿∿∿∿∿∿∿∿∿∿

Table 8.3   Key Aspects to Consider When Calling Families

Culture	Milieu	Social System
Consider your beliefs about family communication and involvement.	Consider what you know about the characteristics of the families.	Consider the kind of relationship you want to establish with families and make sure that your words convey that.
Do you believe that families should be called only when a problem arises?	Do they have a phone at home?	When you call, are you just relaying information (one-way, hierarchical), or are you actively involving the family in the conversation (two-way, parallel)?
Or do you believe families should be called for both good and bad news?	What are the family's routines?	How are you inviting the family members to share their perspective?
	What time of day would be a good time to call?	

establish connections with families, remember that you can use the phone to relay positive news: perhaps something the student did well that week, or information on upcoming class events. Using the Weiss and Edwards (1992) framework, this differing purpose for communication of helping establish a partnership rather than just calling when a problem exists depicts a collaborative school *culture*. Consider it an opportunity to build your foundation for future communication with the family. Table 8.3 depicts key aspects to consider when telephoning families.

Using Technology

Educators are using a variety of technological options to communicate with families: (a) the Internet, (b) videotapes, and (c) audiotapes. The Internet offers a growing number of ways to communicate with families. As a result, many schools now provide each of their teachers with a computer and Internet access. Educators may create group e-mail messages to students' families to quickly notify them of upcoming events or to survey them for input on a variety of topics. Some educators may also create Web sites where students and their families can get information about assignments and classroom or school policies and events. Although many caregivers appreciate the opportunity to communicate via e-mail, and an e-mail bulletin board system for all families or a restricted e-mail system for each family may be quite effective, many families have neither the access nor skills for communicating via e-mail. For example, a recent survey reported that only 63 percent of adults in the United States have a computer with e-mail or Internet access (Madden 2000). Hence, it will be necessary for you to consider whether you wish to communicate with families without computers or Internet access and to provide more traditional ways to send out information, and/or to convey information to them about sources in your community (such as the public library) where they might gain Internet access.

E-mail messages serve many of the same purposes as other forms of written communication. In addition, e-mail messages can be distributed to family members at home or at work. One middle school in Florida e-mailed parents an initial summary of the semester assignments for each course and a weekly update of assignments and due dates (P. K. Yonge 2007). One hazard of using e-mail to communicate with families or other professionals is that your e-mail message to them may be read by an unintended audience. Hence, you need to communicate confidential information using more secure communication methods. A second hazard of using e-mail is that we have noticed that some individuals do not think about how their message will impact their intended audience as deliberately as when they are writing a letter or making a phone call.

Web sites are also becoming an increasingly popular way for educators to communicate with families. Web sites provide a location on the Internet for family members to visit, to access information, and, in some cases, to communicate with each other. Web sites can be used by family members or others to raise questions, share ideas, plan classroom activities, learn about school activities, express their concerns, ask questions, or organize their own meetings or activities (Beghetto 2001). Web sites can also provide links to information to address specific child-rearing issues or to describe recommended practices with children who have specific needs.

Videotapes are a second technological medium for communicating with students' caregivers. Videos of children's behavior or of classroom activities can give caregivers an understanding of how a child is functioning socially in the classroom, with whom they are interacting, or what level of social skills they have developed. A study of video use with families of students in three early childhood classrooms found that both caregivers and teachers benefited from this means of communication (Hundt 2002).

Videotapes can also be used to picture a child's progress or to illustrate classroom instructional activities. Because they do not rely upon reading or writing, videotapes can be a particularly effective method for communicating to families with limited English proficiency or low literacy (Guidry, van den Pol, Keely & Nielsen 1996). In addition, videotapes allow families who cannot come into the classroom during the school day to learn what is going on.

Audio cassette recorders are a third technological tool for communicating with families. Audiotapes allow students, family members, and school staff to exchange information and ideas. Students and other family members can listen at home to recorded messages from friends or teachers and can find out what happened during the school day. Because they do not rely upon written communication, audiotapes can be a quick and inexpensive way to communicate with families.

Back-to-School Night/Open House

Most schools host some type of back-to-school night or open house at the beginning of each school year. Often these events involve meeting the teachers, followed by the teachers shouldering much of the direction for the evening, explaining their hopes and plans for the school year. This way of managing open house is consistent with the remediation paradigm of family involvement. Although this method may be informative for some families, members of the family do not usually have an opportunity to actively participate in the event and share their knowledge of their students. In fact, at times family members are discouraged from making any personal contact with the teacher and instead asked to schedule a meeting at a later time if they have questions or information to share. In many cases, students do not attend the open house, and if they do happen to be there, they do not actively participate in the event.

Often individual teachers do not have control over the scheduling of the date and time of back-to-school night or open house. Additionally, the length of time parents are expected to spend in their students' classrooms may be organized for them. Yet the possibility still exists to redesign your open house meeting format so as to create an event that is more meaningful and collaborative.

What might an open house look like when working from a collaborative paradigm? Weiss and Edwards (1992) provide a brief example of an activity that could be included in collaborative orientation programs: Parents and students could work together to create goals for the school year, take turns sharing their goals with the group, and then discuss their goals with the group. The teacher could work as the facilitator of the group discussion, asking open-ended questions and making sure all who want to share have the opportunity to do so. Then, the teacher can summarize the information shared by the students and caregivers and tie that in with his or her goals and plans for the class. See Table 8.4 for a comparison of a traditional or col-

Table 8.4   Comparison of Traditional and Collaborative Back-to-School Night Programs

	Separation/Remediation Paradigm	Collaborative Paradigm
Who is typically involved?	Teacher, caregivers	Teacher, caregivers, students
What kinds of activities are generally included?	Teacher-led presentation	Teacher introduces a meaningful activity that encourages active participation of all caregivers and students.
Who holds most of the control and responsibility for the program?	Teacher	Teacher, caregivers, and students share control and responsibility for the program.
How are caregivers and students involved in the program?	Passively (if at all); communication is one-way, caregivers and students listen to information presented by the teacher	Actively; communication is two-way, with caregivers and students sharing information with, as well as receiving information from, the teacher
How is seating arranged in the classroom?	In a manner that is conducive for a teacher-led presentation/ lecture—e.g., desks lined up in rows	In a manner that is conducive for teacher/caregiver/student interaction—e.g., desks in a circle or small clusters

laborative orientation. (Also, refer back to Reflective Exercise 2.1 in Chapter 2, to read a parent's description of and response to a collaborative fall orientation.)

When you create an open house experience under the collaborative paradigm, you send the message that you value family involvement. Additionally, it takes some pressure off of you as the teacher. Under either the separation or remediation paradigms of family–school relations, communication is one-way, with the teacher being responsible for telling the parents how the school year is going to go. Such an experience can be quite intimidating, especially for a novice teacher who may feel responsible for everything that is said and for answering all of the questions asked! Under the collaborative paradigm, ideas, plans, and goals can be established collectively, with the caregivers, students, and teachers formulating answers together. In this model, communication is two-way, with teachers sharing information with families and families sharing information with teachers. Table 8.5 depicts some key dimensions of the collaborative climate that you hope to convey in your orientation.

Table 8.5   *Aspects to Consider in Designing Back-to-School Night Programs*

Culture	Milieu	Social System	Ecology
Consider your beliefs about family communication and involvement.	Consider what you know about the characteristics of families.	Consider the kind of relationship you want to establish with families.	Consider how to set up your classroom and how this encourages or discourages partnerships with families.
	What kinds of activities would be meaningful for families?	What kinds of interactions with families do you want to have at Back-to-School Night?	What kinds of pictures, posters, and work are displayed on your classroom walls?
	What kinds of activities would allow families to share their perspectives and funds of knowledge?	How do you see your role?	Is this work inclusive of all students in your classroom?
		Will you be the leader of the night? Will you be a guide-on-the-side? Will you be a member of the team? Will you be doing most of the talking?	What are the seating arrangements in your classroom?
		How will family participation and sharing be encouraged?	Are the chairs in rows facing the teacher's desk (set up for one-way communication), in a circle (promoting large group interaction), or in clusters (small group interaction)?

Now, let us take the key points and considerations depicted in Table 8.5 on page 223 and evaluate two different back-to-school night scenarios in the Case Study 8.1. Swap (1993) provides additional suggestions to help make such large group events with families more successful. These suggestions include using strategies for reaching parents, using strategies for making attendance easier, and planning events carefully to promote informal communication.

CASE STUDY 8.1

Varying Characteristics of Two Back-to-School Night Programs

Read the following scenarios describing two different Back-to-School Night programs, and think about what your expectations and feelings might be as a caregiver of an elementary school child.

Scenario One

Since the children would not be participating in Back-to-School Night, I had to drop them off at my mother's house after work. I drove to my son Matthew's elementary school for the Back-to-School Night program. I parked my car, and as I approached the school I consulted the school map that was placed outside to find Matthew's 2nd grade classroom. I had hoped to make it to the school a bit early so that I could talk with Matthew's teacher, Ms. Jones, for a moment about Matthew's performance in math. When I arrived at the classroom, I noticed that the walls were neatly decorated with the students' classwork. Before I had a chance to find Matthew's work, Ms. Jones introduced herself to me and asked me to have a seat at Matthew's desk. Once all of the parents were seated, Ms. Jones welcomed us to her classroom and began her presentation. Ms. Jones briefly described her education and training, her classroom rules, and her hopes and goals for the school year. She also described how she would be helping to prepare our children for the annual standardized tests required by the state. Ms. Jones talked about the curriculum and books she would be using this year, and the field trips she was planning. She had arranged each child's textbooks on their desks so we could scan through them as she talked. She also shared some photographs of various activities that her students participated in last year. Ms. Jones concluded her 25-minute presentation by thanking us all for attending and providing us with a handout of "helpful hints"—suggestions for activities we could do at home with our children to help supplement what they will be learning in the classroom. I tried to catch Ms. Jones to speak with her about Matthew, but I could see that other parents had the same idea. Ms. Jones explained to the parents that she was not able to talk with us individually about our children tonight, but that she would try to set up individual appointments with us if we contacted her. I decided to wait for my weekly work schedule to come out before trying to set up a time to meet with her.

Scenario Two

I arrived at the school for Back-to-School Night with my son Alan and his younger brother and sister. Although in previous years the students were not invited to Back-to-School Night, Alan's current teacher, Ms. Stevens, encouraged the students to attend. Ms. Stevens also let us know that food would be provided (especially nice since I had to leave straight from work to get to the school on time) and that high school student volunteers would be available to provide child care for Alan's younger siblings. I parked the car, and the children and I approached the school. Older elementary school students and some parents were on hand as guides, and they first escorted me and the children to the child care station and then to Alan's 2nd grade classroom. One of the first things I noticed when I walked into the classroom was the photographs of each student's family on the walls. Alan showed me the pictures of our family and led me to his desk. Ms. Stevens introduced herself and then told us that Back-to-School Night was going to look a little different from what many of us parents were used to seeing. First, Ms. Stevens had us move our chairs so that we were all seated in a big circle. Then she had each of us (parents and students) think of one word that came to mind when we thought of school. My word was learning, and Alan's word was recess! Ms. Stevens had a "go around" where she asked us each to introduce ourselves and share our words. Next, Ms. Stevens told us that she found it to be very useful to begin the year by hearing what our goals were (both students' and parents') for the school year; that way, she could figure out what she could do as the classroom teacher to work toward them. Ms. Stevens gave us a few minutes to work together, and (following a short outline provided by Ms. Stevens) Alan and I talked about his goals for the school year, my goals for Alan for the school year, and what both of us could do to help Alan reach those goals. After talking with Alan, I was surprised to learn that he wanted to improve in reading. Then Ms. Stevens began another "go around" where each of us shared our goals and plans. As we shared, Ms. Stevens wrote down our key words and ideas on the board. After we all had the opportunity to share, Ms. Stevens looked over our list and began to talk about ways that she could help us reach those goals. For example, one parent said that he wanted his son to learn study skills this year; Ms. Stevens explained the different strategies she would be using to help students improve their planning and study habits. I noticed that Ms. Stevens made a point to hear from each of the parents and students and tried to address all of the key points and ideas shared. After this group discussion, the scheduled time for Back-to-School Night was almost over. Ms. Stevens thanked everyone for attending, and then she said that she would be available for the next 30 minutes to talk to families. She invited us to stay, eat, and mingle if we were able to do so. I had a chance to meet some of the families of the friends Alan had spoken about.

Questions to Consider

■ How are the two Back-to-School Night programs different with regard to *culture?* With regard to *milieu?* With regard to *social systems?* With regard to *ecology?*
■ If you were a parent, which Back-to-School Night program would you prefer to attend? Why?
■ What other kinds of activities or tasks could you use in planning a collaborative Back-to-School Night program?
■ As a future teacher, how do you envision your ideal Back-to-School Night program?

Swap's strategies for reaching parents include providing advanced notice (two to four weeks) for events, preparing personal invitations, and scheduling some events outside of regular school hours. We have found that invitations created by students are received positively by their families. To make attendance easier for parents, Swap suggests assisting with transportation and child care needs and providing food. Although some may feel that offering food to families serves as a "bribe" to get them to attend various events, providing food is a practical way to make attendance easier for families—especially if caregivers must come to the school directly from work or other commitments. Additionally, food can serve as a point of connection between families and school staff. Gathering over food can make the atmosphere less formal and more welcoming.

Swap also offers suggestions regarding the ecology of the events. She encourages planning events carefully to promote informal communication by giving consideration to seating arrangements and activities. For example, Swap suggests having teachers and parents sit at tables together during a potluck dinner, rather than a more typical tendency to migrate toward "staff" and "parent" tables. Swap also suggests designing activities that encourage parents and teachers to interact informally or programs that ask for parents' and teachers' contributions. Although the interactions may appear rather informal, they are still meaningful in that they help build a positive relationship between school staff and families. We have found that any program or event that also features student and staff "performances" draws many family participants.

Family–School Conferences

In addition to open house, many schools require some type of parent–teacher conference at least once during the school year. Often a conference is a time for families and teachers to briefly meet (sometimes for the first time) and discuss students' progress in school. Again, often teachers are the ones who feel responsible for carrying the conferences, making sure that they have gathered all of the necessary student information to report to the families. This information may include scores, grades, and some work samples. Students do not generally attend these meetings. Although this type of parent–teacher meeting may be adequate for some families, other families may leave these brief interactions with unexpressed questions, feelings, and concerns. They may not have a clear understanding of what their student is learning and how their student is performing, especially because the student is not present to share his or her perspectives.

A more collaborative alternative to this traditional conference format is the student-led conference. This conference is an opportunity for families to develop a richer, more meaningful picture of what their children are learning at school, and, at the same time, this arrangement is an opportunity for students to actively participate and take ownership for their work. Student-led conferences are described in detail in Chapter 10.

Problem-Solving Meetings

At times, some of your students may experience difficulties at school, and it may be appropriate to arrange a meeting with family members to discuss how to help them. Such a meeting can be anxiety-provoking, especially for novice teachers, and especially if there has not been ongoing communication with family members regarding their child's progress. A collaborative approach to conducting such meetings is described in Chapter 11.

Family Visits

One way to get to know the families of the students in your classroom is to conduct visits to their home. Such a visit can serve multiple purposes: (a) It can help build rapport with the family; (b) it can help you as a teacher learn about the student's personal characteristics from the family's perspective (e.g., the student's strengths, resources, areas of concern, and interests); and (c) it can help you learn about the family's worldview and their funds of knowledge. This, in turn, can help you better contextualize instruction for the student, bridging the gap that often exists between home and school learning.

Kyle, McIntyre, Miller, and Moore (2002) promote the use of family visits as a way to get to know and to learn valuable information from families. They prefer to call their visits *family visits,* rather than *home visits.* The latter term has a negative connotation to some, because it has been used by different agencies, such as the Department of Children and Families. According to Kyle et al.:

We call our visits "family visits" instead of "home visits" to differentiate from traditional visits conducted because professionals believed something was wrong in the home. They visited homes to check them out or "fix" problems. Instead, we believe that our families hold information that could *help us improve what we do in school*. (62)

The practice of home visits seems fitting when working from the remediation paradigm, in which the purpose of the visit is for the teacher to take an "expert" role, figure out the deficits at home, and give strategies to improve them. On the other hand, the idea of the family visit is consistent with the goals of the collaboration paradigm. Kyle et al. (2002) provide the following recommendations when considering a family visit:

- Check your assumptions about what you expect to find.
- Keep an open mind before, during, and after the visit.
- Know that your own beliefs may be challenged.
- Go in with respect and appreciation that the family has opened their lives to you.
- View the parents/guardians as the experts on their children, home, and community.
- Go in with questions not answers. (62)

By visiting a family's home, teachers can work as ethnographers to discover information and better understand a family's culture. McIntyre, Rosebery, and Gonzalez (2001) provide several examples of teachers who work as ethnographers and utilize the information that they learned to create contextualized instruction for their students. Additionally, contextualized instruction is further discussed in the next chapter.

Some Practical Considerations

When introducing the idea of family visits to pre-service teachers, we sometimes receive mixed reactions. Some pre-service teachers express apprehension about the amount of time it would take to arrange interviews and visits with each family of the students in their classrooms. Time is a legitimate concern that can be managed in different ways. Although some teachers make the effort to participate in a family visit with each student's family at some point during the school year, it may be more realistic for you to choose a few families to interview/visit. You may decide to choose particular families to interview/visit because they are quite different than your own, because you feel that those students are the ones who would most benefit from a stronger family–school link, or because you feel you already have some rapport with the family.

Another concern often raised by pre-service teachers is that of safety. When first asked to conduct a caregiver interview and home visit, the pre-service teachers often express discomfort with the thought of going to the students' homes. This discomfort is often relieved, however, after the pre-service teacher actually participates in the interview/visit, and the pre-service teachers who make the effort to visit the families at their homes frequently find their experience more rewarding than those who meet with the caregivers elsewhere. Kyle, McIntyre, Miller, and Moore (2002) note that the teachers involved with their family visits often have less fear and develop feelings of safety and security in their students' neighborhoods with time and experience. Kyle et al. also point out that the attitude you go into the interview with can influence how you are received and how safe you feel, as a result. They state:

> We go into the communities seeking families' expertise on their children. If we went into the homes as the experts, as if we had "truth" to share, or went to teach parents how to be with their children, we certainly would not feel welcome. (68)

Being concerned about your safety is okay, and, certainly, some situations warrant it. At the same time, it will benefit you to really consider what is holding you back from wanting to visit a student's home—is it that the family is different from yours? Is it that they live in a neighborhood different from the one you grew up in? Distinguishing between legitimate safety concerns and unwarranted assumptions is important. As Kyle, McIntyre, Miller, and Moore (2002) note, concerns regarding personal safety are to be recognized but should not be used as a blanket excuse to avoid family visits.

If you have concerns regarding safety, you have other options. You may feel more comfortable visiting families with a partner. There may be someone in your school who has had more experience with family visits and who would be willing to go with you, such as another teacher, a school counselor, or a school social worker. Note one caveat: If the person from your school is someone who visits families for remediation or only when problems arise, this will likely influence the tone or perception of the interview/visit. Although you may be there out of genuine interest and a desire to learn from the family, the family may perceive the interaction differently. Although it is most ideal to conduct a caregiver interview in the family's home, there may be circumstances that prevent you from being able to do this. Perhaps you could conduct the interview at another location in the family's community.

A third concern sometimes raised by pre-service teachers is that caregivers may find the questions you ask to be too personal, especially those related to the caregivers' memories of growing up and past learning experiences. You can do several things to prevent the caregivers from feeling this way. One suggestion is to explain to the caregiver, before the interview begins, the reasons for asking these questions and how the information you obtain will help you in teaching his or her child. Another suggestion is to state at the beginning of the interview that the caregiver does not have to answer any questions that he or she does not want to answer. A third suggestion is to use your communication skills during the interview to assess verbal and nonverbal cues. If you feel that a particular question would not be helpful, you can choose not to use it. If you observe that the caregiver does not appear to feel comfortable discussing certain topics, you can steer the interview away from them. You may even find that once you ask a couple of initial questions, the interview may go in an entirely different direction that you anticipate. That is okay! The information you obtain will still be very valuable.

Summary

In this chapter we have presented a variety of skills and routines to help you begin to establish relationships with, and to learn from, the families of your students. Relationship and communication skills are explained, including (a) active listening; (b) paraphrasing, clarifying, and summarizing; (c) focusing on and reflecting feelings; (d) asking appropriate questions; and (e) using facilitative feedback. Building on these basic relationship and communication skills, we then discuss communication patterns that differ among individualistic and collectivist cultural groups. Everyday routines to establish relationships with families were then described, with an emphasis on redesigning traditional family–school routines to enhance family–school collaboration. These collaborative everyday routines include (a) welcome letters, (b) phone calls to the family, (c) back-to-school night, (d) family–school conferences, and (e) family visits. These skills and routines, when put into practice, can help teachers learn from families and create meaningful instruction to help bridge students' school and home environments.

Chapter 9

Using Families' Ways of Knowing to Enhance Teaching and Student Learning

Maria R. Coady

Learning Objectives

After reading this chapter, you will be able to:

- Describe the varying definitions of culture.
- Explain how mainstream cultural expectations of learning and schooling influence our assumptions about family–school roles and relationships.
- Describe the cultural ways of knowing of culturally and linguistically diverse (CLD) students and families and contrast these with the dominant ways of knowing found in mainstream educational setting.
- Describe the benefits of the multiliteracies paradigm.
- Explain how family and community funds of knowledge can be used to contextualize instruction.

> *Watching Susana read in Spanish is like unearthing a gem buried deep in the clay. With a little encouragement, she sparkles and shines as her tongue rolls across the rr's and voice floats effortlessly over tildes and accent marks. Susana begins to read Alma Flor Ada's story,* Me Llamo María Isabel/My Name is María Isabel, *which describes the experiences of a newly arrived Spanish-speaking girl at a school in the United States. The real life connections to María Isabel's situation engage Susana more deeply in the story. She gazes up at me, and with a slight nod of reassurance, continues to read with delight.*
>
> *Susana is a fourth grade girl who has recently arrived in the United States from the state of Chiapas, Mexico. She traveled on foot through the desert with her mother and younger brother for three days, crossing into the United States to be reunited with her father, a migrant farm worker with seven years' experience cutting tobacco, harvesting blueberries, and tending young plants at a plant nursery. Susana enrolled at Carey Elementary School, the district's English for Speakers of Other Languages (ESOL) center school, where she works with a specially trained teacher. She also receives educational support through the Migrant Education Program. Despite being able to read and write in Spanish, as a result of completing three years of schooling in Mexico, her linguistic and cultural resources are not tapped in any way to facilitate her learning or support her bilingual identity in this program.*

How might a teacher discover Susana's linguistic and cultural resources? What role might her family play in helping Susana's teacher discover and use these resources for learning in the classroom? In this chapter, I focus on recent language and literacy initiatives that challenge dominant or mainstream ideologies about what families *should* do and offer alternative ways of working with families. First, I consider the construct of culture and illustrate how assumptions about education and family partnerships traditionally manifest in the culture of U.S. schools. I then describe the cultural ways of knowing of culturally and linguistically diverse (CLD) students and families and contrast these with the dominant ways of knowing found in mainstream educational settings. Next, I examine alternative ways of conceptualizing literacy, with an emphasis on multiple literacies, and examine specific projects, initiatives, and practices that support CLD students and families, particularly those that foster the literacy development of linguistically diverse learners. Finally, I describe specific approaches to learning about and using the funds of knowledge of diverse families in educational settings.

Re-Examining Culture

Educators, anthropologists, and other social scientists who focus on the study of human behavior have long contemplated the concept of culture and its role in human society. Culture has been defined in numerous ways, although definitions of culture typically include reference to objects, values, and beliefs shared by members of a particular group. Geertz (1973), for example, defined culture this way:

> A historically transmitted pattern of meanings employed in symbols, a system of inherited conceptions expressed in symbolic form by means of which men [*sic*] communicate, perpetuate, and develop their knowledge about and attitudes towards life. (89)

Geertz's definition emphasizes meanings that are created as a result of shared human experiences and interactions. His definition underscores the social construction of culture by use of symbols. Symbols, according to Geertz, include uses of language, as well as other means of communication that have been transmitted down through generations. In contrast to Geertz's definition, Nieto (2004) defines culture as

> [t]he values; traditions; social and political relationships; and worldview created, shared, and transformed by a group of people bound together by a common history, geographic location, language, social class and/or religion. (436)

Nieto's definition also underscores the social construction of culture (meaning that humans build, negotiate, and transmit culture), but her definition emphasizes the context of culture as being embedded in social and personal relationships and taking place within a given context (historical, geographical, social, and religious). Most important, Nieto notes that culture is *transformed* by groups of people. In other words, she views culture not as static but rather as a dynamic, ever-changing web of shared understandings about the world and how it works.

Both definitions conceptualize culture as an "invisible web" of meanings and understandings rather than simply conceptualize culture as an array of static items or objects that can be experienced through the five senses. In fact, in these definitions culture is viewed as the lens through which we see and interpret the world. Yet it is difficult to recognize the influence of culture until we come into contact with a culture different from our own, especially one that challenges our beliefs, values, or worldview. Culture, then, is pervasive and shapes our actions and interactions in multiple ways. We may not all share a common definition of culture and may not fully understand the degree to which culture influences our actions and beliefs. However, when working with culturally and linguistically diverse families, confronting existing cultural assumptions and stereotypes to engage in mutually supportive partnerships is vital. By means of Reflective Exercise 9.1 on page 234 consider the differences in the two definitions of culture above and then create your own definition of culture.

Reflective Exercise 9.1

Defining Culture

Part A: In small groups, review the two definitions of culture presented above. Note three ways in which these definitions are alike, then identify three ways in which the definitions differ. Which definition do you prefer? Why?

Part B: Using the group's findings from Part A, write a new definition of culture based on your own personal experiences.

Influence of Culture in Educational Settings

Culture influences how we educate children and what we think of as education as the vignettes in Reflective Exercise 9.2 demonstrate. Different cultural groups have distinctly different ways of conceptualizing education and how children should be educated.

Reflective Exercise 9.2

Cultural Assumptions in Education

Consider the following vignettes. Identify what is "observable" culture in these settings, as well as what invisible values and beliefs inform these behaviors, actions, and contexts.

  A. In an office supply store, many parents and children are busy filling up their shopping carts with school supplies the night before the new school year begins.
  B. A third grade classroom is arranged with the desks in small groups of four to six students. In the corner of the room is a bright, thick rug alongside bookshelves filled with novels and other free reading materials. Two cozy chairs are also located in that corner.

What is "culture" in each vignette? In what ways is it visible and invisible? How does the setting and/or behavior reflect values and beliefs?

Thus, not all behaviors practiced in an educational setting are interpreted the same way across various cultural groups. For example, among certain Asian cultures, children are taught that looking teachers directly in the eye when being spoken to is a sign of disrespect (Bennett 2003). To do so would be interpreted as a sign of challenging a teacher's authority. In contrast, American students are taught to look teachers directly in the eye so as to indicate that they are paying attention and understanding what is being said. The gesture is also viewed as a sign of respect. These two different ways of understanding a student's behavior can have important impacts on the ways in which teachers relate to students in the classroom and on the ways in which students from diverse backgrounds learn and participate in school.

How would you define a *well-educated* person? In mainstream U.S. settings, we typically think of a well-educated person as someone who has had access to and successfully completed many years of education. We might associate being bright or intelligent with someone who is well educated, and this might include having high grades in school. In addition, we might think of that person as having access to economic success and social mobility.

In contrast, the concept of education is defined differently across and among other cultural groups. In her work with newcomer Latino families settling into the North Carolina region of the United States, Villenas (2002) described the significant conflict between Latino families and mainstream educators resulting from their differing conceptualizations of education. Latino parents were faced with negotiating the tensions of enacting *una buena educación* (a good education) for their children that included respect and good conduct against a perceived "morally lax U.S. society" (18). Villenas described how Latinos were often framed by educators in terms of deficits, specifically "what the parents didn't do, didn't have, or didn't care about" (21). Her work questioned the positioning of Latinos as needy clients and, instead, advocated for a "just vision of education that . . . requires the legitimate honoring of Latino parents' human agency" (31).

A study conducted by Coady (2001) investigated language policies and practices in bilingual (Irish Gaelic-English) schools in the Republic of Ireland. She also documented educators' expectations about how families should participate in their children's education and the actual ways in which parents participated. The study found that Irish parents were rarely present in schools during instruction times. In fact, participants in the study defined parental participation as acting on school committees outside of school hours. During school hours, parents could be present for events and activities (e.g., art and school assemblies) but were not permitted in the classroom when instruction or grading took place. These practices contrast with U.S. schools in which parents of children from middle-class backgrounds are frequently encouraged to work as volunteers in the classroom, to grade student work, and to assist the teacher in the classroom.

Taking a broader view, Hoover-Dempsey et al. (2001) investigated parental participation in children's homework by analyzing fifty-nine individual studies on parental participation in homework. Their findings showed that, in general, parental involvement reflected parents' expectations and beliefs about what they felt they should do to support the education of their children. Moreover, the researchers found that parents who helped their children "believed that their help positively influenced student outcomes" (201). In contrast, parents were less willing to engage in homework assistance when they did not view that help as beneficial to their children's learning.

These studies illuminate how varying expectations about the roles families should play in their children's schooling are constructed and reinforced by a particular cultural lens. Working with diverse families requires deconstructing dominant expectations and ideologies (i.e., what is valued and why) and recreating new relationships that reflect families' cultural and linguistic resources and ways of knowing.

Challenging Unidirectional, School–Family Relationships

Although families from culturally and linguistically diverse backgrounds may hold differing assumptions about the process of education and what their role is in their children's education, unearthing the cultural assumptions embedded in school–family communication is not easy. Often, communication and information that comes from schools to families is unidirectional, that is, flowing from one place (the school) to another place (the home). Moreover, interactions are frequently based on dominant, mainstream assumptions about what education is, what constitutes literacy, and what families should do to support the education of children. Unearthing those assumptions and challenging them requires reflection and insight into how relationships can be reconceptualized as working partnerships that are culturally and linguistically responsive and beneficial to children. Read the school letter depicted in Figure 9.1 and then identify, by means of Reflective Exercise 9.3, the cultural values and assumptions about parental participation held by the educators who wrote this letter.

Reflective Exercise 9.3

Educators' Cultural Assumptions about Parental Participation in Education

In local school districts, it is not uncommon for parents to receive information, materials, and suggestions about the ways in which families can support children's education. Consider the two documents below. The first document, in Figure 9.1, is a letter composed by educators at a local school and sent home to parents. It describes four Key Principles for Parents. Embedded in that document are many assumptions about what is important for parents to know and to do. The following questions might help your analysis of the mainstream.

A. What values and beliefs does the school make about parental participation?
B. What cultural assumptions are embedded in the four Key Principles for Parents?
C. What cultural values are associated with "winning" (i.e., gift certificates and/ or a pizza party)?
D. What implicit message does this letter send to parents from different cultural backgrounds? Different linguistic backgrounds?

In the previous activity, you probably identified the school's emphasis on competition (and using games to encourage participation) in the family letter. The letter describes how classrooms compete with each other, with the winner receiving a pizza party. This emphasis on competition contrasts with a collaborative approach that is often found among other cultural groups (Gudykunst & Kim 2003). A less competitive approach might seek to understand how the family environment and caregivers' experience can support learning in the home. Another assumption implicit in the letter is that the schools determine what is "successful" in terms of parenting and academic achievement. Implicit in this letter is the message that diverse definitions and approaches to success are not valued. (See Figure 9.1.)

Now look at the survey depicted as the Awesome Parent Report Card in Figure 9.2 on page 238. What mainstream assumptions about education, literacy, and learning are reflected in it?. By means of Reflective Exercise 9.4 on pages 238–239, identify the cultural values and assumptions about learning and education conveyed in this "report card."

~~~~~~

Figure 9.1   Letter to Parent: "A School for Every Child"

"A School for Every Child"

November 1

Dear Parent,

A part of our School Improvement Plan this year includes a Parent Involvement Component. We all know that parents are their child's "first teacher" and school is their child's "first job." We also know when parents are involved in their child's education, students are more successful.

At the beginning of the school year, we sent home a poster of the four Key Principles for Parents that would help the school assist your child in having a successful school year. The Key Principles focused on Academics, Social Development, Responsibility and School Communication.

Coming home today with your child's Report Card is the Parent Report Card. Please take a moment to rate yourself on the Four Key Principles. Then cut off the bottom portion of the self-assessment with your name and your child's name and return it to school. The tear off will then be placed in a drawing and the winning student will receive a $25.00 gift certificate to Toys R Us, and the winning parent will receive a $25.00 gift certificate to Publix Food Store. The teacher, whose class has the highest percentage of returned signatures, receives a pizza party.

We hope all of our parents will participate in this program as a way of helping your child be successful. Your continued support is always appreciated.

Sincerely,

~~~~~~

Figure 9.2   The Awesome Parent Report Card

The Awesome Parent Report Card
Please rate yourself the following way:
3 = Always   2 = Sometimes   1 = Seldom   0 = Never

Key Principle #1: Focus on Academics

_____ I read with my child several times each week and sign his/her agenda or folder.
_____ Our family has a library card and we use it at the public library.
_____ I check my child's bookbag nightly reviewing the papers and Agenda.
_____ My child has a consistent time and place to do homework and I ensure homework is completed.

Key Principle #2: Focus on Social Development

_____ I have conversations with my child regularly.
_____ I monitor and limit the amount of time my child spends watching television.
_____ I teach, expect, and reinforce appropriate manners, language and behaviors.

Key Principle #3: Focus on Responsibility

_____ I help my child maintain a daily routine (ex. certain time for dinner, homework, bath, reading, bedtime).
_____ I encourage my child to accept responsibility for his/her actions.
_____ I ensure that my child is in attendance and on time each day. When my child is sick, I notify the school.

Key Principle #4: Focus on School Communication

_____ I communicate with my child's teacher in person, on the phone, or through written communication.
_____ I attend PTA meetings, school events, School Improvement Meetings and/or parenting workshops.

_____ Total Score

Grade: 32–36 points =   A   Awesome
            25–31 points =   B   Better than Average
            16–24 points =   C   Climbing
            0–15 points =   D   Do Keep Trying

~~~~~~

Reflective Exercise 9.4

Educators' Cultural Expectations about Learning and School

The second document, Figure 9.2, is a parent self-administered survey that assesses the Key Principles mentioned in the letter depicted in Figure 9.1. The survey also reflects expectations about learning and school. The following questions can guide your reflection:

A. What are the underlying values and beliefs associated with the Awesome Parent Report Card?

B. Who do you think determines what an Awesome Parent is? Who benefits from that definition? How? Who does not benefit?

C. Imagine you are a newcomer parent from a non-mainstream-U.S. background. What implicit messages are sent in the survey? What assumptions does the school make about what good parents do and how one "assesses" good parents?

D. How can this document be modified to reflect more collaborative school–family partnerships?

For example, Principle 1, Focus on Academics, reflects specific home literacy practices (reading together at bedtime and signing the child's agenda) that may typically occur among many mainstream families but may be unusual among other groups. For example, among certain cultures, storytelling and oral communicative practices are the favored language development practices (Heath 1983). Parents who have had limited formal schooling or who do not speak English may feel uncomfortable attending PTA meetings or school events. Single-parent families may have many life demands that preclude them from attending. The household functioning of diverse, nonmainstream families contrasts with several of the assumptions delineated in this survey. Although well-intended, documents such as these may do more damage than good to CLD families. Indeed, it would not be difficult to imagine parents or families who judged themselves as "not performing well" in their role as parents or as "first educators" of their children after reading such a survey.

Moreover, students' home language and culture are frequently judged to be adequate only if they match the language and culture of the school (Cummins 2001). When communication from the school is unidirectional, and assumptions about education (and what makes parents "good" participants in education) are left unexamined, little chance exists to create genuine and positive partnerships with families that support their children's education. In other words, to create effective school–family partnerships, educators must begin with a genuine curiosity and willingness to learn about a student's home language and family and community culture using a nonjudgmental stance, and then they must use that knowledge as a bridge into teaching school concepts and skills.

Using Families' Funds of Knowledge to Support Learning

The work of Moll et al., described earlier in Chapters 1 and 3, is an example of a way in which home "knowledges" can be used as resources for learning and engaging children in school. I use the word *knowledges* in the plural here to underscore the multiple dimensions of knowledge and that no single, supreme knowledge exists. In his study, Moll et al. (1992) described students' home culture and identified their funds of knowledge or nonmainstream forms of knowledge that were used for home and family functioning and well-being. They defined *funds of knowledge* as "historically accumulated and culturally developed bodies of knowledge and skills essential for household or individual functioning and well-being" (133). Some of these skills include cooking, gardening, home construction, agriculture and mining, household management, folk medicines, and religious and moral knowledge.

In Moll's project, teachers and university researchers visited families to learn about the culture, knowledge, and skills that Latino families in the Southwest possessed. To identify families' funds of knowledge, Moll emphasized the importance of discovering the ways that the families operated and of appreciating their views, values, and beliefs. The primary method used to learn about families' funds of knowledge was through home visits. However, the intention of the home visits was not to bring families news about the problems encountered in school with their child; rather, home visits were meant to be places of discovery whereby teachers could learn about the skills and knowledge areas that families possess and the ways that families or households use these skills. Teachers then use this information to build classroom activities and curricular units around these skill and knowledge areas (McIntyre, Rosebery & González 2001; Moll & González 1993).

Moll and González (1993) noted three outcomes resulting from this project. First, teachers became skilled as qualitative researchers. Second, new relationships were formed with families. Third, students' households were redefined as containing deep social and intellectual resources that could be tapped into for teaching and learning purposes. The third outcome had implications for working with children in schools and forming partnerships with families in the community. Rather than viewing families' knowledge areas as deficits and barriers to learning, these knowledge areas were seen as resources for engaging children more fully in school learning.

The methods used by Moll et al. (1992) to understand families' ways of knowing underscore the importance of educators' efforts to understand the cultural background and ideologies of CLD students and to form partnerships with families that reflect and value their ways of knowing. In brief, Moll's work illuminates the ways in which home–school partnerships can work: as a two-way, symbiotic, or mutually beneficial partnership rather than a unidirectional, one-way relationship, in which the school asks students to leave their language, culture, and identity outside the school house door.

Expanding Notions of Literacy to Support Learning

One additional dimension of Moll's project was that teachers investigated the various languages and literacies used by families in the home. The participants in Moll's early study were Mexican and Yaqui families. Moll et al. (1992) discovered that alternative literacies, such as numeracy, were part of the cultural and linguistic resources of the family. Similarly, other researchers have worked to expand and redefine traditional notions of literacy. In 1996, a group of international educators and scholars examined notions of literacy in education. The group, which initially met in New London, New Hampshire, was aptly named The New London Group (1996). The group recognized that literacy practices in a global world needed to include both new technologies, multilingual abilities, and an appreciation of the alternative literacies practiced throughout the world. This meant moving beyond a narrowly defined construct of literacy to a more broadly defined conception of literacy.

Auerbach (1997) identified three distinct paradigms of family literacy that have evolved over the past twenty-five years. Moll's funds of knowledge project and other similar projects, including the work of Shockley, Michalove, and Allen (1995) reflect a "multiple literacies" paradigm (156). For example, Shockley, Michalove, and Allen sought to connect the home and school domains through the use of parent–teacher dialogue and home–school journals. In the multiple literacies paradigm, the starting point for literacy development is with students, and educators investigate the home language and cultural backgrounds of students to connect home literacies with school learning. Teachers assume that (a) every child is an individual with a wealth of cultural knowledge; (b) that by using that knowledge to contextualize instruction, students become more fully engaged in learning; and (c) that students' families and communities can help teachers learn about that cultural knowledge.

A second paradigm discussed by Auerbach is *intervention–prevention* (similar to the remediation paradigm discussed in Chapter 2). In this paradigm, families from culturally and linguistically diverse backgrounds are viewed as lacking sufficient literacy practices. As a result, some form of intervention or remediation is provided to bring CLD children "up to speed." Because parents are charged with being their children's first teachers, programs shaped by the intervention–prevention paradigm typically include parenting classes and other skills-based interventions that target parents as well as children. Many of the current government funded family literacy initiatives fall within this paradigm, such as the Parent and Child Together (PACT) program that sets specific guidelines for parent–child reading. Although well-intentioned, these projects are based on a deficit view of nonmainstream families (Auerbach 2001). This deficit view becomes more evident when educators begin to analyze and question basic school to home communications, such as the Awesome Parent Report Card and key principles presented earlier in the chapter.

The third paradigm proposed by Auerbach is that of *social transformation*. The purpose of the literacy projects in this paradigm is the resolution of societal inequities through teaching. These literacy projects are collaborative in that they do not proscribe skills or a unidirectional style of interaction from experts to learners. Auerbach (1997) cites McCaleb's (1994) work in which parents discuss critical themes, which are then used as a starting point for literacy with children. Additionally, Freirean approaches to literacy, originally designed to teach literacy to poor adult learners in Brazil and addressed societal inequities (Freire 1998), are illustrative of this paradigm.

Programs and Projects Using a Multiple Literacy Paradigm

The Multiliteracy Project

The work of Cummins et al. (2007) is one project that demonstrates the ways in which educators can work with multilingual children to engage them in cognitively challenging learning tasks in educational settings. Cummins, a university researcher, and his group sought to address two questions: (a) What forms of literacy should be used by teachers with multilingual children? (b) Which pedagogical options are most appropriate for use with multilingual children in urban educational settings? The Multiliteracy Project challenged three assumptions that characterize instruction in education throughout North America: (a) Literacy equates to English literacy; (b) the cultural knowledges and language abilities that students bring to school have little relevance; and (c) culturally and linguistically diverse parents lack the skills to assist their children in their literacy development.

The Multiliteracy Project not only challenged those assumptions, but also was conceptualized to discover alternative methods that could be used with CLD children in educational settings. One teacher in the project, Lisa Leoni, engaged her students in a writing project in which students integrated children's literature with academic content (in this case, social studies). Students then collaborated in small groups and created *dual language identity texts,* which were designed for younger children with whom they could later share the texts. As Cummins et al. (2007) reported, these texts became cognitively engaging and culturally reflective learning opportunities when

> Students invest their identities in the creation of these texts which can be written, spoken, visual, musical, dramatic, or combinations in multimodal form. The identity text then holds a mirror up to students in which their identities are reflected back in a positive light. When students share identity texts with multiple audiences (peers, teachers, parents, grandparents, sister classes, the media, etc.), they are likely to receive positive feedback and affirmation of self with these audiences. (6, 7)

A key outcome of this work was the interaction that was fostered between the children and the families. Children, whose selected works can be viewed at www.multiliteracies.ca, were able to connect home language and culture with school learning. Sulmana, a seventh grade Pakistani girl, noted:

> I had forgotten many of the words in the last three years so my vocabulary improved a lot too. I had to ask my Mom a lot of words when we were writing it in Urdu but also before that, when I realized that we were going to be writing

it in both languages, I went home from that day and started reading more books in Urdu because I hadn't been doing that so much, so I had forgotten some words and I wanted my writing to make sense. (Cummins et al. 2007, 16)

The Multiliteracy Project exemplifies what educators can do with children academically while using their home knowledges (language and culture) as a resource that connects CLD students to the curriculum.

The "Libros de Familia" (Family Books) Project

How can educators foster collaboration with families in ways that nurture children's cultural and linguistic identities and simultaneously enhance learning in the home? In the chapter's opening vignette, I presented Susana, a newcomer migrant farm-working child in Florida. In fact, Susana is one of fifty-one children who partici-pated in the *Libros de Familia,* or Family Books, project in 2005–2006. In this project, university student volunteers brought books into the homes of migrant families and engaged in reading with children (Coady 2007). The project was a collaborative effort between University of Florida, the Harvest of Hope Founda-tion, the Migrant Education Program, and the local library.

All of the children in the *Libros* project are Spanish-language-dominant, and most of the participants were recent arrivals to the United States. Although their situations were unique, these students were considered "migrant" under federal definitions, that is, they had parents who worked in agriculture and related indus-tries and moved across district lines more frequently than once every thirty-six months (Pappamihiel 2004). As we know, the migrant lifestyle brings unique chal-lenges to educators, students, and families. Migrant families face numerous and difficult social realities, including poverty, mobility, housing, transportation, health care, and, of course, education (Riley 2002).

Given the unique needs of migrant families, one of the objectives of the *Libros* project was to work with children and families in ways that were sensitive to the migrant lifestyle and that did not prescribe what families should do. We explic-itly rejected mainstream assumptions about what families should do to foster language and literacy. Instead, we recognized the multiple ways in which literacy was interwoven into the lives of the participants (Taylor 1983) and varied among different groups (Heath 1983). In addition, the project attempted to foster first language (Spanish) literacy use. Unlike what occurs frequently in mainstream educational settings, in which instruction is monolingual and reflects the dominant U.S. culture, in the *Libros* project, migrant children's language, culture, and life experiences informed the work and interactions of the participants. In short, the lives of the children were reflected in the pages of the books.

University student volunteers were grouped in pairs or small groups in which at least one member was Spanish–English bilingual and then matched with migrant families. Volunteers were introduced to families by the Migrant Education Program advocate. During weekly visits, the university volunteers brought bilingual and multicultural children's literature to the homes during fall and spring semesters. During the visits, volunteers engaged in reading with children, translated school documents, and assisted children with homework when requested. Volunteers left books behind for children to read during the week and returned the following week with new books. The volunteers were encouraged to identify the interests and knowledge areas of the children and were taught how to use these to engage children in reading.

One unanticipated outcome of the project was that many families engaged in reading the books together, a reflection of Barrera's (2005) finding that Latino families do enjoy and engage in reading. During the project, several of the families became engaged in reading. Ryan, a graduate student in ESOL and volunteer in the *Libros* project, described how one parent became engaged in reading and interacted with her daughter.

> By the third week we were able to speak to Rosa, the mother, about the books we had been leaving, and were delighted to hear that she hadn't known until recently that they were in Spanish and English but had begun to read each night with her daughter. Melissa had begun to put the books close to the door, next to other school supplies, and was constantly bugging her parents to read them to her. Rosa assumed they were only in English (as is most of the literature that Melissa brings home) but one night looked at them and saw that they were bilingual books that she could read to Melissa in Spanish. Not only did Rosa seem happy about this, but also Melissa. Even the father mentioned with a sly grin that he had been listening in on the readings. (Coady 2007)

Another volunteer, Matt, noted that the father of two children listened in on his children's reading and was especially intrigued by Joe Hayes' bilingual book, *A Spoon for Every Bite*. The father enjoyed the cleverness of the main character and the cultural message that the story imparted. In fact, the father asked if he could keep a copy of the book.

We also recognized that student learning could be enhanced when teachers also have information about families' cultural and linguistic resources. We arranged for several of the volunteers who were education majors to work with students in classrooms as tutors, aides, and researchers. Teachers in the ESOL center schools, where many of the migrant children were bused each day, were provided with some of the books used in the project so that they might keep them in the classroom. Several teachers subsequently made home visits to learn more about the children and communicated with us regarding upcoming events and information that could be conveyed to parents. From our side, we informed teachers of harvest season demands on families and what we learned about children's interests that could further engage the children in the classroom.

Future efforts in the *Libros* project include distributing transportable home libraries to children using donated reading materials; training tutors on reading strategies and post-reading activities with bilingual children; and working with families to promote reading in the home using culturally and linguistically appropriate materials. Given the life demands on migrant parents, we aim to work with parents in ways that support their children's learning.

Both the Multiliteracy Project and the *Libros de Familia* project revealed ways in which educators can engage CLD students in the classroom and at home. A key point of these projects was that students' linguistic and cultural resources can be used as starting points for learning. Additionally, students' identities were valued and promoted in both of these initiatives. Other projects have demonstrated how similar strategies work. For example, in the Kamehameha Early Education Program (KEEP), Hawaiian students' participation in school was enhanced when students were allowed to engage in "talk story" or turn-taking in story narration, a feature of Hawaiian storytelling. This structure differed from practices that favor a single narrator. The strategy encouraged collaboration among students and teacher and reflected a more appropriate and culturally relevant participation structure (Au & Jordan 1981).

Using Family and Community Funds of Knowledge to Contextualize Instruction

In recent years, educators have recognized that students' developing understanding of school concepts builds on two foundations: new academic material presented by the school and what students bring to academic topics in terms of everyday experience and knowledge. Drawing upon students' life experiences and knowledges and connecting, or contextualizing, them to the school will enhance student learning. As Tharp, Estrada, Dalton, and Yamamuchi (2000) suggest, "Contextualized instruction motivates students and builds on what the children already know, increasing the likelihood that the children will learn" (23).

As a result of this knowledge about how learning is most effective, educators have begun seeking out and including the contexts of students' experiences and their local communities and incorporating those into the curriculum and their instruction. Specifically, teachers are exploring ways of using culturally and linguistically diverse students' household-based funds of knowledge as resources or bridges for learning in school. Designing curriculum around compelling and practical problems provides opportunities for teachers alongside caregivers and students to work together in ways that have meaning at the personal, class, school, and community levels. In one example, Ayers, Fonseca, Andrade, and Civil (2001) described how a middle school math teacher discovered the mathematical funds of knowledge of Latino students in working-class neighborhoods and used them to develop an architecture project, called *Build Your Dream House*. The project engaged his students in a range of mathematical practices.

Three levels of contextualization have been described in the education literature. The first level is that of teaching, or pedagogical, strategy. This level recognizes that "effective instructional strategy invokes children's existing schema that has been developed in their own environment and experience and then relates it to the conceptual material being presented" (Tharp et al. 2000, 28). The second level is a curriculum level in which teachers use culturally relevant materials and skills to foster high degrees of literacy, numeracy, and science. That is, the curriculum is contextualized for CLD students such that it facilitates their learning. Tharp et al. note that "drawing on personal, community based experiences affords students opportunities to apply skills acquired in home and school contexts" (28). The work of González and Moll in studying the funds of knowledge in students' families and community is an excellent example of this form of contextualization.

Finally, a third level of contextualization, the policy level, has focused on contextualizing the school itself by recognizing that "school learning is a social process that affects and is affected by the entire community" (Tharp et al. 2000, 28). More long-lasting progress has been achieved with children whose learning has been explored, modified, and shaped in collaboration with their parents and communities. McCaleb's (1994) work, mentioned earlier, is an example of contextualizing schooling at the policy level through involvement of families.

The Center for Research on Education, Diversity, and Excellence (CREDE) delineated guidelines that educators can use in attempting to contextualize instruction for CLD students. A teacher who contextualizes instruction

- Begins activities with what students already know from home, community, and school
- Designs instructional activities that are meaningful to students in terms of local norms and knowledge
- Acquires knowledge of local norms and knowledge by talking to students, parents or family members, community members, and by reading pertinent documents
- Assists students to connect and apply their learning to home and community
- Plans jointly with students to design community-based learning activities
- Provides opportunities for parents or families to participate in classroom instructional activities
- Varies activities to include students' preference from collective and cooperative to individual and competitive learning activity formats
- Varies style of conversation and participation to include students' cultural preferences, such as co-narration, call-and-response, and choral, among others (CREDE 2006)

The projects presented in the chapter highlight several of the CREDE indicators for contextualizing instruction. For example, the Multiliteracy Project draws on what CLD students know, including home language and culture. Ms. Leoni, the students' teacher, utilizes dual language identity texts as an instructional activity that brings students' backgrounds and life experiences directly into the classroom; this activity facilitates her students' learning. The *Libros de Familia* project further demonstrates several CREDE indicators. The project brings together community organizations, educators, and university volunteers who engage in literacy development and reading with Spanish-speaking, migrant children in the home. The project draws on students' cultural and linguistic knowledges through the use of multicultural literature. As a collaborative effort, the project fosters mutual learning among the participants and bridges the home context with school learning.

How can educators begin to learn about families' funds of knowledge? First, teachers can be vigilant of students' apparent learning styles and participation in educational settings. Often, keen observation of students' engagement and participation in learning offers insight into home practices (González, Andrade & Carson 2001). In addition, teachers can carefully listen to and critically read students' writing. Coady and Escamilla (2005) describe how the writing of Spanish-speaking children about their life experiences demonstrates a sophisticated understanding of social realities and justice. What students write, therefore, reveals much about the lives of CLD children.

Educators can engage in a family interview of home funds of knowledge, adapting the work of Moll et al. (1992) to local settings. Gonzalez, Andrade, and Carson (2001) advocate a multidimensional approach to funds of knowledge research, including a neighborhood observation, educational sessions, and home interviews. The interviews themselves focus on labor histories, regular household activities, and parental views about their roles as caregivers.

Amatea (2007) has designed a family educational knowledge survey used to interview families and investigate funds of knowledge. She describes three phases of the interview: (a) learning about families' history and labor history; (b) learning about families' regular household activities; and (c) learning about the caregivers' views of parenting and their own school experiences. Reflective Exercise 9.5 depicts some questions that you may find useful when gathering information about these three areas during a family visit .

Reflective Exercise 9.5

Potential Questions to Use in a Family Visit

Questions to raise with parents or caregivers to gain information about the student:

- What strengths or positive qualities do you see in your child?
- Tell me a little bit about your family. Is this your only child or do you have other children? How old are they? What kinds of home responsibilities do you expect your child to complete?
- Tell me about your child's friendships. Who does he or she play with (i.e., socialize with) outside of school?
- What does your child say about school?

- What kinds of activities, at school or elsewhere, excite and interest your child? What does he or she like to play?
- What is your child's favorite subject or activity? Does he or she like to read? If so, what are his or her favorite books or stories?
- What kinds of activities, at school or elsewhere, seem to upset or frustrate your child? How does he or she react when upset?
- What kinds of skills or things would you like for your child to learn this year?
- What else would you like me to know about your child? Do you have any concerns about your child that you would like me to know?

Questions to gain information about the caregivers' learning experiences and expectations about family–school interactions:

- What are some of your earliest memories of learning in your own family growing up? How and what did the members of your family teach you?
- Who do you remember as a wise person in your family or community? What valuable knowledge did they possess? How did they share their knowledge with others?
- What are your earliest memories of school? Did school learning seem similar to or different from the kinds of learning you had participated in before in your family? How would you describe yourself as a student?
- What was your family's involvement in your school experience? How did the school expect parents to be involved in education? Looking back, do you think that was an appropriate expectation?
- What are some of the activities that you like to do together with your child?
- In what ways do you feel that you teach your children? What and how do they teach you? What important things do you feel are your responsibility to teach them?
- What do you feel your children learn from other members of your family? How do other members of your family teach your children?

Source: Amatea (2007) Workshop Handout. Gainesville, FL: University of Florida.

If, as a teacher, you have been able to implement the communication strategies covered in the previous chapter, you will be well on your way to establishing a connection with the families of students in your classroom. It will be important to have promoted two-way interaction with families before requesting to interview them or visit their home. If the proper foundation is not laid with your communication skills, and your philosophy on family involvement has not been appropriately conveyed, these requests may be seen as invasive by some families. Your interview/visit should be scheduled in advance, during a time that is convenient for both you and the family. It may be beneficial to send a couple of casual reminders to the family confirming the day and time, so that they will not be surprised by your visit.

Although you will not want your visit with a family to feel scripted or rehearsed, it may be worthwhile to consider some questions to ask while you are getting to know the family at their home. This will be an opportunity for you to use your communication skills to actively listen and reflect on what the family is sharing with you. In the process, you will discover the attributes that define each family and each family's potential strengths and resources.

Potential Interview Questions

What do you want to learn about each family? What questions will help you gain a better understanding of the family so as to better connect home and school environments for the student? Not only will interview questions, such as the ones in Reflective Exercise 9.5, help you understand a family's educational history, such questions can also be used to understand the local community and the labor history and family functioning patterns of CLD students. Educators who hope to unearth families' funds of knowledge may seek to learn about the local industry and migration patterns, as well as the history of the community. For example, in North Florida, the agricultural base includes hay-baling, blueberries, plant nurseries, and peanuts. These industries attract migrant farm-working families, which are typically mobile, economically disadvantaged, and have specific knowledge areas related to the work they do. Such knowledge about the community will allow educators to connect family and local knowledge areas to school learning.

Additionally, knowing about the cultural and linguistic diversity in the community, as well as the background of the family, should guide the interview process. For example, it may be culturally appropriate to ask families about household activities, but specific personal questions (such as marital status or income level) of a family or other topics may be considered *taboo*. Thus, for educators to engage in funds of knowledge interviews, it is important that they (a) understand the local community context, (b) learn about the cultural and linguistic background of families so that questions are culturally appropriate, and (c) approach the interview with genuine curiosity and a nonjudgmental stance. Culturally and linguistically diverse families may function in ways that are dissimilar from mainstream habits. Understanding those differences can become a rich source of information, one that educators can use.

Bridging Family Funds of Knowledge and School Settings

Learning about household functioning and families' knowledge areas (including language and culture) is a first step that educators can take to bridge the home and school contexts and form partnerships with families. The next step is for educators to use this information in the school setting. Moll et al. (1992) have described how teachers use families' household knowledges to create lessons that value diverse learners. The researchers also fostered parental participation by inviting parents to share their knowledge with the classroom, one example of how educators can build on home and enhance the home–school connection.

Language is another resource that teachers can tap into as a learning resource. English language learners have knowledge about how a language other than English works. Research has shown that using the first language to acquire English is a positive pedagogical practice that can support the acquisition of English (Krashen & McField 2005). Thus, rather than limiting the use of the first language in school, educators can work with students to continue to develop the first language. Having access to multicultural and bilingual children's literature, writing bilingual stories, and creating bilingual books are some ways that educators can take positive steps to supporting bilingual students' identities (Cummins 2001). Bilingual education programs, designed to develop both students' first language and English, are another example of how first languages can support learning and the academic achievement of linguistically diverse learners (Krashen & McField 2005).

Not only are families' knowledge areas a source of inspiration and connection to classroom curriculum, but also they become a forum for children to converse about and demonstrate their preexisting competencies and knowledge. Moreover, this relationship can be a vehicle for modifying the perceptions that teachers may develop about families who come from marginalized cultural groups by creating a means for families to work as equal partners with teachers.

Finally, educators can challenge the existing deficit view of families and assumptions made about CLD children and families and work toward making the world more socially just and opportunities more equitable. One size fits all curricula do little to support the unique and rich backgrounds of children and connect with families in educational partnerships. Rather, they send implicit messages to children that their home language and culture are not valued or of use in school. Educators can work with colleagues and community members to (a) reflect on current practices that are inherently inequitable and that promote mainstream ideologies, (b) address negative and inaccurate views of diverse families, (c) challenge social and educational inequities, and (d) advocate for and implement programs and practices that promote diversity and support partnerships with families.

Summary

The chapter presented information about families' ways of knowing, including notions about education, school learning, and literacy. Educators who work with CLD families and children can use numerous strategies and actions to enhance learning. First, however, educators need to understand how culture shapes values and beliefs, education, and the process of educating children. Culture is socially constructed, and interacting with children from culturally and linguistically diverse backgrounds means challenging dominant ideologies that deny children the full development of their identities. In addition, schools often send implicit messages to families about what they *should* do and what parental participation in children's education must look like. This deficit approach encourages culturally and linguistically diverse children and families to leave their identities outside the schoolhouse door. As educators, we must question and challenge deficit models of education and literacy programs that position families as lacking and limited. The rich cultural and linguistic resources that families possess are opportunities for student learning and cognitive engagement in schools.

In contrast to this deficit approach, an approach that uses families' ways of knowing, including their linguistic and cultural knowledges, as a resource is more likely to engage children in learning and to foster partnerships with CLD families. The Multiliteracy Project and the *Libros de Familia* initiative are recent examples of the ways in which educators can work with CLD children in classroom and home settings as we begin to foster a socially just and more equitable process of education. Partnerships with families require collaboration that is culturally and linguistically responsive and bidirectional in nature. Working with CLD families means providing translation and interpretation services to foster communication with families. It also requires learning about families' ways of knowing using a nonjudgmental stance. Finally, we must begin to think about the ways in which social inequities manifest in schools and work toward schools that are more equitable and socially just.

Resources

The National Center for Culturally Responsive Educational Systems,
www.nccrest.org
The National Center for Culturally Responsive Educational Systems (NCCRESt), a project funded by the U.S. Department of Education's Office of Special Education Program, provides technical assistance and professional development to close the achievement gap between students from culturally and linguistically diverse backgrounds and their peers, and to reduce inappropriate referrals to special education. The project targets improvements in culturally responsive practices, early intervention, literacy, and positive behavioral supports.

Chapter 10

Fostering Student and Family Engagement in Learning Through Student-Led Parent Conferences

Ellen S. Amatea and Kelly M. Dolan

Learning Objectives

After reading this chapter, you will be able to:

- Explain the purpose and benefits to students, parents, and teachers of having students lead a conference.
- Describe the varying formats of student-led conferences and the changes in roles and responsibilities for students, parents, and teachers that are necessary for a successful conference experience.
- Describe how to organize, schedule, and evaluate student-led conferences.

■ Discuss the steps involved in preparing students and parents to participate in student-led conferences.

As a 10-year veteran fourth grade teacher, I thought back on my conference with Tim's mother and father, the Winstons. They were the eleventh family I had scheduled to meet with during the day set aside for conferences at our school. Although each conference was expected to take fifteen minutes, I often had difficulty conveying the fine points I wanted to share about students' work, their participation in class, and their progress in that period of time. In addition, I often felt there was little opportunity to deal with the feelings engendered in parents by my report or to make plans together to improve children's learning. The Winston family's conference was a case in point.

Mr. and Mrs. Winston were both professionals in their early forties who were very involved in the job of raising Tim, their only child. They had brought him to their conference admitting that they had made no other child care arrangements. I had welcomed Tim but wondered how comfortable he was feeling about being there. Tim was a fragile looking little boy who was quite intelligent but resisted getting involved in many classroom activities. Underneath his blasé exterior, Tim often seemed angry. It came out in lots of little ways. He dragged his feet in starting to do written assignments and often seemed irritable in dealing with the other kids. When the conference began I had invited Tim to join us, but he had gone over to his desk instead. Later, however, he drifted over to the table where the conference was being held. He listened intently to what was being said and moved toward and then away from the conference table, obviously unsure of what to do. I had wondered: "Why wouldn't he join in?" When I described Tim's classroom performance and his test scores (which were strong in some areas and weak in others), I had asked him what his opinion was about his performance. But Tim had silently put his head down and moved away from the table when I questioned him. I had noticed that Mrs. Winston had tears in her eyes and wondered how much pressure she was feeling. How discouraged or disappointed did she feel? None of these feelings were acknowledged, only evaluative information was shared.

Looking back I could easily see that this had been a tension-filled time. Communication by all involved parties had been constrained. Tim's actions showed that he was thinking: "I'm frightened. I'm not sure what they are going to say about me. I don't know how to answer their questions about my performance at school!" Although Tim was there to hear my compliments and concerns, he was too anxious to take these in. Tim's parents were probably feeling anxious as well. Surely they wanted to communicate how invested they were in their child's education, but because Tim was shutting down and not talking, they were feeling frustrated as well. As I thought about this experience, I wondered: "How could I have made this a more positive experience for this family? What could I have done so that Tim would have believed he had something to say about his own learning? How could I have prepared him to comfortably share his perspective on his learning with his parents?"

Since that time, I have been introduced to a concept then new to me: the student-led conference in which students are prepared to lead their parents through a discussion of their work collected over time and organized into a portfolio. Introducing this practice with my students has not only resulted in parents gaining a more extensive picture of what their child is learning, it has also become a powerful tool for fostering student and family engagement in my students' learning.

Communicating to parents about what their children have been working on in school and what learning progress they have made is one of a teacher's most challenging responsibilities. Although a number of time-honored procedures are established—such as the grade report card and the parent–teacher conference—for reporting student progress toward meeting classroom goals and standards, many teachers have begun to question the effectiveness of these traditional reporting procedures. The opening vignette is one author's reflection that best describes how we began to reconsider our usual approach to conducting parent–teacher conferences.

A growing number of educators (Austin 1994; Bailey & Guskey 2001; Benson & Barnett 1999; Picciotto 1996) have begun to question the effectiveness of traditional conference formats as they have become aware that the most important person—the student—was missing from these conversations. These educators are experimenting with different approaches for including students in teachers' conversations with parents as a result of believing that only by involving the student can there be an accurate, relevant, and meaningful conversation about student learning. The student-led parent conference is one such approach. As the name implies, student-led conferences are conferences held at traditional report card time, or other times during the year, which are led by students themselves. Parents come to the conferences to hear about their child's progress. Through demonstration and discussion, students show their parents what they have been learning (Austin 1994; Picciotto 1996).

Such a conference can consist of a variety of different formats: (a) the student-involved conference in which the teacher takes primary responsibility for directing the conversation, although the student is present to add comments or answer questions; (b) the presentation or showcase conference in which the student presents a collection of work to a group or panel that includes teachers, parents, and other adults; (c) the portfolio night in which an entire class of students showcases their portfolios at the same time for viewing by families; and (d) the simultaneous student-led conference in which several family conferences conducted by students occur at one time.

We, a fourth grade teacher and a university professor of counselor education, decided to write about our experiences with the fourth type, the simultaneous student-led conference, because we discovered that this conference approach can be a powerful tool for engaging students and their families more fully in learning. We have now assisted other teachers in the first through tenth grades at our school in introducing this practice into their classrooms. As a result, we know that this practice can successfully be modified to serve the needs of different aged students. In this chapter we describe our experience of introducing the simultaneous student-led conference practice into our fourth grade classroom. To address the practical issues involved in implementing a student-led conference, we first focus on the purpose and benefits to students, parents, and teachers of having students lead a conference. We then describe in great detail what our student-led conferences "look like" and discuss the change in roles and responsibilities necessary for a successful conference experience. We then discuss the logistics of preparing, organizing, scheduling, and evaluating such conferences.

Purpose and Benefits of Student-Led Conferences

When we first embarked on the process of introducing student-led parent conferences to our fourth grade students and parents, we assumed that the real value to be derived from students conducting conferences with their parents would be its *communication* value—that is, for parents to gain a fuller view of their child's progress. We expected that when students were given a voice in the conference, parents would more fully understand and appreciate what their children were learning and achieving and thus could more adequately encourage them, and students would feel heard and understood.

However, we soon found that the student-led conference was also a powerful motivational tool for fostering greater student engagement in learning because it heightened the personal relevance of learning for our students. Teachers know that for learning to be relevant, students must be able to (a) see the importance of the concepts they are learning and (b) connect those concepts to prior learning and to the world outside of the classroom. We discovered that our students could more easily see the relevance of their daily work when they knew that an audience beyond the walls of the classroom was going to see and review their work. Because students knew they would be reporting to parents or other significant adults about their learning, they began to see the relevance of completing work, keeping track of work, and making sure work was done well.

Second, giving students control over the selection and discussion of their academic work gave our students a greater sense of personal agency or efficacy. Rather than merely be a "passenger" in an effort that a teacher exclusively directed (i.e., with the teacher making all the decisions about what students are to learn or how they are to be evaluated), we invited students to select the work they valued doing, to actively engage in reviewing and assessing their own learning, and to feel a sense of ownership of their portfolio. To do this, rather than have the portfolio of their work chosen and managed by us, we gave students an opportunity to select their own work. We used the portfolio development task as an opportunity to teach our students how to reflect upon and describe their work, using questions, such as the following:

> How can you best show your parents what you are learning and how you are
>   behaving in school?
> How does your work show how you have improved?
> What task or assignment was the most challenging, and why?
> What do you think you need to work on and improve?

As Wiggins and McTighe (1998) suggest, as a result of engaging in such self-reflection, students can learn something important that is typically not an intentional part of the curriculum; how to assess for self-knowledge, learning what they do and do not understand about a given subject and what they might do to enhance that understanding. As a result of these activities, the process of selecting and discussing a collection of their work becomes a significant mastery experience for students. As Herbert (1998) notes:

> What we didn't know then (when we started this practice) was that the
> process of selecting samples of one's own work and assembling them into a
> portfolio is profoundly important to children. We also learned that all children
> have a natural ability and desire to tell their story through the contents of a
> portfolio. Even now, we remain excited about capturing the individual voices
> of our students through portfolio collections. (583)

A key ingredient essential to the cultivation of students' sense of personal agency or efficacy is the tone of "celebration" of student work that must be infused into the student-led conference. Both through the message home to parents about the conference and through the student-led conference itself, parents and students learn that the conference is an opportunity to celebrate rather than just evaluate students' learning progress. As Herbert (1998) described, the conferences led by students in her building are "celebrations of student competence . . . opportunities for children to present their portfolios to their own parents . . . ways that children and parents hear that learning is worth celebrating, and that children can be competent participants in that celebration" (585).

Finally, we found that student-led conferences were an excellent method for increasing parent engagement and participation in school. Bailey and Guskey (2001) reported that student-led conferences significantly increased parent attendance. Having now conducted student-led conferences in Grades 1 through 10 at our school, we also found a significant increase in parent participation, with 100 percent of our parents attending our first, second, third, and fourth grade conferences, 95 percent attending our fifth, sixth, and seventh grade conferences, 85 percent participating in our eighth grade conferences, and 80 percent attending our ninth and tenth grade student-led conferences (Amatea 2003).

Similar benefits of enhanced student and parent engagement in learning have been reported by a number of practitioners (Austin 1994; Bailey & Guskey 2001; Benson & Barnett 1999). For example, Bailey and Guskey noted: "The real power of student-led conferences is that they require students to take most of the responsibility for reporting what they have learned. To do this, students must evaluate and reflect upon their work on a regular basis, organize their work into a thoughtful collection, and organize their thoughts about their learning well enough to articulate these thoughts to others" (4).

The Student-Led Conference: A Change in Roles and Responsibilities

How exactly does a student-led conference differ from a traditional parent–teacher conference? What do teachers and students and parents need to do differently? To be successful, student-led conferences require teachers, students, and parents to change their usual conference roles. Teachers must become facilitators and coaches. Students must become leaders. Parents must become active listeners, questioners, encouragers, and supporters. Let us first describe what our student-led conferences look like and then discuss the new roles and responsibilities necessary for a successful conference experience.

Nature of the Student-Led Conference

Our conferences were designed both to showcase student work and progress and to help students and parents learn how to actively plan together for future student learning. We designed our student-led conferences based on the simultaneous student-led conference format described by Benson and Barnett (1998) in their book, *Student-Led Conferencing Using Showcase Portfolios*. Each conference event consists of six steps: (a) a large-group introduction to the conference event conducted by the teacher, followed by (b) a large-group discussion and demonstration of parent and student conference roles, (c) the individual family discussion of student work conducted by the student, (d) the joint development by the student and parent(s) of a goal setting plan, (e) the parent and student writing of personal feedback letters to each other and the parent completing a conference evaluation form, and, finally, (f) family members exchanging letters and enjoying refreshments. We allocate 45 minutes for each conference session, expecting the first two steps to take approximately 10 minutes, steps three and four to take approximately 25 minutes, and steps five and six to take 10 minutes.

We schedule our conferences at two different times during the school year—once in the fall and once in the late spring. For each conference event we select four sixty-minute time periods in the afternoon, after school, or in the evening over a two-day period. (Elementary teachers often schedule five to seven families at a time in each session, whereas secondary teachers often schedule forty to fifty students' families at a time in each session and meet in a large room, such as a school

⌃⌄

Figure 10.1a   Letter Orienting Parents to Student-Led Conferences

Dear Parent/Guardian:

We are going to be trying out an exciting new format for parent–teacher conferences this year, called the *student-led parent conference*. This new format is designed to help students develop a greater sense of ownership and responsibility for their learning and their school progress. These conferences will provide an opportunity for your child to take an active role in reflecting on and evaluating his or her performance, discussing his or her academic progress with you, and showing you examples of what he or she has learned.

Why are we trying this new format? Although parent–teacher conferences have been an integral part of school programs for a long time, students are usually left out of these important conversations about their learning. Second, even when they have a fifteen-minute conference with a teacher, parents often feel that they have an incomplete picture of their child's learning progress.

The idea behind the student-led conference is that these conferences with you can be an opportunity for students to learn how to assess their learning progress and to share their learning triumphs and struggles with you. These conferences also provide you and your child with a regular structure for talking about their learning. Given these powerful results, I hope you will be interested in participating in this new practice with us. We will be scheduling these conferences immediately after school or in the evening on two consecutive days. The students will be responsible for conducting his or her conference with you. We view this as an important opportunity for students to learn how to talk about their strengths, to acknowledge their weaknesses, and—with you guiding them—to think about how they can plan to improve their learning.

Please make every effort to be part of your child's conference. This is an opportunity to strengthen the lines of communication with your child about his or her learning. We know you will want to be a part of this new conferencing process.

Thank you.

Sincerely,

Kelly Dolan   Ellen Amatea
Fourth Grade Teacher   Counselor

---

library or cafeteria.) Parents are sent a letter inviting them to choose a preferred time from one of the four sessions listed. (See Figures 10.1a and 10.1b for samples of the introductory letter and the appointment letter.)

At each of the conference sessions, the teacher or teaching team opens the conference event by introducing themselves to the families in attendance and explains the purpose of the conference, the agenda of activities, and the conference goal setting/action planning task that the student and parent will complete together. In addition, the teacher(s) discusses particular strategies parents might use to assist their children to be successful in their conference and gives them a handout that

~~~~~~

Figure 10.1b   *Family Appointment Time Letter*

Dear Parents,

Here is an update on our conferencing plans. The children are really coming along in getting prepared for their student-led conferences with you. Each child has been working on putting together a portfolio, which they are thinking of as their "scrapbook about fourth grade," and they plan to share with you. When you come in your child will be showing you his or her portfolio and talking with you about his or her strengths, progress, concerns, and goals.

We have set the dates of October 30 and November 1 for our first student-led conferences. On the bottom half of this letter you will see a form. Please look at the four times listed, and return the form to us indicating which time you prefer.

We know that this concept is new for you, too, but don't worry. We will start each conference session with a role-playing activity that will provide you with some suggestions for talking with your fourth grader.

It is exciting to see the children really thinking of themselves as learners. We are looking forward to sharing with you soon. By the way, please remember that if you ever have any questions or concerns, I would be happy to set up an individual conference with you.

Sincerely,

Kelly L. Dolan

------------------------- **Cut here and return to me** --------------------------

Please look at the following choices of conference dates and appointment times and indicate yours and your child's first and second choice dates and times for their conferences with you.

Tuesday, October 30	**Thursday, November 1**
3:30–4:30_____	5:30–6:30_____
or	or
5:00–6:00_____	7:00–8:00_____

describes these strategies (see Figure 10.2 on page 260). A humorous role-play is then conducted, depicting how a parent might effectively use these strategies during the conference.

Students then pick up their portfolios from a central location in the room and direct their parents to one of a series of tables that have been set up somewhat apart from one another so as to ensure some family privacy. Once they are at their table, each student then explains the purpose of the conference and then proceeds through a conference agenda, showing, explaining, and demonstrating what they have learned in school through a discussion of their portfolio. (In addition to the portfolio, teachers and students often set up learning centers or displays of student work around the perimeter of the room before the conference so that students can show their parents examples of their classroom learning activities during the

~~~~~~

Figure 10.2   Strategies for Helping Your Student Take Charge of His or Her Conference

Let your student steer by listening rather than leading the conversation. Ask your student, rather than tell, what he or she wants to plan to improve.

Keep your student talking by asking questions, which will open up his or her thinking to you. Some possible questions might be

What are some things you are learning in this class?

What do you have to do in this assignment?

What do you think you did well?

What did you enjoy about this (project, unit, activity, book writing piece)?

How might you improve in this area?

How can I help you?

Help your student not get derailed by self-consciousness and self-criticism by supporting rather than criticizing: Tell your student what you like about what he or she is planning and doing, rather than talking only about what he or she is not doing well. Some possible ideas might be

"I feel proud because . . ."

"I know that sometimes you have difficulty with . . . but . . ."

"I am glad to see you are taking an active role in your learning by . . ."

"I am glad to see that you are making an extra effort in . . ."

---

conference or point out their work on bulletin boards or other classroom displays.) Once they have reviewed their work, students and parents are asked to create a goal-setting plan together, using a goal-setting form as a guide (see Figure 10.3) in which (a) they identify what they judge to be the student's strengths and areas in need of further development, (b) together they set some specific goals for what students may want to work on learning, and (c) they decide on actions that the student and parent might take to advance those goals.

These four steps take approximately 35 minutes. At the end of these activities, students are directed to an adjoining classroom to write a thank-you note to their parents and to bring back refreshments for themselves and their parents. During this time, parents are invited to write a letter to their child, commenting on the student's conference performance. To encourage parents to give constructive feedback to their child, we give parents a handout that lists some prompts and sentence starters they might use. (See Figure 10.4 on page 262 for a sample of the post-conference family feedback handout.)

~~~~~~

Figure 10.3   Conference Goal-Setting/Planning Form

Dear Student:

What goals might you agree on and see yourself working toward together with your parent to improve your learning? Your parent can help you think about what goals you might set for yourself next and what you might do to meet your goals.

Step 1. STRENGTHS

What might we agree that I (the student) am strong in?

Student's Ideas   Parent's Ideas

_____   _____

_____   _____

_____   _____

Step 2. GOALS

What might I (the student) most want or need to work on?

Student's Ideas   Parent's Ideas

_____   _____

_____   _____

_____   _____

Step 3. ACTION PLAN

What specific action steps might we agree on right now that we could start doing to help me meet my goals?

Student's Action Steps   Parent's Action Steps

_____   _____

_____   _____

_____   _____

Student Signature_____

Parent Signature _____

We also ask parents to complete a brief one-page questionnaire for evaluating the overall conference. (See Figure 10.5 on page 263 for a sample of the parent conference evaluation form.)

Our student conferences end when students return to the room, exchange letters with their parents, and eat refreshments. During the next day at school we ask our students to complete an evaluation of the conference and then discuss the conference experience with them (see Figure 10.6 on page 264).

〰〰〰〰〰〰〰〰〰〰〰〰〰〰〰〰〰〰〰〰〰〰〰〰〰〰〰〰〰〰〰〰〰〰〰

Figure 10.4   *Post-Conference Family Feedback*

Dear Family and Guests,

After the conference please take a moment and write a short note to your child describing your reactions to his or her performance during the student-led conference. (We will furnish the note paper.) Some items for discussion that you may want to use in your note are listed below. Please plan to share your note with your child tonight. Your note will become part of your child's portfolio. Thank you again for choosing to take an active role in this aspect of your child's education/learning. Your participation sends the message to your student that you believe that his or her school performance is important to you and to his or her future.

Ideas for discussion in the letter:

"I felt proud because . . ."

"Keep up the good work on . . ."

"I know that sometimes you have difficulty with . . . but . . ."

"I am glad to see you are taking an active role in your learning by . . ."

"I am glad to see that you are making an extra effort in . . ."

"Some ways I can help you are . . ."

"I enjoyed your conference because . . ."

"I learned a lot from you about your work in . . ."

Sincerely,

Kelly Dolan   Ellen Amatea

The Teacher's Role

To successfully implement this new conferencing practice, teachers must help students take over the leadership of their conferences. To do this effectively, we learned that we had to give up some of the control that we were used to having. For example, in planning our first student-led conferences, we envisioned that we would either "drop in" on each student-led conference and answer parents' questions or have the parent and child drop by a table for teacher input after the child's presentation. However, in our reading of various authors (Austin 1994; Benson & Barnett 1999; Picciotto 1996), they caution that such a role inadvertently organizes parents to continue to see the teacher as the "real" authority on their children's learning. To avoid the authority during the conference automatically reverting to the teacher and away from student, these authors suggest that teachers play a more unobtrusive role when the individual family conferences are going on. As a result, although we would have an important role in helping students prepare for their conferences, our role at the event itself would be as stage managers who direct the action of the event from afar.

∿∿∿∿∿∿∿∿∿∿∿∿∿∿∿∿∿∿∿∿∿∿∿∿∿∿∿∿∿∿∿∿∿∿∿∿∿∿

Figure 10.5   Family Evaluation of Our Student Goal-Setting Conference

Please help us evaluate our new practice of student-led parent conferences by completing this form. Thank you! (Please circle your answer.)

1. The time allowed for the student-led conference was

| **Too little** | **About right** | **Too much** |

2. Please rate how much the conference helped you learn more about your child's thinking about his or her achievement and learning in school. (Circle number.)

Not at all helpful   **Very helpful**

    1   2   3   4   5

3. Please rate how much the conference helped you learn more about your child's thinking about setting goals for learning. (Circle number.)

Not at all helpful   **Very helpful**

    1   2   3   4   5

4. Please rate how much the information we provided about student-led conferences helped you support your child's learning and goal-setting. (Circle number.)

Not at all helpful   **Very helpful**

    1   2   3   4   5

5. Please comment on the **goal-setting portfolio** itself, such as its organization, contents, changes you would like to see, and so on.

_____

_____

_____

_____

6. Please comment on the **student-led parent conference** itself, such as its benefits, its organization, and any changes you would suggest we consider making for next time.

_____

_____

_____

_____

7. Please write any additional comments on the other side of this paper.

Signature _____

We took that advice to heart, and on conference night we greeted parents, opened the conference event, describing the conference activities and the particular roles that student, parent, and teacher would play, and explained that, as teachers, we would be staying out of the individual conversations that students and parents would have about each student's learning. (However, we stressed that we would be available

∧∧

Figure 10.6   *Student Conference Feedback Form*

After the Conference: Student Reflections

The best thing about my conference was:

_____

_____

Things would have gone better if:

_____

_____

As I look back on my conference and preparations for it, I feel I gained:

_____

_____

I think my parents learned:

_____

_____

Additional comments:

_____

_____

Name_____ Date_____

---

for individual conferences if that need arose.) Then, rather than participate in any of the individual student conferences, we stepped back, let our students conduct the conferences, and were amazed by the results!

We did, however, have a very important preconference role in preparing students, parents, and the conference environment to guarantee success. This entailed (a) orienting parents to the new conference format, (b) developing and implementing a series of lessons to introduce students to the idea of the student-led conference and portfolio development process, (c) guiding students' portfolio development, (d) rehearsing with students, and (e) arranging the classroom space to accommodate families. We will describe these responsibilities in greater detail in the next section.

The Student's Role

The student's role changes dramatically in the student-led conference. Rather than function as a nonparticipant or passive observer (as we saw Tim do in the opening case of the Winston family), the student becomes an active leader and spokesperson. Rather than listen to the teacher's view of what the student is learning, the student gives his or her views. To prepare for this new role, students must develop skills in talking about their work with their parents, describing their view of what they are learning, identifying their learning strengths and needs, collecting evidence illustrating their learning progress, and learning to set goals and make plans for their future learning. In addition, students often help with the many organizational details of the actual conference: inviting parents and scheduling their conference appointment, role-playing and rehearsing what they plan to say at their conference, preparing and arranging the physical space of the classroom for the conference, and taking home important information to parents, both before and during the conference.

We have found that students at all grade levels, third through tenth, reported increased self-confidence and pride, and some amount of surprise in their ability to explain their work, to set goals, and to express their ideas about school and learning to their parents. In gathering feedback from students after their conferences, we found that many students commented about the effects they observed of their conference on themselves and on their parents. One student said: "I liked the conference because I was not nervous talking about my work." Another said: "I liked the conference because there were no distractions." Another student noted: "My conference really went smoothly because I wasn't trying to talk really fast or to race anybody." Other students emphasized the benefits: "It gave me more confidence" and "I got closer to my mom about everything I've done in school. Now she doesn't have to ask so many questions about school." Another fourth grader noted how it has led to an increased focus on skill building: "I am trying to improve my reading skills with my mom now." Students also reported effects the conference had on their parents. One fourth grade student wrote: "My mom and dad were really excited and proud. They thought my portfolio was very organized and that I've been doing good work." Another student said: "My parents got to understand what we do in class." Other students noted: "I liked having my parents come and listen to stuff I've been doing" and "My parents found out how well I was doing in school" and "My mom felt good when she heard about my work."

The Parent's Role

The parent's role also changes dramatically in the student-led conference. Rather than just function as passive listeners or receivers of teachers' expert advice, parents have an active role in encouraging their child to share their views about their learning and to help them make plans to improve their learning. To do this effectively, the parent must listen attentively, ask questions, provide encouragement, and jointly develop learning plans with their child. Often the role of listening to their child and encouraging them to take the lead in managing the conversation is a new one for parents. Hence, we emphasize and model strategies of active listening, asking open-ended questions, and providing positive feedback.

Parents consistently comment on the beneficial impact of the conference experience on their child and themselves. Many parents noted that the conference experience gave them a chance to see how their children operate in their classroom. Not only did they see the classroom materials (such as books) that were available, but also they learned about some of the learning routines their children engaged in, they saw their children interact with the teacher and classmates, and they heard what their children think about their learning. One parent reported: "This was a wonderful way for parents to see what their children are doing 'in their own words.'" Another parent said: "The specific examples in my child's portfolio helped me understand what my child is expected to learn." Not only did the student-led conferences provide a context for parents to hear more about their children's learning and classroom context, but also they allowed parents to see their children take responsibility for their learning. For example, one parent said: "This was great! Student-led conferences really gave my son a chance to show responsibility for his actions concerning this learning!" Another said: "Not only does the conferencing process encourage more responsibility for her work, it really contributed to my child's sense of pride in and awareness of herself as a learner." Many parents commented that their child displayed a sense of accomplishment and excitement about learning. One parent said: "The conferences were well rehearsed and presented. They gave the children a real sense of accomplishment." Another parent said: "This is a great idea. It builds confidence and teaches organization." Parents also commented on their child's candor and directness in talking about their weaknesses and strengths. One parent said: "This was an important event for my child. Not only was she proud to show me what she was strong in, but she shyly showed me and talked to me about her weaknesses too."

In addition, many parents reported valuing the time spent alone with their children at the student-led conference. Children loved the attention, of course, but parents also came to appreciate their child in a new way. One parent commented: "It was great to 'slow down' and talk with my child about their learning. This doesn't usually take place in our busy life!" Finally, parents often come away from these conferences quite amazed by their children. Not only are their children able to do more than their parents had thought, but also they are able to articulate their progress quite clearly. As one parent noted: "I was astonished by the way my child took charge of his conference. I have not seen that side of him before."

Preparing Students and Parents for Their New Roles

Preparing Students

As we thought more deeply about our conferencing and portfolio development plans for our students and the implicit judgment of performance inherent in them, we realized that our students would have an opportunity to assess themselves only in terms of a narrow range of traditional academic domains, if we focused on school subjects only. As a result, they might develop a narrow and negative view of their own competencies and avoid becoming fully engaged in the conferencing process. We knew that students might be inspired to discuss their learning accomplishments more readily if they focused initially on their areas of strength, both in academic and in nonacademic areas. We decided to make the portfolio develop-ment and presentation process a vehicle for helping students develop confidence in their competencies and strengths in a variety of different nonacademic areas as well as showcase their academic accomplishments. We wanted students to conclude not whether they were smart, but where they were smart. Consequently, we designed a series of five lessons that introduces the conference idea and then focuses on students developing a portfolio that answers four questions: (a) What are you like? (b) What do you want to learn? (c) What have you been learning? (d) What do you plan to work on learning next?

Introducing the Idea of Student-Led Conferences

In our first lesson we introduced the idea of student-led parent conferences and its potential benefits. Our goal was to help the students understand what it was like for parents who were curious about what their child did at school all day. The teacher simulated this idea by introducing a teddy bear as a "pretend child," having it leave the classroom for part of the day, and then facilitating a classroom discussion of when the "child" was picked up. In the discussion the teacher likened the children's curiosity about their bear child's day to the feelings their parents have when their children return from school. The teacher then introduced the idea that student-led conferences and portfolios could be a means for helping their parents understand more about their own school day experiences.

Exploring Multiple Intelligences

In our second lesson we invited our students to see themselves as learners with unique abilities and skills. Because we wanted students to assess themselves in terms of a fuller range of competencies than just the traditional academic ones, in our second lesson we introduced the concept of multiple intelligences. Gardner (1983; 1999) developed a theory of multiple intelligences in which eight different intelligences account for the broad range of human potential in children and adults. These intelligences are lin-guistic intelligence (word smart), logical-mathematical intelligence (number/reason-ing smart), spatial intelligence (picture smart), bodily-kinesthetic intelligence (body smart), musical intelligence (music smart), interpersonal intelligence (people smart), intrapersonal intelligence (self smart), and naturalist intelligence (nature smart). Gard-ner contends that our schools and culture typically focus most of their attention on two forms of intelligence—linguistic and logical-mathematical intelligence. How-ever, he recommends that we place equal attention on individuals who show gifts in the other intelligences: artists, architects, naturalists, designers, dancers, entrepreneurs, and others who enrich the world in which we live.

In our classroom we explained the eight established intelligences in a language that made it easy for our fourth graders to distinguish them and then assigned students to seek out a person high in one of these different intelligences. The students were then asked to identify an adult they knew (e.g., a parent) who had one of the eight intelligences and interview him or her in terms of their hobbies, their favorite school subjects, and the jobs they like. As students reported their interview findings back to the class, they developed a clearer picture of the distinctions between the different intelligences. Next, we asked students to assess themselves in terms of the different intelligences, identifying the intelligences in which they were strongest, those in which they would like to get better, and discussing what they might do to help themselves improve a particular intelligence. Not only did this lesson provide our students with a language for talking about differences in abilities without putting anybody down, but also it provided us with a greater awareness of the types of activities and styles of learning that our students valued.

Becoming Navigators

We also wanted to encourage our students to begin viewing themselves as active planners and observers of their own learning. Children often have few opportunities to set goals and make conscious choices themselves about what they will learn. Instead, they are expected to go along with their teachers' decisions and plans. We wanted to encourage students to begin viewing themselves as active agents who can set their own learning goals, make plans for how they might work toward their goals, and assess their progress. To do this, we needed to have students notice whether they had goals for their learning and to show them how they might set goals and develop strategies to meet those goals. Intrinsic in this step was the message that goal setting is a responsibility of the student as a learner. If they did not set their own goals for learning, who would?

Thus, in our third lesson we introduced the idea of having students view themselves as navigators rather than passengers on the ship traveling through the learning experiences of fourth grade. We asked each student to develop a learner's "passport" that would serve as the introduction to their conference portfolio. In this passport, students would describe their interests and "smarts," set goals for their future learning, and develop plans for reaching those goals. We modeled the development of this passport by depicting how an imaginary fourth grade student would assess his or her hobbies, interests, the school subjects he or she liked and those he or she found difficult, the types of skill areas (both in and out of school) in which he or she wanted to improve, and the personal learning goals he or she set and planned and developed. (See Figure 10.7 for a sample passport.)

Selecting and Reflecting on Student Work

We introduced the idea that each student would develop a showcase portfolio, called a *learning album*. We had the students include their learning passport that described their individual learning strengths and interests as one way to personalize their portfolios. Next came the task of deciding what types of work products would be included. To give our families a clearer picture of daily and weekly school life, we decided that we would have students showcase their performance on ordinary class-

ᐱᐱᐱᐱᐱᐱᐱᐱᐱᐱᐱᐱᐱᐱᐱᐱᐱᐱᐱᐱᐱᐱᐱᐱᐱᐱᐱᐱᐱᐱᐱᐱᐱᐱᐱᐱ

Figure 10.7   Sample Learning Passport

MY LEARNING PASSPORT

My Name_____

My Grade_____   My Age_____

My Teacher_____

Where I Was Born _____

When I Was Born _____

My Family _____

_____

**My Photo
(Student photo)**

Five Things I Like to Do (my interests):

1. _____

2. _____

3. _____

4. _____

5. _____

Two Islands of "Smarts"
I Am Now Strong In (skills and abilities I now have which I may want to develop further):

First Island of "Smarts":

_____

Second Island of "Smarts":

_____

Learning Goal 1: (What I would like to learn more about in one of the areas I am strong.)

_____

Two Islands of "Smarts"
I Want to Travel to So that I Can Strengthen My Skills and Abilities in Those Types of "Smarts":

First Island of "Smarts" I Want to Strengthen:

_____

Second Island of "Smarts" I Want to Strengthen:

_____

Learning Goal 2: (What I would like to learn more about in one of the areas I want to strengthen)

_____

room learning activities—those routines already in place within the classroom structure. Examples would include reading logs, fluency progress ratings, test scores in different subject areas, homework participation charts, writing samples, and journal entries. Because we were worried about the need to make sure that each student has a variety of *work products* for the portfolio that are worthy of review, deciding to report out on learning activities that were already in place created a sense of relief for us. To further personalize their portfolios, we also gave our students an opportunity to select one or two particular projects to add to their portfolio and reflect on. Now the only new products that we needed to help students generate were ways of individually recording and analyzing progress in these class activities.

To help our students learn how to reflect on and assess their learning performance and progress and to make plans for their future learning, we introduced in our fourth lesson the use of a student commentary sheet, which we adapted from the commentary format described by Benson and Barnett (1999). (See Figure 10.8 for samples of commentary sheets.) By means of the commentary sheets, we established a general portfolio format for reporting the common events that students were involved in during each day. The sheets also became our way to help each child personalize his or her portfolio.

Students were asked to write commentaries about their accomplishments in each school subject. The commentary sheets allowed for individual student interpretation of (a) the requirements of their initial assignment; (b) their reflection of their effort and achievement; and (c) their opinion about the ways they might strengthen their performance. When asking the children to reflect on their performance on particular activities, we emphasized that the students might notice variations in their performance on school tasks based on their particular learning strengths and "intelligences." Allowing for and encouraging students to talk about these differences in their commentaries further personalized each child's portfolio. Thus, when a student completed a commentary for a particular assignment or subject, they revealed their individual attitudes, accomplishments, and goals.

Because we expected a thorough effort in each commentary, we carefully paced the development of the commentaries. We knew that if we wanted to obtain authentic, meaningful responses from the students, we would need to allow adequate time to complete each commentary about the different activities they wished to showcase. Several days before the conferences, students sorted and organized their work samples and completed commentaries about them.

Rehearsing for the Conference

Our fifth lesson was focused on helping our students learn the skills necessary for presenting their work to their parents. We developed an agenda outlining a formal introduction and an arrangement of portfolio contents. (See Figure 10.9 on page 272 for a sample of this agenda.)

We had our students organize the contents of their portfolio according to this agenda. We then modeled a student following this agenda as she talked with her

〰〰〰〰〰〰〰〰〰〰〰〰〰〰〰〰〰〰〰〰〰〰〰

Figure 10.8   Sample Commentary Sheet for Reading and for Behavior

Commentary Sheet for Reading Log Sheets, Fluency

Step 1: Describe this assignment (What did Ms. Dolan ask us to do?)

Log Sheets _____

_____

Fluency_____

_____

Step 2: How do I feel about my skills in reading?

_____

_____

_____

_____

Step 3: What things am I doing in class to improve and challenge my current reading skills?

_____

_____

_____

_____

Commentary Sheet for Behavior

Step 1: These are the student and teacher behaviors that I think are necessary for our classroom to run smoothly and fairly.

_____

_____

_____

Step 2: Describe your activities during the day when you are on task and productive.

_____

_____

_____

Step 3: Describe your activities during the day when you need reminders and/or consequences regarding your behavior.

_____

_____

_____

Step 4: There are some things I can do to help myself and my classroom. They are:

_____

_____

_____

_____

Figure 10.9   *Student Conference Agenda*

1. Role-playing:

Help your guests find seats in the circle. Ms. Dolan and Ms. Amatea will "act out" a quick conference so your guests will know what to do.

2. Getting Started:

Collect your materials (folder, book, pencils, etc.) for your conference. If you're missing anything, let a teacher know.

3. Introduce Conference Planning Form:

Show your guests the "Conference Planning Form." Let them know that you will fill it out together after you look through your portfolio.

4. Self-Awareness Section:

Share your self-awareness commentary. Show your guests your "Smarts" sheet. Show your guests your "Passport." Discuss the skill areas you have identified as strengths and the skill areas you have selected as areas that need to be strengthened.

5. Reading Section:

Share your reading commentary. Read one of the entries from your reading log sheets to your guests. Read a selection from your book to your guests. Talk to your guests about your reading fluency.

6. Writing Section:

Share your writing commentary. Read the writing pieces you have selected. Discuss the point sheets we use to evaluate your writing and the points you earned for that particular writing piece.

7. Math Section:

Share your math commentary. Discuss your work in the math book, your problem solving (algebra!) in the mornings, and your math warm-ups. Show your guests your Mad Minutes folder and the dated mastery sheet.

8. Science Section:

Share an entry from your science composition book. Take a moment to discuss what we do in Science Lab.

9. Grade Graphs:

Go over your grade graphs and reflection sheets for math, Florida history, and science. Remember to discuss the things you noticed about your learning progress when you connected the scores on your graphs.

10. Behavior:

Go over your behavior commentary.

11. Conference Planning Form:

Look back at your conference planning form. Think about all of the things you've shared, and fill out your part. Get your guest's ideas about your strengths, goals, and action steps, and have them fill out their part. Then both of you sign it.

12. Wrap-up:

Tell your guests you will be right back with some refreshments. Go to Mr. Hollinger's room for the refreshments.

"parent" about her portfolio. As students observed this demonstration, we asked them to take notes on statements that the student model made, which they might like to use in their own conference. We arranged to have older students (e.g., eighth grade) from our school volunteer to serve as surrogate parents for our rehearsal session. The older students observed the model conference as well. Then each of our students was paired up with an eighth grade student for about twenty to twenty-five minutes for a conference "dress rehearsal." The older students, by means of asking questions and giving encouragement, guided the students through their conference presentation.

Preparing Parents

We explained the benefits of this new conference format to parents through an announcement at our fall back-to-school night and in a series of letters sent home to parents over several months. Our first letter asked parents to (a) understand and support the idea that students can explain their learning progress, (b) recognize that this method of reporting seeks to put the child in a more active stance regarding accountability for his or her work, and (c) show belief in their child by their attendance at the conference. Although parents had received information about the student-led conference at the beginning of the year at the parents' information meeting, they needed a formal invitation as the conference time drew near. The teachers sent home a letter restating the purpose and significance of the conference, informing parents of when and where the conference would be held, and suggesting who should attend. The letter contained a response portion that offered parents a choice of one of four possible appointment times scheduled during after school and after work hours. Parents returned the response portion to the teacher, indicating whether they can come and choosing one of the four appointment times. Several days before the conference, the teacher followed up with phone calls to those parents who did not send in a response and encouraged them to attend or send someone else (e.g., an aunt, an older brother or sister) in their place if necessary.

We knew that parents would appreciate some tips on how to help their child conduct an effective conference. Our goal was to introduce parents to a more open-ended, reflexive style of questioning that might be more empowering for the student. We introduced parents to these new, more reflexive ways of talking with their children through discussion, role-playing, handouts, and letter-writing prompts.

Discussion

All of our fourth grade students had parents or relatives who came for their conferences. After our students conducted their conferences, we noticed a curious phenomenon. Our students seemed to feel more confident about themselves and their learning. A number of them spoke more deliberately about their efforts to prepare themselves for a test or a project. Others seemed more ready to undertake an activity that was difficult for them rather than avoid it as they had done in the past. To what could we attribute this? We began to realize that it was not just "doing the conference" that seemed to make the difference; it seemed that the experience of talking about themselves and their learning as they responded to our questions called a more confident student into being. What was different about these questions?

As we thought back over what we had done to help students prepare for the event, we realized that we often used (and coached parents to use) questions and other metacognitive strategies (Costa & Kallick 2000) that allowed the student to *become an observer* of their own experience. Becoming an observer of your own thoughts and behavior is a necessary first step toward teaching or changing a behavior. Asking certain types of reflection-enhancing questions can often "open the eyes" of students and facilitate the development of a new awareness of their competencies or of their situation by scaffolding particular metacognitive strategies. For instance, we often asked questions, such as "Just how did you go about doing this assignment? How did you feel about your effort?" This enhanced students' awareness of how they went about their work. We also asked questions that helped our students develop a greater awareness of their previous successes, such as "What kinds of things have you done in the past when you tackled something that was hard for you to do?" and "How were you able to stick with something that was hard for you to do and see it through to the end?" and "What might you have learned about yourself from doing something hard in the past that you can use here?" As our students worked with us, busily preparing their portfolios and rehearsing what they were going to say to their parents about their learning, we believed that they became more aware of their unique interests, their "smarts," and their strengths and weaknesses. In addition, they became more skilled in thinking and talking about what they had learned, examining how they had progressed, and in thinking of themselves as self-directed learners—able to set their own learning goals, judge their own work, and determine what they need to do to improve.

As we engaged in this process with our students, observing how actively they worked to develop their portfolios and to explain them to their parents, our views of our students and their parents changed. We began to look at our students more often in terms of their competencies and strengths rather than in terms of deficits we needed to address. As we did this, our own role changed. Rather than thinking that we had to make all of the decisions about our students' learning goals, design the activities necessary to reach those goals, or supply what was needed to help orchestrate the conference experience, we realized that we could share the responsibility for goal setting and planning with our students and their parents.

Another benefit of using this conferencing practice is the opportunity it presents to assess your own practice and program carefully as you decide what to include in the conference and how to prepare your students for it. What is really important? What activities or work samples might you encourage students to present that will help parents really see what we are doing in our classroom? How can you organize the conference activities so that students and parents are comfortable and confident in their new roles? What do you want students to learn from this experience? In addition, implementing this new conferencing practice provides a curricular benefit. Having students reflect on their learning activities provides important feedback to teachers. Do most students understand the objectives of your assignments? Do they understand how they can improve their work? How can you, as an educator, plan assignments that are useful measures of curricular objectives as well as meaningful experiences for children? By listening to the conversations that students have with their parents and observing their interactions, teachers can learn what a student is thinking about particular lessons. Does the student understand the goals of a lesson? How do they talk about their performance? Can they explain their performance to their parents? What are they learning from this?

A further benefit is that of seeing how particular students and parents interact. By observing their interactions, teachers can discern how parents interact with their children around school matters. Are they supportive and encouraging? Are they impatient? Are they controlling? Another benefit is seeing how much of a resource the parent can be to the child in completing school tasks. Does the parent understand the particular classroom activities and assignments? Do they understand the ways that the child is recording and gauging their progress? Observing parents' reactions may influence us to adjust our curricular program or to provide clearer information about particular instructional activities or routines.

A final benefit of such conferences is that teachers have an opportunity to interact with parents in a more relaxed, nonproblematic context. Parents indicated that this new conference format felt more personal and engaging than the traditional teacher-centered conference. In addition, by asking parents to participate actively in helping their child assess their areas of strength, set goals, and make plans for future learning, we created a more visible role for them in their children's learning process. We know that parents really are their children's earliest and most enduring teachers. Educators cannot possibly give students the individual attention they need to help them realize their full potential. By involving parents in activities, such as student-led conferences, we can help them become more aware of their children's needs and signal the parents' importance in this endeavor.

We do recognize that the impact of this type of conference may differ, depending upon the ethnic–cultural background of the family. Although the development of children in leadership roles aligns very closely with individualistic value structures, this role may not be a role for children valued in families having more collectivistic values. In this latter group of families, children are expected to look to parents for leadership and guidance (Quiroz, Greenfield & Altchech 1999). We do believe that these cultural traditions may be bridged so that dominant-cultural strategies are combined with those that are more familiar to parents of non-dominant cultural traditions. For example, at the elementary school level we structured our conference format as a group conference in which the teacher first presented information and then allowed the children to share their work. We assumed that such a conference format might build on collectivist values and might be less threatening and allow parents to gain insights and information from one another as questions and discussions ensued during the conference. It would also be important to address language differences by providing a translator for families.

Summary

In conclusion, when we initially decided to introduce our students and their parents to student-led conference practices, we initially saw the conference as a reporting activity and language only as a tool through which our students would describe the external reality of their performance. As we helped our students generate new and different knowledge about themselves, we found our own role as educators changing as well. Not only were we concerned with helping students report on their learning, but also we invited students to think about themselves in new ways. As a result, we found the student-led conference to be a powerful learning strategy for helping students view themselves differently and engage more fully in their learning.

Part IV

Building Relationships Through Joint Decision Making and Problem Solving

To effectively partner with students' families, educators must include families in their decision making and problem solving about a student. To do so, educators need to learn how to jointly solve problems with families so as to help them determine whether their children require special education services or the families require outside resources to address their unique needs. Chapter 11 describes a process of jointly problem solving with families. Chapter 12 depicts how educators can partner with families when deciding whether a student needs special education services and developing and implementing an educational plan for a student. Chapter 13 considers how educators can assist families who face crisis situations that affect their capacity to care for their children. Chapter 14 considers how educators might work together in a school to create more culturally responsive ways of relating to the families of their students.

Chapter 11

Engaging in Collaborative Problem Solving with Families

Ann A. Rai and Ellen S. Amatea

Learning Objectives

After reading this chapter, you will be able to:

- Describe the four styles of conflict management.
- Discuss the common barriers to engaging in collaborative family–school meetings to resolve student problems and difficulties.
- Explain the principles that underlie collaborative family–school problem solving.
- Describe the steps involved in conducting collaborative family–school problem-solving meetings.
- Describe specific techniques for blocking the blaming that often characterizes family–school problem-solving efforts.

■ Discuss the use of the skills of structuring, listening, brainstorming, and consensus building in the facilitation of family–school meetings.

■ Discuss the applicability to family–school problem-solving meetings with culturally diverse families.

> *My approach is to "let sleeping dogs lie." I don't meet with a parent unless I absolutely have to. Instead I try and do everything I can to resolve a child's difficulty myself, and pray either that those things work or that the problem will take care of itself. (A 5th grade teacher.)*
>
> *When I call parents in to meet with me about a problem their child has, I have a specific idea in mind of what I need for them to do to help me resolve it. My job in the meeting is to convince them to do what I think is needed. (A 6th grade teacher.)*
>
> *I often find that when I meet with parents about a problem their child is having, I have a difficult time having them understand my point of view. Rather than their doing what I think is needed, I end up agreeing to do what they want to avoid hard feelings. (A 1st grade teacher.)*
>
> *I believe it is important to have both students and their parents work with me to figure out how we might resolve a difficulty the student is experiencing. I firmly believe that three heads are better than one. I know that together we can often come up with ways of solving a problem that I would never be able to think of by myself. (A 3rd grade teacher.)*

Teachers are often the bearers of unpleasant information to parents. Letting parents know about bad or inappropriate behavior, or that students are failing or need to be retained, is never easy. These and other difficult communication tasks can engender feelings of apprehension and discomfort in both parents and teachers. As the preceding comments depict, educators vary in their style of handling these matters with parents.

Some educators, like the one depicted in the first comment, try to *avoid* conflict by not talking with parents about a child's difficulty unless they absolutely must. These individuals tend to withdraw when faced with the possibility of conflict, perceiving their own goals and those of the child and family to be of much less importance than the fear of experiencing conflict. Feeling hopeless and helpless to address a child's problem or to address and resolve conflicting views about the problem, these educators often maintain a facade that all is well until problems have reached such a critical stage that they cannot be ignored any longer.

Other educators, like the one depicted in the second comment, use a competitive style of conflict management in which they perceive their perspective and goals as highly important and place little value on preserving the parent–educator relationship. These individuals try to *overpower* others by forcing them to accept the solution that they favor. Having a "win–lose" mindset, they believe in a "taking a hard line" and getting others to do things their way even at the expense of their relationship with them. In contrast, educators who believe that preserving the harmony of the family–school relationship is more important than their own personal goals often *accommodate* to parents' perspectives to avoid conflict. This "soft" cooperative, nonassertive style, depicted by the third teacher's comments, is labeled as an accommodating style of conflict management because the respondent favors "giving in," or accommodating to others' demands, rather than risk conflict in the relationship.

A *collaborative* style of conflict management is depicted in the fourth teacher's comment. Viewing a student's problems and conflicting perspectives as an opportunity to seek better outcomes and build more effective relationship with families, this individual invites parents and students in to share their ideas openly, to collectively discuss alternative perspectives, and to manage differences constructively. Obviously, the extent to which educators and family members can engage in such problem solving is dependent upon the degree of trust present in the relationship. In Reflective Exercise 11.1 we ask you to consider which style of conflict management you use most frequently.

Reflective Exercise 11.1

Conflict Management Style

What style of managing conflict did you see modeled in your family when you were growing up?

How comfortable are you with people who display a very different style of conflict management?

Although no one style of conflict management will be effective in every situation, we believe that a collaborative style of conflict management offers the greatest possibility for both effectively resolving students' problems and building trusting relationships with students' families. However, we know from our own lives that the collaborative style of conflict management is not commonly illustrated in many of our day-to-day interactions. Instead we often see the hard, competitive style of conflict resolution or the soft accommodating style modeled in our school, work, or family lives.

As a result, despite the best of intentions for working with students and families, many teachers may feel unprepared and uneasy when it comes to working with families in resolving children's problems. Because knowledge of this way of managing conflicts is not commonly available, in this chapter we describe the steps and skills involved in conducting collaborative family–school problem-solving meetings. In addition, we investigate the applicability of engaging in such problem solving with culturally diverse families. But first, let us discuss some of the barriers to using this style of problem solving and conflict management.

Barriers to Collaborative Problem Solving

Four significant barriers exist to effectively implementing collaborative problem solving in today's schools: (a) the emotionally charged nature of such meetings, (b) the tendency to blame, (c) the monocultural and monolingual orientation of the school, and (d) the traditional style of conducting such meetings. Let us look at each of these more fully.

Emotionally Charged Nature of Family–School Meetings

The typical parent–teacher meeting convened to discuss a child's problem inevitably is charged emotionally. Why is this so? To parents, their child is the most important person in their lives, the one who arouses the deepest passions and greatest vulnerabilities, the one who inspires their fiercest advocacy and protection. And the teachers, deemed society's adults (Lightfoot 2003), are with whom parents must seek an alliance and support in their efforts to rear their child. Parents know that for their child to prosper at school, they must be willing to release their child into the hands of this perfect stranger. Parents also know that they must be willing to have their efforts to rear their child scrutinized and evaluated by that teacher. However, parents' fears and expectations about their interactions with teachers are colored by their own childhood experiences with teachers and with learning. Can I trust this teacher with my child? Will she or he care for my child as I do? Hence, parents often feel very exposed emotionally at such meetings. Teachers also often dread their problem-focused encounters with parents. As Lightfoot (2003) explains:

> The parent–teacher conference is also the arena in which teachers feel the most uncertain, exposed, and defensive, and the place where they feel their competence and professionalism most directly challenged. Beneath the polite surface of parent–teacher conferences, burns a cauldron of fiery feelings made particularly difficult because everyone carefully masks them and they seem inappropriate for the occasion. (21)

Given this emotional context, it is not surprising that misunderstandings between parents and teachers are commonplace. Teachers and parents often have access to different sources of information, have different goals and values (Schmidt & Tannenbaum 2000), and can come from different backgrounds (Fisher & Ury 1991). Each person sees the world from his or her own perspective and assumes that that perspective is the correct version of reality. When differences do occur, strong feelings can contribute to a loss of objectivity and a threatening of egos. The relationship between the parties is often put in jeopardy (Schmidt & Tannenbaum), and solving the problem becomes a series of emotional reactions and counter reactions in which one party blames the other party for the problem (Fisher & Ury). In the end, the child's problem is never solved.

Tendency to Blame

Many parents and educators do not have a history of trusting each other. Often the only type of communication between schools and families that occurs is when students are having problems. Typically, the decision to invite parents in to deal with a student's emotional or academic problem may be fraught with tension and blaming on both sides. Often a student's problems have progressed to the point in which a crisis occurs that cannot be overlooked. Teachers and parents may have conflicting ideas about the nature of the crisis situation and how best to resolve it. When neither party meets the other's expectations, blame results. For example, teachers may expect parents to do what they suggest, grow frustrated by parents' inaction, and judge the parents to be incompetent. Rather than blame the child or blame themselves, they blame the child's family for the student's continuing difficulties. Parents may believe that the teacher does not understand or care about their child and may push for teachers to demonstrate greater understanding. If the teacher does not comply with the parents' requests, the parents may judge the teacher as uncaring and ineffective and blame the teacher for the child's problem.

We have a history of thinking that we must decide whom is to blame as the cause of a problem as a necessary step in problem solving. Hence, inordinate amounts of time are spent deciding "who is at fault" for a child's problem. Is it a lazy child, an incompetent teacher, or an unresponsive parent? Although such blaming is common in family–school interactions, this activity is counter-productive to building a sense of shared responsibility for solving a student's problem. Hence, we will devote time in this chapter to show you how to circumvent (or block) the blaming common to such meetings.

Monocultural and Monolingual Nature of Schools

As you learned in Chapter 6, many schools are monocultural in their outlook. That is, they embrace the norms and values of the dominant culture. As a result, educators' expectations regarding the role that parents should play in the educational process and in problem solving are often based on a middle-class cultural script that is highly individualistic. Yet many students' families may value more collectivist cultural patterns resulting in valuing behaviors and goals for their child that may differ from those promoted by middle-class teachers and parenting their children differently. A common conclusion is that one form of parenting is superior to others in producing high-achieving children. However such a judgment fails to consider the many positive benefits of collectivist cultural practices. For example, a study of child-rearing beliefs of immigrant parents from Cambodia, Mexico, the Philippines, and Vietnam, as well as native-born Anglo American and Mexican American parents, revealed that Anglo American parents valued autonomy and creativity more than did the other parents (Okagaki & Sternberg 1993). The immigrant parents valued conformity to external standards more than did the American-born parents.

Furthermore, not only may educators use a language unfamiliar to students' families, but also they may engage in a style of communication and problem solving that is unfamiliar to them (Dupraw & Axner 1997). For example, families from more collectivist cultures may favor using high-context communication patterns in which nonverbal communication (e.g., pauses, silence) plays a larger role in meaning making than they do in individualistic cultures. In addition, the respective roles and positions of the communicators may influence the meaning making more strongly. Finally, a preference for indirect talk exists in more collectivistic cultures. Rather than frank and direct disclosure of emotions or personal information, direct acknowledgment of conflict, or use of probing questions, persons from these cultures may be comfortable with indirect acknowledgment of information about their personal lives and perspectives.

Traditional Style of Parent–Teacher Meetings

Not only are the monocultural orientation of schools and the use of blaming major barriers to collaborative problem solving, but also the traditional approach educators have used in conducting meetings with parents in the past impedes the use of a collaborative problem-solving approach. The tradition in many schools is to use a competitive style of problem solving and conflict management in parent–school meetings. Well illustrated by the second comment in the opening of the chapter, educators assume that their job is to decide the nature of the problem and how it is to be solved before the parent–school meeting, and then to convince the parent of the correctness of this problem definition and proposed solution. The Case Study provides an example of such a meeting and highlights some of the problems inherent in this traditional approach. As you read this meeting scenario, think about whether the principal and teacher understand the child and parent's viewpoints and whether the parent and child understand the teacher's viewpoints.

CASE STUDY 11.1

Jack and the Fishbowl

Jack is a fourth grade student at Spring Hill Elementary School. It is two weeks before Christmas break, and his teacher Ms. Radcliff has had enough. Jack has been difficult to handle throughout the entire semester. Although he has scored high on standardized tests, Jack is failing both reading and math. He does not complete his in-class assignments or homework. Not only is he failing important subjects, but also he is disrupting the entire classroom. He is constantly out of his seat, fights frequently with other students, and tells jokes while the teacher is lecturing.

Ms. Radcliff has tried everything she knows to help improve Jack's behavior and academic performance. Among other strategies, she has tried giving him positive reinforcement, getting him a tutor that could help him after school, sending him to the principal's office, giving him time-out, ignoring him, changing his seating arrangement, and giving him after-school detention. Because the principal has suggested that teachers in the school involve parents when there was a problem at the school, Ms. Radcliff has called Jack's mother repeatedly to inform her of Jack's academic and behavioral problems.

However, Ms. Radcliff believes that her efforts to contact Jack's mother are a waste of time. In the beginning, Jack's mother seemed to be cooperative, but, as of late, when Ms. Radcliff calls, Jack's mother, Ms. Nichols, seems angry and defensive. Jack's mother even had the audacity to suggest that maybe Ms. Radcliff was the problem. Ms. Radcliff is at the end of her rope and does not know what else she can do.

Yesterday in the classroom Jack took the classroom fish bowl and threw it onto the floor. Ms. Radcliff met with the principal about this incident, and they decided to emphasize the seriousness of Jack's problems and the need for Jack's mother to control Jack by requiring a parent conference before Jack could return to school.

The principal's secretary calls Ms. Nichols, Jack's mother, and informed her that Jack was in trouble again, needed to be picked up from school, and that she must come to the school for a parent conference before Jack can return to school. The meeting was scheduled for the following day at 11:30 A.M.

Jack's mother is angry and frustrated. She has tried to help Jack but she does not know what else to do. She is beginning to think that Jack's problems are due to Ms. Radcliff. Jack has never had problems in school before, and he does not seem to be a problem at home. In addition, she now has to take two unpaid days off from work. As a single parent, she cannot afford to miss days from work. When Ms. Nichols asks Jack about the incident, he says it was an accident.

Jack is angry and scared that his mother has been called to school. He thinks that Ms. Radcliff does not like him and is trying to get him in trouble with his mother. He did knock over the fish bowl, but it was an accident. Jack has been very frustrated in his classroom. He used to be a very good student, but lately the work seems very difficult and he can't seem to concentrate, and to make things worse, Ms. Radcliff has moved him to the back of the class where he has difficulty with hearing and seeing the board. Jack's parents divorced last summer. He misses his father very much, and some of the boys in the class are teasing him about not having a father.

Ms. Nichols and Jack arrive at the school. Jack is sent to eat lunch with his classmates, and Ms. Nichols waits in the office for the teacher to arrive. After a few minutes, the teacher and the school resource officer arrive and go into the principal's office. After what seems like hours, Ms. Nichols is called in to the office. The principal is sitting behind his desk with the police officer standing beside him and the teacher sitting in one of two chairs facing the desk. Ms. Nichols is seated in the other chair.

The principal begins by introducing himself and the resource officer. He then goes on to describe each of the behavioral incidents that Jack has been involved in throughout the year, culminating with the fish bowl incident. He concludes his statements by saying that he is very concerned about Jack's behavior and that he is considering whether Jack should be assessed for a possible emotional problem (which might entail testing and placement in a special education classroom).

The teacher then echoes what the principal has already said and shares the challenges of having Jack in the classroom as well as her concerns about Jack's lack of academic progress. She suggests that the mother seek counseling for Jack from a mental health professional. Ms. Radcliff's frustration with Jack is clearly evident in the tone of her voice.

Ms. Nichols sits quietly and passively, apparently taking in the conversation but inside she is scared, angry, and overwhelmed. She is scared that Jack will be placed in an EH classroom. She is angry with Ms. Radcliff, who evidently does not like her son and seems to have it out for him, and she feels overwhelmed that she does not know what else she can do to help Jack. Although Ms. Nichols is feeling powerless, she assures the school staff that she will take care of things and that Jack will be punished. The principal thanks Ms. Nichols for coming in, all parties shake hands, and the meeting is adjourned.

Questions to Consider

- Which style of conflict management did the school staff use?
- What were the effects of this style of problem solving and conflict management on the outcomes agreed on and the participants' relationship?

Unfortunately, the meeting described previously is not atypical in today's schools. Problem solving is a difficult endeavor and often involves people getting upset, taking things personally, and misunderstanding each other (Fisher & Ury 1991). Typical methods of resolving conflicts and solving problems often leave people feeling exhausted, dissatisfied, and alienated. People usually understand two ways of problem solving: hard and soft. In the soft accommodating way, one party gives in and is left feeling exploited and bitter, as in the case of Ms. Nichols. In the hard competitive way, resolving the problem becomes a contest of wills. This competition between parties is most often damaging to the relationships between the parties and exhausts available resources (Fisher & Ury).

Schools have traditionally dealt with the challenges of problem solving with families by having the contact between schools and families be short and highly ritualized. Educators assume that they should operate as the experts, somewhat like a doctor might in a medical context. The school is seen as the authority, and the locus of the problem is with the child and his or her family. The child and possibly his or her parents are viewed as deficient and in need of treatment (Silverstein, Springer & Russo 1992). The school only meets with parents of children who are having problems. Calling in the parent for a meeting is used as a threat or punishment to get the child to behave more appropriately. However, children are typically left out of this type of meeting, or, if they are included, they are passive observers of the process rather than active participants. Such meetings are often short, and the main purpose is to report to the parents (usually the mother) the nature of their child's problem and what the school has decided to do about it. This might entail the school reporting what they have decided to do to fix the child's problem or what they expect the parent to do. No decision making or problem solving occurs during the meeting itself, as well as an assumption that a follow-up is needed. Because this traditional style meeting has not been very successful, many educators have begun developing more collaborative ways of increasing problem solving between families and schools.

Collaborative Family–School Problem Solving

In this section, we describe the SOLVES approach to family–school problem solving. It differs substantially from the traditional way that educators structure their meetings with parents. This problem-solving approach is based on four philosophical principles common to other joint problem-solving approaches (Christenson & Hirsch 1998):

1. Educators view their relations with students' families as a means for preparing the child for success in school rather than just a mechanism for gathering

information from parents that would help educators to better prepare the child. Hence, the focus is on home and school sharing the goal of facilitating the child's learning and development and also sharing joint responsibility and ownership for problem solving and problem change.

2. Parents and educators recognize that the child is the central purpose for their collaboration. Hence, a clear boundary is established between the home and school in which parents and educators respect each others' domain and competence yet view their roles as reciprocal and flexible depending on situational demands.

3. If discontinuities and differing views occur between home and school, they are not feared but are seen as important to investigate and understand. As a result, conflicts and differences are communicated openly and directly rather than left to fester. Methods are developed for routinely sharing information and resolving issues of mutual interest or concern.

4. The focus of professional helping shifts from diagnosis and treatment of the child's (or family's) deficits and problem to the development of a cooperative partnership in which each party views the other as having specific strengths and competencies. "The educator sees strengths of the child and family and facilitates problem solving to establish shared ownership for solution identification." (325)

The purposes of the SOLVES family–school problem-solving approach are to achieve a productive outcome for the child and to build a strong working relationship between home and school (Amatea, Daniels, Brigman & Vandiver 2004.) SOLVES, a modification of the family–school meeting format designed by Weiss & Edwards (1992) of the Family–School Collaboration Project at the Ackerman Institute, was developed with input from educators and parents and has been implemented in both suburban and urban elementary and middle school settings.

In the family–school meeting, the child, parent, teacher, and, possibly, other stakeholders, discuss their concerns together, think of possible solutions to resolve the concerns, and develop a concrete plan to solve the problem. The facilitator of the meeting uses specific techniques to block blame so that participants do not lose their objectivity, and relationships are nurtured instead of damaged (Weiss & Edwards 1992). During the thirty to forty-five minutes allocated for the meeting, the goal is not only to work on solving the problem, but also to build positive working relationships between participants. Once positive relationships are solidified, the team can continue to work on solving the problem by developing and implementing new solutions as needed. The collaborative meeting follows a structured sequence of six steps that ensures that all participants in the meeting have a chance to talk about their concerns, offer solutions, and come up with a plan to help the student be more successful in school (Weiss & Edwards). A comparison of the traditional family–school meeting practices and this collaborative family–school problem-solving format is depicted in Table 11.1.

~~~~~~

Table 11.1   Comparison of Traditional and Collaborative Family–School Meetings

	Traditional	Collaborative
Purpose of the Meeting	Parents are called in to punish or threaten the student.	Parents are viewed as an important resource in solving the problem.
Who Is Included	Child is not included or is included to receive punishment.	■ Parent(s), student, teacher, and others ■ Child is key player in decision making.
Roles in the Meeting and in Decision Making	Teachers and administrators decide what to do about the problem before the meeting. Parents hear one of two messages: "This is what we are going to do to fix the problem." Or "You fix your child. He or she is the problem."	Problem solving is a joint process of parent, student, and teacher. Power is shared.
Environmental Features	■ Short meetings ■ No attempt at building relationships ■ Parent feels blamed for the child's problem.	■ Blame blocked ■ Participants sit in circle. ■ Time is committed to the meeting. ■ Meeting process is explained. ■ No one is blamed for the problem.
Result	The consequences of not changing the problematic behavior are spelled out for the child and parent. No plan for change or follow-up is created.	A concrete plan is developed to solve the problem, and follow-up is set to evaluate the progress of the plan.

Implementing the *SOLVES* Family–School Meeting
~~~~~~~~~~
~~~~~~~~~~

Now that you have some understanding of the assumptions and philosophy of the family–school problem-solving meeting, let us look more closely at the specific steps and procedures involved in conducting a family–school problem-solving meeting. Before embarking on planning and carrying out such meetings, it is important to remember that the family–school problem-solving meeting works most effectively when teachers have already built positive relationships with parents using climate building activities, such as student-led parent conferences and regular communication. Your first interaction with parents should not be the problem-solving meeting. As discussed earlier, when parents are called to the school to discuss problems their child is having in school, both the parent and the child often feel quite anxious. It is much easier to discuss problems when the parent already sees you as caring for and supporting their child. Climate-building activities can help you create an atmosphere of trust, goodwill, and cooperation that makes address- ing children's problems much easier.

Six steps are involved in conducting family–school problem-solving meetings. The steps, listed in Table 11.2, form the acronym SOLVES.

Step One: Setting Up the Meeting and Inviting the Student and Family

The first step in conducting a problem-solving meeting is to decide why you want to meet, who is to be involved, and when and where the meeting will occur. You need to first think about why you want to meet. What do you hope to accomplish in the meeting? As you think about what you would like to accomplish in the meeting, think about achieving small, specific goals. Students may have multiple or complex problems at school. Think about one issue that, if solved, might have the most influence on improving the student's academic and social functioning. As you think about what you would like to see happen in the meeting, remember that your perspective of the problem is only one perspective. You may discover information in the process of the meeting that will change your ideas about what you would like to accomplish in the meeting.

Deciding Whom to Invite

Several considerations are involved in deciding whom you would like to invite to the meeting. The most important consideration is to determine the people most concerned about the student's welfare and who have an important stake in solving

~~~~~~

Table 11.2   Steps in the Family–School Problem-Solving Meeting

Step One:	**S**	Setting up the meeting and preparing the student and family
Step Two:	**O**	Orienting to purpose and process and introducing participants
Step Three:	**L**	Listening to participants' concerns and blocking blame
Step Four:	**V**	Validating concerns and creating consensus about meeting goals
Step Five:	**E**	Expanding solution ideas
Step Six:	**S**	Setting up and implementing the action plan and follow-up

the problem. The first person to be included is the student. In traditional problem-solving meetings, the student is often excluded from the process. However, we have found that by actively involving the student in identifying the problem and coming up with the solutions, the solutions arrived at by the meeting participants are better tailored to the student's individuality. In addition, the student is more motivated to carry out the solutions when he or she has been involved in the process. To appreciate the impact that involving the student can have on the meeting process and outcome, imagine that you are having a problem at work. In one instance, your supervisor comes to you and says that he or she has discussed your problem with others and has come up with some specific solutions for you. If you do not carry out these solutions you will be fired, demoted, or otherwise punished. How do you imagine you might feel? What might be your response to the suggestions made by your supervisor? Now consider an alternative situation. You are having the same problem at work, but, in this instance, your supervisor comes to you and asks your perspective on the problem and engages you in solving the problem. What are the differences in how you feel and respond when you are involved in solving the problem?

The next participants to invite to the meeting are the students' parents or caregivers. In most instances, all caregivers and parents should be invited to attend the meeting. Each parent may have different perspectives on the problem and on solutions to the problem that may be helpful in solving the problem. Another reason to involve all caregivers in the process is that, if the plan is supported by all of the major parties in the child's life, the plan is more likely to be carried out. If one of the parents or caregivers cannot attend the meeting, you might want to consider including the caregiver who could not attend by calling them on the phone or by having the student share the plan with the absent caregiver and have that caregiver also sign the plan and return it to the school. More than likely, you may have students who are being raised by grandparents or adults other than their parents or whose parents have divorced. In these cases, plan to first call the primary caregiver of the child to gain their permission to involve other family members. Explain to them the benefits of involving other caregivers of the child. The primary caregiver may want to take the responsibility for inviting the other caregiver, or you may prefer that you call and invite the other caregiver. If the primary caregiver refuses to have other caregivers involved, respecting the caregiver's wishes is important.

Other important stakeholders whom you may want to consider inviting to the meeting are neighbors, mentors, tutors, other teachers in the school with whom the child has a special relationship, guidance counselors, administrators, social workers, ministers, coaches, or others that caregivers suggest might be helpful in solving the problem. Knowing the child and the family beforehand will help you make the best decision about whom to invite to the meeting. The key is to invite people to the meeting who have a stake in solving the problem or who can help the students and caregivers feel more comfortable in the meeting. Be sensitive to the number of people invited to the meeting. You do not want the parent and child to feel intimidated by having too many people from the school involved in the meeting. You may feel that it is essential to have several school staff involved, but consult with the parent about whom you plan to invite to the meeting. Also, be sure to prepare the parent ahead of time regarding the number of people you wish to have participate and invite the parent to bring a support person.

In scheduling a place to conduct the meeting, find a place that is comfortable and inviting. An optimal space is one in which the meeting participants can sit in a circle (without a table dividing them). So look for a space in which the appropriate number of chairs can be placed in a circle.

The last stage in planning the meeting is for you to think about how you will conduct the meeting. You will want to review the steps in the problem-solving meeting to make sure you are comfortable with them. If you think that parents might come into the meeting feeling anxious or angry, think about how you will respond ahead of time. Also, plan to bring the necessary materials to the meeting, such as copies of the family–school problem-solving meeting planning form and a pen or pencil. If materials are available that can help the parent to understand their child's problem in more concrete ways, such as your grade book and samples of the student's work, plan to bring those as well.

Preparing the Student and Parents

Because the tradition in many schools has been to call parents to the school only for the purpose of explaining to them the punishment that the child is to receive or to enlist them in threatening their child with punishment, both students and parents often have negative expectations about family–school meetings. Understandably, many parents expect that decisions will be made without their input, and students expect that their parents have been invited to come to school as punishment for the students' misdeeds. To change these expectations and increase the probability of having a successful meeting, your preparing the student and family prior to the meeting is important.

For the problem-solving meeting to be effective, the caregivers and student must view themselves as important resources for solving the student's problem. For the participants to view themselves in this way, some initial work is required. You will need to explain the purpose of the meeting, describe how the meeting will be conducted, and discuss the roles of the participants. You also need to emphasize that the student and the parent are not being invited in because the school is blaming them for causing the problem. Instead they are being asked to share responsibility for solving the problem.

In explaining the purpose of the meeting to the student or parent, describe the problem as you see it but convey that you need more information to understand what is going on. Explain that the purpose of the meeting is to come up with a plan to improve the problem situation and enlist the support of the student and family in solving the problem. For example: "I'm worried that you are not finishing your reading comprehension questions in class. I think it might be because you are having difficulty finishing reading the passages in time, but you know more than I about what is going on. I would like you and I, and your parents, to work together to see if we can figure out a way for you to do better in reading."

The next step in preparing the student or family is to explain what will happen during the meeting. You might want to show the student a copy of the Family–School Problem Solving Form (see Figure 11.1) that will be used during the meeting.

For example: "The first thing we will do in the meeting is that you, I, and your parents will each be invited to talk about what you are most concerned about and want to talk about in the meeting. After we hear from everyone, we will decide together about which concern to work on in the meeting. Next, we will

〰〰〰〰〰〰〰〰〰〰〰〰〰〰〰〰〰〰〰〰〰〰〰〰〰〰〰〰〰〰〰〰〰〰

Figure 11.1   Family–School Problem-Solving Meeting Form

Student _____   Date _____

Participating Stakeholders:

_____

Initial Concern:

_____

Exploring Stakeholders' Concerns: (What is each of you concerned about?)

Teacher's Perspective: _____

Parent's Perspective: _____

Student's Perspective: _____

Agreed On Problem: (What do we want to work on together first?)

_____

Agreed On Action Plan: (What will we do?)

Student's Task: _____

Parent's Task: _____

Teacher's Task: _____

Follow-Up: (How will we check on how the plan is going?)

Agreed to by:

Signed by Student: _____

Signed by Parent(s): _____

Signed by Teacher: _____

ask everyone for ideas about how we might solve the concern or problem we decide to work on. And, finally, we will put our heads together to come up with a plan to resolve the problem. Once we have a plan, we will give each person in the meeting a job to do to help solve the problem."

The final step is to discuss the student or family's role in solving the problem. For example: "Your job is to tell us what you think the problem is. We are relying a lot on what you say because you are the expert on *you* and what is happening to you. We would also like to hear what you have already done to solve the problem and what else we might be able to do together to try to solve the problem."

Even with this explanation, the student or the family may still worry that they will be blamed for the problem. To prevent them from feeling blamed, you need to clearly tell them that they are not to be blamed for the problem. For example, you might say: "I want you to know that you are not being blamed for the problem. You did not do anything bad or wrong, and I know that you are struggling with the problem. Our job is to come up with a plan to beat the problem."

Step Two: Orienting to the Meeting Purpose and Process and Introductions

You have prepared the student and the caregivers for the meeting ahead of time, and the day has come for the meeting. Make sure that the parents/caregivers are greeted as they enter the school and know where to go for the meeting. You might want to prepare the front office staff to provide a warm greeting and direct them to the meeting room. An even better solution would be for you to meet the family/caregivers when they arrive and walk with them to the meeting place. A warm reception can help anxious caregivers feel more comfortable.

As you enter the meeting room, invite the family members to have a seat. (If you recall, you should arrange the seating in a circle, so that each participants is at the same level.) Participants should sit in a circle, with the child sitting between the teacher and the parent(s). Begin the meeting with a little bit of "small talk" to ease the initial tensions that might exist. After a short period of informal talk, the facilitator of the meeting (who will typically be a teacher) will first ask everyone to introduce himself or herself and then will explain the purpose of the meeting, the roles of each person attending the meeting, and the process that will be followed in the meeting. For example, to explain the purpose and process of the meeting the facilitator might say: "Thank you for coming today. I invited you here to this meeting so that we can 'put our heads together' and come up with a plan to provide the best school experience we can for Jessica. I will be asking each of you to express your concerns. Our hope is that by the end of the meeting we will come up with a plan of action we will work on together to address a couple of concerns. Do you have any questions about the process?"

This information signals, according to Weiss and Edwards (1992), that the participants' concerns are important and will be heard, the meeting is not a punishment, and the meeting has a clear purpose of action (not merely talk) for change. In addition, because the focus is on school issues rather than family life issues, an appropriate boundary is set between home and school.

In communicating this information, the facilitator should speak in a manner that is easy to understand without using technical jargon. If technical terms must be used, the facilitator should make sure to explain each term in a familiar language. The facilitator should also make sure that he or she speaks to the child instead of about the child. Speaking about the child in the child's presence creates an atmosphere in which the child feels powerless and excluded from the meeting.

Step Three: Listening and Clarifying Participants' Concerns and Blocking Blame

In this step, each person who attends the meeting has a turn to voice one or two concerns about the student. Not only will the facilitator probe for factors in the child's life that may be maintaining the child's problem, but also ask about situations in which the problem does not occur, and/or solutions they have attempted to solve the problem. During this phase of the meeting, it may also be necessary for the facilitator or other participants to block the implicit or explicit blame of self or others that may be expressed at this time (Weiss & Edwards 1992). The beliefs of the participants about who is responsible for a problem are often expressed as implicit or explicit blame. This blame can derail joint problem solving from occurring. For example, a parent might say to a teacher: "I don't have problems making John behave at home." Implied in this statement is the message that somehow the teacher does not have the ability that the parent has to effectively control the child's behavior. Teachers might find themselves responding by defending their situation more strongly, thus derailing their efforts at joint problem solving. In the next section of the chapter, we introduce you to strategies for effectively dealing with such blaming statements.

A useful starting point is for the teacher to share his or her concerns because the teacher's style of reporting can serve as a model for the other participants in the meeting. The teacher should focus on no more than one or two specific concerns that are most important. In doing so, in a language the child and family can understand, the teacher needs to be as direct and concrete as possible. The teacher should describe the actions that took place and the context in which they occurred, giving specific examples whenever possible. The teacher may also want to mention areas in which the child is doing well. Here is an example of one teacher's report:

> As you know, John does really well in science. He earns high grades, and his science project on volcanoes was one of the best in the class. However, I am concerned about his math performance. I have noticed that John's math grades have been falling and that John has not been turning in his homework.

We give a quiz each Friday, and his last three grades have been a C, a D, and an F. Also, he has not turned in any homework in the last two weeks. I am surprised about John's recent behavior. During the first nine weeks, he turned in every homework assignment and most of his quiz grades were Bs or Cs.

After the teacher shares his or her concerns, each person at the meeting should be invited to share his or her concerns without being interrupted. As the participants in the meeting share their concerns, the teacher should record their responses on the Family–School Problem-Solving Meeting Form

An important aspect in clarifying each participant's concerns is to make them more understandable to others in the meeting. This can be done by asking each participant to provide sufficient information about (a) when, (b) where, (c) with whom, and (d) under what conditions they view that a problem occurs. The teacher may also want to find out when the problem does not occur. Focusing on the times when the problem does not occur may help the student and others at the meeting recognize the student's strengths and successes (Weiss & Edwards 1992).

Step Four: Validating and Checking for Consensus About Shared Concerns

The goal in this step is find the commonalities among the concerns that participants shared and single out one concern that participants decide to work together to change. This can be accomplished by highlighting areas of agreement around which the parents, educators, and student can work together, and focusing the discussion toward which, of all of the things talked about, would be most helpful to develop a plan of action (e.g., after a concern has been agreed on, write the concern on the planning form).

When choosing a concern, the language that is used to describe the concern can be of critical importance. Change-inducing language can provide the group with hope that change in the concern is possible and create more opportunities for intervention. The following strategies use change-inducing language:

1. One form of change-inducing language is to talk about the problem in the past tense rather than in the future or present tense. Doing this conveys that the present and the future might be different from the past (O'Hanlon 1999). For example, say, "You were getting in fights every day," instead of "You get in fights every day."

2. Because the use of all-or-nothing words, such as *always, never, every time, no one, nothing,* or *everyone* can inhibit change and block creative thinking, substitute all-or-nothing words with partial statements or questions (O'Hanlon 1999). For example, instead of saying, "You never turn in your homework," say, "You usually do not turn in your homework."

3. Avoid talking about a student or parent as the problem. Labels given to students can become a self-fulfilling prophecy (O'Hanlon 1999). For example, instead of saying, "You are a behavior problem," try, "You demonstrate problem behavior at times."

4. Try to separate the person from the problem. This can be accomplished by discussing the problem as if it is external to the person. Externalizing the problem creates an atmosphere in which the student feels less shame and less need to blame others (Winslade & Monk 1999).

5. Use language that creates hope for the future. Some key phrases to use to help create a sense of positive expectancy are "as of yet," "so far," "up until now," "when," and "will" (O'Hanlon 1999). For example, "Up until now, you have been failing math," or "So far you haven't been able to make any friends in the classroom." These phrases communicate that the possibility of a different future exists.

Step Five: Expanding Solution Ideas

Now that the group has come to a consensus about the concern that they would like to address, the next task is to come up with a list of possible solutions to solve the problem. Participants are asked to brainstorm together. Each person at the meeting is asked to come up with one or two ideas to solve the problem. A few rules need to be considered to guide this process of brainstorming together to come up with a list of solutions: (a) Initially, no one is to judge any of the solutions that are suggested, and (b) the person who shares the solution should be given the opportunity to give his or her solution without being interrupted. These guidelines help produce more creative solutions to the problem. Once the group has come up with a list of possible solutions, the facilitator asks the group if they can think of other possible solutions by saying, "What else could we try to solve the problem?" Once a complete list of solutions is generated, the list can be used to assist the group in developing an action plan.

Step Six: Setting Up an Action Plan and Follow-Up

The final step in the family–school problem-solving meeting is for the participants to develop an action plan and arrange for follow-up. The action plan specifies *who* will complete each task to solve the problem, *what* each task will be, *when* each task will be completed, and *how* the tasks will be completed. In discussing how the plan will be completed, particular attention will be paid to the standard of quality expected in completing the assigned tasks. The follow-up is scheduled to evaluate the progress of participants in implementing the plan.

The completed action plan should always involve a task for the child to do and should be focused on a school-related issue as opposed to a family-related issue. All members present at the meeting should be included in the action plan in some way. Including all of the members in the action plan communicates that all parties have some responsibility in solving the problem. Although all members are included in the plan, tasks are assigned that are appropriate to the role and skill level of the participants.

After the plan is completed, the plan should be recorded on the planning form, and all members should sign that they are in agreement of the plan. Once the plan is signed, copies should be given to all participants at the meeting and a follow-up contact should be scheduled two weeks following the first meeting. During the follow-up meeting, the team will review the plan to determine whether tasks were completed, whether the plan is helping the student, and whether anything needs to be added to the plan.

Skills Needed in Conducting Family–School Problem-Solving Meetings

The steps of the family–school problem-solving meeting are fairly straightforward. However, one of the greatest challenges in conducting a problem-solving meeting is handling the emotions that are generated. Emotions often get entangled with the objective aspects of the problem (Fisher & Ury 1991). If there is no mechanism in place to handle strong emotions, problem solving can easily dissolve into a series of interactions in which parties blame each other for the problem. In *Getting to Yes: Negotiating Agreement Without Giving In,* Fisher and Ury (1991) describe four strategies that are used to handle the strong emotions associated with family–school problem solving. They are (a) separating the person from the issue or problem, (b) focusing on mutual interests, (c) generating options prior to making decisions, and (d) basing final decisions on objective criteria.

Approaching negotiation with a win–win ("we versus the problem") mindset is critical rather than a win–lose ("me versus you") mindset. Unfortunately, the win–lose approach to problem solving permeates society. Approaching problem solving as though it were a contest, with the goal of having decisions made your way at all cost, however, perpetuates conflict and can weaken the family–school relationship. To take a win–win perspective, the person (whether educator or family member) and the issue must be viewed separately; families and educators must be viewed as "working together on the same side against the problem." They must attack the problem not each other. The goals of such an orientation to problem solving are to understand the perception and position of the other party and to accept the right of individuals to think differently. Education and information, rather than coercion and force, is preferred. Finally, respect for and acceptance of the other's perspective (not to be confused with agreement with the other's perspective) characterizes this approach. According to Fisher and Ury (1991), if one partner fails to use a behavior, the other partner should not give up but rather continue because it would be good for the other person and the relationship between them.

With respect to the second strategy—focusing on mutual interests—family members and educators share a common interest in the education and development of children and youth. For example, by focusing on how to promote the learning and success of the child (e.g., "What is best for the child? What can we do to help the child be successful?), educators or parents may find less need to defend their position through argument.

Collaboratively generating a variety of options instead of making a one-sided decision is the third strategy needed in effective negotiation and problem solving. Obstacles that can inhibit creative brainstorming of possible options from occurring include (a) premature judgment of a proposed solution (e.g., That can't possibly work!), (b) a search for the perfect or best solution, (c) the belief that options are limited, and (d) the failure to see problems as a shared concern and shared responsibility for problem resolution (Fisher & Ury 1991).

Finally, it is important to remember that, in some circumstances, the interests of educators and families can conflict and may appear irreconcilable. The use of objective criteria to aid shared decision making—such as ethical and fair standards or expert judgment—may increase the probability of "breaking the logjam" and achieving understanding between parties. Such a strategy helps maintain the relationship because the decision is not influenced by who is most powerful or who holds out the longest in an argument.

Skills in Blocking Blame

The effectiveness of family–school problem solving is influenced by the degree to which blocking blame techniques are used (Weiss & Edwards 1992). A sample of typical blaming statements made by parents or by teachers is included in Table 11.3 on page 300. As you read these examples, try to imagine what you might do and feel if these statements were directed toward you. How would you respond if these statements were directed at you?

Some of the most helpful skills for conducting problem-solving meetings are skills for blocking blame. At various times during the family–school problem-solving meeting, the facilitator may need to block blame of both self and others. If blame is present, the solutions arrived at by the team are doomed to failure (Weiss & Edwards 1992). In Table 11.4 on page 301, you will find descriptions and examples of specific strategies developed by Weiss and Edwards of the Family–School Collaboration Project for blocking blame between parents, teachers, and students. They are *direct blocking, reframing, probing, refocusing, illustrating, validating,* and *agreeing.* These strategies help maintain the focus on mutual responsibility for problem resolution.

∿∿

Table 11.3   *Examples of Parents' and Teachers' Blaming Statements*

Parents' Statements of Blame

- The teacher does not understand my child. My son has a unique learning style that requires attention that the teacher is unwilling to provide.
- My daughter's teacher waits to call me until there is a problem. Doesn't he think I can be helpful before the problem arises? I know my child better than he does, yet no one has ever asked my opinion.
- Teachers act as if I know less than they do. I never know what goes on in my child's classroom. Don't they think I would understand?
- The teacher is too hard on my child. She singles him out to make him the example for the rest of the class.
- The teacher treats me as if it is my fault that my daughter is failing. The teacher expects me to teach my daughter at home; I work full time, I don't have time to do my job and hers, too.
- Teachers treat parents as if they are nuisances. I get the feeling that I am not an important part of my child's education.
- The teacher never has time for my child. He gives all the attention to the lower level students; meanwhile, my child is not getting the education she deserves.
- Teachers are hard to reach. I always have to leave a message when I call the school. Sometimes it will be days before they call me back.

Teachers' Statements of Blame

- Parents are demanding. They don't realize that I have 29 other students and many other parents to deal with.
- Some parents don't care enough about their children. How am I supposed to teach a student who hasn't had breakfast? Parents don't send their kids to school ready to learn.
- Parents do not understand my responsibilities and what a busy schedule I have. I teach six classes a day, which means I see 120 kids a day. Parents expect me to keep track of their child and know his or her progress the second they call.
- I am a teacher not a social worker. Yet I am expected to educate and handle my students' emotional needs.
- Parents are hard to reach. They don't like me calling them at work, and I don't get paid to call them after 5:00 P.M.
- Parents don't support my decisions. They undermine my instruction by questioning my judgment in front of their child.
- Most parents don't respect what I do—as if teaching is a less prestigious profession. I bet most parents would not last a day in my classroom.
- Parents are not involved enough with their children's education. They don't even help their child with their homework.

Source: Christenson, S., & Hirsch, J. (1998). Facilitating partnerships and conflict resolution between families and schools. In K. C. Staiber & T. R. Kratchowill (Eds.), *Handbook of group intervention for children and families* (312). Boston: Allyn & Bacon.

For example, to use the *probing* technique, the facilitator listens to the blaming statement and then asks for additional information to help understand the context that is leading to the blaming or anger. For example, a parent might say, "You treat my child unfairly." A probing response by the teacher would be, "I did not intend to treat your child unfairly. What do you see that I am doing that makes you think that I am treating her unfairly? Can you give me some specific examples?"

〜〜〜〜〜〜〜〜〜〜〜〜〜〜〜〜〜〜〜〜〜〜〜〜〜〜〜〜〜〜〜〜〜〜〜〜〜

Table 11.4   Techniques for Blocking Blame

Direct Blocking: Signaling that the purpose of the interaction is not to blame but to solve a problem. *Example:*

- Student: *Johnny always starts the fights—it's not my fault.*
- Teacher: *We're not here to find out who's to blame but to figure out how you and Johnny can get your work done instead of fighting.*

Reframing: Providing an alternate point of view about a set of facts, which gives the facts a more positive, productive meaning. *Example:*

- Teacher: *These parents drive me crazy—all they're concerned about is whether their child is going to get into the top class. It starts in pre-kindergarten.*
- Teacher: *It sounds as if they're trying to be an advocate for their child's education and get them started off on the right track.*

Probing: Eliciting additional information to clarify the context leading to the blaming.

- Student: *The teacher always picks on me.*
- Teacher: *I certainly don't intend to pick on you, David. What do you see me doing that makes you think I'm picking on you? Give me some examples.*

Refocusing: A statement that redirects the discussion from a nonproductive or nonessential area to an area relevant to helping the student. *Example:*

- Parent: *Joe did great last year with Mrs. Johnson. We think that Mrs. Williams is just not as good a teacher.*
- Counselor: *I can see that you're very concerned that Joe has a good year this year, too.*

Illustrating: Giving concrete examples of areas of concern. *Example:*

- Parent: *He doesn't act that way at home. You just don't know how to deal with him.*
- Teacher: *What I've observed is that Johnny acts that way when he is with his friends. They enjoy talking with each other so much that they do not seem to be able to stop when it's time to get down to work.*

Validating: Recognizing the validity of another's perceptions and/or efforts. *Example:*

- Parent: *I know June needs me to spend more time with her—maybe I should quit going to school.*
- Principal: *I can understand your concern about spending time with June but your going to school is also a positive role model for her. Let's see if there are other ways you could be helpful to her.*

Agreeing: Confirming someone's perception of a situation. *Example:*

- Teacher: *It really drives me nuts when people come in and think they can just take over the classroom.*
- Parent: *It would drive me nuts, too, if I thought someone was trying to take over something that I was responsible for.*

Source: Training handout from Howard M. Weiss, Center for Family–School Collaboration, Ackerman Institute for the Family, New York.

A *validating* technique can be used to recognize the legitimacy of another person's efforts or perceptions. In response to a parent's saying, "I am angry because I don't think that Doug is getting the attention in class that he deserves," the teacher might validate the parent by saying, "I can understand that you would feel angry if you thought Doug was being shortchanged in some way."

A somewhat paradoxical technique for blocking blame is to *agree* with someone's assessment of the situation when he or she expects you to get defensive. For example, if a parent says, "It makes me crazy when you tell me how I should be raising my own child," the teacher might respond by saying, "It would make me crazy too if I thought that someone were telling me how to raise my child."

A *refocusing* technique is used to redirect the dialogue from a nonrelevant or nonproductive area to an area relevant to helping the student. If a parent says, "You are a single woman. You can't possibly understand children until you have one yourself," the teacher could respond by asking, "What would you like me to know about your child that would help him do better in school?"

Giving specific, concrete examples to help explain a situation depicts use of the technique of *illustrating*. A parent might say something like, "He never misbehaves at home. I cannot imagine that he would behave the way you say." An illustrating technique used by the teacher might sound like this: "Let me give you a few examples of what I have seen. Johnny has gotten in trouble three times for throwing food in the cafeteria. He also has been stopped two times for running in the hallway." Having the appropriate materials available can also help illustrate your perspective to parents. If the issue is student attendance, you should be prepared with your attendance record. If the concern is work in a specific subject, be prepared to show the parent your grade book and student work samples.

A *direct blocking* technique involves saying directly that the purpose of the interaction is not to blame anyone for the problem but to help the student. To directly block the parent who says, "Danielle is never a problem at Girl Scouts or at church. There must be a problem with the way you are running your classroom," the teacher could say, "We are not here to blame anyone for the problem but to find a way to make things better."

The final blame blocking technique is *reframing*. Reframing is giving an alternative perspective about a set of facts that is more positive and productive. For example, a parent might say, "My child is always trying to do everything the boys down the street do." In response, the teacher might say, "Sounds as if he is trying hard to belong and be accepted by his friends." A quote from Fisher and Ury (1991) aptly summarizes the process of blocking blame:

> If pushing back does not work, how can you prevent the cycle of action and reaction? Do not push back. When they assert their positions, do not reject them. When they say attack, you don't say counterattack. Break the vicious cycle by refusing to react. Instead of pushing back, sidestep their attack and deflect it against the problem. Rather than rely on force, channel that energy into exploring mutual interests and inventing options for mutual gain. (108)

To improve your ability to conduct productive family–school problem-solving meetings, other important skills to master include (a) structuring, (b) listening,

(c) brainstorming, (d) consensus building, and (e) action planning. Structuring skills are the skills used to set up and follow the framework of the meeting and include such skills as being able to follow the process given in the six steps. Providing a clear structure for solving problems helps all participants feel less anxious and helps problem solving work more efficiently.

The listening and communication skills we discussed in Chapter 8 are essential to successful problem solving. These skills include paraphrasing, summarizing, using open questions, and empathic listening. Another way to think about the process of listening effectively is to practice the following: (a) Pay close attention to what is being said, (b) ask for clarification if needed, and (c) repeat what is being said to check for understanding (Fisher & Ury 1991).

In brainstorming, group members give their ideas to solve a problem. No criticism of initial ideas is allowed. Once a list of ideas is developed, promising ideas are starred and, if possible, improvements to these promising ideas are suggested. The process of suggesting ideas without judgment leads to more creative decisions, and the process of improving on the most favored solutions helps dovetail the interests of different parties (Fisher & Ury 1991).

Consensus building is the construction of shared understanding from people with divergent perspectives. Consensus has been achieved (a) when all members of the group feel respected and heard in full; (b) when they have been honest in sharing their concerns and feelings; (c) when all perspectives have been considered without prejudice; (d) when relevant information has been shared equally; and (e) when members of the group give full support of the decisions made and are willing to implement the decision as if it were their own (CIS Training, June 20, 1997). Table 11.5 provides a fuller explanation of the distinctive characteristics of consensus building.

Table 11.5   Consensus Building: What It Is and What It Is Not

What It Is	What It Is Not
General agreement by most of the group, team, or committee	Reached by voting
Encourages everyone to participate	Majority rules
Seeks to erase the imaginary line	Horse trading
Seeks a win–win solution or mutual gain solution	A win–lose solution
The best collective judgment of the group	Averaging
A fusion of information, logic, and emotion	Individual opinions
Hard work	

Source: CIS Training, June 1997.

Using Family–School Problem Solving with Culturally Diverse Families

Given the widely varying communication and conflict resolution preferences of culturally diverse families, it is most important that you gain some understanding of the cultural background and communication preferences of the family with whom you plan to work. For example, having children who have become proficient in English translate for their parents in a family–school meeting may seem practical on the surface. However, "placing children in a position of equal status with adults creates dysfunction within the family hierarchy for Latino parents (and other cultural groups)" (Finders & Lewis 1994, 52).

Quiroz, Greenfield, and Altchech (1999) recommend the following strategies in interacting cross-culturally with parents: (a) Foster a comfortable and respectful conversational tone, (b) use indirect questions, (c) recognize collectivistic values, (d) communicate a message of caring, and (e) cultivate empathy. To foster a comfortable and respectful conversational tone, keeping the tone informal is often helpful. Be sure to start off with a little small talk, whether in a phone contact or a meeting. This does not mean undue familiarity, however. You still need to address the family members with proper respect. Because some families are not comfortable with direct questions or requests to share their perspective or concerns, even the request to talk about their concerns or goals for their child must be done sensitively. A more indirect way to approach this might be to say, "Sometimes parents say it is hard to get their child to sit down and do homework at night because of so many other people living in the home." Parents might be relieved to hear that other people face a similar problem and therefore may feel less embarrassed to think about it.

Recognizing that parents may value behaviors that you do not is important. For example, because modesty is valued by many immigrant families, teachers may want to talk with such families about the goal of student achievement in the context of the classroom group and emphasize how such achievement is socially valued. When Gandara (1995) interviewed high-achieving Latinos, he found that being identified as "gifted" or "high achieving" in comparison to their classmates was made bearable only if there was an acknowledgment of the contribution their achievement brought back to the group.

To communicate a message of caring, the language the facilitator/educator uses is crucial. Often the pronoun *I* or *you* conveys a sense of separation between teachers and parents. In talking about the child, using the pronoun *we* makes it clear to the parents that the teacher has something in common with them and that they share responsibility for ensuring the child's successful school performance. Finally, most important, teachers must learn about the culture of the family and come to understand the expectations parents have for their child and for their role in the school.

Getting Started with Family–School Problem Solving

Now that you have learned the steps and skills necessary to conduct family problem-solving meetings, you are ready to try it out. But where do you begin? The most important ingredient for the successful implementation of family–school problem-solving meetings in your school is your own enthusiasm and commitment to seeing your ideas come to fruition. The philosophy of the family problem-solving meeting may be quite different than the prevailing culture of the school. The process of changing a culture in a school can be a slow process. Do not become discouraged if it takes time for others to share your excitement (SACES presentation, October 2001). As others in the school hear you talk about your experiences in working with students and families, they may become more open to trying out these new ideas.

As you begin to try out the family–school problem-solving meeting, gaining administrative support can help create the collaborative culture that makes implementation easier and help nurture the relationships between school staff and families (Weiss & Edwards 1992; SACES presentation, October 2001). Share your ideas with your colleagues, and try to find others in your school who are open to trying out new ways of working with students and their families. After you conduct a problem-solving meeting, having others in the school with whom you can discuss your efforts will help you become more proficient in conducting the meetings (Barth 1990).

As with learning any new skill, do not expect perfection the first time you try to conduct a meeting. The skills required to conduct a problem-solving meeting will take practice and refinement. As you practice the skills and reflect on your experience, you will become more confident and adept at utilizing the family–school problem-solving meeting to collaborate with families to solve problems. Finally, to continually improve your skills in conducting family–school problem-solving meetings, gathering evaluation data can be extremely helpful. When you collect feedback information from students and parents and other caregivers, you can use it to fine-tune the process to work most effectively with other staff and the families you serve. Included in Table 11.6 on page 306 is a sample parent evaluation. Similar evaluations for students and teachers should also be utilized.

Discussion

Problem solving in schools is, at its best, a challenging endeavor. At its worst, problem solving can escalate into an emotional battle in which parents, teachers, students, and administrators blame each other for a child's problem. When parties blame each other, the results are most likely to be alienation, frustration, and ineffectiveness. The

〜〜〜〜〜〜〜〜〜〜〜〜〜〜〜〜〜〜〜〜〜〜〜〜〜〜〜〜〜〜〜〜

Table 11.6 Family–School Problem-Solving Meeting Feedback Form: Parent Version

We would like to hear your feedback about participating in this family–school problem-solving meeting. Circle one of the following responses that best describes your reaction to the process and meeting: *Strongly Agree, Agree, Disagree,* or *Strongly Disagree.*

1. I was worried about what might happen in the meeting.

   Strongly Agree   **Agree**   **Disagree**   **Strongly Disagree**

2. I felt heard and involved in deciding what problem we would work on solving.

   Strongly Agree   **Agree**   **Disagree**   **Strongly Disagree**

3. The problem we agreed to work on was important.

   Strongly Agree   **Agree**   **Disagree**   **Strongly Disagree**

4. I know what others expect me to do to solve this problem.

   Strongly Agree   **Agree**   **Disagree**   **Strongly Disagree**

5. I now know what others are going to do to solve this problem.

   Strongly Agree   **Agree**   **Disagree**   **Strongly Disagree**

6. I am satisfied with what we accomplished during this meeting.

   Strongly Agree   **Agree**   **Disagree**   **Strongly Disagree**

7. I believe the plan we developed together will help us solve this problem.

   Strongly Agree   **Agree**   **Disagree**   **Strongly Disagree**

8. I would be willing to participate in another family–school problem-solving meeting.

   Strongly Agree   **Agree**   **Disagree**   **Strongly Disagree**

9. Do you have any other reactions you think we should know about?

   _____

   _____

Source: Amatea, E., Daniels, H. D., Bringman, N., & Vandiver, F. (2004). Strengthening counselor–teacher–family connections: The family–school collaborative consultation project. *Professional School Counseling, 8*(1), 50.

family–school problem-solving meeting offers a structured process in which care-givers, teachers, and students can collaborate as equals to help solve problems so that the student can enjoy more success at school. As teachers begin to think in a collab-orative manner and learn the skills of structuring, blocking blame, brainstorming, consensus building, and action planning, not only can they use the skills to help individual students and their families, but also they can use these same skills in their interactions with other staff members. Over time, the school culture can change from one in which parents and teachers view themselves as adversaries to one in which they grow comfortable working together to help each student be successful.

Summary

- Teachers must often communicate unpleasant information. In fact, the most common communication between school and family is when students are having problems.
- In communicating unpleasant news to families, teachers can favor one of four conflict management styles: avoidant, overcontrolling, accommodating, and collaborative.
- Four major barriers to effective problem solving with families are the emotionally charged nature of the meeting, the use of blaming, the monocultural orientation of the school, and the traditional way that teachers have conducted such meetings. These conditions often result in such meetings leaving students, families, and teachers feeling blamed, incompetent, and frustrated.
- The family–school problem-solving meeting uses a collaborative style of problem solving, whereby both the student and the family are viewed as resources for solving the problem. Power is shared, and blame is blocked. The meeting is structured with the end result being a concrete plan for action.
- The six steps in the family–school problem-solving meeting form the acronym SOLVES. The steps include (a) setting up the meeting and preparing the student and family, (b) orienting the participants to each other and to the purpose and process of the meeting, (c) listening to participants' concerns/ blocking blame, (d) validating concerns and creating a common focus and goal, (e) expanding solution ideas, and (f) setting up an action plan and arranging for follow-up.
- Skills needed to effectively conduct family–school problem-solving meetings include structuring, blocking blame, brainstorming, consensus building, and action planning.
- To implement the family–school problem-solving meeting, it is important to be enthusiastic, to gain administrative support, to share with your colleagues what you are doing, to practice so that you gain skill in conducting meetings, and to evaluate your work.

Chapter 12

Making Decisions and Plans with Families of Students with Special Needs

Crystal N. Ladwig

Learning Objectives

After reading this chapter, you will be able to:

- Explain how parents' and educators' expectations of how parents should be involved in the education of children with special needs have changed over the past century.
- Summarize the child development theory and major federal legislation that have influenced the delivery of special education services and the involvement of caregivers in making decisions and plans for their children.
- Describe the requirements for the development of individual educational plans for children with special needs.

- Discuss the cultural barriers confronted by educators seeking to involve caregivers in the education of their children with special needs.
- Discuss the philosophical shift to a family-centered approach in working with children's special needs and their families
- Describe specific family-centered strategies that educators can use in their classroom to support the families of children with special needs

The family exerts a tremendous impact on the child with special needs. Furthermore, the family is most involved and affected by the child's school career. Research has consistently shown that students who have special needs benefit in multiple respects when their families are actively involved in their education (Berry 1995). Specifically, parental participation in their children's education has a positive effect on academic progress. Students whose parents are involved in school have higher achievement, better behavior, and more motivation than do other students whose parents are not actively involved (Keith 1999). In a recent report to Congress on the implementation of the Individuals with Disabilities Education Act (IDEA), the U.S. Department of Education (2001) indicated that the most accurate predictor of the achievement and development of a student with special needs is the family's ability to become actively involved in their child's education by creating a home environment that encourages learning and by expressing high expectations. Moreover, the study revealed that the most improved educational outcomes for children with special needs were found where school support services were based on the premise that parents are the most important factors influencing their children's development (U.S. Department of Education).

Most scholars in special education accept without argument that parent involvement is a requirement for schools that seek to use best practices. The type of involvement implemented, however, seems to vary considerably. Parent and professional perceptions of the desired types and amounts of parent involvement not only vary among schools but also have evolved since the passage of Public Law 94–142, the first federal law mandating that educational services be provided for students with disabilities. With these variations and the evolution of the concept of family involvement, the roles of parents and family members have changed considerably.

All too often, it seems that the burden is put on families to become involved in their children's schools rather than the schools creating opportunities for families to become involved. Whereas parents with children without a disability may be involved in their child's schooling by volunteering at school, attending parent–teacher conferences, and attending special events such as open house, parents who have a child with a disability must engage in specific planning and decision-making meetings with school staff. Lindsay and Dockrell (2004) state:

Parent involvement in special education includes the (a) assessment process, where parents' knowledge of their child is an important source of information; (b) decision making, where parents have a right to receive full information, call their own experts, and express a preference for [service] provision; and (c) educational intervention, to which parents may contribute. (225)

The purpose of this chapter is to briefly outline the evolution of family involvement in special education and provide strategies to help teachers and schools include families in more family-centered and responsive ways.

A Look Back

The birth of a child is undoubtedly one of the most important and joyful events in the lives of parents. When a child is born with a disability, that joy is often accompanied by sorrow, grief, anxiety, and blame. Historically, much of the blame was placed on parents as the cause of their child's disability (Muscott 2002; Turnbull & Turnbull 1997). For example, in the latter part of the nineteenth century and into the early twentieth century, moral blame was often imposed on parents who implied that their child had a disability because of their poor moral judgment (Ferguson 2002). This concept was even more predominant for poor and female-headed families. For example, Howe (1846; 1976) stated:

> The moral to be drawn from the prevalent existence of idiocy in society is that a very large class of persons ignore the conditions upon which alone health and reason are given to men, and consequently they sin in various ways; they disregard the conditions which should be observed in intermarriage; they overlook the hereditary transmission of certain morbid tendencies; they pervert the natural appetites of the body into lusts of diverse kinds—the natural emotions of the mind into fearful passions—and thus bring down the awful consequences of their own ignorance and sin upon the heads of their unoffending children. (34)

Throughout the nineteenth century, special residential schools or institutions were created "as ways to get children who were disabled or 'vulnerable' away from their parents" (Ferguson 2002, 125). Professionals of the day argued that institutionalizing children with disabilities was the only way to separate deviant families from their children and allow the "experts" to assume parental roles (Ferguson 1994; Katz 1983; Rothman 1971).

As a result of the deinstitutionalization movement, attitudes gradually shifted such that, by the 1970s, parents were expected to assume primary care-giving responsibility for children who had previously been residing in state institutions and to integrate their children with special needs into the community to the greatest extent possible (Winton 1986). They were expected to be *advocates* who, with the help of teachers and therapists, worked to get their children accepted in schools and in society. The child-based interventions of this era assumed that enhancing the child's environment would help the child or, at least, prevent further delay (Barrera 1991).

With the passage of the Education for All Handicapped Children Act in 1976 (now called IDEA) mandating parent participation rights (Fieldler, Simpson & Clark 2007), parents were expected to acquire new skills and competencies to help their child both educationally and developmentally. Throughout the 1980s, the importance of family involvement and empowerment began to emerge, requiring additional skills and responsibilities for parents. However, these early parent involvement activities primarily included parents in activities professionals deemed important (McWilliam, Tocci & Harbin 1998). This theme continued to evolve during the 1990s with parents expected to assume more and more responsibility for all aspects of their children's education. Such shifts in responsibility have resulted in dramatic changes in expectations as to the roles that parents of students with special needs are expected to play in their children's schooling.

Changing Roles of Parents of Children with Special Needs

All parents, whether they have a child with a disability, naturally assume a wide variety of roles. Among the most common are "providers," "caretakers," "teachers," "sharers of information," and "doctors/nurses." Most, if not all, parents agree that assuming all of these roles can be a difficult, yet rewarding, experience. Parents of children with special needs also assume these traditional parental roles, but they have the additional burden of redefining these roles to meet the special needs of their child with disabilities. Providing for the basic needs of a child with severe disabilities may require qualitatively and quantitatively different activities than providing for a child without disabilities. Other roles also exist for parents of children with special needs. Among the most prominent of these is the role of *advocate*. All parents advocate for their children, but for parents of children with special needs, this advocacy takes on an entirely different meaning. Rights that most parents have taken for granted (e.g., child's enrollment in public schools) have not always been afforded to these children. The advocacy of parents of children with special needs has not simply comprised protective factors but a fight for basic civil rights for their children. Their children may not have the skills to fight for themselves, so the burden has fallen on their parents. Most parents are familiar with this when their children are very young. For parents of children with special needs, this may never go away. Especially for children with severe disabilities, parents may continue to carry out their traditional care-giving roles well into their child's adulthood.

With due process provisions built into special education legislation (Individuals with Disabilities Education Act, or IDEA), parents also share the responsibility for ensuring that their child's legal rights are met. With the passage of IDEA, parents of children with special needs acquired the role of *educational planner,* responsible for participating in the development of Individualized Educational Plans (IEPs) and Individualized Family Service Plans (IFSPs). In this role, parents must make educational decisions (e.g., whether to consent to a special education label and placement) that can affect their children's entire future. (It is not surprising, therefore, that the changing and evolving parental roles in special education can lead to confusion and frustration for parents and professionals alike.)

Early attitudes about parent involvement implied that school staffs could decide whether they wanted to involve parents in their child's educational planning. Illustrated in the following statement: "Parents should participate in the activities that professionals deem important" (McWilliam et al. 1998, 206), this attitude toward family involvement is in direct opposition to the current attitudes about family-centered practices (discussed in greater detail later in the chapter) that assert that parents should be given the opportunity to assume the level of involvement they desire by being given a choice and explanation about the educational roles they can assume (Boone & Crais 1999).

Barrera (1991) observed that as interventions change, so, too, do parents' roles. Parents often have assumed the role of *trainee,* observing professionals and trying to copy the intervention activities at home. Other terms often used to describe parents in this role include *therapeutic agents* (Dunst, Leet & Trivette 1988), *intervenors* (White, Taylor & Moss 1992), or *instructors* (Marfo 1996). Within these roles, parents are often pressured to work harder with their children to enhance better developmental outcomes (Marfo 1996). In practice, family decision making often involves simply accepting or rejecting plans (Beverly & Thomas 1999). Therefore, although parents have become decision makers in practice, the quality of that role is not yet ideal.

Clearly, even from this cursory look at changing expectations for parent roles in special education, a gap exists between parental roles in theory and in practice. This limited parent involvement is further illustrated by a review undertaken by White, Taylor, and Moss (1992) in which they examined 172 studies of parent involvement in early intervention and classified most roles and supports for families within 10 categories. As can be seen in Table 12.1, their results show that, although parents have almost always been involved as intervenors, these efforts have not typically yielded positive child outcomes. Interestingly, no studies in this review examined other ways parents might be involved or explored alternative child outcomes (changes in IQ were the most commonly reported outcome). The authors of this review proposed possible reasons for these poor outcomes. All but one study included the parent as *intervenor,* thus ignoring other roles parents could assume that might lead to more positive child and family outcomes. The effects of services on parents and families were not ascertained, and little data were reported within these studies that indicated how well parents implemented the planned interventions at home. Finally, a great deal of the data included in these studies were based on anecdotal reports and poorly designed research. Bennett, Deluca, and Bruns (1997) found that teachers viewed parents as out-of-school resources for addressing the child's

Table 12.1   Parent Roles and Supports to Families

	Parent Assistance to Child
Parent as Intervenor	Parent teaches developmental skills to child.
Parent–Child Relations	Parent engages in activities to enhance attachment, bonding, etc.
Sensory Stimulation	Stimulate senses via activities such as spinning, rolling, or stroking.
Parent as Classroom Aide	Parents serving as classroom aide for their own and other children.
	Help to Parents/Family
Emotional Support	Providing psychological service, counseling, and/or support groups for parents and family.
Resource Access	Assisting parents and family members to access available community and government resources such as child care, medical care, nutrition, and housing.
Parenting Skills	Teaching parents generic child management skills, teaching values, etc.
Job Training	Providing education to parents in job-related skills.
Knowledge of Child Development	Teaching parents about general child development (e.g., Piagetian stages, motor milestones, psychological states, etc.).
Respite Care	Providing respite relief for parents.

Adapted from White, K. R., Taylor, M. J., & Moss, V. C. (1992).

needs and disability. Teachers did not want parents to be more active in school by serving as volunteers within their classrooms. Parents, however, felt that their physical presence at school was important, whereas teachers preferred communication via telephone. In fact, increased parental advocacy often led to poorer relationships among team members. In their analysis of parent participation in special education, Duchnowski et al. (1995) identified a variety of roles parents might assume. Among these were *advocate, teacher, organizational member, decision maker, source of problem,* and *passive recipient of services.* Their review of the literature revealed that educational professionals perceived parents most frequently as the *source of problem* or *passive recipient of services* and least frequently as *partners* and *policymakers.* This finding reveals that if school professionals are to view parents as partners and policymakers, a need exists for professionals to recognize and respect the unique contributions of individuals within unique family systems. These authors suggest that roles could be enhanced through outreach, training for partnerships, participatory research and evaluation, focusing on neighborhoods, and training professionals.

Influence of Current Theory and Legislation

Current theories of family involvement in special education have been identified with a variety of labels, including "family-friendly," "family-centered," "family-oriented," and "family-focused." For the purposes of the chapter, the term *family-centered* will be used to describe these similar labels. The influences of the modern family-centered philosophy can be grouped within two general categories: child development theories and legislation.

Child Development Theories

The importance of child development theories on parent involvement in special education is based on three assumptions: (a) Parents are responsible for meeting their children's basic (i.e., biological) needs; (b) parents are responsible for encouraging their children's development; and (c) parents can impact their children's development. Two theories of child development, in particular, ecological/systems and transactional, have been significant contributors to family-centered theory and practice.

Ecological Systems Theory

Undoubtedly, the best known of the ecological theorists is Urie Bronfenbrenner. If you recall from our earlier discussion of this theory, Bronfenbrenner hypothesized that developing individuals are active participants located within a variety of systems. These systems, ever changing, constitute the different settings that have the potential to impact the developing child (Bronfenbrenner 1979). Bronfenbrenner originally hypothesized four systems. The first and most directly influential to the developing child, the *microsystem* (e.g., home or childcare) comprises activities, roles, and interpersonal relations within specific settings in which the child directly participates. The *mesosystem* includes the relationships between microsystems (e.g., relationship between home and school). Settings in which the child is not an active participant but which may indirectly affect the developing child (e.g., parents' workplaces) are incorporated in the *exosystem*. Finally, the *macrosystem* encompasses the previous three systems through shared beliefs, ideologies, and cultural identities. Bronfenbrenner's later work (1997) includes an additional system, the *chronosystem,* which refers to the changes within systems over time. This theory has become the framework for current assessment and intervention with young children (Bjorck-Akesson & Granlund 1995) and has resulted in a shift from focusing on enhancing a child's environment to improving the interaction between the child and his or her environment.

As Dunst et al. (1990) have pointed out, "An ecological systems perspective of human development considers the ways in which people and their social and nonsocial environments are interrelated and how these interdependencies contribute to the growth and adaptation of a developing person" (204). Consistent with this notion are practices that address family concerns and priorities as an avenue to improving student outcomes. Often this is accomplished by attempting to influence the environment or the interactions between individuals within systems. Influences to the environment may be in the form of individualized interventions with families or initiatives, such as legislation, at a higher system level. Individualized interventions must consider the unique nature of families, as well as how they define their roles within the family and the community.

Role definitions and expectations hold a prominent position within ecological theory. Bronfenbrenner (1979) defined roles as "the expectations for behavior associated with particular positions in society. Roles have a magic-like power to alter how a person is treated, how she acts, what she does, and thereby even what she thinks and feels" (6). Role expectations are influenced by both the content of the activities and the relationships between two interacting parties. This concept illustrates the importance of professional attitudes toward parents and the relationships that form between them. Role expectations affect the perceptions, activities, and relationships that individuals assume within these roles. Outcomes are, therefore, enhanced when parents and professionals agree on the qualities of a particular role. Without such agreement, neither professionals nor parents may be satisfied.

Transactional Theory

The shared component of Bronfenbrenner's ecological theory and the transactional theory, championed by Arnold Sameroff, is that neither nature nor nurture reign supreme. Sameroff's transactional model "was developed in reaction to the prevailing main-effect model for predicting long-term developmental outcomes" (Marfo & Cook 1991, 6). The model emphasizes the changing and bidirectional nature of interactions between the developing child and individuals in the child's environment (Sameroff 1987). This social transaction mediates development. In contrast to other child development theories, transactional theorists assume that children have the potential to influence their own environment. Rather than assume that either the child's nature or the parents' nurturing alone influence development, these two aspects of development are assumed to interact and change over time, influencing each other in a continuous and dynamic process (Sameroff). Therefore, the child's development and interactions cannot be understood without an understanding of the child's environment (Magnusson & Allen 1983), including the physical–geographical, social, and cultural factors, and the actual and perceived situations within the environment.

Like ecological theory, transactional theory emphasizes the uniqueness of the family's larger sociocultural context. Larger systems (e.g., Bronfenbrenner's macrosystem) influence a family's functioning via cultural and societal rules in the same manner in which a family influences the developing child (Fiese & Sameroff 1989). Therefore, child development should be studied within this larger family, sociocultural context and the family's adaptation to that context is critical. For example, a family's "code" develops as a result of how the family perceives its social world, the stories that differentiate its members from others outside of the family, and rituals that define how the family works within its social world (Fiese & Sameroff 1989). When the family code and the child outcomes do not match, intervention becomes necessary.

With these factors in mind, from a transactional perspective, intervention strategies for children with special needs focus on one of three tasks: remediation, redefinition, or reeducation (Fiese & Sameroff 1989). Remediation occurs when the goal is to change the child (i.e., teaching the child to fit the code). Redefinition of the family code may be necessary if the child's behavior cannot be altered to fit the code (e.g., typical development). It may be necessary for the family code to be altered to fit the child's behavior (e.g., acceptance of alternative rates of development). Finally, reeducation implies that the parents must learn a new set of skills to help their children develop such as when a child requires medical procedures (e.g., administration of insulin shots for a child with diabetes) on a regular basis. Parent roles within interventions depend largely on the family code, the intervention strategy required, and legislative requirements. In Case Study 12.1, we describe Nicky and her family and ask you to examine how Nicky both influences and is influenced by her family, her family's relations with educational and medical personnel, the relations between the school and medical personnel, and the larger cultural climate.

∿∿∿∿∿∿∿∿∿∿∿∿∿∿∿∿∿∿∿∿∿∿∿∿∿∿∿∿∿∿∿∿∿∿∿∿∿

CASE STUDY 12.1

Examining the Systems that Impact Nicky

Like most newborns, Nicky was born free of disabilities. That happy state, however, lasted for only about six months. By then, she had been rendered nearly deaf, almost completely blind, and completely dependent on technology to receive food and liquids. The cause of her disability was maltreatment by her father. His actions resulted in many consequences, but perhaps the most unusual result is that Nicky's maternal grandmother Vera is now her legal mother. Nicky's biological mother is Charolette, Vera's daughter. After Nicky was injured at home and then treated at Children's Mercy Hospital in Kansas City, she was released to the custody of a temporary foster parent, for safety's sake. With the support of Charolette (Nicky's mother) and the local child protective agency, Vera petitioned the local courts to adopt Nicky, believing that adoption would forever sever the father's rights and thus protect Nicky.

Although Charolette comes to Vera's home every morning to bathe, dress, and groom Nicky, and remains heavily involved with her, both Vera and Charolette needed help to care for Nicky and raise her brother Tavron. Charolette called her grandparents (Vera's parents) and asked: "I need help. Mother needs help. What can you do?" Without so much as a second thought, Charolette's grandparents Aaron and Marie sold their home outside Greenville, Mississippi, and moved to Lawrence, Kansas, permanently. Physicians, nurses, dietitians, and occupational and physical therapists attend to Nicky's health needs. Teachers have included her in their classes since she was about one year old. That is when Nicky entered the preschool program operated by faculty and staff and the University of Kansas at Lawrence. She spent one year there and then transferred to Raintree Montessori School across town.

Raintree Montessori School had long been committed to include children with disabilities in its programs that teach predominantly children without disabilities. Although no student with severe disabilities had been at Raintree and part of its inclusion program in a long time, Pam Shanks, Raintree's lead teacher, was open to teaching Nicky: "If I can teach her to respond, that in itself is worthwhile. Also, if I can teach the other students in the class to respond to Nicky with compassion, that makes my job all the more worthwhile." Surrounded by family, professionals, and peers without disabilities, Nicky now lives in a "village" where everyone depends on everyone else. If anything goes wrong with Nicky's health, her medication regimen, or the gastrointestinal tubes on which she depends for liquid nutrition, almost everything will go wrong at home and school. Health-care distress will disrupt all other facets of her life.

Questions to Consider

- Who is involved in Nicky's life?
- How have members of the family interacted and organized to support each other in caring for Nicky?
- How have outside professionals interacted with Nicky's family?
- What legislative and cultural practices in the larger system influence the actions of these professionals?
- How would you organize these influences into Bronfenbrenner's system levels?

Source: Turnbull, A., Turnbull, R., Erwin, E., & Soodak, L. (2006). *Families, professionals and exceptionality* (19, 20). Upper Saddle River, NJ: Pearson.

Legislation

Special education services have, to a great extent, resulted from legislation and litigation, which is no less true when we examine the roles of families within special education. Special education roles have been mandated and legitimized (Bronfenbrenner 1979) through legislation and governed by departments of education and other agencies. One act in particular (and its subsequent amendments and reauthorizations) has, without a doubt, had the greatest single impact on the educational services provided to students with disabilities and their families throughout the country.

Public Law 94–142: The Education of All Handicapped Children Act

This groundbreaking piece of legislation guaranteed the rights of all school-aged children with disabilities to a free and appropriate public education in the least restrictive environment. Parent involvement was a part of the legislative requirements from the start, but, initially, parental roles were limited. The earliest version of what we now refer to as the Individuals with Disabilities Education Act (IDEA) simply required that parents be invited to attend IEP meetings and that parents be required to consent to an evaluation and placement of their child before any such evaluation or placement could occur (Harry, Allen & McLaughlin 1995). Parents, at times, also participated with homework, making decisions about school, informal conversations with teachers, and observations.

During the early days of legislated special education, parents assumed two primary roles: decision makers and learners (Winton 1986). Parents made decisions about whether to consent to assessment or placement. They were not active decision makers in policy and rarely were they decision makers in planning or practice. As learners, parents were expected to learn new skills and abilities that would allow them to better teach their children (Winton 1986). The accomplishment of the expectations of the latter role often resulted in the parent assuming the roles of teacher or therapist. Parents did not initially have a great deal of control over their children's education. They were seen primarily as passive and in need of professional assistance. However, the importance of this legislation cannot be overlooked. It was this piece of legislation that first guaranteed educational rights to children with special needs and their families; and it opened the door for parents to become more involved in their children's special education and schooling, as is evidenced in subsequent reauthorizations of IDEA.

The Evolution of IDEA

With each reauthorization of IDEA, Congress has attempted to improve the educational services provided to both students and families in a manner that encourages greater family involvement. The first significant change occurred with the 1986 reauthorization. This law specifically addressed the educational and intervention needs of young children with special needs. A primary purpose was "to enhance the capacity of families to meet the special needs of their infants and toddlers with disabilities" (EHA Amendments of 1986, PL 99–457, 100 Stat. 1145). Inherent in the family-centered nature of this reauthorization were several assumptions: (a) a lack of support for parents, (b) a lack of family services, and (c) projected benefits of family-centered interventions (Dunst 1985; Mahoney, O'Sullivan & Dennebaum 1990). Two components of this law have significantly impacted parent roles within special education. The rationale for these requirements has its roots in the child development theories discussed previously, as well as practices and empirical findings of better outcomes when parents are involved (Shonkoff & Meisels 1990). First, the Individualized Family Service Plan (IFSP) was mandated as a way to help families of young children with special needs as a whole as opposed to focusing on children only. It provided parents with a venue in which their needs and priorities could be heard and addressed. The second requirement, the provision of a service coordinator, was intended to help coordinate the services and therapies a child *and* family receive. It was anticipated that these requirements would help empower parents (Thompson et al. 1997).

Within these requirements are embedded expectations for new parental roles. Parents are now responsible for directing assessment and participating in planning and implementation of the requirements of the legislation (Murphy et al. 1995). Ideally, family concerns and needs are to lead the assessment in a direction that will be most beneficial to the family and, thereby, the child. Following assessment, the parents' priorities are to direct the intervention and services the child and family receives. As a result, parents acquire more active roles within the eligibility and placement processes, as well as in the development and implementation of the IFSP (Beverly & Thomas 1999). This expansion of parental roles and responsibilities, in addition to the priority placed on the family's needs and desires, is evidence of a shift from a primarily child-focused service delivery system to a more family-centered approach (Bailey 1991).

Decision Making and Planning

Individualized Education Plan (IEP)

An Individualized Education Plan (IEP) is a federally mandated document designed to guide the instruction of each student with a disability by setting individual educational goals. In addition, IEPs must include a description of how the student's progress toward meeting these goals would be measured. The IEP team is a group of individuals who meet to discuss the student's overall development and academic achievement and write the IEP. The team must include the following persons:

- The parents of a child with a disability
- At least one regular education teacher (if the child is, or may be, participating in the regular education environment)
- At least one special education teacher/provider
- A representative of the local education agency (LEA) who is qualified to provide, or supervise the provision of, specially designed instruction to meet the unique needs of children with disabilities; knowledgeable about the general education curriculum; and knowledgeable about the availability of resources of the LEA
- An individual who can interpret the instructional implications of evaluation results, who may also be a member of the team described previously
- At the discretion of the parent or the agency, other individuals who have knowledge or special expertise regarding the child, including related services personnel as appropriate
- Whenever appropriate, the child with a disability

Parent involvement in the process of developing the IEP is specifically outlined in IDEA. Parents and professionals alike are bestowed with certain rights and responsibilities. In accordance with IDEA, parents are involved in many aspects of their child's education above and beyond those of parents with typically developing children. Schools must provide ample opportunity for parents of students with disabilities to participate in meetings to determine special education eligibility and placement, make assessment decisions, and write the IEP at least once annually. Schools are further required to provide parents with copies of all official documents. Procedural safeguards exist within IDEA to ensure that both the student's and family's rights are protected. Parents have a right to review any records related to their child's education, including all aspects of special education services. Parents also receive a copy of their procedural safeguards at least once annually. When disagreements occur, both schools and parents have the right to take the matter to due process.

Parent involvement within the IEP process may vary widely depending on the preferences of the IEP team members. At a minimum, IDEA stipulates that parents (a) may request initial evaluation or reevaluation; (b) must provide informed consent for initial evaluation, reevaluation, and services prior to such actions occurring; (c) participate in IEP meetings (providing input and helping make decisions); and (d) receive copies of all official documents. Parents should also participate in the assessment process by providing documents (e.g., medical records) or other information relevant to the evaluation (e.g., the student's early developmental history). Parents are not typically involved in the pre-referral interventions that take place prior to the formal special education procedures (Tam & Heng 2005).

Wertz, Mamlin, and Pogoloff (2002) characterize the IEP process as containing two major elements: IEP meeting and IEP document. The IEP meeting includes traditional parent–teacher conference information, in addition to specific details that will subsequently be included in the IEP document. The IEP meeting is the venue during which parents should be given ample opportunity to express their own opinions of their child's strengths, weaknesses, and needs. During the IEP meeting, it is vital that professionals provide parents with all of the information they will need to make educated decisions regarding their children's special education services. In developing the IEP document, the team must recognize and build on the strengths of the child, the concerns of the parents, results of evaluations, and academic, developmental, and functional needs of the child. As can be seen in Table 12.2, the IEP document includes a wide variety of information, including educational goals, assessment modifications, placement determination (including where the child will be placed and the frequency and duration of services), and evaluation results.

The most recent reauthorization of IDEA occurred in 2004. One of the major goals associated with this reauthorization was to align IDEA with the No Child Left Behind Act of 2002. Schools are required to send home progress reports to document each student's progress toward meeting their individual IEP goals. Additionally, provisions were made to offer, with parental consent and only in some states, a pilot program for multiyear IEPs not to exceed three years. However, there are significant concerns that extending the duration of the IEP may lead to fewer opportunities for students' educational teams to meet with parents.

Table 12.2   Required Components of the IEP

The IEP is a written statement for each student ages three to twenty-one. Whenever it is developed or revised, it must contain statements about the following:

The student's present levels of academic achievement and functional performance, including:

- How the disability affects the student's involvement and progress in the general education curriculum
- How the disability of preschoolers (ages three to five) affects their participation in appropriate activities
- A statement of benchmarks or short-term objectives if the students take alternative assessments

Measurable annual goals, including academic and functional goals, designed to

- Meet the student's needs that result from the disability, to enable the students to be involved in and make progress in the general education curriculum
- Meet each of the student's other disability related educational needs

Measurement of annual goals:

- How the school will measure the student's progress toward annual goals
- How often the school will report the students' progress

Special education, related services, and supplementary aides and services, based on peer-reviewed research to the extent practicable, that will be provided to the student or on the student's behalf and the program modifications or supports for school personnel that will be provided so that the student can:

- Advance appropriately toward attaining the annual goals
- Be involved in and make progress in the general education curriculum and participate in extracurricular and nonacademic activities
- Be educated and participate with other students with disabilities and with students who do not have disabilities in the general education curriculum and extracurricular and other nonacademic activities

The extent, if any, to which the student will not participate with students without disabilities in the regular class and in the general education curriculum and extracurricular and other nonacademic activities

Any individual appropriate accommodations necessary to measure the student's academic achievement and functional performance on state and local assessments of student achievement. If the IEP team determines that the student will take an alternate assessment on a particular statewide or district-wide assessment, the IEP must document why the students cannot participate in the regular assessment and what alternate assessment is appropriate.

Projected date for beginning services and program medications, and the anticipated frequency, location, and duration of each service and modification

Source: Turnbull, A., Turnbull, R., Erwin, E., & Soodak, L. (2006). *Families, professionals and exceptionality* (255). Upper Saddle River, NJ: Pearson.

Student Involvement in the IEP Process

IDEA requires that students be invited to participate in their own IEP meetings beginning at age fourteen. IDEA further includes students themselves by stating that decisions about their future be based on the students' interests and preferences.

Finally, IDEA requires that the IEPs for students age sixteen and over include a transition plan to prepare the student for the transition from school to adult life. Given these mandates, several researchers have studied the extent to which students with disabilities actually do participate in IEP meetings and how their interests and preferences guide the planning process for their transition from school to adult life. *Self-determination* has become the predominant term used to describe student involvement in special education planning. Brotherson, Cook, Conconan-Lahr, and Wehmeyer (1995) defined self-determination as "the opportunity and ability to make choices and decisions regarding one's quality of life" (3). Research has shown that parents and caregivers agree that students with disabilities should be informed participants in their IEP meetings (Grigal et al. 2003). A significant body of research now exists documenting the benefits of self-determination for students with a wide range of disabilities (Durlak, Rose & Bursuck 1994; Hoffman & Field 1995; Kaiser & Abell 1997; Serna & Lau-Smith 1995; Wehmeyer 1996). Students who are more involved in decision making about their education are more likely to achieve their goals, improve their academic skills, develop self-advocacy skills, graduate, and gain employment than those who do not (Mason et al. 2004).

How can parents and educators include students in these meetings? It has proved to be very difficult. The attendance mandate within IDEA has not proved sufficient to meet the intent behind the mandate. Martin et al. (2006) observed 109 middle and high school IEP meetings that included students and reported that less than half of the students shared their interests during the meetings and even fewer discussed the goals they had for themselves. A low level of student engagement at these meetings was observed. Martin et al. recommended that students be taught how to effectively participate in these meetings and that the meeting structure be modified to encourage greater student participation. Additionally, they concluded that the traditionally teacher-led meetings may not be the most effective format for engaging students. Having students themselves chair or co-chair the meetings may be a more effective strategy for encouraging greater student participation.

Suggestions for effectively including students with disabilities as both members of the IEP team and as active participants in the creation of the IEP document are depicted in Table 12.3.

Culture and Disability

The concept of disability is largely shaped by the culture in which the disability exists. Societies in general tend to be rather ethnocentric with disabilities being generally defined as deviation from the norm. The norm, however, may differ widely from one culture to another. Additionally, the source of disabilities may be attributed to a wide range of causes. Most of the research on disabilities, especially in special education, has focused on specific interventions, theories, and practices

Table 12.3   Strategies for Including Students with Disabilities in Planning Meetings

- Before the meeting:
  - Invite the student and parents to the meeting.
  - Explain to the student (and parents if they are new to the process) what the IEP meeting is, who will be there, and what will occur at the meeting.
  - Help the student prepare for the meeting by preparing a list of items that he or she would like the team to consider (e.g., My Goals for the Future, What I Want to Be When I Graduate, My Hobbies and Interests, Things That are Difficult for Me).
  - Give the student several opportunities to practice sharing these lists. It can be very intimidating to sit at a table with your parents and all of your teachers.
- During the meeting:
  - Ask the student to introduce the teachers and his or her parents. If necessary, the teachers can introduce any remaining participants to the parents.
  - Start with the student's list of priorities, then the parents' priorities, and, finally, the school's priorities.
  - Invite the student to participate in each topic that comes up.
  - Have the student sign the IEP document.
- After the meeting:
  - Discuss the IEP meeting and document with the student to make sure he or she has an opportunity to have any remaining questions answered or concerns addressed.
  - Provide the student with a copy of the IEP document.

designed to remediate or accommodate students. Recently, a relatively large body of literature has begun to emerge, documenting the experiences of minority groups within the special education system. Most notably, significant discrepancies have been documented in the placement and discipline decisions of African American students versus Caucasian students. The "civil rights" movement of the larger population of individuals with disabilities is known as Disability Studies. This area of study and advocacy views disability as a unique cultural identity, without consideration of racial, ethnic, or socioeconomic factors (Harry 2002). The result of this movement and the ethnocentricity that exists in much of the discourse is that the interaction of culture and disability has not been as widely studied as many other topics within special education.

Harry (2002) conducted an extensive review of the nature of disability within a cultural context. She found that cultural views of disability varied widely and also depended upon the severity of the disability. Parents' views of child development strongly predicted the expectations they have for their children with mild disabilities. They further found that parents' beliefs about the etiology of their children's severe disabilities differed widely. Harry concluded that "a strong implication of these findings is that the acculturation process has a powerful effect on both parenting styles and on parental beliefs about child development" (133).

Lamorey (2002) reviewed several studies that examined the perceptions and beliefs of several specific cultural groups (including parents from Korea, China, Mexico, Australia, and Africa) with regard to having a child with a disability (e.g.,

Cho, Singer & Brenner 2000; Gray 1995; Ryan & Smith 1989; Mardiniros 1989; Olubanji 1981). Many of these parents attributed their child's disability to a deity (either as punishment or as part of God's plan), magic, their own mistakes or short-comings, and biomedical causes, among others.

The impact of these findings cannot be overlooked. Parents do not always view disability in the same manner as teachers and schools. When a parent's or child's beliefs about the nature and severity of a disability are in conflict with the schools' beliefs, disagreements between parents and schools will arise. This is especially true with regard to mild disabilities in which parents from some cultural groups (e.g., Puerto Rican American and African American) may perceive a larger range of "normal" development than the clinical view held by many professionals (Harry 2002; Lamorey 2002). The result is that parents may be perceived by professionals as "denying their child's problems" and hence as part of the problem rather than part of the solution (Hopfenberg et al. 1993). Teachers must be careful not to repeat history, blaming parents for their child's disabilities. Rather, they should consider the family's view of the child's development and respect the family with its unique characteristics.

Harry (2002) determined that six areas of difficulty often arise when attempting to provide culturally sensitive services to families of children with special needs who are from different cultures:

- Cultural differences in definitions and interpretations of disabilities
- Cultural differences in family coping styles and responses to disability-related stress
- Cultural differences in parental interaction styles, as well as expectations of participation and advocacy
- Differential cultural group access to information and services
- Negative professional attitudes to, and perceptions of, families' roles in the special education process
- Dissonance in the cultural fit of programs (136)

It is virtually impossible for teachers to learn the cultural beliefs, attitudes, and values of every culture they may come in contact with during their career. However, without this information, it may seem difficult, if not impossible, to truly be culturally sensitive. Teachers must attempt to understand families' cultural views about disability and bridge the gap that may exist between those cultural views and the practices and policies of the school system. Several general principles can serve to guide teachers to be more culturally sensitive when working with parents of students with special needs who are from other cultures. First, teachers have a great cultural resource in the Internet. Conducting searches about specific cultures can help teachers learn much about the cultural beliefs, practices, and values of their students and families, including their perceptions about disabilities. Second, when thinking about culture, think broadly. Do not limit searches to cultures in other countries. Note that cultural subgroups have formed within the United States that should be considered as well. Third, when appropriate, ask the parents themselves. Once a teacher has formed a good relationship with his or her students' families, there may be opportunities where it would be appropriate to ask the parents for more information about their cultural beliefs. Finally, use culturally sensitive language and avoid idioms. Using such cultural and family-friendly language will help prevent miscommunication and will encourage collaboration and openness between teachers and parents, especially during the IEP process.

Parent Roles Within a Family–Centered Approach

The impact of child development theories, legislation, and past practices on current views of working with families is extensive. From ecological theory, an understanding exists of the importance of families as unique systems in which children grow and develop and recognition of the influence parents and extra-familial factors have on children. From the transactional perspective, the interactions between the developing child and his or her environments have been acknowledged as bidirectional and dynamic, emphasizing the changing nature of relationships over time. From early legislation in special education (i.e., PL 94–142), the birth of special education policy arose as we know it today. Additionally, this legislation mandated much of the parent involvement that we see today in policy and practice. Later legislation, particularly Part H of PL 99–457, expanded this legislative view of parent involvement by focusing on parental needs and priorities for assessment and planning, intervening with the family instead of focusing only on the child, and providing more opportunities for parental involvement. From existing practices, child-focused planning and interventions are clearly not adequate and that professional control is inappropriate. Finally, from research on the interaction between culture and disability, evidence shows that culture has a significant impact on the way parents perceive their child with a disability and their roles in their child's education. The interrelatedness of these factors cannot be overlooked. The combination of and interaction between these factors has formed the basis of what is currently referred to in the special education literature as "family–centeredness."

What Is Family–Centeredness?

For most of the history of special education, services and decisions were primarily dictated by individual school systems with the sole focus being the child. The 1986 reauthorization of IDEA changed this. This update included provisions for providing special education services to infants and toddlers with disabilities *and* their families. This concept has gradually moved upward from infants and toddlers, to preschool programs, elementary schools, and so on.

A family–centered philosophy for working with children with disabilities and their families cannot be easily defined or described. Certain qualities and characteristics seem typical of all views of family–centeredness. No clear-cut definition has been identified, although several have been proposed within the literature. Murphy et al. (1995) identified family–centered practices as those that (a) include families in decision making, planning, assessment, and service delivery at family, agency, and systems levels; (b) develop services for the whole family and not just the child; (c) are guided by families' priorities for goals and services; and (d) offer and respect families' choices regarding the level of their participation (25).

Dunst et al. (1991) stated: "The term *family–centered* refers to a combination of beliefs and practices that define particular ways of working with families that are consumer-driven and competency-enhancing" (115). Finally, Bailey, McWilliam, and Winton (1992) refer to family–centered care as a concept based on family support, empowerment, coordinated services, normalization, and cultural sensitivity.

Family–centered practitioners seek to involve parents as partners and see parents as the central figures in the lives of the students with whom they work (Mahoney et al. 1990). As such, family–centered teachers are concerned not only with the needs of the child, but also with the needs of the family with whom they live. This is based on the belief and supporting evidence that children will experience greater success when the families' needs are met (Muscott 2002). "Family–centered practice emphasizes families' strengths rather than deficits, family choice over resources and services, and collaborative relationships between schools and families" (66).

Summers et al. (2005), Rupiper and Marvin (2004), McBride (1999), and Dunst (2002) have all characterized family–centered services as responsive to families' choices with an emphasis on family–professional collaboration and the provision of services to children and families. Of course, school districts are greatly limited in the services they may offer directly to families outside of the typical educational arena. However, teachers and schools are typically more aware of outside resources that may be available to help a family in need. Often, just putting the parent in contact with the proper resource can open many doors. The nature of family–centered services also changes throughout a student's educational career as adolescents begin to assert their independence and become involved in their own educational planning. Most notably, when professionals implement family–centered practices, parents tend to be more satisfied with the services the family receives (Rupiper & Marvin 2004; McNaughton 1994; Romer & Unbreit 1998).

The definitions discussed previously all have in common a philosophical shift from practices and interventions that were child-focused to those that are now more family–centered. Simeonsson and Bailey (1991) suggested four factors that contribute to this shift: (a) lack of evidence in support of child-focused interventions; (b) recognition that infants and young children are best understood within a family context; (c) belief that families are appropriate recipients of service and intervention; and (d) influence of parent–child interactions. Mahoney and Filer (1996) proposed a similar list of contributing factors, with the addition of changing parental roles and expanding knowledge of the complex issues encountered when raising a child with special needs.

The concept of family–centeredness encompasses both a philosophy (i.e., beliefs and attitudes) and behaviors (i.e., practices). Using these definitions and rationales for change, certain qualities and characteristics inherent in family-centered practice begin to emerge. The primary emphasis is on collaborating with and supporting families (Mahoney & Bella 1998). Considering parent knowledge, competencies, capabilities, and resources (Powell et al. 1997) while focusing on parent needs and priorities will encourage collaboration and support. Due to the unique nature of family systems, individualization becomes necessary when working with families similar to the individualization that occurs when working with children. The presumption is that family control is enhanced when utilizing a family–centered philosophy. Parents should choose their desired level of involvement, have their priorities, goals, and needs considered and respected by professionals (Bailey et al. 1992), and become the decision makers for their children's educational programming.

Family-Centered Roles

Parent roles within a family-centered philosophy are largely defined by the unique perspective that parents bring to the process, including information about the family members' ecology, strengths, goals, histories, culture, and values (Powell et al. 1997). As depicted in Table 12.4 on page 328, parents are viewed as experts on their children and their families. This realization is important if parents are to become the decision makers. Inherent in this role is a clear understanding of options available to children with special needs and their families. It is often the professionals' responsibility as family supporter to help make parents aware of the available options from which to choose. As experts on their children and families, parents become active in information gathering, eligibility and placement decisions, and development and implementation of plans (Beverly & Thomas 1999). As true partners within special education circles, parents should be recognized as being capable of influencing development, designing and monitoring services, and formulating policies (Murphy et al. 1995). These roles should be present in all areas of special education from assessment and eligibility to planning and implementing services and follow-up activities. The presumption is that the acquisition of these roles results in improved child and family outcomes.

Table 12.4   Parent Roles and Responsibilities

Family–Centered	Traditional
Experts—Sharing information, needs, and priorities about child and family with other team members	Resources—Providing information to professionals to assist them in their assessment, planning, intervention, and decision-making responsibilities
Decision makers—Deciding what is best (in all areas of assessment, planning, and intervention) for child and family	Decision makers—Making choices from options presented by professionals
Partners—Participating in all assessment, planning, and intervention activities with equal status as professionals	Trainees—Learning from professional model
	Source of problem—Cause of child and family problems
Active organizational members/advocates—Participating in all levels of policy and practice determination	Therapeutic agents, intervenors, or instructors—Teaching and conducting therapy

Family–Centered Educational Practices

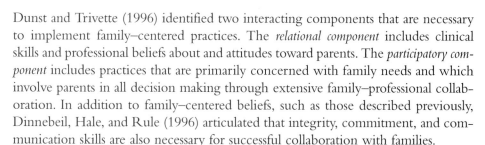

Dunst and Trivette (1996) identified two interacting components that are necessary to implement family–centered practices. The *relational component* includes clinical skills and professional beliefs about and attitudes toward parents. The *participatory component* includes practices that are primarily concerned with family needs and which involve parents in all decision making through extensive family–professional collaboration. In addition to family–centered beliefs, such as those described previously, Dinnebeil, Hale, and Rule (1996) articulated that integrity, commitment, and communication skills are also necessary for successful collaboration with families.

The key theme that runs throughout all family–centered practices is decision making. Ultimately, special education legislation mandates that parents be involved in decision making. The family–centered beliefs and subsequent practices provide parents with the information and resources necessary to make the best decisions for their children and families. Bailey (2001) asserts that practices should enable families to become competent advocates for their children. "Professionals who use family-centered practices help families in making decisions about their children by providing complete and unbiased information; supporting these families emotionally; and developing service systems that are responsive to individual family needs and respectful of cultural, racial, and ethnic diversity" (Kaczmarek et al. 2004, 213).

Many of the strategies for family involvement within the special education system are similar, if not the same, as the strategies that would be beneficial when fostering family-centered practices with all students and families. Table 12.5 on page 330 outlines content area topics that are worthy of consideration for family–centered practitioners. The discussion that follows includes specific family–centered practices within the context of special education.

1. *Organize your classroom to help families become advocates.* Parents often expect to play a traditional role in family–school interactions in which parents come to school, hear what the teacher has to say, and then deal with it as best they can at home. Family–centered classrooms are organized from the beginning to encourage a more open dialogue and greater collaboration. To implement this practice, the teacher must explain to parents and caregivers how a specific classroom is run, what is expected of parents, and the varied opportunities they have to become involved. Seeking out parental input at nontraditional times is one of the best ways this is done. It demonstrates to parents that their opinions are valuable and helpful to the teacher.

2. *Build flexibility within service delivery.* To ensure the greatest potential for effective collaboration and to meet individual families' needs, teachers need to think outside of the box when planning and scheduling classroom and collaborative activities. This may involve the teacher making himself or herself available to families at nontraditional times and in nontraditional ways. For example, Nelson et al. (2004) identified a continuum of relationships between families and professionals. Those teachers with more fluid boundaries made themselves available at times other than traditional work hours and were willing to meet outside of the school and/or regular school hours. Single, working parents, for example, may not be able to come to the school grounds for an IEP meeting or other parent–teacher conference during the typical school day. Scheduling the meetings in the evenings or meeting with parents in their homes or other locations may allow parents to be more involved. Unfortunately, many school districts do not build in these types of collaborative activities into their planning for teachers. As a result, teachers and other school personnel who utilize these strategies often must do so on their own time and at their own expense. This can also become problematic during scheduling of IEP meetings if some professionals are available after school hours and others are not.

3. *Establish effective communication.* Martin and Hagan-Burke (2002) suggest seven steps to facilitate effective communication between schools and parents, including: (1) assigning a facilitator; (2) acknowledging accomplishments; (3) meeting routinely; (4) establishing predictability; (5) keeping it simple; (6) making informed decisions; and (7) assessing acceptability and treatment integrity. Often, the informal conversations between teachers and parents are where the seeds of this type of communication are planted. Additionally, it takes time for effective communication to develop, such as when establishing predictability.

4. *Individualize to the needs of the entire family.* Each family enters school with its own unique experiences, values, beliefs, needs, and desires. Some parents may feel very comfortable in assuming the role of advocating for their child and being a true partner in the decision-making and planning processes that occur throughout the school

~~~~~~

Table 12.5   Content Categories Related to Family–Centered Services

Knowledge of Families	Systems/ecological theory
	Families as systems
	Diverse family cultures & systems
	Impact of disability on family functioning
	Families of child with disabilities (infants/toddlers, preschool, and school-age)
	Parent rights/involvement options
Individualized Family Service Plans/Individualized Education Plans	Identifying and utilizing the strengths and resources of family members
	Targeting family-identified concerns and priorities
	Coordinating services for and with families
	Utilizing existing/natural family routines/environments
	Supporting family as primary decision maker
	Adhering to ethical practices
Respecting Diversity	Respect for various cultural/familial beliefs, values, and practices
	Awareness/reflection of own cultural and family values and biases
	Respect for the family as the focus of early intervention services
	Respect for the family as a competent resource
Communication Skills	Utilizing culturally sensitive communication skills
	Utilizing appropriate interviewing strategies
	Implementing negotiation skills
	Using effective listening skills
	Using appropriate question types
	Using appropriate explanation types and strategies
	Applying problem-solving process
Knowledge of Team Work	Interdisciplinary roles and responsibilities of various professionals
	Interagency roles/responsibilities
	Discipline: specific roles and responsibilities
	Team models and team functions
	Principles of role release
	Models of consultation/collaboration

Adapted from Rupiper, M., & Marvin, C. (2004). Preparing teachers for family centered services: A survey of preservice curriculum content. *Teacher Education and Special Education, 27(4),* 384–395.

career of a child with a disability. Other parents may place all of their trust in the teacher and believe that he or she is best qualified to make educational decisions for their child. Teachers and other school personnel must recognize that such variances exist and honor them. At the same time, family–centered teachers should continually provide parents with opportunities to become more involved as their comfort level rises and as they become accustomed to the nontraditional organizational strategies.

Services to children should be clearly outlined in each student's IEP. IDEA requires that the decisions that are made and documented within the IEP be individualized. That is, that the services offered to students must be solely based on their needs. One premise that underlies family–centered practices is that family needs must also be considered. If, for example, professionals on the IEP team determine that the child is best served in a full-time special education classroom, but the family strongly believes in inclusion, every effort should be made to include that child with typically developing peers as much as possible. The opposite holds true as well. Not all parents believe that inclusive classrooms will best meet the needs of their children.

5. *Understand that families of children with disabilities often go back and forth through various stages of coping and grief.* Before a child is born, parents dream of the child that is to come. They often think about the things they want to do with their child, the things they will teach their child, and what their child will be when he or she grows up. When parents suddenly learn that the child they have imagined is different from the child that is born, parents often go through a grieving process. The dream they had of their child's future life is gone and parents must learn to cope with a new reality. Throughout the child's lifespan, events will occur that will thrust the parent back into this grieving process. Typically, this happens when the child does not meet milestones typical of children his or her age (e.g., walking, talking, reading, writing, driving, dating, getting a job) or when younger siblings or other younger children close to the family begin to developmentally surpass the child with a disability. During these times, it may be especially difficult for families to collaborate and be involved at school. Attending an IEP meeting where they hear how their child is struggling may only exacerbate these feelings of grief. It is vital that teachers and other school personnel understand that these times will occur for families and respond empathically when these situations arise.

6. *Respect the uniqueness of families and treat them with dignity.* Acknowledge the cultures, values, and traditions of families (McWilliam & Bailey 1993). Parents come to the table with more knowledge of and experience with their child than anyone else. Teachers will learn more about individual children (e.g., likes, dislikes, interests, strengths, weaknesses) from parents than perhaps any other source. Demonstrating respect and treating parents with dignity will go a long way toward establishing the effective communication skills discussed previously. Inherent in this is the assumption that teachers will not make judgments on families for the way they live their lives or for having nontraditional families (e.g., grandparents raising children because the parents are in prison). Also, schools should provide interpreters for parents who do not speak fluent English.

7. *Establish parent–professional collaboration and partnerships.* Communication in and of itself will not guarantee collaboration and partnerships with families. Teachers

and schools must provide multiple and varied opportunities for parent involvement (Muscott 2002). If parents are invited to come to school only for IEP meetings and traditional parent–teacher conferences, they will never learn to think of themselves as active agents and decision makers in their child's schooling. As such, collaboration will be limited and partnerships may be nonexistent. Parents need to be given opportunities to become involved in planning for their child's education and working with professionals to implement the plans (Bailey 2001). This could be accomplished by asking parents what activities they do with their children at home to help them, or it could involve planning with parents and having them come to school to share in the instruction (e.g., a parent who is a veterinarian may lead a lesson on pet care).

8. *Share information with parents and students.* It is unreasonable to assume that families (parents and students) will be able to make the difficult decisions about the education of their child with special needs without all of the relevant information. For example, if a family is not fully aware of the range of placement options (e.g., full-time special education classrooms through full-time inclusive classrooms), then that family will not have all of the information needed to determine which placement is best for their child. Families should be provided with *all* relevant information that they may need to make decisions for their child (Dunst 2002). Additionally, this information should be conveyed to families in a supportive manner that respects the families' unique qualities, including their cultural and religious values (Bruder 2000).

9. *Emphasize family choice and decision making.* Families should be involved in all aspects of decision making (Pretti-Frontczak et al. 2002; Smith 2005). As stated previously, in essence, this is what family-centeredness is all about. Family–centered programs emphasize family choice and decision making, including program practice and intervention options (Dunst 2002). During certain times parental choice and decision making are mandated (e.g., consenting to placement in special education programs). Family–centered parental choice and decision making extend beyond the federal mandates to include family involvement in less formal areas of the student's education.

10. *Use responsive practices.* Family–centered practices are responsive to families' identified needs, desires, and decisions. Involving families in discussions only to ignore the families' input will ultimately result in a total lack of collaboration and partnership. Families need to see, not just hear, that teachers are responsive to their opinions and ideas. The old adage holds true: Actions speak louder than words. Families need to see that teachers' actions reflect family input.

Challenges and Barriers

Encountering difficulties when translating theories into practical applications is not uncommon. Such is the case with family–centered approaches and practices. Bailey et al. (1992) conducted a study of professionals in four states who were asked to rate their current practices in terms of how family–centered they felt they were and should be. A clear discrepancy was observed. Professionals consistently rated ideal practices as much more family–centered than they actually were. They attributed most of the barriers that impeded greater family–centeredness to parents and the larger special education system. The authors cautioned, however, that professional biases about family desires and abilities should be tempered as parents choose their own level of involvement. Bjorck-Akesson and Granlund (1995) replicated this study with professionals and parents in Sweden. Not only was the same professional discrepancy observed, but also a discrepancy between parents' and professionals' ratings of ideal roles. Professionals rated ideal roles reflecting greater client empowerment more highly than did parents in the areas of decision making and participation in child assessment and identification of family goals and services. Furthermore, they reported that parents often assumed roles with the responsibility to simply approve assessment plans, provide information about the child, and suggest goals. The support that was typically provided was based on professionals' perceptions of family needs instead of parent communication of their needs. Barriers to implementation included legislation, litigation fears, administrative policies and regulations, and a lack of resources (i.e., time, money, and staff). One must consider the reasons for these discrepancies, particularly that parents reported a desire for less family–centered practices than professionals did. Perhaps parents truly feel this way, or perhaps parents, through years of services that were not family-centered, have been conditioned to fear control, depend on professionals, and doubt themselves functioning competently within more family–centered roles. If the latter is the case, teachers and other school personnel must take a closer look at their own practices and the implications for families. Teachers must also consider whether cultural and/or familial factors account for these differences.

Several additional barriers have been identified by other researchers (Dunst 2002; Kaczmarek et al. 2004; Rupiper & Marvin 2004; Wertz et al. 2002). Mahoney et al. (1989; 1990) concluded that many barriers limit the implementation of family-centered practices, including: (a) the difficulty involved in changing the focus of a child and classroom-based system to a family-focused one; (b) inadequate time for teachers to implement family–centered practices; (c) insufficient preparation of teachers to implement family–centered practices; and (d) an absence of family–centered materials. Mahoney and Filer (1996) concluded that an unclear concept of needs exists. "Needs" are assumed to be those things parents need to support their child and his or her development. In practice, the determination of family needs is usually done by asking parents what services they want to receive. This places parents in the position of choosing from a menu of options instead of communicating their individualized needs and having those needs met.

The majority of the barriers center on the teacher's knowledge, skills, and practical implementation of services. Teachers who may have been trained in family–centered practices may find them difficult to implement given the many directions in which teachers are pulled on a daily basis (Rupiper & Marvin 2004). Additionally, it may be difficult to convince parents to step outside of their traditional roles to take on these new roles and responsibilities. Some parents may simply feel that their place is not to take such ownership of their child's education, rather it is the teacher's responsibility to ensure that families are made fully aware of the desired level of participation when it is outside of the traditional level with which most parents are familiar.

Despite these difficulties, the consensus within special education is that higher quality parent involvement is beneficial to students. Our ultimate commitment as educators must be to the welfare of our students. The responsibility falls on individual teachers to implement the best family–centered practices. Teachers must take on the role of educating parents about how they can be more involved as partners in their child's educational planning. Teachers must work within the system as best they can to meet families' needs. Finally, teachers must commit to learning more about other cultures, parenting styles, and be open to new ideas. McWilliam et al. (1995) summarized:

> One implication for practice is that addressing family-level concerns might be a developmental process: the more professionals attend to families' priorities the more likely they are to develop close relationships with families. With such a relationship, a family is more likely to see [interventionists] as a potential resource for addressing family-level needs. (57)

Empowerment in Practice

Empowerment is a concept discussed frequently in the family–centered special education literature. Dunst and Trivette (1988) defined empowerment as "family identification and recognition of needs, the ability to deploy competencies to obtain resources to meet needs, and self-attributions about the role family members played in accessing resources and meeting needs" (94). In their discussion of enabling case-management strategies, they noted that the client empowerment approach promotes parents as competent decision makers who are actively involved in their child's education. This strengths-based approach places control in the parents' hands, allowing them to identify their own needs and resources while becoming self-sufficient.

Although at first glance, this may appear family-centered, an argument can be made to the contrary. Shonkoff and Meisels (1990) argued as much when they stated that "the concept of empowerment itself can be paternalistic if it is viewed as the giving of power to parents by professionals, rather than the assumption of power by parents themselves" (26). This implication is present when language such as "professionals empower parents" is used (e.g., Thompson et al. 1997). Such a statement implies that professionals have the power and control and that they choose to give it to parents. Evidence of this can be found in a longitudinal study of the participation of African American parents of twenty-four preschool children in special education programs (Harry, Allen & McLaughlin 1995). Initially, parents were very involved in their children's education and schooling. By the end of the study, all roles except parental monitoring of work had decreased significantly. The most commonly reported parental role was receiving information and signing documents. Parents no longer saw the need to attend IEP meetings, because they knew the information and paperwork would be sent home for them to sign. Parents reported that the family-friendly atmosphere had diminished between preschool and first grade, a finding that is consistent with others (Mahoney, O'Sullivan & Dennebaum 1990; McWilliam et al. 1995). Such disillusionment was related to less parent participation. Although a few parents did remain involved, "it seems reasonable to assume that, given some encouragement to see their roles as influential, and given adequate avenues for communication, other parents may have been inclined to become more vocal on issues that concerned them" (Harry, Allen & McLauglin 1995, 374). This conclusion was further reinforced by Turnbull and Turnbull (2001) and Wertz et al. (2002), who asserted that the IEP process can be disempowering, but that individual teachers can have a significant effect on the quality of the collaboration that occurs between parents of students with special needs and their families.

The concept of power and its implications within this context cannot be overstressed. "The greater the degree of power socially sanctioned for a given role, the greater the tendency for the role occupant to exercise and exploit the power and for those in a subordinate position to respond by increased submission, dependency, and lack of initiative" (Bronfenbrenner 1979, 92). Teachers and parents alike must respect the power that the other possesses. Only through such respect and sharing of roles can the students' and families' needs be met.

Summary

Family involvement in special education has been proven to have significant, positive outcomes for students and families alike. Parents should be involved in all aspects of decision making, planning, and program implementation. Unfortunately, this has not always been the case. Historically, parents were blamed for their children's disabilities and were perceived as harmful to their own children. For this reason, parents of children with disabilities were often encouraged to institutionalize their children from a very early age. Often, children with special needs were not allowed to enter public schools, and parents were left with very few options.

These beliefs gradually changed, and in 1976 the Education for All Handicapped Children Act became law. With this single piece of legislation, children with disabilities were now entitled to a free and appropriate public education in the least restrictive environment. Their education was to be individualized to their needs and guided by Individualized Education Plans created by a team of parents and professionals. Each reauthorization of this legislation, now called the Individuals with Disabilities Education Act (IDEA), has refined special education services and attempted to include families more. The most recent reauthorization also includes provisions to align IDEA with No Child Left Behind.

Current best practice for family involvement in special education is based on IDEA requirements, child development theories, including Bronfenbrenner's ecological/systems theory, and the transactional theory championed by Sameroff. The resulting family-centered approach is founded on the belief that parents and families are the single most influential component in a child's life. Supporting the families and respecting their cultural and personal beliefs are vital to supporting the child's education. Including parents and the students with disabilities in school activities that fall outside of the traditional roles will help families and students retain control of their own lives. The professional's responsibility is to serve, support, and respect the family. This includes putting aside cultural biases and ethnocentrism and recognizing that cultural values and beliefs about disability and education may vary widely.

In a family–centered approach, families are seen as experts, decision makers, partners, advocates, and active members of educational teams. The teacher's responsibility is to make parents aware of the new roles available to them while respecting a parent's desire to limit their own roles until they become more comfortable. This can be accomplished by utilizing ten basic family–centered practices:

- Organize your classroom to help families become advocates.
- Build flexibility within service delivery.
- Establish effective communication.
- Individualize to the needs of the entire family.
- Understand that families of children with disabilities often go back and forth through various stages of coping and grief.
- Respect the uniqueness of families, and treat them with dignity.
- Establish parent–professional collaboration and partnerships.
- Share information with parents and students.
- Emphasize family choice and decision making.
- Use responsive practices.

Chapter 13

Creating a Support Network for Families in Crisis

Catherine Tucker and Sondra Smith-Adcock

Learning Objectives

After reading this chapter, you will be able to:

■ Explain how an educator might assess whether a family is experiencing difficulties.
■ Identify resources within the school or larger community to assist families.
■ Describe the steps educators might use to help families access outside help.
■ Discuss how educators might build strong working relationships with the helping professionals in the broader community.
■ Describe the innovative "full services" programs for families.

Teachers see children every day and get to know them very well. As a result, they are often the first to notice when children's classroom behavior is being impacted by their families' difficulties. As a teacher gets to know a child's family, that teacher may discover that the family is attempting to handle an extremely stressful life situation. Mental health issues, such as substance abuse, family violence, divorce, child maltreatment or neglect, homelessness, and unemployment, are among the many stressful life circumstances that can overwhelm a family's capacity to care for and rear its children. When a teacher notices that a family is facing stressful situations, he or she may want to help. Often, however, the stressors that affect students' families are complex and exceed the resources of any one teacher or school. Moreover, traditionally, schools have not been organized to help children and their families address complex problems (Dryfoos 1994). Therefore, learning how to provide emotional support to families under stress and how to link them to community resources outside of the school are important skills for teachers to master.

How can teachers access the resources of schools and the larger community to help students and their families? First, the teacher needs to discover what is occurring within the family by closely observing the child and his or her family. Learning about the family entails discovering the difficulties it is facing and how it is coping with those issues without judging or blaming the family members. Second, once a teacher has identified that a family needs assistance, he or she will want to identify resources to assist the members within the school or larger community. In this chapter, we describe the steps teachers might use to help families access outside help. We then discuss how educators can build strong working relationships with the helping professionals in the broader community and showcase several of the innovative "full-services" programs for families that schools and communities are developing.

Assessing Family Strengths and Difficulties

As a first step to helping families in crisis, assessing their current strengths and needs is important. Examine the Case Study 13.1 of Vance and his family and identify what you consider to be the strengths and the difficulties faced by this family. We will revisit this case throughout the chapter to illustrate the various skills involved in working with families in crisis.

In first examining this case, you might notice the considerable number of stressors that Vance's family is facing. However, turning your attention to this family's strengths, you might notice several strong coping strategies they have developed. First, Mr. Tyler is very committed to his children's success at school. He is as involved at school as he can be, given his demanding work schedule and his role as a single parent. He is also forthcoming with information when talking with the teacher and obviously feels a level of trust in communicating with her. It also

〰〰〰〰〰〰〰〰〰〰〰〰〰〰〰〰〰〰〰〰〰〰〰〰〰〰〰〰

CASE STUDY 13.1

Vance and His Family

Read the following case and identify this family's strengths and stressors.

Vance Tyler is a second grade student in Ms. Farmer's class. Ms. Farmer is a first year teacher and has her hands full learning the "in's and out's" of school policy and procedure. Vance is presenting her with a particular challenge. He is a bright, verbal boy who tells her he "wants to do good" at school. However, Vance is constantly fighting with other students in the class. It seems that he wants to be in control during any group activity and reacts badly when others balk at his "orders." He also rarely brings in homework, although when he applies himself in class, he is easily able to do the work. Ms. Farmer is frustrated by Vance's lack of academic progress and the disruptions he often causes in the classroom. Ms. Farmer asks her mentor teacher for help. Mrs. Parsons has been teaching for twenty years and has been very successful with students like Vance. She advises Ms. Farmer to invite Vance's family in for a problem-solving meeting to find out what is going on at home that could be leading to some of Vance's behavior at school. Ms. Farmer knows that Vance lives with his younger sister Nora and their father. She phones Mr. Tyler and explains that Vance is having trouble getting along with others and she invites him to come to school to make a plan together to help Vance be successful at school. They arrange a mutually convenient time to meet. Prior to the meeting, Ms. Farmer prepares Vance by explaining when and why his father is coming to school, emphasizing to him that the meeting is designed to find ways to make school better, not to punish him. Ms. Farmer also makes sure to have a problem-solving form ready. When Mr. Tyler arrives, Ms. Farmer welcomes him warmly and explains the family–school problem-solving meeting steps. Then she goes over in some detail concrete examples of Vance's recent behavior. When she asks for Mr. Tyler's input, he explains that he has been punishing the child for doing poorly at school but realizes that the punishment (sending him to his room and taking away TV watching) has not helped much. When Ms. Farmer probes to find out more information about Vance's history, his father reveals that he is a single father of two young children. Mr. Tyler and his children, Vance and Nora, live on what he makes as a technician at an automobile tire store. It has been easier financially for them this year, because Nora started kindergarten in the fall, so he's no longer paying for day care. The three of them live in a rental house near the school, although Mr. Tyler hopes to eventually move into a place he can own instead of renting. However, since Vance and Nora's mother left, his finances have been in a tangle. John says his wife Michelle has a serious alcohol and drug problem. At this point, Ms. Farmer remarks that the stress of being a single parent must be difficult to cope with, and asks when Mrs. Tyler left. He replies that she left "for good" after she got out of jail for a DUI about three months ago. When Michelle got out of jail, the marriage continued to deteriorate, and her drug use continued to escalate. After a few more weeks, Michelle left to live with a new

boyfriend in a nearby town. Her calls and visits to him and the children are probably the root cause of Vance's current problems at school, since he did well in day care
and in kindergarten. Ms. Farmer comments that this must be a very hard time for
the family. She asks Mr. Tyler if he would like to talk to a family counselor about the
problems with his wife. He replies that he is willing to do anything to help his children. Ms. Farmer makes a list of a few counseling centers in the area, along with the
number for Al-Anon and says she will ask the school counselor to start seeing Vance
at school. Then the conversation shifts back to the issues in the classroom. Ms.
Farmer explains to Vance that although he may feel upset, they will work together
to help him achieve in school. Together, Ms. Farmer, Mr. Tyler, and Vance decide to
implement a reward system, so that on days Vance does well, he can earn extra free
choice time. His father agrees to reward his improvements at home as well.

Question to Consider

What are this family's strenghts?

---

appears that he sets reasonable and clear expectations for his children. Finally, Mr.
Tyler, Vance, and Nora seem close and have developed ways to meet their daily
needs, in spite of their limited resources. It takes some training to see the strengths
demonstrated by different families. Take a moment by means of Reflective Exercise 13.1 to consider what strengths the families you know demonstrate.

Reflective Exercise 13.1

Family Strengths

What are your family's strengths? Are they similar or different from Vance's family's
strengths? Is it more difficult to find a family's strengths when they are different from
your own?

Working with the Family to
Seek Help from the Community

Teachers often notice behavioral changes in the classroom when children are experiencing stress in their home environment. Yet how a child demonstrates the impact
of a family problem is often difficult to predict or interpret. Children manifest
changes in their behavior for many reasons; however, noticing a significant change

in a child's behavior should always trigger the teacher to consider whether a problem at home exists that needs attention. The child's change in behavior can first be addressed directly with the child, by simply asking: "Is there anything you want to talk about?" during a private moment.

If a child does disclose a family problem, it is important to be supportive and accepting, not judgmental. Simply acknowledging that you are there to listen can relieve a great deal of stress for a child. Referring the child to the school counselor, social worker, or psychologist for further assessment of the child may be helpful when behavioral changes occur, especially if the child's behavior seems extreme and/or you suspect the child might be neglected or abused. When a child discloses problems the family is experiencing, the teacher will need to follow up with parents to determine what, if any, help is needed. When teachers reach out to parents in these circumstances, parents are often cautious. Parents who are undergoing stressful situations are often reluctant to talk to school personnel about their circumstances for fear of being judged or pitied. Furthermore, families who are from marginalized groups (e.g., low income or cultural or ethnic minorities) are often suspicious of school personnel who inquire into their personal life as a result of prior experiences with agencies that have discriminated against them (Boyd-Franklin, 1989). As is true with the various family stressors discussed in this chapter, it is crucial not to view the family with disdain or pity, but to search for their strengths and resiliencies. Many parents fear they will be blamed and seen as "less than" if school personnel know about their situation. Whether based on previous experiences or hearsay, this fear of judgment is a very real issue for parents who are responding to teachers' well-meaning questions.

Conveying an open and nonjudgmental stance with families may seem simple and straightforward, but it often requires teachers to rethink how they might approach families. School personnel who have embraced the separation and remediation paradigms, as discussed in Chapter 2, may expect that students and parents will accommodate to the school's viewpoint without resistance. When parents do not "come when called" or do not respond favorably to the school's recommendations, parents may be viewed as "not caring, deficient, hard to reach, and as having little to offer to the education of their children" (Davies 1988; Leitch & Tangri 1988; Lott 2001).

When parents at first do not respond to phone calls or notes, make sure your communications are caring and nonjudgmental, and try not to leap to conclusions that the parents are deficient in some way. We recommend that if parents do not "come" the first time they are called, that teachers continue to reach out and re-iterate to parents/caregivers that they are available to listen and may be able to help them get needed assistance. What are effective ways to invite families to disclose issues to you as a teacher? How do your words or actions help families develop trust with you? What words and actions should you avoid when trying to build trust with families? Answer these questions in Reflective Exercise 13.2 on page 342.

Reflective Exercise 13.2

Teacher–Family Communication Skills

What are effective ways to invite families to disclose issues to you as a teacher? How do your words or actions help families develop trust with you? What words and actions should you avoid when trying to build trust with families?

Some forms of communication are facilitative and help you build trust with others. When asking people to disclose sensitive information, adopting a physical posture of listening and attention is important. For most people, if you lean forward and make eye contact, they feel that you are listening to and accepting of them. Also, if you are surrounded by a large group of school staff, do not expect parents to feel comfortable or to disclose much. To reduce feelings of intimidation for parents, plan to keep the number of school staff attending meetings with you and a caregiver/parent to a minimum. Privacy is also important, so be sure you are not meeting in a place with a lot of foot traffic or other interruptions. When listening, be sure to use furthering responses (e.g., nodding, using responses of affirmation such as "yes" or "OK"), ask open-ended questions, and refrain from replying with judging or blaming statements (e.g., "You really should think of seeking some help for this problem; your child is not doing well in school."). If people perceive that you are judging them for their personal problems, little will be disclosed, and they will be unlikely to allow you to help them. You may recall the discussion of these communication skills in Chapter 8. They are most essential to apply in dealing with families experiencing stress or crises.

Common Family Challenges

Families today face numerous stresses that can make parenting an even more difficult task. Dealing with natural disasters, financial problems, family violence, child maltreatment, or mental health problems, such as substance abuse, can create a very stressful family environment, which, in turn, can create stress for children's lives in school. When families encounter these nonnormative stressors (as discussed in Chapter 5), the family's usual organization and roles are rendered "off-balance." As a result, they often need assistance in a variety of areas to help them restabilize and function effectively. Also, keep in mind that families of all ethnic and most cultural groups can experience these problems. However, educators should familiarize themselves with the beliefs and practices of the cultural and ethnic groups represented in their schools to create strong positive relationships with families from diverse backgrounds (Boyd-Franklin 1989; Boyd-Webb 2003; Loue 2003). In the following section we describe several stressful circumstances that families may experience, discuss the impact of these circumstances on family functioning, and suggest some possible intervention strategies. In addition, we list a variety of school and community resources found in Additional Resources at the end of this chapter that teachers may consider when linking families in crisis to helping professionals.

Financial Problems

Although any family can experience financial stress, it has the most profound impact upon working class and poor families, who tend to have the fewest resources to fall back on. Poverty has been defined as "a condition that extends beyond the lack of income and goes hand in hand with a lack of power, humiliation and a sense of exclusion" (Raphael 2005, p 36). Seeing poverty in this way means that a considerable number of children and their families often feel ashamed and excluded from the institutions that are positioned to assist them. In 2002, 16 percent of American children lived in poverty (defined as earning less than $19,157 for a family of four by the U.S. Census Bureau in 2005), and one in four families in the United States with young children earned less than $25,000 a year (Child Welfare League of America, October 23, 2005).

   Living in poverty often puts a great deal of stress on the family, making sustaining effective family functioning more challenging (as discussed in Chapters 4 and 6). For example, families who are living with financial strains are frequently more engaged with survival issues, such as keeping a roof over their heads and putting food on the table, rather than responding to notes from their children's teachers. This should not cause the teacher to believe that the parents are uninterested in their child's education, but that the parents are currently more focused on meeting basic needs. For some families, this situation is temporary, caused by loss of a job or unexpected expenses due to divorce, illness, natural disaster, or other life-altering event. In other cases, living in poverty or near poverty is a long-term problem. In either case, family emotional resources are often stretched thin along with family income.

   Families from any cultural group or socioeconomic class can experience financial distress and may handle stress differently, so generalizations are hard to make. However, some characteristic reactions to family financial distress demonstrated by students are listed to help teachers begin to think about what might be triggering a child's atypical behavior. The child

- May either act out aggressively or withdraw from friends
- May have fewer extracurricular activities than before
- May seem very upset over lost or broken items
- May seem embarrassed about clothes, toys, or other social status items
- May not invite other children over to his or her house
- May become upset if any money is needed for field trips, and so on
- May not have appropriate clothes for weather (e.g., coat, boots)

How might you respond to a student reacting to his or her family's financial distress? Some useful tips for working with students or families in financial distress are

- Be sensitive to lack of money for field trips, extra outings, and so on. You may wish to find out whether your PTA or other school group has money to cover such expenses.
- Do not embarrass the child or parent by discussing their financial problems when other people are present.
- If you notice the child seems hungry, underfed, or is not wearing clothes appropriate for the weather (e.g., has no winter coat), consult with your school counselor or social worker to learn of ways to link the family with community resources. These can be symptoms of a financial crisis or possible signs of neglect.
- Find out about other resources and strengths the family has and build on them. Families in financial crisis often feel ashamed of their circumstances. Hence, it is very important to recognize their positive attributes to enhance the parents' feelings of self-worth and lessen their reluctance to work with you and the school.

Divorce

About half of all first marriages in the United States end in divorce (U.S. Census Bureau 2005). Each year, about one million American children under age eighteen experience the divorce of their parents. These rates have remained fairly stable over the past thirty years, following a dramatic increase during the 1970s. What these statistics mean for educators is that it is highly likely that many of your students will live in single-parent homes or blended families, and that you will have students in your classroom who are currently experiencing the divorce of their parents. Although rather commonplace in today's society, divorce is a highly stressful experience for both parents and children. Although all families are unique, and therefore, will experience divorce and remarriage in different ways, the children always experience a period of loss and grief. Some common consequences for children of divorce are

- Reduction in family income
- Moving to a new home, neighborhood, and school
- Legal battles, often involving child custody
- Having to learn two sets of rules for operating in two different homes
- Trying to maintain loyalty to both parents
- Confusion and sense of loss
- Fear of not seeing one parent as often, or at all
- Being used as a go-between to relay messages or, worse, as a "spy"

How might you respond to children and families who are experiencing a divorce? Here are some suggested actions you might consider:

- Acknowledge to the child, in private, that you are aware of the situation and are available to listen.

- Keep classroom routines as "normal" and stable as possible. School is often the calm place within a storm for children.
- Consider referring the child to your school counselor, social worker, or psychologist if he or she displays ongoing symptoms of sadness, anger, or becomes withdrawn.
- Do not "take sides" with either parent.
- Be sure to stay in touch with both parents, unless and until one of them is awarded sole custody of the child. Parents have the legal right to request and receive all school records and correspondence. If legal custody arrangements change, the parent is responsible for notifying school personnel. Always keep a copy of any legal documents that parents bring to school, and share a copy with your principal, school counselor, social worker, or other designated person.

Death in the Family or Community

Of all possible family or community tragedies that teachers may encounter, death may be the most difficult to respond to. Death is, of course, a natural part of the life cycle; however, it continues to be a taboo topic in many cultures and usually takes a significant emotional toll on a family. When a student faces a death in his or her family or close social network, many types of reactions are possible and normal. Some children may react with anger toward the deceased, whereas others may primarily exhibit sadness or withdrawal (Kübler-Ross 1997). Many factors influence how children respond to the death of a person close to them. Some of these include

- How the person died. Was it a sudden death, or a death following a long illness? Sudden, violent losses, rather than losses that result with aging, are often more difficult for children. Being able to say good-bye to a loved one sometimes helps children cope better with that person's death.
- How well the child knew the person, or how often he or she saw the deceased. Obviously, the loss of a parent, sibling, or other very close family member is likely to be more difficult to grieve than the loss of someone who is not as close. The death of a parent can also have long-term financial implications.
- The way the family explained the death and dealt with the aftermath. Culture plays an important role in determining how a family deals with death and grief. Rituals of closure, such as funerals, wakes, or sitting shiva, can be comforting and help restore order following the chaotic time after a loved one dies (Kübler-Ross 1997). If the family does not allow the child to express a full range of post-trauma emotion, or denies the death, the grieving process for the child can become extremely difficult.
- The age and developmental level of the child. Very young children do not have an understanding of time or permanency and may expect the dead person to return (Piaget 2001).

Following the death of a loved one, children generally go through several stages of grief (Kübler-Ross 1997). These stages are not linear, meaning a person can go back and forth through the stages many times before finally gaining a sense of peace and acceptance. The stages of grief are different for each individual and can vary even for individuals according to the circumstances of the loss. The five stages of grief identified by Kübler-Ross include denial, anger, bargaining, depression, and acceptance. The stage of denial usually means that the person is still in shock, and the true nature of the loss has not yet "sunk in." The person may feel numb or emotionless. This stage can last quite a while, particularly if the death was sudden. Anger, especially in children, can include the feeling that the deceased has abandoned them. Anger is an emotion that is often misunderstood, hence it is sometimes discouraged. However, anger is a very normal reaction to loss and should not be stigmatized. During the bargaining phase, people, especially children, who are still "magical thinkers," sometimes will try to bargain with God to return their loved one. Depression and extreme sadness usually signal that the impact of the loss is being truly felt. This stage can last a long time and, in some cases, may require attention from a mental health professional if it continues to interfere with normal activities after a period of several months. Once the depression improves, a grieving person will feel a sense of acceptance of the loss. They may retain a sense of sadness but are now able to return to their "normal" way of life and integrate the loss into their life story.

In working with bereaved students,

- Allow students to express sadness, anger, and so on, without judging them.
- Refer the student to the school counselor for extra support.
- Try to have the students' schedule remain as normal as possible; maintaining routines can be very comforting to children.
- Consider having other students in the class make cards for the child and his or her family to express support and care.
- Do not be surprised to see some regressive behavior (e.g., thumb sucking, crying easily) for a while after the loss.

Be prepared for questions about death and loss from your students. The school counselor, school psychologist, or local hospice staff can help you prepare to discuss these issues.

Family Violence

The American Psychological Association (1996) defines family violence as, "acts of physical, sexual, or psychological maltreatment, aggression, and violence that occur in a family unit whereby one family member with more power or authority attempts to gain control over another family member" (cited in Boyd-Webb 2003, 316). Women represent 73 percent of all victims of family violence in the United States, and 76 percent of perpetrators are male About half of all violent crime in the United States between 1998 and 2002 involved violence between spouses, and another 11 percent occurred between parents and children (U.S. Department of Justice, Office of Justice Programs, 2006).

Although the number of violent incidents between family members has decreased over the past decade (OJP 2006), family violence is still a widespread societal problem that continues to affect schoolchildren. Children who witness violence between their parents or other adult caretakers are at greater risk for depression, anxiety, and aggressive behavior (Jaffe & Sudermann 1995). Moreover, children who have witnessed violence often have frequent nightmares, sleep problems, changes in appetite, and are at higher risk for school failure and delinquency (Gil 1991). In addition, children who witness violent acts are at risk for developing physical health problems, such as asthma, gastrointestinal disorders, allergies, and headaches (Graham-Bermann & Seng 2005).

The probability that a teacher will have a child in the classroom who has witnessed at least one act of violence in his or her home is extremely high. Graham-Berman and Seng (2005) surveyed children in a low-income area in Michigan and discovered that 46.7 percent had been present during one or more violent incidents in their homes by the time they entered preschool. If a teacher suspects a child is witnessing domestic violence at home, the teacher should immediately contact the school counselor, principal, psychologist, or social worker. Most states require educators to report suspected domestic violence to child protective services. In working with children whose families may have experienced violence, consider the following guidelines:

- Safety is always primary. Do not meet alone with any person you know has, or is suspected of having, a history of violent behavior. Always have others present and meet in an open, public place. Do not go to the home of any person whom you suspect may have been violent toward others.
- Be sure you have the most recent copies of any restraining orders and emergency custody decrees on file, and leave explicit information on this matter for substitute teachers.
- People who are victims of domestic violence may go to great lengths to cover up the violence in their home, sometimes due to fear of reprisal or personal shame. If someone discloses violence to you, he or she is taking a risk and needs to be treated with the utmost respect.
- Abused partners are at the highest risk for attacks, including homicide, just after leaving a violent situation. Monitor the child carefully, especially on field trips and when leaving for the day during this time.

Child Maltreatment

Unfortunately, many children not only witness family violence, but also are its victims. In 2002, 2,450 children were abused or neglected each day in the United States (NCCAN 2006). An average of four American children died every day from maltreatment in 2002, and teachers reported 16 percent of all cases of abuse and neglect that year (NCCAN). The psychological damage inflicted by neglect and emotional abuse can be equally as serious as physical maltreatment (Kagan 2004). Children who suffer from parental neglect often develop insecurities about how others will respond to them. Milder cases of children suffering from neglect include symptoms such as clinging to adults, being very shy and withdrawn, and being fearful of new situations. When more severe neglect or maltreatment exists, more serious symptoms such as rage, aggression, lying, stealing, and lack of concern for others can occur (Cassidy 1999; Kagan 2004; Karen 1998).

Neglect from caregivers early in life can also lead to slower brain development, reduced language skills, and difficulty interpreting social cues in later life (Cassidy 1999; Karen 1998; Karr-Morse & Wiley 1997). Some researchers believe that many learning disabilities may stem from early parental neglect or abuse (Karr-Morse & Wiley). Children who have been neglected or abused may appear to be less attentive and/or more aggressive in the classroom. Abused or neglected children sometimes exhibit symptoms of inattention or hyperactivity, when in fact they are suffering from the effects of trauma. Common indicators of family violence and/or child maltreatment demonstrated by children are that he or she

- Appears fearful or hyper vigilant
- Has unexplained bruises, burns, or other injuries not common among children in their age group, or in unusual places (neck, stomach, and thigh)
- Acts out sexually, talks about or draws sexually explicit situations
- Complains of genital pain or itching
- Shifts from usual behavior to being withdrawn or aggressive
- Often comes to school dirty, hungry, or inappropriately dressed for weather
- Reports going home to an empty house (younger children)
- Is avoidant of police or other authority figures
- Acts too mature for age, such as taking care of classmates
- Is anxious about being picked up at school by certain individuals

To work with children who might be abused or neglected, consider the following:

- Children who have been abused often have trouble trusting adults. Be extremely careful not to break promises, no matter how small, to build a trusting relationship.
- Depending on the circumstances surrounding the abuse, children may be fearful of the dark, of being alone in small spaces, of being alone in the bathroom, or of certain types of people (e.g., tall men). Be alert to these issues and report them to the nonoffending parent and mental health care provider for the child. Do not punish the child for a fearful reaction.
- Children who have been sexually abused sometimes act out their abuse on other children. If this occurs, contact the child's parent and your principal right away. Calmly explain to the child that this behavior is not acceptable at school, but avoid being overly harsh or punitive with the child, as he or she is acting out a traumatic memory, not being intentionally malicious.

One of your major obligations as a teacher is to recognize and report situations in which you suspect maltreatment of a child. However, you must use caution when developing a hypothesis about what is happening in a child's home. On the one hand, educators need to be conscientious about reporting suspected child maltreatment or family violence, and, on the other hand, you must be sure not to alienate the family by making erroneous reports. This requires extreme delicacy and diplomacy.

So what should you do if you suspect a child has been maltreated? First, make sure that your suspicions are based on facts and that you have reasonable grounds for concern. Second, be aware of your school's policy and procedures regarding reporting child maltreatment within the school. For example, in some schools, you may be required to report to the school counselor, social worker, nurse, or principal, depending on school procedures. Some schools have developed the policy that the principal or another person (e.g., a school counselor or social worker) has been designated as the one required to place the call to social services, although the teacher is responsible for notifying this person of a problem. In other schools, the policy is that teachers must make their own reports to social services. Third, call the local or state child protection agency. If you are unsure of what agency to call, contact your school counselor, social worker, or principal. Every state requires people who have any child-care responsibility to report maltreatment. If you do not report it, you are violating the law and are subject to civil or criminal punishment. When you are making a direct report, you will need to have the following information on hand:

- Child's name, date of birth, and home address
- Parents' or caregivers' names, addresses, and telephone numbers
- Suspected perpetrator's name and any contact information you have
- Names of siblings who live with the child and where they are in school

If you are missing any of this information, make the report anyway. Having complete information makes investigating alleged child maltreatment cases easier, but you should not delay reporting a potentially dangerous situation if you are missing some contact information.

As with so many issues in society, an ounce of prevention in family violence is worth a pound of cure. Many states have implemented formal curricula designed to help children identify and avoid potentially dangerous situations and give them skills for reporting abuse to trusted adults. If your school system does not have a formal program, you can take the initiative in teaching your class about safety planning. This might involve talking with your students about (a) how (and when) to call 911, (b) the differences between good and bad touches, and (c) how to tell an adult they trust if someone hurts or scares them. Many Web-based resources are available for teachers interested in developing such prevention programs that can be accessed through the government clearinghouse (e.g., www.childwelfare.gov).

Substance Abuse

Alcohol and drug addiction exacts a devastating toll on our nation. Approximately 14 million adults are alcoholics or abusers of alcohol, and one in four of our children are exposed to alcoholism or alcohol abuse in their families before age 18. Three million children between the age of 14 and 17 drink regularly and face future problems with alcohol.

President G. W. Bush, November 11, 2001

The first exposure some children have to alcohol and other drugs may be before birth. Mothers who use alcohol and/or other drugs during pregnancy pass the drugs onto the fetus, which can cause birth defects such as mental retardation, learning disorders, and behavioral problems (Steinhausen & Spohr 1998). Due to the stigma and possible legal repercussions for pregnant women admitting to substance abuse problems, the number of children who are affected by prenatal drug and alcohol abuse is difficult to determine. However, the U.S. Department of Health and Human Services (1990) estimates that between 1.3 and 2.2 out of every 1,000 live births every year in the United States have fetal alcohol syndrome, and another 3 or 4 per 1,000 have some less serious birth defects caused by prenatal exposure to alcohol.

Children who are living in families where substance abuse is an issue face many challenges regardless of whether they were exposed to drugs and alcohol before birth. According to Boyd-Webb (2003), some common stressors children encounter in substance abusing families are

- Living in dangerous neighborhoods, often with unstable housing arrangements and frequent moves
- Financial strain and often homelessness
- Lack of family or other social support systems
- Parents with poor coping and management skills
- Addicted parents are sometimes so consumed with the need to obtain and use drugs that children may be neglected, abandoned, or abused
- Parents who have active drug use problems may be arrested and jailed often, leaving children as wards of the state if no relatives can care for them
- Family life is often chaotic, leaving children anxious and unsettled (288)

At school, the anxiety and chaos of living in a substance abusing family can manifest in many different types of behavior. Teachers might observe children sleeping in class, being disorganized or poorly prepared for class, seeming distracted or daydreaming, or acting out aggressively. Children in substance abusing families may also seem "older than their years" and may assume a care-taking role (Loue 2003).

In the case of substance abuse, families are often defensive or secretive about the problem, largely due to fear of legal reprisal and/or social embarrassment. If you have established a positive relationship with a parent, he or she may be more likely to discuss the issue with you. However, many factors determine whether a person is ready to enter treatment. Some general guidelines in working with children of families with substance abuse problems are

- As the child's classroom teacher, you can provide a positive environment at school by keeping daily schedules consistent to counterbalance a chaotic home life, being firm but fair with school rules, and being a listening ear for the child when needed.

- Often, homes where one or more people struggle with addictions are not well organized. Rules and schedules, which are highly reassuring to young children, are not well established and the child may feel like he or she is living in a whirlwind of emotion, conflict, and chaos.
- Families with addictions often have financial and legal problems as well as the addiction itself, which add stress to the child's environment.
- Addicted adults often suffer from mood swings and may have erratic behaviors. Teachers can help ameliorate children's stress in these situations by being extremely organized, consistent, and compassionate.
- Do not make different rules or exceptions for a child based solely on a parent's addiction. Treat the child the same way you treat all of the other students. This will help the child feel "normal" and lessen his or her possible feelings of not fitting in due to family difficulties.

Natural Disasters

Although fires, hurricanes, floods, earthquakes, and other forms of natural disasters have always been a part of the human experience, the effect that living through one of these frightening events might have on children has only recently been acknowledged by professionals. The struggles of child survivors of extreme weather events, such as the tsunami in Southeast Asia in 2005 and Hurricane Katrina in September 2006, brought international attention to the difficulties that children sometimes face in the wake of such events.

Many factors contribute to how well a child will cope with a natural disaster. Children are generally highly resilient and recover at least as quickly as adults following a disaster (Kirschke & van Vliet 2005). However, some children do suffer with various emotional disturbances in the aftermath of traumatic events. According to the National Association of School Psychologists (NASP) (2005), some common symptoms children may exhibit following a natural disaster might include

- In young children, thumb sucking, bed-wetting, reverting to baby-like behaviors, eating more or less than normal, nightmares, irritability
- In older children (ages six to twelve, or so), aggression or withdrawal, changes in eating or sleeping patterns, clinging to adults, distractible, irritable behavior, nightmares
- In teenagers, changes in eating or sleeping patterns, less interest in favorite activities, increase in irritability, headaches, and stomach upset

Children who exhibit some or all of these symptoms generally begin to feel better in two weeks to a month. If symptoms persist, or cause major disruptions in a child's school or family life, teachers should advise parents to seek help from a licensed mental health professional.

School personnel can do a lot to help children recover from the terrifying experience of a natural disaster. Schools often have crisis response teams in place, comprised of school and emergency personnel, to deal with the aftermath of natural disasters as well as other traumatic events, such as the death of a teacher or student. Crisis plans are developed by crisis response teams and are specific, written documentation of what should be done in the case of an emergency. If your school does not have a crisis plan, talk to your administrative team about creating one. Crisis response plans defuse much of the distress of deciding how to handle a trauma by giving clear guidelines to teachers and providing a list of support resources available in the community. Some general guidelines for handling the aftermath of a natural disaster in the classroom include

- Keep school schedules and routines as normal as possible. Decreasing the amount of change and chaos is critical following a disaster.
- Allow children to talk about their feelings or create artwork about the event and discuss how similarly you all feel about the event. Normalize the children's feelings of anxiety and sadness, and let them know that most people feel better within a month or so after such an event.
- Talk about child survivors of other disasters who have now returned to their normal routines. Illustrate that, although it is not easy to do, people do return to "normal" after a hurricane, tornado, earthquake, and so on.
- Communicate with parents as often as possible. Share information from credible sources, such as the Red Cross or NASP, about helping children cope.
- Talk about healthy ways to relieve stress and cope with difficult situations.

In Reflective Exercise 13.3, we ask you to identify the particular problems that Vance's family faces, and to consider how these problems might be affecting Vance's in-school behavior. Also, if you were his teacher, what might you intervene?

Reflective Exercise 13.3

Impact of Stressors and Challenges on Family

Which problem areas affect Vance's family? How might these stressors affect his behavior at school? As his teacher, what would you do to help?

Vance's family is struggling with divorce, financial problems, and substance abuse. Vance is acting out his feelings of distress and lack of control, by trying to control other children. The distress also contributes to his becoming easily frustrated and very distractible. His teacher can refer him to the school counselor and refer his family to services in the community for family counseling. The teacher can also work with Vance in the classroom to better control his distress by (a) rewarding him for positive coping by talking to her when he feels upset instead of acting out; (b) allowing him to take short "time-outs" as needed; and/or (c) assigning grade level appropriate reading about dealing with emotions positively and/or anger management.

Assessing Available Resources

As stated in Chapter 4, families have multiple functions and roles. Families raise and socialize children; provide food, clothing, and shelter to members; provide daily care, spiritual, and emotional support to each other; shape members' personal identity; share recreational activities; and provide life skills to members. All of these functions are critical in the life of a family, especially to children within the family. When a crisis occurs, some or all of these areas of function can be negatively impacted by the stress of the changes caused by the crisis. Students may exhibit a need for extra help and support due to stress experienced by the family and the temporary loss of family functioning in one or more areas. To facilitate a family's return to effective functioning, teachers need to be aware of existing resources within the school or the larger community that might assist them. The following is a listing of various resources commonly found in schools and communities.

Inside the School

Often professionals within the school can be helpful to families in crisis or to teachers seeking to assist them. Although each school will, in all probability, have its own set of rules about how and whom to refer a student or student's family, these professionals can be helpful to families in times of crisis in a variety of ways. For example, school counselors, school social workers, and school psychologists can provide emotional support during and after a crisis and offer further referrals for such care. Nurses and social workers can assist students and families with health care issues, including helping families access specialized care for children with disabilities. Special educators and speech pathologists can assist families of children with special needs to identify and access services that can help their child be successful in school as well as help the families connect with support services for emotional needs they may have as a result of the child's condition. Administrators, counselors, psychologists, special educators, reading specialists, mentor teachers, attendance officers, and behavior specialists can assist teachers in managing a child's behavioral or academic needs in the classroom and can act as consultants for problem solving with teachers and families as well. Hence, teachers are well advised to identify and access these school-based professionals early and often.

Although titles and functions may differ between states and school districts, most schools employ some or all of the following professionals: counselors, psychologists, social workers, nurses, truant officers and/or attendance coordinators, special education teachers and directors, behavior resource teachers, reading specialists, speech and language pathologists, principals, assistant principals, and mentor teachers. Teachers need to be familiar with the professionals in their buildings and districts. Find out what each person's specific responsibilities include and how to go about referring students to that person.

In the Community

In many communities in the United States, the local United Way produces and distributes a directory of community service agencies. Usually, the United Way directory includes descriptions of the services provided, hours of operation, and location. These directories are tremendously helpful to teachers and others who need to refer families to a variety of local services. If your community has a United Way directory, much of the legwork described here is already done for you. You need only to obtain and read the most recent version of the directory to get an overview of local resources. (*Note:* Because United Way determines to which community agencies funding is given, some concern exists that agencies in low-income communities may not be adequately supported.) If your community does not have such an agency that has developed such a service directory, your job becomes a bit more complex. You need to first find out what types of service agencies exist in your area. Most communities will have at least some of the types of services listed in Figure 13.1.

Once you have identified key local resources, you need to become familiar with the following information about each agency:

- What services are provided?
- What fees are charged?
- What are the hours of operation?
- Where are they located?
- Are translators available for non-English speakers and/or deaf parents?
- Who is the main contact person within the agency for the school?
- Is transportation available? Are they on a bus or train line?

Having a personal relationship with key agency staff is often crucial for helping families access services. If your school has a social worker or school counselor, in all likelihood, that person has cultivated such relationships with local agency personnel and can guide teachers to the key people in each agency. Furthermore, in some schools or districts, policies exist about which staff members may make referrals for services outside of school, and teachers are encouraged to defer to the school's social worker or counselor to streamline the referral process. Be sure to become aware of your school's policies.

In Reflective Exercise 13.4 on page 356 we ask you to consider what resources within your school or in your community might be available to you and the families. Do you know how and when to contact them? What resources might you link Vance's family with? (*Answer:* Vance's family might be connected with a counseling service for divorce counseling. If available, his father might enjoy learning from parenting classes. If their financial problems are serious, they might also benefit from using either emergency aid from the Department of Children and Families or from consumer counseling services.)

Figure 13.1   Types of Community Service Organizations

United Way is an umbrella agency that receives and distributes funding to various community human service agencies. Most local United Way agencies will have a published directory that lists most or all local human services agencies, contact information, and other helpful information. Some local United Way agencies also operate referral hotlines.

Public Health Department is a governmental agency that provides basic health care services, such as immunizations and prenatal care to people with low income. Public health departments also employ health educators who may visit schools to conduct information sessions about health and wellness topics. School nurses are also hired by the local public health department.

Family and Children's Mental Health Services/Mental Health Center is an agency that provides low-cost counseling services and educational programs. In some states, this agency may be a government entity, and in others it is privately funded. Some family and children's counseling centers may also operate family violence shelters or homeless services.

Department of Social Services/Department of Families and Children is the state agency charged with investigating allegations of child abuse and neglect and operating and licensing group and foster care homes. Social service agencies also determine who is qualified for the state children's health insurance program, food stamps, and the state's welfare program. This agency may be called by various titles in various states, and may be broken up into divisions, but all fifty states have some version of it.

Domestic Violence Shelter is a home-like setting where women and young children can go after being attacked by violent partners. Usually, there is no fee for staying at the shelter. Shelters often provide counseling services and help women find jobs and permanent housing.

Alcoholics Anonymous/Narcotics Anonymous/Al-Anon are support groups for people with substance abuse problems. They are free of charge and run by group members, not helping professionals. Their primary goal is to help each other stay sober one day at a time.

Hospice is an organization that assists people with terminal illnesses and their families. Hospice provides in-home end-of-life care and counseling services to patients and families.

Council of Churches/Ministers is a local group of clergy who band together to address community problems such as substance abuse or homelessness. These organizations vary greatly by community. Sometimes they may directly operate food banks or shelters.

Homeless Shelters/Feeding Centers are a feeding and housing help for the homeless, which can be found in most communities. The size and range of services offered depend largely on the size of the city where they are located and the number of homeless people in the area. Most provide at least one hot meal a day and some type of sleeping shelter. Some also provide counseling and medical services.

Lion's Club is a fraternal organization whose main focus is vision. They can be very helpful in obtaining glasses for low-income children.

Parks and Recreation Department, found in most communities, is government funded and runs swimming pools, public parks, and after-school care and youth sports programs. They often do not charge fees for youth sports and after-school care.

Reflective Exercise 13.4

Linking Family with School and Community Resources

What resources within your school or in your community might be available to you and the families. Do you know how and when to contact them? With what resources might you link Vance's family?

Engaging with Families in Crisis

Regardless of whether a crisis currently exists, engaging with families is not a discrete, one-time occurrence. As stated many times in previous chapters, collaborative family–school relationships are built over time using a variety of skills and methods. Hopefully, the teacher will have already built a respectful, caring relationship with the family prior to the family facing a crisis so that helping the family now find and access school- and community-based resources will be far easier because the family and teacher already trust and understand each other.

Once a crisis surfaces, whether it is a school-based issue with the child or a family-based issue, the teacher will need to use her or his communication skills and the strength of her or his relationship with the family to be of help. When the teacher and family are racially and/or culturally different, the issue is particularly critical. Due to a long history in this country of maltreatment, discrimination, and abuse of minority and low-income people by the European American and more affluent people, building trust between a Caucasian middle-class teacher and a low-income African American family (for example) takes more effort on the part of the teacher to prove that he or she is trustworthy and has the child's and family's best interests in mind (Boyd-Franklin 1989; Gibson & Abrams 2003).

When engaging with families who are experiencing a crisis, whether it is a mental health problem, loss of a parent's job, or a natural disaster, keep in mind that people in crisis may not respond the same way as they did prior to the crisis, or in the same way another person would in the same circumstance. Common effects of experiencing a crisis are numbness, or feeling inhibited in your ability to experience and express emotions, fear, helplessness, and shame (Brewin 2001).

When speaking with families in crisis, remember to be a good listener—ask for clarification when needed, probe for more information when appropriate, and paraphrase to show you are hearing their message. Also, it is important to identify the underlying emotions parents are feeling. For example, a teacher might respond to a story about a family member's death by saying, "It sounds like this has been a very sad and difficult time for you and your family." Acknowledging and naming their emotions can help people recognize and clarify their own feelings and let them know you truly comprehend the situation. Expressing your own feelings about the situation as a means of supporting the family is also appropriate. By expressing genuine caring for the family, you build trust and facilitate communication with its members.

If appropriate, a teacher may choose at this point to refer the family to another professional in the school or to a community-based service agency. Crisis situations often lower a person's abilities to remember facts and issues, so be sure to write down all relevant information about the referral for a family member. Caregivers in crisis may anger more easily than usual, so take care not to sound judgmental or blaming when making referrals. Use the blocking blame skills described in Chapter 11 to avoid making a parent feel that you are accusing him or her in some way.

After making the referral, create a plan to follow up with the caregiver/parent about his or her progress in accessing services. Remember that, unless you ask the caregiver to sign a form granting permission to obtain information from a community agency, you will not be able to get any feedback from the agency as to whether the family has made an appointment or has received services. If a family has not followed up on your recommendation, you will want to contact the family and ask what you can do to help them access the services or inquire about any barriers they may have encountered. In some cases, you may need to make the appointment for the family and help them arrange transportation. However, you must also remember that families cannot be forced to follow a school professional's recommendations. Creating negative consequences for not following your recommendations will not make family members more likely to comply and will negatively impact your relationship with them. By means of Reflective Exercise 13.5, identify the steps the members of the school staff took to respond to the Tyler family's crisis.

Reflective Exercise 13.5

Responding to a Family Crisis

What steps did Ms. Farmer take to help Mr. Tyler? Which of her words or actions do you feel most facilitated communication? How do you think you would have handled the situation? What would be the most difficult aspect of the conversation for you?

As you probably noticed, Ms. Farmer did not jump to conclusions about Vance's behavior. She listened carefully and was open to input from his father and from Vance. She worked with the family in a nonjudgmental way to facilitate collaborative problem solving.

Community and School Service Delivery Models

〰〰〰〰〰
〰〰〰〰〰

Creating a network of community resources means teachers can help families respond to stressors that can affect their children's schooling. The efforts of classroom teachers to link families to community services can bring about remarkable changes in children's overall academic and psychosocial development and the families' ability to care for and rear their children. As individual teachers and other school personnel try to help children and families confront stressors in their life, they often develop ongoing relationships with staff at community agencies. These relationships have varying degrees of formality, but many are helpful and function smoothly to help schools reach out to and support families. While creating these relationships is important and beneficial for schools and families, many communities are formalizing these relationships into a continuum of community service delivery models.

Some schools and school districts have developed specific community partnership initiatives that are systematic and ongoing. These *School–Family–Community Partnerships* are action teams organized at the school level or the district level that comprise members of the school community and the larger community (Epstein 2005). Other school districts have developed *Full-Service Community School* models, which bring community agencies and schools together into one entity (Dryfoos 2000). Each of these models will be discussed in more detail in the following section.

School–Family–Community Partnerships

School–Family–Community Partnerships are structured ways to organize school efforts to meet the needs of students and families. The National Network of Partnership Schools (NNPS) developed the model under the direction of Joyce Epstein, professor of Sociology at Johns Hopkins University (Vogel 2006). Over the last decade, these partnerships have grown in number. School–Family–Community Partnerships are now in place in 100 school districts, 1,000 schools, and 17 state departments of education (Epstein 2005).

Family–School–Community Partnerships are based on improving student achievement. The first step in creating these partnerships is to form an action team. Action teams comprise school personnel and community agency representatives. These action teams can be organized at the school, district, or state department of education. The action team is responsible for developing specific plans for the partnership and getting the work of family–school–community collaboration started. Because the collaboration is different across communities, these plans vary. However, according to Vogel (2006), these partnerships usually aim to change the interaction of the school, family, and community in several ways. First, schools can redefine family involvement in schools. Although many schools define family involvement as getting the parents to visit the school, family involvement can be much more extensive than parents attending a book fair or PTA meeting. For example, the school might help parents improve their child-rearing skills or get parents more involved in decision making about their children's immediate educational program or state-level initiatives. Changing the ways that schools collaborate with the community is also important. Collaborating with the community involves coordinating resources and services for families, students, and the school with businesses, agencies, and other groups, and providing services to the community. Support and encouragement for school personnel, family members, and community partners and building relationships are crucial as these shifts in school, family, and community involvement are made.

Some detailed and ongoing research efforts have shown that School–Family–Community Partnerships yield positive results. The NNPS at Johns Hopkins University has conducted studies over the past five years that have shown that family, community, and school partnerships improve students' achievement and other indicators of success (Epstein 2005). By improving community collaboration, schools addressed the problems of more of the families that traditionally have been considered "hard to reach" families (Sheldon 2003). The success of family–school–collaboration efforts means that traditional ideas of community–school relationships have to be reconsidered. The school is no longer positioned to address only educational questions but also facilitate the development of children in a much more systemic and profound way. This requires changing the way that schools have traditionally reached out to families, but, moreover, this shift requires thinking about education differently. According to Joyce Epstein, founder and director of NNPS:

> It's nice to have parents feel more comfortable in the school, or have local stores support the football team. But considering the depth of resources that parental and community involvement can bring to a school, it's a mistake to pass on the opportunity to harness this energy to provide a better education. (Cited in Vogel 2006, 68)

Full-Service Community Schools

Full-Service Community Schools combine quality education and comprehensive support services at the same site (Dryfoos 1994). In her book, *Full-Service Schools: A Revolution in Health and Social Services for Children, Youth, and Families*, Dryfoos further describes the full-service model. In full-service schools, children are provided high-quality education through individualized instruction, team-teaching, cooperative learning, parent involvement, and a healthy school climate. Support services, such as child care, health screenings, dental programs, nutrition education, crisis intervention, community mentoring, mental health services, and basic welfare assistance, are included at the school. These schools operate at longer hours and through the summer. Full-service schools are organized according to the presenting needs of children and families in a particular school community, such that no two full-service schools are the same (Dryfoos 2005). Recently, however, the DeWitt-Wallace Reader's Digest Extended Services Schools Initiative selected four full-service school models as exemplary (cited in Dryfoos 2005). Full-service schools can take a variety of forms. For example, the following initiatives were recognized:

Children's Aid Society Community Schools

These *schools* partner a community agency with a school system. Each community school has a built-in primary health center and mental health services. Two schools have been designed with family resource centers and after-school activities (Moses & Coltoff 1999).

University-Assisted Community Schools

These *efforts* partner the University of Pennsylvania with the West Philadelphia Improvement Corps (WEPIC). The resulting partnership, called the Center for Community Partnerships, brought university faculty, students, principals, and teachers together to transform school buildings into community centers (Somerfield 1996).

Beacon Schools

Developed in New York City, these provide grants to community-based agencies to go into school buildings and open them to the neighborhood from early morning until late evening throughout the year. Each of the seventy-six schools is different. After-school programs, family and cultural events, health centers, drug prevention programs, small business programs, tutoring, literacy, and parent education are examples of the on-site services offered (Dryfoos 2005).

Bridges to Success

Founded by the United Way, this project partners public and nonprofit agencies with educational programs to establish schools as learning and community centers. In this model, local United Way agencies extend their services into schools. Each school has a council that plans and organizes services and is made up of the principal and other school staff, service providers, parents, and community members. A wide variety of services have been offered, including health and dental care, case management, after-school activities, mental health services, community-service learning, tutoring, and job-readiness training (United Way 1999).

Research evidence suggests that full-service schools have many benefits. In these schools, students are less truant and mobile and have higher academic achievement than children in comparable schools without social services on-site (Whalen 2002). Other research shows that full-service schools can also improve parent involvement, teacher involvement, counseling services, and parent development (Boston Children's Institute 2003).

Summary

The connection between children's health and well-being and their academic achievement is clear (Adelman & Taylor 2000; Whalen 2002). Learning is optimal when children's needs are met and their families are not worried about financial problems, physical or mental health issues, or other problems. Teachers connect with students in schools every day, so they are in a unique position to help children and families who are experiencing stressors. Because schools are not always expected to help families in crisis, teachers may find it challenging at first to support families in crisis. Furthermore, the enormity and range of emotions faced by families in crisis can make helping these families seem overwhelming.

In this chapter we attempted to describe the steps educators can take to link families with effective community supports. Increasingly, schools are also being called on to systematically provide a wide range of services to children and families. Ideas about family–school–community collaboration have been evolving over the last decade. Therefore, models that go beyond the efforts of the classroom teacher to more system-wide efforts are also needed. Dryfoos (2005) predicts, "We can see the emergence of creative ideas and partnerships, and, in the future, we can expect many more new versions and visions of community schools" (17).

Additional Resources

Books for Children about Divorce

Brown, L. K., & Brown, M. (1986). *Dinosaurs divorce.* Boston: Little Brown.

Heegard, M. (1991). *When Mom and Dad separate: Children can learn to cope with grief from divorce.* Minneapolis: Woodlands Press.

Heegard, M. (1993). *When a parent marries again: Children can learn to cope with family change.* Minneapolis: Woodlands Press. Heegard's books are interactive coloring and reading books for elementary-age children to use with adult guidance.

Levins, S., & Langdo, B. (2005). *Was it the chocolate pudding? A story for little kids about divorce.* Alexandria, VA: APA Press.

Macgregor, C. (2004). *The divorce help book for teens.* Atascadero, CA: Impact Publishers.

Masurel, C. (2003). *Two homes.* Cambridge, MA: Candlewick. For very young children.

Pickhardt, C. (1997). *The case of the scary divorce: A Jackson Skye mystery.* Washington, DC: Magination Press. This book is designed for children about nine to eleven years old and is written as a mystery story, in which the "detective" lends support to a friend whose parents have separated.

Prokop, M. (1996). *Divorce happens to the nicest kids: A self-help book for kids.* Warren, OH: Algera House Publishers. For older elementary or early middle school students.

Books for Children about Family Violence and Child Maltreatment

Burber, L. (1995). *Family violence: The Lucent overview series.* Hoboken, NJ: Lucent. For children ages twelve to eighteen.

Davis, D. (1984). *Something is wrong at my house.* Seattle, WA: Parenting Press. For children ages five to ten.

Holmes, M. (2000). A *terrible thing happened: A story for children who have witnessed violence or trauma.* Washington, DC: Magination Press. For children ages four to eight.

Namka, L. (1995). *The mad family gets their mad out: Fifty things your family can say and do to express anger constructively.* Minneapolis: Educational Media Corp. For parents and children ages four to twelve.

Schor, H. (2002). *A place for Starr: A story of hope for children experiencing family violence.* Indianapolis, IN: Kidsrights. For children ages five to ten.

Velasquez, R. (1998). *Rina's family secret: A Roosevelt High School book.* Houston, TX: Pinata Books. For children ages eleven to fourteen.

Books for Children about Family Substance Abuse

Black, C. (1997). *My dad loves me, my dad has a disease: A child's view: Living with addiction* (3rd ed.). San Francisco: Mac.

Brotherton, M. (2006). *Buzz: A graphic reality check for teens dealing with drugs and alcohol* (FlipSwitch series). Colorado Springs, CO: Multnomah.

Hastings, J. (2000). *An elephant in the living room, the children's book.* Center City, MN: Hazelden.

Heegard, M. (1993). *When a family is in trouble: Children can cope with grief from drug and alcohol addiction.* Chapmanville, WV: Woodland Press.

Hornik-Beer, E. (2001). *For teenagers living with a parent who abuses alcohol/drugs.* Lincoln, NE: BackinPrint.com.

Kulp, J., & Kulp, K. (2000). *The best I can be: Living with fetal alcohol syndrome-effects.* Minneapolis: Better Endings New Beginnings.

Leite, E., & Espeland, P. (1989). *Different like me: A book for teens who worry about their parent's use of alcohol/drugs.* Center City, MN: Hazelden.

Books for Children about Natural Disasters

Mark, B., & Layton, M. (1997). *I'll know what to do: A kid's guide to natural disasters.* Washington, DC: Magination Press.

Holmes, M. (2000). *A terrible thing happened: A story for children who have witnessed violence or trauma.* Washington, DC: Magination Press.

Books for Children about Disabilities

Meyer, D. (Ed.). (2005). *The sibling slam book: What it's really like to have a brother or sister with special needs.* Bethesda, MD: Woodbine.

Penn, S. (2005). *Disabled fables: Aesop's fables*. Retold and illustrated by artists with developmental disabilities. Long Island City, NY: Star Bright.

Porterfield, K. M. (2003). *Straight Talk about learning disabilities (Straight Talk about)*. New York: Facts on File.

Thomas, P. (2005). *Don't call me special: A first look at disability*. Hauppauge, NY: Barron's.

Woloson, E. (2003). *My friend Isabelle*. Bethesda, MD: Woodbine.

Useful Websites

LD on Line,
www.ldonline.org
Leading Web site on learning disabilities, dyslexia, attention deficit disorders, special education, learning differences, and related issues for families, teachers, and other professionals

National Association of School Psychologists,
www.nasponline.org/NEAT/naturaldisaster_teams_ho.html

National Clearinghouse on Child Abuse and Neglect Information,
http://nccanch.acf.hhs.gov/index.cfm
Organization that collects, organizes, and disseminates information on all aspects of maltreatment

National Coalition for the Homeless,
www.nationalhomeless.org/facts.html
Focuses on public education, policy advocacy, and technical assistance to end homelessness and increase economic and social justice for all citizens

The American Red Cross,
www.redcross.org/services/disaster/0,1082,0_319_,00.html

The National Institutes for Mental Health,
www.nimh.nih.gov

Chapter 14

Seeing the Big Picture: Creating a School Climate that Strengthens Family–School Connections

Linda S. Behar-Horenstein and Frances M. Vandiver

Learning Objectives

After reading this chapter, you will be able to:

- Describe the specific ways that the school as a whole might create a more inviting and responsive family–school climate.
- Explain the key steps involved for school staff members to change how they work with families.
- Discuss how the school administrator influences the development of a more inviting family–school climate.
- Describe key methods that faculty might use to make their school more welcoming to students' families.

■ Discuss the challenges faced by beginning teachers in changing how their school works with families.

■ Describe the levels of change by which a school might make its family–school climate more inviting.

> *Researchers who explore what motivates parents to be involved in their children's education consistently report that invitations made by the school as a whole as well as by individual teachers are powerful motivators of parents' involvement (Hoover-Dempsey, Walker, Sandler, Whetsel, Green, Wilkins & Closson 2005). But what exactly do schools do that motivates families to become more involved in their children's education? More important, how do school staffs change their ways of interacting so as to give a collective message of how they wish to work with families, especially culturally diverse families? In this final chapter we briefly summarize what school staffs are doing to enhance their ways of working with students' families. We then look at how school staffs are organizing their efforts to change their ways of working with students' families. Finally, we consider how these school-wide practices influence the roles of the school administrator and the beginning teacher.*

Creating a More Inviting Family–School Climate

For nearly two decades researchers have suggested that student commitment to learning is enhanced when collaboration between families and school becomes the normative practice (Swap 1993). Although a variety of conceptualizations of parental involvement have been researched, findings from these studies have consistently shown a positive relationship between parental involvement and student academic achievement. For example, student academic and social competence improve when schools, families, and communities work together to promote student success (Clark 1993; Dornbush & Ritter 1998; Epstein & Hollifield 1996; Garbarino 1997). Several researchers have also reported a positive relationship between parent involvement in conjunction with student learning and achievement (Christenson & Sheridan 2001; Epstein 1991). In addition, improvement in language and literacy skills (Senechal & LaFevre 2002), acceptable school attendance (Epstein & Sheldon 2002), and reduction in grade retention have been reported by researchers to be positively related to greater parent involvement (Miedel & Reynolds 1999). However, Sheldon (2005) cautions that fostering family–school partnerships should not be solely directed at improving student achievement. He recommends directing efforts at understanding how schools can develop a supportive climate and how schools can support families and partner together to enhance students' holistic development. As a result, a number of steps have been taken by school staffs as a whole to make their school environment more responsive and inviting to parents.

Rethinking Concepts of Family

Although family–school collaboration is a doable practice, it involves school personnel rethinking their notions of family and of family–school involvement (Bronfenbrenner 1991). For example, the notion of "family" has traditionally been referred to biological parents. Yet family–school researchers suggest that the identification of "parent" should be broadened to include any caregiver over age eighteen who has the primary responsibility of promoting the child's physical, emotional, social, and educational development (Musti-Rao & Cartiedge 2004). As a result, many schools are creating bulletin boards and school displays that depict the wide variety of families that compose their student population—including families parented by two mothers or two fathers, families for whom English is not their first language, and families with children who have physical or mental disabilities. These educators view this practice as one way that they can send the message that all types of families are valued by the school staff.

Examining Current Family–School Practices

Many educators are beginning to examine their current family–school practices and the underlying beliefs implicit in them. Harry (1992), for example, conducted an ethnographic study of twelve Puerto Rican families and their children who received English as a second language instruction and services for mild disabilities. She reported that the parents typically played a very passive role in educational decision making, with school staff characterized by one-way communication from the school staff to the parents. To invite parents to play a more meaningful and active role in such interactions, Harry recommended that educators and administrators draw on parents' expertise and utilize their understanding of their child's experiences and cultural aspects that might help them better understand the child's development, behavior, and ways of learning. During these conversations, school personnel could authentically convey how they valued and needed the parents' involvement by providing avenues for sharing the ways in which the school and home environments might differ and/or be similar, and how this might impact the child's learning.

Learning About Families' Perspectives and Circumstances

Understanding who are the families of the students that the school serves is an important first step to building stronger connections with students' families. All families have stressors that pull them in multiple directions in our fast-paced society. School personnel must consider the resources often associated with low socioeconomic status (SES) families and recognize that family demands may impact higher and lower income families differently. For example, the time and energy of low-income parents for involvement in their children's schooling are often influenced by their work schedule that often requires long or unpredictable hours (Collignon, Men & Tan 2001; Garcia Coll, Akiba, Palacios, Bailey, Silver, DiMartino & Chin 2002; Griffith 1998; Machida, Taylor & Kim 2002; Weiss et al. 2003). In addition, the school-related knowledge of low SES families is typically influenced by less schooling and less access to extra-familial or professional support (Horvat, Weininger & Lareau 2003). Moreover, their available time, energy, knowledge, and skills may be mitigated by disparities in their physical and emotional health that are often associated with low income, such as increased susceptibility to chronic and debilitating stress and depression (Grolnick, Grolnick, Benjet, Kurowski & Apostoleris 1997; Grolnick, Kurowski, Dunlap & Hevey 2000; Kohl, Lengua & McMahon 2002; Weiss et al. 2003).

Lower income families may also find involvement in schools difficult because school personnel sometimes make unwarranted assumptions about their level of participation. For example, teachers sometimes assume that low-SES families lack the ability, interest, skills, time, motivation, or knowledge to participate (Collignon et al. 2001; Eccles & Harold 1993; Gonzalez, Andrade, Civil & Moll 2001; Griffith 1998; Hoover-Dempsey, Walker, Jones & Reed 2002; Horvat et al. 2002; Moll, Amanti, Neff & Gonzalez 1992; Pang & Watkins 2000; Pena 2000; Weiss et al. 2003). As Phelan, Davidson, and Yu (1998) pointed out, parents whose cultural backgrounds differ from the mainstream within the school district places them at distinct disadvantage by creating sociocultural borders. Equalizing the balance of power between parents and educators allows them "… to co-construct a bigger picture about the conditions of the child's life vis-à-vis learning and development" (cited in Christenson & Sheridan 2001, 48).

One dilemma that was identified at a K-12 school, where the second author (FV) serves as the school leader, was the need to provide additional support for students who were identified as struggling readers. In 2000, a pilot program was begun with thirty middle school students who had volunteered to come for four weeks in the summer to an intensive reading program, entitled Summer Adventures In Literacy (SAIL). One component of the program was a weekly Family Night in which the students taught their parents some of the reading strategies that they themselves were learning in the program. As the principal described: "We knew that getting parents to come to school for several hours after work would not be possible without providing dinner for them and the children in the program. Our parent organization solicited our business partners to provide dinner for those in attendance and the SAIL teachers and school leaders attended each Family Night session." This program has been very successfully supported by families and has grown to include over a hundred students each summer in kindergarten through grade nine, and the Family Night sessions continue to be a positive time for students sharing with their parents as well as a social time for faculty, students, administrators, and parents. This program "speaks" loudly to the parents about the commitment of the school to the academic growth of the students and the family collaboration that is essential to their children's success.

Welcoming and Inviting Parent Participation

Families need to feel welcome and wanted to participate in the school. They need to know how they can participate meaningfully and actively in their child's education. Feeling welcome will increase the likelihood of parental participation. When parents feel welcome, they are also more likely to support the work of educators and to share their own ideas, especially if they feel that educators will listen to them. For example, in one local school district, parents were not allowed to observe their children's classes or help their children in the classrooms. The school staff decided to modify that situation to ensure that parents (whose taxes support public education) could have an opportunity to observe their children's classrooms except on days when tests were administered.

In one local school with which the first author (LBH) of the chapter is familiar, each child and parent who come through the school door each day is greeted with a warm smile and hug by the school principal. Parents are invited to contribute to the classroom by assisting with weekly reading groups, grading homework, making scenery for classroom plays, answering the phone in the office, administering annual tests to children who were absent on test days, or helping maintain the school grounds by painting, creating a playground area for younger children, and building ramps or stairs for other units. At this school, parents not only feel welcome, but also they volunteer their time in whatever way they want to and can contribute.

Creating Meaningful Co-Roles for Families

Developing specific policies that create a more equal role for caregivers and educators and clearly recognizing these co-roles in school policies and practices is another way that school staffs are creating more collaborative family–school roles. Traditionally, educators have regarded parents as volunteers, fund-raisers, and homework helpers (Christenson & Sheridan 2001). Assigning parents to institutionally determined roles ignores the potential of parents and families to contribute in meaningful ways to their children's education. Moreover, traditional practices ignore the assets that families have. Attitudes often characterize families as either fitting into the Euro-American lifestyle or being judged deficient. Many schools continue to perpetuate the norms, practices, and values of families that fit into the dominant culture (Christenson & Sheridan 2001). Thus, families who differ from these norms are seen as deficient (Davies 1993). Poor and disadvantaged families are described as those who are failing their children.

Yet the centrality of families has been recognized as a crucial component to student achievement. National educational goals have identified the partnering of family and school as central to the prevention of school failure among students. Underscoring this imperative, Pianta and Walsh (1996) asserted that to create a culture of success, all school personnel must recognize that at the core of school failure is "an inability or an unwillingness to communicate—a relationship problem" (24). To ensure the healthy cognitive, social, and emotional development of children, family and school resources—fiscal, time, physical, personnel—must be dedicated to these efforts (Wang, Haertl & Walberg 1997).

Because schools as a whole exert a powerful influence on parents' and educators' normative expectations for working together, developing school structures and practices that support collaborative parent–school relationships is important. For example, practices that forge collaborative parent–school relationships are letting parents know that they are welcome, keeping them informed about their children's progress, and conveying to them that school personnel respect them, their concerns, and suggestions (Adams & Christenson 1998; Christenson 2004; Comer 1985; Griffith 1996, 1998; McNamara, Telzrow & DeLamatre 1999; Soodak & Erwin 2000).

Examining the way families and educators currently connect and then altering existing structures to ensure that there is a shared responsibility for students, parents, and educators are another way to build trust and communication. For example, homework has been identified as one indicator of successful schools and successful students. Involving parents in their children's homework encourages students to spend more time completing assignments with higher quality work and promotes positive communication between the parent and child (Epstein 2001; Hoover-Dempsey et al. 2001). Involving parents reinforces the importance of schoolwork and can also stimulate conversations between parents and family members and students about student learning. These conversations may bring parents and children together as they exchange ideas (Acock & Demo 1994) and show children how parents support schoolwork (Bali, Demo & Weidman 1998; Gonzalez, Andrade, Civil & Moll 2001; Levin, Levy-Schiff, Appelbaum-Peled, Katz, Komar & Meiran 1997; Martens & Woods 1994).

Teachers can regularly assign homework that encourages students to work with family members to complete assignments (Bali et al. 1998; Epstein, Salinas & Jackson 1995; Van Voorhis 2000). In one local school with which the first author (LBH) of the chapter is familiar, students in grades five through eight were assigned to work together in history groups to write and present plays that depict their interpretation of historical events, to create art projects that depict how people lived during particular time periods, and to write reports. Students called on their parents for assistance in organizing their findings or in sewing costumes and then invited their parents to their history presentations. The combination of group work, creating and producing, designing or finding customs, and acting allowed and encouraged students with varying cognitive styles to contribute in ways that showcased their individual and collective talents. In another project at the same school, families and children in grades two through four worked together to create math games that required their application of basic mathematical operations, and then the children's families were invited to solve problems and earn prizes.

Providing Opportunities for Teacher Skill Development

Teacher self-efficacy and training in parental involvement strongly influence the degree to which parents are invited to observe in classrooms (Hoover-Dempsey, Bassler & Brissies 1992; Swick & McKnight 1989). Yet few teachers receive pre-service training in how to work collaboratively with families (Graue & Brown 2003; Morris & Taylor 1998). Providing in-service training for teachers in working collaboratively with families is one strategy that the principal can provide to ensure the frequency and effectiveness of parent–school communication. Parent efficacy is also important. Parents who feel efficacious are more likely to volunteer their involvement in classrooms than those who do not. When parents' values and beliefs clash with those of educators for parents who are already stressed, even messages of invitation by educators are unlikely to be heard (Christenson & Sheridan 2001). Parental role construction is also an important factor to consider when attempting to enhance parental involvement in their children's schooling. Parental role construction refers "to parents' beliefs about what they are supposed to do in relation to their children's education and the patterns of parental behavior that follow those beliefs" (Hoover-Dempsey, Walker, Sandler, Whetsel, Green, Wilkins & Closson 2005, 107; Hoover-Dempsey & Sandler 1995, 1997; Hoover-Dempsey, Wilkins, Sandler & O'Connor 2004; Walker, Wilkins, Dallaire, Sandler & Hoover-Dempsey 2005).

How Schools Change Themselves

An increasing body of research has demonstrated the importance of family involvement as a crucial component that influences students' academic achievement. Moreover, research reveals that most teachers, administrators, and parents believe that family involvement is important (Epstein 2001; Shumow & Harris 2000). However, it takes a real change in thinking, as well as practice, for a school to become one where parents, teachers, staff, administration, and students are partners and co-facilitators in the learning process. The first step toward this goal is the commitment to the belief that working on developing a more positive relationship with students' families is important enough that it requires a focus of time, energy, and resources. A second step is the development of the faculty's awareness of the current state of family–school relationships and the circumstances of families who attend their school. A third step is that of the faculty identifying areas for improvement and developing a plan to move forward. Obviously, the leadership of the principal is essential not only to developing a faculty's awareness of the current state of family–school relationships, but also to identifying areas for improvement, developing a plan to move forward, and committing resources to this effort.

The Principal's Role

Principals play a central role in establishing the school climate. They set the tone for parental involvement and program implementation. They also empower teachers and parents to reach for effective involvement (Soodak et al. 2002). Principals will undoubtedly face resistance to implementing change to family–school discourse because human beings, by nature, attempt to maintain equilibrium and maximize their autonomy vis-à-vis their environment (Schein 2004). But just like parents who must maintain their positions when giving consequences to a misbehaving child, principals must be unwavering in their quest for change. To help a faculty become more aware of the types of barriers that families and school staff may experience in attempting to work together, the principal needs to invite faculty to talk about the issues, needs, and constraints faced by educators in the school building (Christenson & Sheridan 2001). Changing staff assumptions about working with families can begin with exploring current practices and modes of communication with families. The principal can suggest to faculty and staff that it is crucial to look school-wide and to ask themselves whether current school practices systematically include or exclude families. To answer this question, the principal and teachers can work together, looking at the structure of current family–school activities, such as Back-to-school Night and assessing the tone of family–school communications depicted in the school handbook and archived newsletters and letters to determine whether these activities and communications are inviting or distancing. Staff can also evaluate the everyday procedures within each office of the school to determine whether they are inviting and "user-friendly."

Principal leadership lays the foundation for how families and others perceive schools and gives a collective message about the type of school and its reputation. Principals communicate to staffs how they expect school personnel to work with students and families. Thus, when principals convey the message that involving families as partners with school personnel is a valued priority, parents are more apt to engage with school personnel (Epstein 2005). Effective principals let parents know when and where to contact them, thus creating an open-door policy (Christenson & Sheridan 2001). For example, in a special educational facility for severely disturbed boys, ages twelve to sixteen, where the first author was the middle school principal, she regularly invited parents to come in and visit with her about their children's progress. She began each conversation by welcoming the parents and asking about how they were doing. The tenor of those meetings always focused on the child's cognitive, social, and emotional development, and about the positive strides that the child had made. Then the author sought input into how the school and family could work together to enhance the student's emotional maturation. A nonblaming policy framed the conversation. She emphasized the philosophy that the purpose of their child's school experiences was to ensure that the child learned enough to get a good job, a nice place to live, and have a nice life. The principal used these forums to learn more about the child's community and family life. The nature of this school's leadership and cultural norms influenced the type of family–school collaboration.

The implementation and effectiveness of family–school programs depend on several elements operating together simultaneously (Desimone 2002; Newmann, King & Youngs 2000). The longevity of principal leadership is central to the efficacy of these programs. For example, Van Voorhis and Sheldon (2002) found that there was a negative relationship between principal turnover and program quality. However, they also found that disruption to leadership is decreased if there is a well-implemented program that is buttressed by broad support and adequate funding. Berends et al. (2002) reported that support and principal leadership are probably the most influential factors in determining a school's capacity to implement new programs (cited also in Berends, Kirby, Naftel & McKelvey 2001; Kirby, Berends & Nafetl 2001). Principal leadership is vital, because principals establish school priorities, direct the allocation of funding, and establish and influence the attitudes and morale of school staff (Knapp 1997; Newmann et al. 2000).

Principals can also influence the staff's expectations for meaningful family participation. They establish the tone for interactions by modeling positive communication with all families and encouraging the staff to develop opportunities for sustained positive interactions between families and educators (Edmonds 1979). For example, holding biweekly breakfasts with grade level teachers can increase the interaction between students, parents, and educators in a relaxed environment. Principals can also serve as advocates to ensure that system-level policies are enacted to support strong family–school interactions (Christenson & Sheridan 2001). School leaders also convey to their staff the importance of providing opportunities to reach out to all families. In Table 14.1 you see an array of opportunities to enhance family–school communication developed by the principal and staff of one school.

When the principal required that the staff develop opportunities for families to interact with staff outside of the traditional school day, the number of families who became involved with faculty and staff doubled. As shown in Table 14.1, back-to-school nights were scheduled to allow more active roles and sustained contact between educators and families. Seasonal school fairs and student performances resulted in educators and families working together and having an opportunity for

Table 14.1   How Principal Leadership Can Facilitate Opportunities for Family and School Communication

- Offered back-to-school nights in which families had active roles
- Developed and presented seasonal school fairs and student performances for families
- Provided teacher-led and student-led conference meeting times during evening hours and by video
- Provided opportunities for families to meet to problem solve with teachers before and after school
- Scheduled beginning or mid-year parent–educator interviews and collaborative assessments of their children's skills

mutual enjoyment and informal communication about their children. Parents appreciated having an opportunity to attend student-led and teacher-led parent conferences during evening sessions after their workday. Varied and flexible time schedules were also offered to parents to enhance their opportunities to resolve problems and to contact the staff by phone or in-person. Flexible schedules were enhanced when the principal and school personnel utilized the available technology— such as online grade book programs, teacher Web sites with e-mail addresses and unit plans, and a school Web site with policies, activities calendars, pictures of family activities, newsletters, parent organizations/volunteer activities, and printable forms— to foster other ways of communicating.

Increasing Faculty Awareness

One of the dilemmas that almost every faculty across the country faces is the disconnection between the backgrounds of the faculty and the students. The trend is one of a middle-class, White female teaching professional and an ever-increasing multicultural student body. The dynamics of this situation make it imperative that district and school leaders take deliberate steps to help the teachers, students, and parents better understand each other's cultural differences and common goals. The principal's role is to articulate the common goal of collaborating to meet the needs of each child as the foundation for all decisions at the school. This immediately underscores the need for greater understanding of students' cognitive styles—connecting abstract concepts to the concrete world of the child's experiences—and for developing a dialogue with families. Although this is easy to pronounce, it takes deliberate, yet realistic efforts, to make strides in this area. Teachers do not have time to devote to extensive study. Many school districts are restrictive regarding release time for teachers. The universal difficulty in finding quality substitutes often makes it impossible to release teachers even when plans have been made to do so.

As a result, school staffs committed to making their schools more responsive to all families might first attempt to gain a greater awareness of family and student needs by using existing data that are readily available. As a next step, staff will need to reach beneath the surface of these data and develop doable plans for improving their family–school relationships. To do this, the following strategies can be used:

- Examine available demographic data on your school or class to develop a *living profile* that depicts who your students are demographically; then develop a demographic profile of your faculty and staff and identify relevant gaps between your students and faculty.
- Analyze the patterns of academic success of various student subgroups at your school and identify those teachers who are having success with specific student groups; then utilize their expertise to help other staff develop strategies to reach these students.
- Utilize faculty book study to learn more about teaching culturally diverse groups.

- Interview parents and students about the difficulties of school and how they think the faculty could be more successful.
- Emphasize how you, the classroom teacher (or the faculty), do not have all of the answers and that you not only welcome family involvement, but also need family involvement to be successful. This, of course, must be followed up with respect for all families and a welcoming culture for all.
- Examine your beliefs, individually and as a faculty, regarding families that come from different cultures and economic situations than you. Decide what actions need to be taken, individually and collectively, to become more effective in areas of need.

The only way to have continuous progress in the area of family–school relationships is to have a continuous examination of that relationship as an integral component of the school conversation. The conversation then has to result in some action that involves parents as partners.

How can we change the fundamental assumptions, practices, and relationships to improve student learning? First, there must be a recognition that the types of changes needed are those that will result in restructuring as opposed to reform or change initiatives. Restructuring requires a fundamental shift in attitudes and practices that can result in improved student learning. One example of restructuring involved a middle school where the second author (FV) served as the principal. Concerned that the current textbooks available for adoption did not adequately meet their students' learning needs, one eighth grade teaching team decided to develop its American history course so as to more actively involve the diversity of its students. The team wanted the course to be focused around Essential Questions (EQ) that would pique student interest and require the students to read primary and secondary sources to solve the EQ. Acting as the school's advocate, the principal proposed to the school district that the monies allotted from the district for textbooks be spent for technology support and classroom libraries for this course, and the district agreed. The teachers were provided release time to develop the curriculum and all of the parents of the eighth graders were sent a personal letter about the upcoming new course and were invited to help with the curriculum development. The parental support and enthusiasm for an American history course that was not the European version of American history helped keep the teachers enthusiastic with a project that took most of one summer to complete. When the course was implemented in the fall, the teachers and parents were "on the same page," and a course without a textbook was enthusiastically received.

Changing Assumptions About Teaching

The principles of pedagogy and their relationship to teaching and learning are generally absent from and infrequently modeled in the continuum of teacher development, beginning in pre-service through in-service levels (Dalton & Mori 1992, 1996; NCTAF 1996). Statistics have shown that nearly one quarter of newly hired teachers in 1991 were unable to deliver effective instruction with higher proportions of urban and rural isolated schools that served minority at-risk students (Darling-Hammond & Falk 1997). Pedagogy means that teachers need to learn about students' home and community lives to understand how they as educators can draw on local funds of knowledge to enhance student learning. As Dalton (1998) has observed:

> Standards that acknowledge pedagogy's central role, notably the National Science Education Standards, provide unambiguous guidance for teachers about how to comment, how to involve students in content activities, and how to assess student progress continually. (Cited in National Research Council 1996)

Changing assumptions about teaching means that teachers begin to view the assets that all families bring. For example, encouraging beginning teachers to observe family dynamics or ways of communicating is one approach to helping teachers learn about the different modes of communicating and learning in families of socio-culturally diverse learners.

To learn more about socio-culturally diverse families, teachers may be introduced to ethnographic methods. First, working together with veteran teachers, beginning teachers might survey parents of their students. By working with the survey information they gather—identifying trends, outliers, and developing plans together—beginning teachers might develop a working profile of the students' families with whom they will be working throughout the year. Teacher inquiry could focus on learning about the family's ways of communicating, teaching, routines, habits, values, their priorities, and how they assist children with reading or homework, in general, and with understanding the world around them. This information can be instrumental to ensuring that families and educators share the same vision for enhancing student development, learning, and behavior.

For example, teachers might want to conduct a family visit, such as that outlined in Chapters 8 and 9 to see a description of the routines and practices that children and parents engage in around homework. Is the house busy and full of people or quiet during homework completion? Is the radio or television playing? Where does the child complete homework? Who helps the child and in what way? After teachers have made several observations in the child's home and written their own reactions, they can analyze the findings and reflect on what they have learned. After sharing their observations with the family and/or grade level team members, they can work collaboratively to develop strategies, as needed, to assist in the child's learning, development, and behavior. These experiences can help teachers change unclear or stereotypic views about how culturally diverse families facilitate student learning. They can also demonstrate the teacher and school's commitment to establish co-roles for families and educators. Principals can support this practice by providing staff development for training or by bringing in a consultant to conduct a series of in-service workshops.

In Case Study 14.1 on Ellman Middle School, note how the principal worked with her staff to change their parent–teacher conference practices.

CASE STUDY 14.1

Restructuring Parent—Teacher Conferences

As a new principal arriving at Ellman Middle School (pseudonym), she noticed how teachers interacted with parents. Ellman had a large faculty that was invested in their practices, ways of communicating, and ways of thinking. Additionally, there was a top-heavy administrative structure that made school functions and structures complex. One commonplace practice was that teachers contacted parents only when there was a problem with their child. Teachers then expected the parents to remedy the child's behavior. Often students were not included in these conversations. Teachers rarely reflected about how their own behaviors may have influenced the child's behavior or their communication with the parents (Amatea & Vandiver 2004). To restructure this practice, teachers at Ellman MS instituted parent—teacher conferences that involved students. A family—school problem-solving format was used. The teachers implemented a task-focused approach, involved all members as individuals who could contribute in a meaningful way to resolve the student's problems, and blocked blame. During the 2000–2001 school year, the problem-solving format and strategies were introduced in a school-wide staff training session. The principal's role in this process was to continue dialogue with faculty about the importance of including families and students in the teacher—parent conference format. One expectation of this initiative was that each teaching team would use some written format to guide parent—teacher conferences. Also, the principal was asked to make *success stories* visible in faculty communication (Deal & Peterson 1999). The implementation of this action helped children significantly. However, the more important outcome was the change in student, school staff, and family members' relationships (Amatea & Vandiver 2004). The development of the process took nearly three and a half years, and the change was a slow and enduring process. Planning for this change in practice took up to one year; however, in this circumstance, the planning and implementing resulted in tangible change that was successful.

Question to Consider

How did this principal guide the staff in changing their parent—teacher conferences?

Entering as a New Teacher

Entering a new school as a beginning teacher is a daunting experience. With the burgeoning size of our public schools, just finding your classroom can be a challenge. A first-year teacher's work-a-day life is consumed with learning the routines of the school, organizing the classroom, getting books ready to be assigned to students, learning students' names, and creating daily lessons, among other responsibilities. As a newcomer, different ideas will capture your attention. Observing what people say and do and who talks and who does not is an important step in making the transition into a new setting. Listening at faculty meetings and identifying the issues that are most prominent in the discussion can also facilitate your enculturation into your new school. Depending upon your own cultural background, it may be difficult to determine how to identify the learning needs of culturally diverse students. To acquire an understanding of your students' cultural backgrounds, it is important to talk with the school principal and to ask about the racial/ethnic composition of the school. Another useful strategy is to talk with your grade level team leader and other grade level teachers about how they have worked successfully with culturally diverse students. In Case Study 14.2, a beginning teacher seeks out the counsel of a more experienced teacher. What are your reactions to the suggestions made by the more experienced teacher?

∿∿∿∿∿∿∿∿∿∿∿∿∿∿∿∿∿∿∿∿∿∿∿∿∿∿∿∿∿∿∿∿∿∿∿∿∿∿

CASE STUDY 14.2

Susan and the Student Peer Approach

Susan, a beginning teacher, found herself struggling with her second grade students. "You can't believe how long it took my class of twenty-two children to turn to page 19 in our reading book today. Most of the children did not even know what the number 19 looked like."

"What happened?" asked another new teacher, Cindy, who teaches fifth and sixth grade students.

"I don't understand it," Susan stated. "I thought that by working with second grade students, I could help assure that they would do well. But I am not so sure after today!"

"I have an idea that you might want to try" Cindy replied. "What if you selected four or five of your students who are capable and make them team captains for the remaining students? You would use them as captains to assist their peers."

"I'll give it a try!" Susan said. Using this peer approach, Susan soon discovered that the team captains were able to help their classmates follow directions more quickly and adjust to the school routines more rapidly. Talking with Cindy a few days later, Susan described how successful the approach had been with her students.

"If this process continues to be successful," Cindy said, "You may want to consider rotating the role of team captain with other students within their group." Susan presented this idea to her class, and the students agreed that this was an idea worth trying. As the school year progressed, Susan saw more students taking on leadership roles within their group and a greater amount of collaboration and helpfulness among the students. She felt like her classroom was beginning to develop its own sense of community.

Questions to Consider

Why do you think using team captains was successful?

What approach would you have used? Why?

How did the use of team captains contribute to development of the classroom climate?

Sometimes a new teacher might be concerned about a student who appears to have potential but is not doing well in or outside of the classroom. In the scenario described in Case Study 14.3, a new teacher decides how to respond to a student who seems aggressive and unmotivated.

CASE STUDY 14.3

Shelly and the Family Visit with Romano and His Mother

Shelly, a beginning fourth grade teacher, found herself overwhelmed within the first few weeks of school by a Hispanic boy, Romano, who intimidated the other boys in her classroom with threats of violence. "He threatened to hit me at recess," reported Jawan. Shelly continued to carefully monitor Romano's behavior and jotted down her observations over the next four days. A summary of her notes follows:

August 10—Romano worked quietly at his desk while reading a novel. At recess, he told all of the other boys what position they could play during soccer. During science, he put his head down on his desk, throughout the video on the scientific method.

August 11—Romano entered the classroom angry and seemingly upset. He had a difficult time staying in his seat during the morning announcements. During science class he seemed to daydream. I had to remind him three times during the assignment that he needed to complete his worksheet. When he left the classroom, I heard him yell to Jawan, "I am going to punch you."

August 12—Again, Romano entered the classroom appearing agitated. When I asked him if anything was wrong, he said, "No, just some guy stuff. I can handle it."

August 13—Romano read his book and remained quiet. At recess, he grabbed the soccer ball from David and yelled at the other boys, telling each of them that they were assigned to a particular position on the field. He fell asleep during science and left the classroom almost as quickly as the bell rang.

Romano's inattentiveness in class and aggressive behavior with his peers concerned Shelly more each day partly because she did not want to give up hope on Romano and partly because she was passionate about him feeling successful academically. She went next door to a 4th grade teacher, Jane, and explained the situation. "Sometimes," Jane said, "it helps to sit with the student during lunch, and get to know him a little bit. In this way, you can begin to let Romano know that you genuinely care. After doing this a few times, you can write to his family and ask if you can come over to their home to visit with them. When you arrive at his house, greet Romano with a smile and then sit down together and learn the names of those family members." Initially nervous about visiting the family, Shelly considered sending the home liaison to visit Romano's home. After talking with the liaison who reassured her that she would be glad to accompany her, Shelly decided to go visit the family by herself.

At the front door, Romano and his mother Mrs. Ramirez greeted Shelly. Shelly thanked Mrs. Ramirez for meeting with her. They sat down in the living room and talked. Shelly explained her concern about Romano and her desire to help him. She also listened to Mrs. Ramirez as she explained how the departure of Mr. Ramirez had impacted her son. "My husband told my son to be the man of the family and watch over your mother, brothers, and sisters," Mrs. Ramirez explained. She reported that Romano had recently become more controlling during his father's absence and quite "bossy" with his friends. Shelly then described what she had observed of Romano's behavior at school and during recess. During the family visit, Shelly observed how diligently he cared for three younger siblings. He carried them around their house, consoled them when they fell or cried, and played with them. Shelly offered to develop a plan of action with Romano and his mother that could assist Romano and boost his engagement in his work. They built in a time when she would be phoning Romano's mother to see whether their plan was working. Shelly approached Mrs. Ramirez in a nonblaming manner and with an earnest desire to help Romano. After the 45-minute visit, not only did Shelly leave with a better understanding of Romano but also with a plan for helping him become more engaged at school.

Questions to Consider

What did Shelly do that helped her better understand Romano?

How did the family visit help her better understand Romano's behavior at school?

How did the family interactions at Romano's home differ from the peer interactions at school? Why?

Examining the Depth of School Change Required

As discussed in the chapter and illustrated by the previous two case studies, schools have developed and utilized a wide variety of methods for making themselves more welcoming and inviting to families. These methods range in terms of the breadth and depth of change required of all staff members in the school. The following methods are arranged from those that require a relatively low depth of change to those that require a greater depth and breadth of change:

1. Some schools employ a parent/parent volunteers/family liaison person who can provide other parents with information on how the school works and may speak the language or come from the ethnic minority group represented by many families in the school. The liaison person's role is to serve as a go-between, explaining the school to families and families to the school via translation services and home visits, for example. While such a professional can make an individual family's experience less nerve-racking, one consequence of utilizing such a person is that the rest of the staff is not required to change their practices and can remain unchanged in their ways of thinking (Comer 1985).

2. A school may emphasize having its office staff develop skills with a more positive consumer orientation in which all families, students, and other visitors are treated with friendliness and respect (Hoover-Dempsey et al. 2005).

3. A school staff may take steps to depict a more representative picture of cultural groups and family structures in visual displays in the school (e.g., school bulletin boards, books, and correspondence) and demonstrate a warmer, friendlier tone to families in such displays and correspondence.

4. A school staff may develop friendlier, more effective and efficient methods for keeping families informed of student progress by using the latest technologies (e-mail, voice mail) to keep parents abreast of student expectations and progress. A staff might also utilize available technology to communicate more effectively with families such as online grade book programs; teacher Web sites with e-mail addresses and unit plans; and a school Web site with policies, activities calendars, pictures of family activities, newsletters, volunteer activities, or activities sponsored by parent organizations. However, these methods typically involve one-way communication from the school to the family rather than seek out two-way communication.

5. The school staff can establish opportunities for two-way communication with families that complement their work schedules. For example, teachers can hold conferences on evenings or with more varied and flexible schedules. Individual parent and educator conferences can offer opportunities for interview and collaborative assessment of the child's skills.

6. Staff can create opportunities for two-way communication by redesigning the traditional school-wide family–school routines (e.g., Back-to-school Night, school letters) to enhance getting input from students and parents about their goals, perspectives, and circumstances, and by increasing opportunities for meaningful interaction.

7. Staff can seek out families' perspectives—learning about what parents and students see as their goals, perspectives on their child's learning, and identifying needs that are consistent with families' special circumstances and culture. In addition, staff can follow through on families' suggestions by designing interventions that support children's learning in ways that are consistent with parents' circumstances.

8. Staff can seek out parent/family knowledge to build curriculum that connects students' home knowledge with school learning.

Summary

Although the research paints a positive picture of the relationship between parent involvement and student success in school, the actualization of a positive school culture that is truly inviting to parents to become partners with the school and its faculty is hard to accomplish. The reason is not because teachers, counselors, and administrators do not want parental help—school folks need all of the help they can get in the high stakes, high visibility arena that public education currently finds itself. The truth is that the traditional way of "doing school," the *in loco parentis* model, does not have traditional structures or dispositions to make meaningful involvement of parents in the academic lives of their children an easy strategy to accomplish. In essence, it takes a real shift in school culture for a school to become one where parents, teachers, staff, administration, and students are partners and co-facilitators in the learning process. Given these challenging circumstances, it is *not impossible* to improve the current conditions of the school–family relationship in any school. The first step toward restructuring is a belief that working on developing a more positive relationship is important enough to focus time, energy, and resources to begin this process. The leadership of the principal is essential to developing the faculty's awareness of the current state of family–school relationships, to identifying areas for improvement, and to helping the faculty not only develop a plan for improvement but also provide whatever resources are needed for the implementation of the plan.

Working to overcome the challenges of involving themselves with low-income and socio-culturally diverse families is difficult and challenging for most school staff (Sheldon 2005). Research is still needed to explore how principals' actions and decisions foster strong programs of family, school, and community partnerships. Also, additional research is needed to assess the quality of partnerships that draw from multiple resources, such as teachers' and principals' perceptions of implementation and parents' and students' perceptions of their experiences with school partnerships (Sheldon). As the book comes to an end, we would like you to consider, by means of Reflective Exercise 14.1, the first steps you might likely take as a new educator to promote more collaborative family–school relations in your workplace.

Reflective Exercise 14.1

Collaborative Teaching Approach

Imagine yourself as a first-year teacher in an elementary school where most other teachers have been employed for over ten years and worked from a fairly traditional paradigm of education. What are two ways you might introduce and promote a collaborative approach to teaching throughout the school?

Resources

Tools for School Improvement Planning,
www.annenberginstitute.org/tools
The Annenberg Institute has funded a research project to develop everything that schools might need to collect, analyze, and interpret the data necessary for successful school change and advocacy efforts.

Constructing School Partnerships with Families and Communities,
www.ncrel.org/sdrs/areas/issues/envrnmnt/famncomm/pa400.htm
This site is a resource from the North Central Regional Educational Laboratory (NCREL) on strengthening home and school partnerships.

Bibliography

Chapter 1

Amatea, E., Daniels, H. D., Bringman, N., & Vandiver, F. (2004). Strengthening counselor–teacher–family connections: The family–school collaborative consultation project. *Professional School Counseling, 8*, 47–55.

Austin, T. (1994). *Changing the view: Student-led parent conferences.* Portsmouth, NH: Heinemann.

Ayers, M., Fonseca J. D., Andrade, R., & Civil, M. (2001). Creating learning communities: The "build your dream house" unit. In E. McIntyre, A. Rosebery, & N. Gonzalez (Eds.). *Classroom diversity: Connecting curriculum to students' lives* (pp. 92–99). Portsmouth, NH: Heinemann.

Bempechat, J. (1998). *Against the odds: How "at risk" students EXCEED expectations.* San Francisco: Jossey-Bass.

Benson, B., & Barnett, S. (1999). *Student-led conferencing using showcase portfolios.* Thousand Oaks, CA: Corwin Press.

Beyer, L. E. (1996). *Creating democratic classrooms: The struggle to integrate theory and practice.* New York: Teachers College Press.

Bloome, D., Katz, L., Solsken, J., Willett, J., & Wilson-Keenan, J. (2000). Interpellations of family–community and classroom literacy practices. *The Journal of Educational Research, 93*, 155–164.

Brand, S. (1996). Making parent involvement a reality: Helping teachers develop partnerships with parents. *Young Children, 51,* 76–81.

Children's Defense Fund. (2005). *The state of America's children: Yearbook 2005.* Washington, DC: Author.

childstats.gov. (2007). America's children in brief: Key national indicators of well-being, 2007. Retrieved September 26, 2007, from www.childstats.gov/americaschildren.

Christenson, S. L., & Sheridan, S. (2001). *Schools and families: Creating essential connections for learning.* New York: Guilford Press.

Christenson, S. L., Rounds, T., & Franklin, M. J. (1992). Home-school collaboration: Effects, issues and opportunities. In S. Christenson & J. Conoley (Eds.). *Home-school collaboration: Enhancing children's academic and social competence.* (pp. 19–51). Bethesda, MD: National Association of School Psychologists.

Clark, R. (1983). *Family life and school achievement: Why poor black children succeed or fail.* Chicago: University of Chicago Press.

Clark, R. (1990). Why disadvantaged students succeed: What happens outside school is critical. *Public Welfare, 48,* 17–23.

Cochran-Smith, M. (2004). *Walking the road: Race, diversity, and social justice in teacher education.* New York: Teachers College Press.

Collignon, F., Men, M., & Tan, S. (2001). Finding ways in: Community-based perspectives in Southeast Asian family involvement with schools in a New England state. *Journal of Education for Students Placed at Risk 6*, 27–44.

Comer, J. P., & Haynes, N. M. (1991). Parent involvement in schools: An ecological approach. *Elementary School Journal, 91*, 271–277.

Cox, D. (2005). Evidence-based interventions using home-school collaboration. *School Psychology Quarterly, 20*, 473–497.

Darling-Hammond, L., & Youngs, S. (2002). Defining "highly qualified teachers": What does "scientifically-based research" actually tell us? *Educational Researcher, 31*(9), 13–25.

Darling-Hammond, L., & Sclan, E. M. (1996). Who teaches and why. In J. Sikula (Ed.). *Handbook of research on teacher education* (pp. 67–101). New York: Simon & Schuster-Macmillan.

Darling-Hammond, L. (2000). How teacher education matters. *Journal of Teacher Education, 51(3),* 166–173.

Dauber, S. L., & Epstein, J. (1993). Parents' attitudes and practices of involvement in inner-city elementary and middle schools. In N. F. Chavkin (Ed.). *Families and schools in a pluralistic society* (pp. 53–71). Albany: State University of New York Press.

Davies, A., Cameron, C., Politano, C., & Gregory, K. (1992). *Together is better: Collaborative assessment, evaluation and reporting.* Winnipeg, Canada: Peguis.

Davies, D. (1988). Low-income parents and the schools: A research report and a plan for action. *Equity and Choice, 4,* 51–57.

Delpit, L. (1995). *Other people's children: Cultural conflict in the classroom.* New York: New Press.

Dornbusch, S., Ritter, P., Leiderman, P., Roberts, D., & Fraleigh, M. (1987). The relation of parenting style to adolescent school performance. *Child Development, 58,* 1244–1257.

Dryfoos, J. (1994). *Full service schools: A revolution in health and social services for children, youth and families.* San Francisco: Jossey-Bass.

Eccles, J. S., & Harold, R. D. (1996). Family involvement in children's and adolescents' schooling. In A. Booth & J. F. Dunn (Eds.). *Family–school links: How do they affect educational outcomes?* (3–34) Mahwah, NJ: Lawrence Erlbaum.

Edin, K., & Lein, L. (1997). *Making ends meet: How single mothers survive welfare and low-wage work.* New York: Russell Sage Foundation.

Epstein, J. (1990). School and family connections: Theory, research, and implications for integrating sociologies of education and family. In D. Unger & M. Sussmann (Eds.). *Families in community settings: Interdisciplinary perspectives.* New York: Haworth.

Epstein, J. (1991). Effects on student achievement of teacher practices of parent involvement. In S. Silvern (Ed.). *Advances in reading/language research: Literacy through family, community and school interaction* (Vol. 5, pp. 261–276). Greenwich, CT: JAI Press.

Epstein, J. (1995). School/family/community partnerships: Caring for the children we share. *Phi Delta Kappan, 76,* 701–711.

Epstein, J. (2001). *School, family and community partnerships: Preparing educators and improving schools.* Boulder, CO: Westview Press.

Epstein, J., & Van Voorhis, F. (2001). More than minutes: Teachers' roles in designing homework. *Educational Psychologist, 36,* 181–193.

Finders, M., & Lewis, C. (1994). Why some parents don't come to school. *Educational Leadership, 51,* 50–54.

Furstenberg, F., Cook, T. D., Eccles, J., Elder, G. H., & Sameroff, A. J. (1999). *Managing to make it: Urban families and adolescent success.* Chicago: University of Chicago Press.

Gay, G. (2000). Culturally responsive teaching: Theory, research and practice. New York: Teachers College Press.

Goodwin, A. L. (2000). Teachers as (multi)cultural agents in schools. In R. Carter (Ed.). *Addressing cultural issues in organizations: Beyond the corporate context* (pp. 104–114). Thousand Oaks, CA: Sage.

Gonzalez, N. E. (1995). The funds of knowledge for teaching project. *Practicing Anthropology, 17,* 3–6.

Heath, S. B. (1983). *Ways with words: Language, life and work in communities and classrooms.* Cambridge: Cambridge University Press.

Henderson, A., & Mapp, K. L. (2002). *A new wave of evidence: The impact of school, family and community connections on student achievement.* Austin, TX: Southwest Educational Development Laboratory.

Hodgkinson, H. (2002). Demographics and teacher education. *Journal of Teacher Education, 53,* 102–105.

Hoover-Dempsey, K., Bassler, O., & Burow, R. (1995). Parents' reported involvement in students' homework: Strategies and practices. *Elementary School Journal, 95,* 435–450.

Hoover-Dempsey, K. V., & Sandler, H. (1997). Why do parents become involved in their children's education? *Review of Educational Research, 67,* 3–42.

Hoover-Dempsey, K. V., Walker, J. M., Sandler, H. M., Whetsel, D., Green, C. L., Wilkins, A. S., & Closson, K. (2005). Why do parents become involved? Research findings and implications. *Elementary School Journal, 106,* 105–130.

Irvine, J. (1997). *Constructing the knowledge base for urban teacher education.* Washington, DC: American Association of Colleges for Teacher Education.

Jeynes, W. H. (2003). A meta-analysis: The effects of parental involvement on minority children's academic achievement. *Education and Urban Society, 35,* 202–218.

Kozol, J. (1991). *Savage inequalities: Children in America's schools.* New York: Harper & Row.

Krasnow, J. (1990). *Improving family–school relationships: Teacher research from the Schools Reaching Out Project.* Boston: Institute for Responsive Education.

Ladson-Billings, G. (1995). Multicultural teacher education: Research, practice and policy. In J. A. Banks & C. A. Banks (Eds.). *Handbook of research on multicultural education.* (pp. 747–761). New York: Macmillan.

Lareau, A. (1989). *Home advantage: Social class and parental intervention in elementary education.* London, England: Falmer.

Lareau, A., & Horvat, E. M. (1999). Moments of social inclusion and exclusion: Class, race and cultural capital in family–school relationships. *Sociology of Education, 72,* 37–53.

Leitch, L., & Tangri, S. (1988). Barriers to home–school collaboration. *Educational Horizons, 66,* 70–74.

Lindle, J. C. (1989). What do parents want from principals and teachers? *Educational Leadership, 47,* 12–14.

Lopez, G. R., Scribner, J. D., & Mahitivanichcha, K. (2001). Redefining parent involvement: Lessons from high-performing migrant-impacted schools. *American Educational Research Journal, 38,* 253–288.

Lott, B. (2001). Low-income parents and the public schools. *Journal of Social Issues 57,* 247–259.

McCaleb, S. P. (1994). *Building communities of learners: A collaboration among teachers, students, families and community.* New York: St. Martin's Press.

McCarthey, S. (1997). Connecting home and school literacy practices in classrooms with diverse populations. *Journal of Literacy Research, 29,* 145–182.

McCarthey, S. (2000). Home–school connections: A review of the literature. *Journal of Educational Research, 93,* 145–154.

McIntyre, E., Rosebery, A., & Gonzalez, N. (2001). *Classroom diversity: Connecting curriculum with students' lives.* Portsmouth, NH: Heinemann.

Moll, L. C. (1992). Bilingual classrooms and community analysis: Some recent trends. *Educational Researcher, 21,* 20–24.

Moll, L. C., & Gonzalez, N. (1994). Lessons from research with language minority children. *Journal of Reading Behavior, 26,* 439–456.

Moll, L., Amanti, C., Neff, D., & Gonzalez, N. (1992). Funds of knowledge for teaching: Using a qualitative approach to connect homes and classrooms. *Theory into Practice, 31,* 132–141.

Murry, V. M., Brody, G. H., Brown, A., Wisenbaker, J., Cutrona, C., & Simons, R. (2002). Linking employment status, maternal psychological well-being, parenting and children's attributions about poverty in families receiving government assistance. *Family Relations, 51,* 112–120.

National Center for Education Statistics. (2005). *2005 Condition of Education.* Washington, DC: Department of Education.

National Center for Education Statistics. (2005). *Estimates of resident population by race/ethnicity and age group: Selected years, 1980 through 2005.* Washington, DC: Digest of Education Statistics.

Orfield, G. (2004). *Dropouts in America: Confronting the graduation rate crisis.* Cambridge, MA: Harvard Education Press.

Patton, J. R., Jayanthi, M., & Polloway, E. A. (2001). Home–school collaboration about homework: What do we know and what should we do? *Reading and Writing Quarterly, 17,* 227–242.

Peterson, N. L., & Cooper, C. S. (1988). Parent education and involvement in early intervention programs for handicapped children: A different perspective on parent needs and the parent–professional relationship. In M. J. Fine (Ed.). *Advances in parent education: Contemporary perspectives* (pp. 197–236). New York: Academic Press.

Pianta, R., & Walsh, D. (1996). *High-risk children in schools: Constructing sustaining relationships.* New York: Routledge.

Scott-Jones, D. (1995). Parent–child interactions and school achievement. In B. A. Ryan, G. R. Adams, T. P. Gullotta, R. P. Weissberg, & R. L. Hampton (Eds.). *The family–school connection: Theory, research, and practice* (vol. 2, pp. 75–107). Thousand Oaks, CA: Sage.

Sheldon, S., & Epstein, J. (2002). Improving student behavior and school discipline with family and community involvement. *Education and Urban Society, 35,* 4–26.

Swap, S. M. (1993). *Developing home–school partnerships: From concept to practice.* New York: Teachers College Press.

Taylor, D., & Dorsey-Gaines, C. (1988). *Growing up literate: Learning from inner city families.* Portsmouth, NH: Heinemann.

Trumbull, E., Rothstein-Fisch, C., Greenfield, P. M., & Quiroz, B. (2001). *Bridging cultures between home and school: A guide for teachers.* Mahwah, NJ: Lawrence Erlbaum.

Valdes, G. (1996). *Con respeto: Bridging the distances between culturally diverse families and schools.* New York: Teachers College Press.

Velez-Ibanez, C., & Greenberg, J. (1992). Formation and transformation of funds of knowledge among U.S. Mexican households. *Anthropology and Education Quarterly, 23,* 313–335.

Villegas, A., & Lucas, T. (2002). Preparing culturally responsive teachers: Rethinking the curriculum. *Journal of Teacher Education, 53,* 20–32.

Weiss, H., & Edwards, M. (1992). The family–school collaboration project: Systemic interventions for school improvement. In S. Christenson & J. Conoley (Eds.). *Home—school collaboration: Enhancing children's academic and social competence* (pp. 215–243). Silver Spring, MD: National Association of School Psychologists.

Chapter 2

Barnard, W. M. (2004). Parent involvement in elementary school and educational attainment. *Children and Youth Services Review, 26,* 39–62.

Brand, S. (1996). Making parent involvement a reality: Helping teachers develop partnerships with parents. *Young Children, 51,* 76–81.

Brody, G. J., Flor, D. L., & Gibson, N. M. (1999). Linking maternal efficacy beliefs, developmental goals, parenting practices, and child competence in rural single-parent African American families. *Child Development, 70,* 1197–1208.

Bronfenbrenner, U. (1979). *The ecology of human development.* Cambridge, MA: Harvard University Press.

Bronfenbrenner, U. (1997). Ecology of the family as a context for human development: Research perspectives. In J. L. Paul, M. Churton, H. Rosselli-Kostoryz, W. Morse, K. Marfo, C. Lavely, & D. Thomas (Eds.), *Foundations of special education: Basic knowledge informing research and practice in special education.* Belmont, CA: Brooks/Cole.

Bruner, J. (1996). *The culture of education.* Cambridge, MA: Harvard University Press.

Children's Defense Fund. (2005). *The state of America's children 2005.* Washington, DC: Author.

Christenson, S. L., Rounds, T., & Franklin, M. J. (1992). Home-school collaboration: Effects, issues and opportunities. In S. Christenson & J. Conoley (Eds.), *Home-school collaboration: Enhancing children's academic and social competence* (pp. 19–51). Silver Spring, MD: National Association of School Psychologists.

Christenson, S. L., & Sheridan, S. M. (2001). *Schools and families: Creating essential connections for learning.* New York: Guilford Press.

Clark, R. (1990). Why disadvantaged students succeed: What happens outside school is critical. *Public Welfare,* 17–23.

Coleman, J. (1987, August–September). Families and schools. *Educational Researcher, 16,* 32–38.

Comer, J. P. (1980). *School power.* New York: Free Press.

Comer, J. P., & Haynes, N. M. (1991). Parent involvement in schools: An ecological approach. *Elementary School Journal, 91,* 271–277.

Comer, J. P., Haynes, N. M., Joyner, E. T., & Ben-Avie, M. (Eds.) (1996). *Rallying the whole village: The Comer process for reforming education.* New York: Teachers College Press.

Dauber, S. L., & Epstein, J. (1993). Parents' attitudes and practices of involvement in inner-city elementary and middle schools. In N. F. Chavkin (Ed.), *Families and schools in a pluralistic society* (pp. 53–71). Albany: State University of New York Press.

Davies, D. (1988). Low-income parents and the schools: A research report and a plan for action. *Equity and Choice, 4,* 51–57.

Delpit, L. (1995). *Other people's children: Cultural conflict in the classroom.* New York: New Press.

Deslandes, R., Royer, E., Potvin, P., & Leclerc, D. (1999). Patterns of home and school partnership for general and special education students at the secondary level. *Exceptional Children, 65,* 496–506.

Eccles, J. S., & Harold, R. D. (1993). Parent-school involvement during the early adolescent years. *Teachers College Record, 94,* 568–587.

Epstein, J. (1987). Parent involvement: What research says to administrators. *Education and Urban Society 19,* 119–136.

Epstein, J. (1990). School and family connections: Theory, research, and implications for integrating sociologies of education and family. In D. Unger & M. Sussmann (Eds.), *Families in community settings: Interdisciplinary perspectives.* New York: Haworth.

Epstein, J. (1995). School/family/community partnerships: Caring for the children we share. *Phi Delta Kappan, 76,* 701–711.

Epstein, J. (2001). *School, family and community partnerships: Preparing educators and improving schools.* Boulder, CO: Westview.

Epstein, J. L., & Van Voorhis, F. L. (2001). More than minutes: Teachers' roles in designing homework. *Educational Psychologist 36,* 181–193.

Fan, X., & Chen, M. (1999). Parental involvement and students' academic achievement: A meta-analysis. *Educational Psychology Review, 13,* 1–22.

Frome, P. M., & Eccles, J. S. (1998). Parents' influence on children's achievement-related perceptions. *Journal of Personality and Social Psychology, 74,* 435–452.

Glasgow, K. L., Dornbusch, S. M., Troyer, L., Steinberg, L., & Ritter, P. L. (1997). Parenting styles, adolescents' attributions, and educational outcomes in nine heterogenous high schools. *Child Development, 68,* 507–529.

Goals 2000: Educate America Act, Public Law 103–227.

Gonzalez, A. R., Holbein, M., & Quilter, S. (2002). High school students' goal orientations and their relationship to perceived parenting styles. *Contemporary Educational Psychology, 27,* 450–470.

Grolnick, W. S., Ryan, R. M., & Deci, E. L. (1991). Inner resources for school achievement. Motivational mediators of children's perceptions of their parents. *Journal of Educational Psychology, 83,* 508–517.

Harrison, A. O., & Minor, J. H. (1978). Inter-role conflict, coping strategies, and satisfaction among Black working wives. *Journal of Marriage and the Family, 40,* 799–805.

Heath, S., & McLaughlin, M. (1987). A child resource policy: Moving beyond dependence on school and family. *Phi Delta Kappan, 68,* 576–580.

Henderson, A. (1987). *The evidence continues to grow: Parent involvement improves student achievement.* Columbia, MD: National Committee for Citizens in Education.

Henderson, A., & Mapp, K. L. (2002). *A new wave of evidence: The impact of school, family, and community connections on student achievement.* Austin, TX: Southwest Educational Development Laboratory.

Henderson, A., Jones, K., & Raimondo, B. (April, 1999). The power of parent partnership. *Our Children: The National PTA Magazine,* 36–39.

Hill, N. E., & Craft, S. A. (2003). Parent–school involvement and school performance: Mediated pathways among socioeconomically comparable African American and Euro-American families. *Journal of Educational Psychology, 95,* 74–83.

Hoover-Dempsey, K. V., & Bassler, O., & Burow, R. (1995). Parents' reported involvement in students' homework: Strategies and practices. *Elementary School Journal, 95,* 435–450.

Hoover-Dempsey, K. V., & Sandler, H. (1997). Why do parents become involved in their children's education? *Review of Educational Research, 67,* 3–42.

Hoover-Dempsey, K. V., Walker, J. M., Sandler, H. M., Whetsel, D., Green, C. L., Wilkins, A. S., & Closson, K. (2005). Why do parents become involved? Research findings and implications. *Elementary School Journal, 106,* 105–130.

Kellaghan, T., Sloane, K., Alvarez, B., & Bloom, B. (1993). *The home environment and school learning: Promoting parental involvement in the education of children.* San Francisco: Jossey-Bass.

Kuhn, T. (1970). *The structure of scientific revolutions.* (2nd ed.). Chicago: University of Chicago Press.

Lareau, L., & Horvat, E. M. (1999). Moments of social inclusion and exclusion: Race, class, and cultural capital in family–school relationships. *Sociology of Education, 72,* 37–53.

Lareau, L. (1989). *Home advantage: Social class and parental intervention in elementary education.* London, England: Falmer.

Leitch, L., & Tangri, S. (1988). Barriers to home-school collaboration. *Educational Horizons, 66,* 70–74.

Lewis, A. E., & Forman, T. A. (2002). Contestation or collaboration? A comparative study of home–school relations. *Anthropology and Education Quarterly, 33,* 60–89.

Lindle, J. C. (1989). What do parents want from principals and teachers? *Educational Leadership, 47,* 12–14.

Ma, X. (1999). Dropping out of advanced mathematics: The effects of parental involvement. *Teachers College Record, 101,* 60–81.

Marcon, R. A. (1999). Positive relationships between parent school involvement and public school inner-city preschoolers' development and academic performance. *School Psychology Review, 28,* 395–412.

McIntyre, E., Rosebery, A., & Gonzalez, R. (2001). *Classroom diversity: Connecting curriculum with students' lives.* Portsmouth, NH: Heinemann.

Merriam-Webster, Inc. (1985). *Webster's ninth new collegiate dictionary.* Springfield, MA: Merriam-Webster.

Moles, O. (1993). *Building family-school partnerships for learning: Workshops for urban educators.* Washington, DC: Office of Educational Research Improvement, U.S. Department of Education.

National Educational Goals Panel. (1999). *The national educational goals report: Building a nation of learners.* Washington, DC: U.S. Government Printing Office.

No Child Left Behind Act. (2001). Retrieved July 15, 2006, from www.nochildleftbehind.gov/

Peterson, N. L., & Cooper, C. S. (1989). Parent education and involvement in early intervention programs for handicapped children: A different perspective on parent needs and the parent–professional relationship. In M. J. Fine (Ed.), *The second handbook on parent education: Contemporary perspectives* (pp. 197–236). New York: Academic Press.

Reich, R. (1983). *The next American frontier.* New York: Penguin.

Seeley, D. S. (1985). *Education through partnership.* Washington, DC: American Enterprise Institute for Public Policy Research.

Seeley, D. S. (1991). The major new case for choice is only half right. *Equity and Choice, 7(1),* 28–33.

Sheldon, S. B., & Epstein, J. L. (2002). Improving student behavior and school discipline with family and community involvement. *Education and Urban Society, 35,* 4–26.

Smrekar, C., & Cohen-Vogel, L. (2001). The voices of parents. Rethinking the intersection of family and school. *Peabody Journal of Education, 76,* 75–100.

Snow, C., Barnes, W., Chandler, J., Goodman, I., & Hemphill, L. (1991). *Unfulfilled expectations: Home and school influences on literacy.* Cambridge, MA: Harvard University Press.

Swap, S. M. (1993). *Developing home-school partnerships: From concept to practice.* New York: Teachers College Press.

Trusty, J. (1999). Effects of eighth-grade parental involvement on late adolescents' educational experiences. *Journal of Research and Development in Education, 32,* 224–233.

U.S. Department of Education. (2002). *No child left behind.* Available at: www.nochildleftbehind.gov/next/overview.html

U.S. Department of Health and Human Services. (1997). *Health United States, 1996.* Washington, DC: U.S. Government Printing Office.

U.S. Congress. (1999). IDEA: Rules and regulations. *Federal Register, 64,* 12406–12672. Washington, DC: Author.

U.S. Congress. (2004). IDEA: Rules and regulations. *Federal Register, 69,* Washington, DC: Author.

Vygotsky, L. S. (1978). *Mind in society: The development of higher psychological processes.* Cambridge, MA: Harvard University Press.

Weiss, H., & Edwards, M. (1992). The family–school collaboration project: Systemic interventions for school improvement. In S. Christenson & J. Conoley (Eds.), *Home-school collaboration: Enhancing children's academic and social competence* (pp. 215–243). Silver Spring, MD: National Association of School Psychologists.

Chapter 3

Amatea, E., Daniels, H. D., Bringman, N., & Vandiver, F. (2004). Strengthening counselor–teacher–family connections: The family–school collaborative consultation project. *Professional School Counseling, 8(1),* 47–55.

Amatea, E., & Vandiver, F. (2004). Strengthening counselor–teacher–family connections to promote children's learning: A case study of organizational change. *Journal of School Leadership, 14,* 327–344.

Austin, T. (1994). *Changing the view: Student-led parent conferences.* Portsmouth, NH: Heinemann.

Christenson, S., & Hirsch, J. (1998). Facilitating partnerships and conflict resolution between families and schools. In K. C. Stoiber & T. R. Kratchowill (Eds.), *Handbook of group intervention for children and families* (307–344). Boston: Allyn & Bacon.

Christenson, S. L., & Sheridan, S. M. (2001). *Schools and families: Creating essential connections for learning.* New York: Guilford Press.

Cook, T. D., Murphy, R. F., & Hunt, H. D. (2000). Comer's school development program in Chicago: A theory-based evaluation. *American Educational Research Journal, 37(2),* 535–597.

Epstein, J. (1995). School/family/community partnerships: Caring for the children we share. *Phi Delta Kappan, 76(9),* 701–712.

Epstein, J. (1990). School and family connections: Theory, research, and implications for integrating sociologies of education and family. In D. Unger & S. Sussmann (Eds.), *Families in community settings: Interdisciplinary perspectives.* New York: Haworth.

Fullan, M. (1996). Professional culture and educational change. *School Psychology Review, 25,* 496–500.

Henderson, A. (1987). *The evidence continues to grow: Parent involvement improves student achievement.* Columbia, MD: National Committee for Citizens in Education.

Hoover-Dempsey, K.V., & Sandler, H. (1997). Why do parents become involved in their children's education? *Review of Educational Research, 67,* 3–42.

Kyle, D., McIntyre, E., Miller, K., & Moore, G. (2002). *Reaching out: A K-8 resource for connecting families and schools.* Thousand Oaks, CA: Corwin Press.

Lareau, L. (1989). *Home advantage: Social class and parental intervention in elementary education.* London, England: Falmer.

McCaleb, S. P. (1994). *Building communities of learners: A collaboration among teachers, students, families and community.* New York: St. Martin's Press.

McCarthey, S. (1997). Connecting home and school literacy practices in classrooms with diverse populations. *Journal of Literacy Research, 29,* 145–182.

McCarthey, S. (2000). Home-school connections: A review of the literature. *Journal of Educational Research, 93,* 145–154.

Merriam-Webster OnLine. (2006). Accessed October 2006 at www.m-w.com.

Moles, O. C. (1993). *Building family-school partnerships for learning: Workshops for urban educators.* Washington, DC: Office of Educational Research Improvement, U.S. Department of Education.

Moll, L. C. (1992). Bilingual classrooms and community analysis: Some recent trends. *Educational Researcher, 21,* 20–24.

Moll, L. C., & Gonzalez, N. (1994). Lessons from research with language minority children. *Journal of Reading Behavior, 26,* 439–456.

Moll, L., Amanti, C., Neff, D., & Gonzalez, N. (1992). Funds of knowledge for teaching: Using a qualitative approach to connect homes and classrooms. *Theory into Practice, 31,* 132–141.

Sattes, B. (1985). *Parent involvement: A review of the literature.* (Occasional paper No. 21) Charleston, WV: Appalachia Educational Laboratory.

Shockley, B., Michalove, B., & Allen, J. (1995). Creating parallel practices. In B. Shockley, B. Michalove & J. Allen (Eds.) *Engaging families: Connecting home and school literacy communities* (pp. 18–27). Portsmouth, NH: Heinemann.

Seeley, D. S. (1989). A new paradigm for parent involvement. *Educational Leadership, 47,* 46–48.

Swap, S. M. (1993). *Developing home-school partnerships: From concept to practice.* New York: Teachers College Press.

Taguiri, R. (1968). The concept of organizational climate. In R. Taguiri & G. H. Litwin (Eds.), *Organizational climate: Explorations of a concept* (pp. 10–32). Cambridge, MA: Harvard University Press.

Tharp, R., & Gallimore, R. (1993). *Rousing minds to life: Teaching, learning and schooling in a social context.* Cambridge, MA: Cambridge University Press.

Tharp, R. G., Estrada, P., Dalton, S., & Yamauchi, L. (2000). *Teaching transformed: Achieving excellence, fairness, inclusion and harmony.* Boulder, CO: Westview.

Weiss, H., & Edwards, M. (1992). The family–school collaboration project: Systemic interventions for school improvement. In S. Christenson & J. Conoley (Eds.), *Home–school collaboration: Enhancing children's academic and social competence* (pp. 215–243). Silver Spring, MD: National Association of School Psychologists.

Weiss, H. (1996). Family–school collaboration: Consultation to achieve organizational and community change. *Human Systems: The Journal of Systemic Consultation and Management, 7,* 211–235.

Chapter 4

Amatea, E. (1989). *Brief strategic intervention for school behavior problems.* San Francisco: Jossey-Bass.

Amatea, E., Daniels, H., Bringman, N., & Vandiver, F. (2004). Strengthening counselor–teacher–family connections: The family–school collaborative consultation project. *Professional School Counseling, 8,* 47–55.

Aspinwall, L., Richter, L., & Hoffman, R. (2001). Understanding how optimism works: An examination of optimists' adaptive moderation of belief and behavior. In E. C. Chang (Ed.), *Optimism and pessimism: Implications for theory, research and practice* (pp. 217–238). Washington, DC: American Psychological Association.

Baldwin, A. L., Baldwin, C., & Cole, R. E. (1990). Stress-resistant families and stress-resistant children. In J. Rolf, A. S. Masten, D. Chichetti, K. H. Neuchterlein, & S. Weintraub (Eds.), *Risk and protective factors in the development of psychopathology* (pp. 257–280). New York: Cambridge University Press.

Barber, B. L., & Eccles, J. S. (1992). Long-term influences of divorce and single parenting on adolescent family- and work-related values, behaviors and aspirations. *Psychological Bulletin, 111,* 108–126.

Baumrind, D. (1989). Rearing competent children. In W. Damon (Ed.), *Child development today and tomorrow* (349–378). San Francisco: Jossey-Bass.

Baumrind, D. (1991). Parenting styles and adolescent development. In R. M. Lerner, A. C. Petersen & J. Brooks-Gunn (Eds.), *The Encyclopedia on adolescence* (746–758). New York: Garland.

Bemak, F., & Cornely, L. (2002). The SAFI model as a critical link between marginalized families and schools: A literature review and strategies for school counselors. *Journal of Counseling and Development, 80,* 322–331.

Bempechat, J. (1998). *Against the odds: How "at risk" students EXCEED expectations.* San Francisco: Jossey-Bass.

Brody, G. J., Flor, D. L., & Gibson, N. M. (1999). Linking maternal efficacy beliefs, developmental goals, parenting practices, and child competence in rural single-parent African American families. *Child Development, 70,* 1197–1208.

Bugental, D. B., Blue, J., & Cruzcosa, M. (1989). Perceived control over care-giving outcomes: Implications for child abuse. *Developmental Psychology, 25,* 532–539.

Bukatko, D. & Daehler, M. (1995). *Child development: A thematic approach.* Boston: Houghton Mifflin.

Carlson, C. J., Hickman, J., & Horton, C. (1992). From blame to solutions: Solution-oriented family–school consultation. In S. Christenson & J. Conoley (Eds.), *Home–school collaboration: Enhancing children's academic and social competence* (pp. 193–213). Silver Spring, MD: National Association of School Psychologists.

Christenson, S. L., & Sheridan, S. (2001). *Schools and families: Creating essential connections for learning.* New York: Guilford Press.

Clark, R. (1983). *Family life and school achievement: Why poor black children succeed or fail.* Chicago: University of Chicago Press.

Clark, R. (1990). Why disadvantaged students succeed: What happens outside school is critical. *Public Welfare,* 17–23.

Coleman, J. S., Campbell, E., Hobson, C., McPartland, J., Mood, A., Weinfeld, F., & York, R. (1966). *Equality of educational opportunity.* Washington, DC: U.S. Office of Education, National Center for Educational Statistics.

Collignon, F., Men, M., & Tan, S. (2001). Finding ways in: Community-based perspectives in Southeast Asian family involvement with schools in a New England state. *Journal of Education for Students Placed at Risk 6,* 27–44.

Comer, J. (1984). Home–school relationships as they affect the academic success of children. *Education and Urban Society, 16,* 323–337.

Conger, R. D., & Conger, K. J. (2002). Resilience in Midwestern families: Selected findings from the first decade of a prospective, longitudinal study. *Journal of Marriage and the Family, 64,* 361–373.

Conger, R. D., & Elder, G. H. (1994). *Families in troubled times.* New York: Aldine de Gruyter.

Cox, R. P., & Davis, L. L. (1999). Family problem solving: Measuring an elusive concept. *Journal of Family Nursing, 5,* 332–360.

Crosnoe, R., Mistry, R. S., & Elder, G. H. (2002). Economic disadvantage, family dynamics, and adolescent enrollment in higher education. *Journal of Marriage and the Family, 64,* 690–702.

Crouter, A., MacDermid, S., McHale, S., & Perry-Jenkins, M. (1990). Parental monitoring and perceptions of children's school performance and conduct in dual and single-earner families. *Developmental Psychology 26,* 649–657.

Delgado-Gaitan, C. (1991). Involving parents in schools: A process of empowerment. *American Journal of Education, 100,* 20–46.

Desimone, L. (1999). Linking parent involvement with student achievement: Do race and income matter? *Journal of Educational Research, 93,* 11–30.

Deslandes, R., Royer, E., Potvin, P., & Leclerc, D. (1999). Patterns of home and school partnership for general and special education students at the secondary level. *Exceptional Children, 65,* 496–506.

Doerries, D. B., & Foster, V. A. (2001). Family counselors as school consultants: Where are the solutions? *The Family Journal: Counseling and Therapy for Couples and Families, 9,* 391–397.

Dornbusch, S., Ritter, P., Leiderman, P., Roberts, D., & Fraleigh, M. (1987). The relation of parenting style to adolescent school performance. *Child Development 58,* 1244–1257.

Dornbusch, S., & Ritter, P. (1992). Home–school processes in diverse ethnic groups, social classes, and family structures. In S. L. Christenson & J. C. Conoley (Eds.), *Home–school collaboration: Enhancing children's academic and social competence* (pp. 111–125). Silver Spring, MD: National Association of School Psychologists.

Eccles, J. S., & Harold, R. D. (1996). Family involvement in children's and adolescents' schooling. In A. Booth & J. F. Dunn (Eds.), *Family–school links: How do they affect educational outcomes?* Mahwah, NJ: Lawrence Erlbaum.

Echevarria-Doan, S. (2001). Resource-based reflective consultation: Accessing client resources through interviews and dialogues. *Journal of Marital and Family Therapy, 27,* 201–212.

Edin, K., & Lein, L. (1997). *Making ends meet: How single mothers survive welfare and low-wage work.* New York: Russell Sage Foundation.

Ensminger, M. E., & Slusarcick, A. L. (1992). Paths to high school dropout: A longitudinal study of a first grade cohort. *Sociology of Education, 65,* 95–113.

Epstein, J. L. (1995). School/family/community partnerships caring for the children we share. *Phi Delta Kappan, 76(9),* 701–711.

Fan, X., & Chen, M. (2001). Parental involvement and students' academic achievement: A meta-analysis. *Educational Psychology Review, 13,* 1–22.

Frome, P. M., & Eccles, J. S. (1998). Parents' influence on children's achievement-related perceptions. *Journal of Personality and Social Psychology, 74,* 435–452.

Furstenberg, F., Cook, T. D., Eccles, J., Elder, G. H., & Sameroff, A. J. (1999). *Managing to make it: Urban families and adolescent success.* Chicago: University of Chicago Press.

Garcia Coll, C., Akiba, D., Palacios, N., Bailey, B., Silver, R., DiMartino, L., & Chin, C. (2002). Parental involvement in children's education: Lessons from three immigrant groups. *Parenting: Science and Practice, 2,* 303–324.

Garmezy, N. (1981). Children under stress: Perspectives on antecedents and correlates of vulnerability and resistance to psychopathology. In A. I. Rabin, J. Aronoff, A. M. Barclay & R. A. Zucker (Eds.), *Further explorations in personality.* (pp. 196–269) New York: Wiley Interscience.

Gonzalez, A. R., Holbein, M., & Quilter, S. (2002). High school students' goal orientations and their relationship to perceived parenting styles. *Contemporary Educational Psychology, 27,* 450–470.

Grolnick, W. S., Ryan, R. M., & Deci, E. L. (1991). Inner resources for school achievement: Motivational mediators of children's perceptions of their parents. *Journal of Educational Psychology, 83,* 508–517.

Herzog, E., & Sudia, C. (1973). Children in fatherless families. In B. Caldwell and H. Ricciuti (Eds.), *Child development and social policy* (141–232). Chicago: University of Chicago Press.

Hetherington, E., Featherman, D., & Camara, K. (1981). *Cognitive performance, school behavior, and achievement of children from one-parent households.* Washington, DC: National Institute of Education.

Hill, N. E., & Craft, S. A. (2003). Parent–school involvement and school performance: Mediated pathways among socioeconomically comparable African American and Euro-American families. *Journal of Educational Psychology, 95,* 74–83.

Hoover-Dempsey, K. V., Bassler, O., & Burow, R. (1995). Parents' reported involvement in students' homework: Strategies and practices. *Elementary School Journal, 95,* 435–450.

Hoover-Dempsey, K. V., & Sandler, H. (1997). Why do parents become involved in their children's education? *Review of Educational Research, 67,* 3–42.

Hoover-Dempsey, K. V., Walker, J. M., Sandler, H. M., Whetsel, D., Green, C. L., Wilkins, A. S., & Closson, K. (2005). Why do parents become involved? Research findings and implications. *Elementary School Journal, 106,* 105–130.

Horvat, E., Weininger, E., & Lareau, A. (2003). From social ties to social capital: Class differences in the relations between schools and parent networks. *American Educational Research Journal, 40,* 319–351.

Izzo, C., Weiss, L., Shanahan, T. & Rodriguez-Brown, F. (2000). Parental self-efficacy and social support as predictors of parenting practices and children's socio-emotional adjustment in Mexican immigrant families. *Journal of Prevention and Intervention in the Community, 20,* 197–213.

Jackson, A. P. (2000). Maternal self-efficacy and children's influence on stress and parenting among single Black mothers in poverty. *Journal of Family Issues, 21,* 3–16.

Jencks, C., Smith, M., Acland, H., Bane, M., Cohen, D., Gintis, H., Heyns, B., & Michelson, S. (1972). *Inequality: A reassessment of the effect of family and schooling in America.* New York: Basic Books.

Kellaghan, T., Sloane, K., Alvarez, B., & Bloom, B. (1993). *The home environment and school learning: Promoting parental involvement in the education of children.* San Francisco: Jossey-Bass.

Kraus, I. (1998). A fresh look at school counseling: A family-systems approach. *Professional School Counseling, 1,* 12–18.

Kriesberg, L. (1967). Rearing children for educational achievement in fatherless families. *Journal of Marriage and the Family, 29,* 288–301.

Lam, S. F. (1997). *How the family influences children's academic achievement.* New York: Garland.

Leitch, M. L., & Tangri, S. S. (1988). Barriers to home–school collaboration. *Educational Horizons, 66,* 70–74.

Lyons, J., Uziel-Miller, N., Reyes, F., & Sokol, P. (2000). Strengths of children and adolescents in residential settings: Prevalence and associations with psychopathology and discharge placement. *Journal of American Academy of Child and Adolescent Psychiatry, 39,* 176–181.

Luthar, S., Cicchetti, D., & Becker, B. (2000). The construct of resilience: A critical evaluation and guidelines for future work. *Child Development, 71,* 543–562.

Machida, S., Taylor, A., & Kim, J. (2002). The role of maternal beliefs in predicting home learning activities in Head start families. *Family Relations, 51,* 176–184.

Mandara, J. (2006). The impact of family functioning on African American males' academic achievement? A review and clarification of the empirical literature. *Teachers College Record, 108,* 206–223.

Mandara, J., & Murray, C. B. (2002). Development of an empirical typology of African American family functioning. *Journal of Family Psychology, 16,* 318–337.

Marjoribanks, K. (1979). *Families and their learning environments: An empirical analysis.* London: Routledge and Kegan Paul.

McCubbin, M., Balling, K., Possin, P., Frierdich, S., & Byrne, B. (2002). Family resiliency in childhood cancer. *Family Relations, 51,* 103–111.

McCubbin, M., & McCubbin, H. (1996). Resiliency in families: A conceptual model of family adjustment and adaptation in response to stress and crisis. In H. McCubbin, A. Thompson & M. McCubbin (Eds.), *Family assessment: Resiliency, coping and adaptation—inventories for research and practice* (pp. 1–64). Madison, WI: University of Wisconsin System.

Minuchin, S., Nichols, M., & Lee, W. (2007). *Assessing families and couples: From symptom to system.* New York: Pearson.

Moynihan, D. (1965). *The negro family: The case for national action.* Washington, DC: U.S. Department of Labor, Office of Policy Planning and Research.

Murray, C. B., & Mandara, J. (2003). An assessment of the relationship between racial socialization, racial identity and self-esteem in African American adolescents. In D. A. Y. Azibo (Ed.), *African-centered psychology* (293–325). Durham, NC: Carolina Academic Press.

Murry, V., & Brody, G. H. (1999). Self-regulation and self-worth of Black children reared in economically stressed, rural, single-parent families: The contributions of risk and protective factors. *Journal of Family Issues, 20,* 458–484.

Murry, V., Brody, G. H., Brown, A., Wisenbaker, J., Cutrona, C., & Simons, R. (2002). Linking employment status, maternal psychological well-being, parenting and children's attributions about poverty in families receiving government assistance. *Family Relations, 51,* 112–120.

Murry, V. M., Kotchick, B. A., Wallace, S., Ketchen, B. A., Eddings, K., Heller, L., & Collier, I. (2004). Race, culture and ethnicity: Implications for a community intervention. *Journal of Child and Family Studies, 13,* 81–99.

National Center for Educational Statistics. (1997). *Findings: Involvement of residential parents.* Washington, DC: National Center for Educational Statistics, Department of Education.

Nicoll, W. G. (1997). A family counseling and consultation model for school counselors. In W. Walsh & G. R. Williams (Eds.), *Schools and family therapy* (pp. 75–133). Springfield, IL: Charles C. Thomas Publications.

Orthner, D. K., Jones-Sanpei, H., & Williamson, S. A. (2004). The resilience and strengths of low-income families. *Family Relations, 53,* 159–167.

Quiero-Tajalli, I., & Campbell, C. (2002). Resilience and violence at the macro level. In R. R. Greene (Ed.), *Resiliency: An integrated approach to practice, policy and research* (217–240). Washington, DC: NASW Press.

Salem, D. A., Zimmerman, M. A., & Notaro, P. C. (1998). Effects of family structure, family process and father involvement on psychological outcomes among African American adolescents. *Family Relations, 47,* 331–341.

Santrock, J. W., & Tracy, R. L. (1978). Effects of children's family structure status on the development of stereotypes by teachers. *Journal of Educational Psychology, 70,* 754–757.

Scott-Jones, D. (1995). Parent–child interactions and school achievement. In B. A. Ryan, G. R. Adams, T. P. Gullotta, R. P. Weissberg & R. L. Hampton (Eds.), *The family–school connection: Theory, research, and practice* (vol. 2, pp. 75–107). Thousand Oaks, CA: Sage.

Scheier, M. F., & Carver, C. S. (1992). Effects of optimism on psychological and physical well-being: Theoretical overview and empirical update. *Cognitive Therapy Research, 16,* 201–228.

Seccombe, K. (2002). Beating the odds versus changing the odds: Poverty, resilience, and family policy. *Journal of Marriage and Family, 64,* 384–394.

Seefeldt, C., Denton, K., Galper, A., & Younoszai, T. (1998). Former Head Start parents' characteristics, perceptions of school climate, and involvement in their child's education. *The Elementary School Journal, 98,* 339–349.

Seligman, M. (1991). *Learned optimism.* New York: Knopf.

Seligman, M. (1996). *The optimistic child.* New York: Houghton Mifflin.

Sigel, I. E., McGillicuddy-DeLisi, A. V., & Goodnow, J. J. (Eds.) (1992). *Parental belief systems: The psychological consequences for children* (2nd ed.). Hillsdale, NY: Erlbaum.

Snow, C., Barnes, W., Chandler, J., Goodman, J., & Hemphill, L. (1991). *Unfulfilled expectations: Home and school influences on literacy.* Cambridge, MA: Harvard University Press.

Steinberg, L., Lamborn, S. D., Darling, N., Mounts, N. S., & Dornbusch, S. M. (1994). Over-time changes in adjustment and competence among adolescents from authoritative, authoritarian, indulgent and neglectful families. *Child Development, 65,* 754–770.

Steinberg, L., Lamborn, S. D., Dornbusch, S. M., & Darling, N. (1992). Impact of parenting practices on adolescent achievement: Authoritative parenting, school involvement and encouragement to succeed. *Child Development 63,* 1266–1281.

Sui-Chu, E. H., & Willms, J. D. (1996). Effects of parental involvement on eighth-grade achievement. *Sociology of Education, 69,* 126–141.

Taylor, D., & Dorsey-Gaines, C. (1988). *Growing up literate.* Portsmouth, NH: Heinemann.

Walberg, H. J. (1984). Families as partners in educational productivity. *Phi Delta Kappan, 65,* 397–400.

Walsh, F. (2003). Family resilience: A framework for clinical practice. *Family Process 42,* 1–18.

Weiss, H., & Edwards, M. (1992). The family–school collaboration project: Systemic interventions for school improvement. In S. Christenson & J. Conoley (Eds.), *Home–school collaboration: Enhancing children's academic and social competence* (pp. 215–243). Silver Spring, MD: National Association of School Psychologists.

White, K. R. (1982). The relationship between socioeconomic status and academic achievement. *Psychological Bulletin, 91,* 461–481.

Wigfield, A., Eccles, J. S., & Rodriguez, D. (1998). The development of children's motivation in school contexts. *Review of Research in Education, 23,* 73–118.

Wiley, A. R., Warren, H. B., & Montanelli, D. S. (2002). Shelter in a time of storm: Parenting in poor rural African American communities. *Family Relations, 51,* 265–273.

Young, V. H. (1970). Family and childhood in a Southern Negro community. *American Anthropologist, 72,* 269–288.

Xu, J., & Corno, L. (2003). Family help and homework management reported by middle school students. *Elementary School Journal, 103,* 503–517.

Chapter 5

Becvar, D. S., & Becvar, R. J. (2000). *Family therapy: A systemic integration.* Boston: Allyn & Bacon.

Blackburn, A. C., & Erickson, D. B. (1986). Predictable crises of the gifted student. *Journal of Counseling and Development, 64,* 552–555.

Borders, L. D., Black, L., & Pasley, B. K. (1998). Are adopted children and their parents at greater risk for negative outcomes? *Family Relations, 47,* 237–241.

Bozhovich, L. I. (2004). Developmental phases of personality formation in childhood (III). *Journal of Russian and East European Psychology, 42,* 71–88.

Carter, B., & McGoldrick, M. (2005). *The changing family life cycle.* Boston: Allyn & Bacon.

Centers for Disease Control and Prevention. (2007). *America's children in brief: Key national indicators of well-being, 2006.* National Center for Health Statistics.

Emerson, J., & Lovitt, T. (2003). The educational plight of foster children in schools and what can be done about it. *Remedial and Special Education, 24,* 199–203.

Finders, M., & Lewis, C. (1994). Why some parents don't come to school. *Educational Leadership, 51,* 50–54.

Fitzgerald, B. (1999). Children of lesbian and gay parents: A review of the literature. *Marriage and Family Review, 29,* 57–75.

Garcia-Preto, N. (2005). Transformation of the family system during adolescence. In B. Carter, & M. McGoldrick (eds.). *The changing family life cycle* (274–286). Boston: Allyn & Bacon.

Gladding, S. T. (2001). *The counseling dictionary: Concise definitions of frequently used terms.* Upper Saddle River, NJ: Prentice Hall.

Jackson, Y., Sifers, S. K., Warren, J. S., & Velasquez, D. (2003). Family protective factors and behavioral outcome: The role of appraisal in family life events. *Journal of Emotional and Behavioral Disorders, 11,* 103–111.

James, R. K., & Gilliland, B. E. (2001). *Crisis intervention strategies.* Belmont, CA: Wadsworth.

Lamme, L. L., & Lamme, L. A. (2001/2002). Welcoming children from gay families into our schools. *Educational Leadership, 59,* 65–69.

Lamme, L. L., & Lamme, L. A. (2003). *Welcoming children from sexual minority families into our schools.* Bloomington, IN: Phi Delta Kappa Educational Foundation.

Mandara, J. (2006). The impact of family functioning on African American males' academic achievement: A review and clarification of the empirical literature. *Teachers College Record, 108(2),* 206–223.

Miller, B., Fan, F., Christensen, C., Grotevant, H., & van Dulmen, M. (2000). Comparisons of adopted and nonadopted adolescents in a large, nationally representative sample. *Child Development, 71,* 1458–1473.

Nichols, M. P., Schwartz, R. C. (2001). *The essentials of family therapy.* Boston: Allyn & Bacon.

Nichols, W. C., & Everett, C. A. (1986). *Systemic family therapy: An integrative approach.* New York: Guilford Press.

Pantin, H., Coatsworth, J. D., Feaster, D. J., Newman, F. L., Briones, E., Prado, G., Schwartz, S. J., & Szapocznik, J. (2003). Familias unidas: The efficacy of an intervention to promote parental investment in Hispanic immigrant families. *Prevention Science, 4,* 189–201.

Patterson, J. M. (2002). Understanding family resilience. *Journal of Clinical Psychology, 58(3),* 233–246.

Pittman, F. S. (1987). *Turning points: Treating families in transition and crisis.* New York: W. W. Norton & Company.

Prevatt, F. F. (2003). The contribution of parenting practices in a risk and resiliency model of children's adjustment. *British Journal of Developmental Psychology, 21,* 469–480.

Ray, V., & Gregory, R. (2001). School experiences of the children of lesbian and gay parents. *Family Matters, 59,* 28–34.

Senge, P., Cambron-McCabe, N., Lucas, T., Smith, B., Dutton, J., & Kleiner, A. (2000). *Schools that learn* (35–58, 71, 77–97). New York: Doubleday/Currency.

Sharf, R. S. (2000). *Theories of psychotherapy and counseling: Concepts and cases* (2nd ed.). Belmont, CA: Brooks/Cole.

Smith, A. B., & Dannison, L. L. (2007). Selected bibliography on custodial grandparent families. Western Michigan University. Retrieved from www.wmich.edu/grs/reference.htm on October 15, 2007.

Tasker, F. (1999). Children in lesbian-led families: A review. *Clinical Child Psychology and Psychiatry, 4(2),* 153–166.

U.S. Department of Commerce, Census Bureau. (2006). American families and living arrangements. Retrieved from www.census.gov/population/www/socdemo/hh-fam/cps2006.html on April 16, 2007.

U.S. Department of Labor. (2006). *Family roles are changing in the U.S.* Bureau of International Information, U.S. Department of State. Retrieved from www.usinfo.state.gov on April 16, 2007.

Walsh, F. (1998). *Strengthening family resilience.* New York: Guilford Press.

Chapter 6

Addams, J. (1998). *Twenty years at Hull-House.* New York: Penguin Books.

Atkinson, D. R. (2004). *Counseling American minorities* (3rd ed.). New York: McGraw-Hill.

Baca Zinn, M., & Wells, B. (2000). Diversity within Latino families: New lessons for family social science. In D. H. Demo, K. R. Allen, & M. A. Fine (Eds.), *Handbook of family diversity* (pp. 252–273). New York: Oxford University Press.

Bailey, D. B., Simeonsson, R. J., Winton, P. J., Huntington, G. S., Comfort, N., & Isbell, P. (1986). Family-focused intervention: A functional model for planning, implementing and evaluating individual family services in early intervention. *Journal of the Division for Early Childhood, 10*, 156–171.

Banks, J. A. (1994). *Multiethnic education: Theory and practice* (3rd ed.). Boston: Allyn & Bacon.

Barbour, C., Barbour, N. H., & Scully, P. A. (2005). *Families, schools, and communities: Building partnerships for educating children.* Upper Saddle River, NJ: Pearson.

Brown, C., & Jones, L. (2004). The gender structure of the nursing hierarchy: The role of human capital. *Gender, Work and Organization, 11*, 1–25.

Casas, J. M., & Pytluk, S. D. (1995). Hispanic identity development: Implications for research and practice. In J. G. Ponterotto, J. M. Casas, L. A. Suzuki, & C. M. Alexander (Eds.), *Handbook of multicultural counseling* (155–180). Thousand Oaks, CA: Sage.

Casanova, U. (1996). Parental involvement: A call for prudence. *Educational Researcher, 25*, 30–32.

Collignon, F. F., Men, M., & Tan, S. (2001). Finding ways in: Community-based perspectives on Southeast Asian family involvement with schools in a New England state. *Journal of Education for Students Placed at Risk, 6*, 27–44.

Cowdery, J., Ingling, L., Morrow, L., Wilson, V. (2007). *Building on student diversity: Profiles and activities* (178–180). Thousand Oaks, CA: Sage

Dalton, S. S. (1998). *Pedagogy matters: Standards for effective teaching practice.* Santa Cruz, CA: University of California; Center for Research on Education, Diversity & Excellence (CREDE).

Davis, N. T., & Blanchard, M. R. (2004). Collaborative teams in a university statistics course: A case study of how differing value structures inhibit change. *Social Science & Mathematics, 104*, 279–287.

Delgado-Gaitan, C. (1992). School matters in the Mexican-American home: Socializing children to education. *American Educational Research Journal, 29*, 495–513.

Delgado-Gaitan, C. (1994). Socializing young children in Mexican-American families: An intergenerational perspective. In P. M. Greenfield & R. R. Cocking (Eds.), *Cross-cultural roots of minority child development* (pp. 55–86). Hillsdale, NJ: Erlbaum.

Derman-Sparks, L., & Brunson-Phillips, C. (1997). *Teaching/learning anti-racism: A developmental approach.* New York: Teachers College Press.

Derman-Sparks, L., Ramsey, P., Edwards, J., & Brunson-Day, C. (2006). *What if all the kids are white? Anti-bias multicultural education young children and families.* New York: Teachers College Press.

Developmental Studies Center. (1995). *Homeside activities.* Oakland, CA: Developmental Studies Center.

Dryfoos, J. G. (1994). *Full-service schools: A revolution in health and social services for children.* San Francisco: Jossey-Bass.

Dunlap, C. Z., & Alva, S. A. (1999). Redefining school and community relations: Teachers' perceptions of parents as participants and stakeholders. *Teacher Education Quarterly, 26*, 123–133.

Dunst, C. J. (1985). Revisiting, rethinking early intervention. *Analysis and Intervention in Developmental Disabilities, 5*, 165–201.

Evans, W. P., & Carter, M. J. (1997). Urban school-based family counseling: Role definition, practice applications, and training implications. *Journal of Counseling & Development, 75*, 366–374.

Fawcett, L. M., & Garton, A. F. (2005). The effect of peer collaboration on children's problem-solving ability. *British Journal of Educational Psychology, 75*, 157–169.

Fernandez, C. (2002). Learning from Japanese approaches to professional development: The case of lesson study. *Journal of Teacher Education, 53*, 393–405.

Furstenberg, F., Cook, T. D., Eccles, J., Elder, G. H., & Sameroff, A. J. (1999). *Managing to make it: Urban families and adolescent success.* Chicago: University of Chicago Press.

Garrahy, D. A. (2001). Three third grade teachers' gender-related beliefs and behavior. *Elementary School Journal, 102*, 81–94.

Gay, G. (2000). *Culturally responsive teaching: Theory, research and practice.* New York: Teachers College Press.

Gollnick, D. M., & Chinn, P. C. (2002). *Multicultural education in a pluralistic society* (6th ed.). Upper Saddle River, NJ: Merrill/Prentice Hall.

Goodnow, J. J., & Collins, W. A. (1990). *Development according to parents: The nature, sources, and consequences of parents' ideas.* Hillsdale, NJ: Erlbaum.

Goodwin, A. L. (2000). Teachers as (multi)cultural agents in schools. In R. Carter (Ed.), *Addressing cultural issues in organizations: Beyond the corporate context* (pp. 104–114). Thousand Oaks, CA: Sage.

Gonzalez, N. E. (1995). The funds of knowledge for teaching project. *Practicing Anthropology, 17,* 3–6.

Gordon, B. (1997). Curriculum policy and African American cultural knowledge: Challenges and possibilities for the year 2000 and beyond. *Educational Policy, 11,* 227–242.

Hale-Benson, J. E. (1986). *Black children: Their roots, culture, and learning styles* (Rev. ed.). Baltimore: Johns Hopkins University Press.

Harris, M. M., & Hoover, J. H. (2003). Overcoming adversity through community schools. *Reclaiming Children & Youth, 11,* 206–211.

Helms, J. E., & Cook, D. A. (1999). *Using race and culture in counseling and psychotherapy: Theory and process.* Boston: Allyn & Bacon.

Hoover-Dempsey, K., Bassler, O., & Burow, R. (1995). Parents' reported involvement in students' homework: Strategies and practices. *Elementary School Journal, 95,* 435–450.

Ivey, A. E. (2000). *Developmental therapy.* San Francisco: Jossey-Bass. (Original work published in 1986.)

Joe, J. R., & Malach, R. S. (1998). Families with Native American roots. In E. W. Lynch & M. J. Hanson (Eds.), *Developing cross-cultural competence: A guide for working with young children and their families* (pp. 127–164). Baltimore: Paul H. Brookes Publishing.

Kemmis, S., & McTaggart, R. (2000). Participatory action research. In N. K. Denzin & Y. S. Lincoln (Eds.), *Handbook of qualitative research* (2nd ed.) (pp. 567–605). Thousand Oaks, CA: Sage.

Lamont, M., & Fournier, M. (1992). *Cultivating differences: Symbolic boundaries and the making of inequality.* Chicago: University of Chicago Press.

Lamont, M., & Small, M. L. (2006). *How culture matters for poverty: Thickening our understanding.* National Poverty Center Working Paper Series #06–10. Retrieved August 30, 2006 from www.npc.umich.edu/publications/working_papers/.

Lawson, H. L. (1999). Two frameworks for analyzing relationships among school communities, teacher education, and interprofessional education and training programs. *Teacher Education Quarterly, 26,* 5–67.

LeBaron, Michelle. (2003). *Bridging cultural conflicts: A new approach for a changing world.* San Francisco: Jossey Bass.

Lewis, C., & Tsuchida, I. (1988). A lesson is like a swiftly flowing river: How research lessons and the improvement of Japanese education. *American Educator, 22,* 12–17, 50–52.

McMahon, T., Ward, N. L., Pruett, M. K., Davidson, L., & Griffith, E. H. (2000). Building full-service schools: Lessons learned in the development of interagency collaborations. *Journal of Educational & Psychological Consultation, 11,* 65–92.

Moll, L. C., & Gonzalez, N. (1994). Lessons from research with language minority children. *Journal of Reading Behavior, 26,* 439–456.

Murry, V. M., Kotchick, B., Wallace, S., Ketchen, G., Eddings, K., Heller, L., & Collier, I. (2004). Race, culture, and ethnicity: Implications for a community intervention. *Journal of Child and Family Studies, 13,* 81–99.

National Collaborative on Diversity in the Teaching Force. (2004). *A call to action: Assessment of diversity in America's teaching force.* Washington, DC: National Education Association.

Neal, L. I., McCray, A. D., Webb-Johnson, G., & Bridgest, S. T. (2003). The effects of African American movement styles on teachers' perceptions and reactions. *Journal of Special Education, 37,* 49–57.

Nieto, S. (1999). *The light in their eyes: Creating multicultural learning communities.* New York: Teachers College Press.

Nieto, S. (2004). *Affirming diversity: The sociopolitical context of education.* White Plains, NY: Longman.

Nobles, W. (1997). African American family life: An instrument of culture. In H. P. McAdoo (Ed.), *Black families* (3rd ed., 83–93). Thousand Oaks, CA: Sage.

Olatunji, C. A. (2000). Culturally and developmentally appropriate interventions for the alternative school. In V. A. Anfara & P. C. Kirby (Eds.), *Voices from the middle: Decrying what is, imploring what could be.* Dubuque, IA: Kendall/Hunt.

Olsen, G., & Fuller, M. L. (2003). *Home-school relations: Working successfully with parents and families* (2nd ed.). Boston: Allyn & Bacon.

Papp, L., Goeke-Morey, M., & Cummings, M. (2004). Mothers' and fathers' psychological symptoms and marital functioning: Examination of direct and interactive links with child adjustment. *Journal of Child and Family Studies, 13,* 469–482.

Payne, R. K. (1998). *A framework for understanding poverty.* Highlands, TX: RFT Publishing.

Perlstein, D. (1990). Teaching freedom: SNCC and the creation of the Mississippi freedom schools. *History of Education Quarterly, 30,* 297–324.

Phan, L. T., Rivera, E. T., & Roberts-Wilbur, J. (2005). Understanding Vietnamese refugee women's identity development from a sociopolitical and historical perspective. *Journal of Counseling and Development, 83,* 305–312.

Phillips, C. B. (1993). The movement of African-American children through sociocultural contexts. In B. Mallory & S. New (Eds.), *Diversity and developmentally appropriate practices* (pp. 137–165). New York: Teachers College Press.

Pittman, K., Irby, M., Yohalem, N., & Wilson-Ahlstrom, A. (2004). Blurring the lines for learning: The role of out-of-school programs as complements to formal learning. *New Directions for Youth Development, 2004,* 19–41.

Prevatt, F. (2003). The contribution of parenting practices in a risk and resiliency model of children's adjustment. *British Journal of Developmental Psychology, 21,* 469–480.

Ramirez-Smith, C. (1995). Stopping the cycle of failure: The Comer model. *Educational Leadership, 52,* 14–19.

Roysircar, G. (2004). Child survivor of war: A case study. *Journal of Multicultural Counseling and Development, 32,* 168–180.

Roysircar-Sodowsky, G., & Maestas, M. V. (2000). Acculturation, ethnic identity, and acculturative stress: Evidence and measurement. In R. H. Dana (Ed.), *Handbook of cross-cultural and multicultural assessment* (pp. 131–172). Mahwah, NJ: Erlbaum.

Santiago-Rivera, A. L., Arredondo, P., & Gallardo-Cooper, M. (2002). *Counseling Latinos and la familia: A practical guide.* Thousand Oaks, CA: Sage.

Schinke, S. P., Cole, K. C., & Poulin, S. R. (2000). Enhancing the education achievement of at-risk youth. *Prevention Science 1,* 51–60.

Shindler, J. V. (2004). "Greater than the sum of the parts?" Examining the soundness of collaborative exams in teacher education courses. *Innovative Higher Education, 28,* 273–283.

Sirin, S. R., & Rogers-Sirin, L. (2004). Exploring school engagement of middle-class African American adolescents. *Youth & Society, 35,* 323–340.

Skinner, C. H., Pappas, D. N., Davis, K. A. (2005). Enhancing academic engagement: Providing opportunities for responding and influencing students to choose to respond. *Psychology in the Schools, 42,* 389–403.

Slentz, K. L., & Bricker, D. B. (1992). Family-guided assessment for IFSP development: Jumping off the family assessment bandwagon. *Journal of Early Intervention, 16,* 11–19.

Stevahn, L., Johnson, D. W., Johnson, R. T., Oberle, K., & Wahl, L. (2000). The effects of conflict resolution training integrated into a kindergarten curriculum. *Child Development, 71,* 772–784.

Sudarkasa, N. (1997). African American families and family values. In H. P. McAdoo (Ed.), *Black families* (3rd ed., pp. 9–40). Thousand Oaks, CA: Sage.

Sue, D. W., & Sue, D. (2003). *Counseling the culturally diverse: Theory and practice* (4th ed.). New York: John Wiley & Sons.

Taylor, B. M., Pearson, P. D., Peterson, D. S., & Rodriguez, M. C. (2003). Reading growth in high-poverty classrooms: The influence of teacher practices that encourage cognitive engagement in literacy learning. *Elementary School Journal, 104,* 3–28.

Trumbull, E., Rothstein-Fisch, C., Greenfield, P. M., & Quiroz, B. (2001). *Bridging cultures between home and school: A guide for teachers.* Mahwah, NJ: Erlbaum.

Turnbull, R., Turnbull, A., Shank, M., & Smith, S. (2004). *Exceptional lives: Special education in today's schools* (4th ed.). Upper Saddle River, NJ: Merrill/Prentice Hall.

Tsaparlis, G., & Gorezi, M. (2005). A modification of a conventional expository physical chemistry laboratory to accommodate an inquiry/project-based component: Method and students' evaluation. *Canadian Journal of Science, Mathematics, and Technology Education, 5,* 111–131.

Tutwiler, S. W. (2005). *Teachers as collaborative partners: Working with diverse families and communities.* Mahwah, NJ: Erlbaum.

Unger, D., Jones, C., Park, E., & Tressell, P. (2001). Promoting involvement between low-income single caregivers and urban early intervention programs. *Topics in Early Childhood Special Education, 21,* 197–212.

Vermette, P., Harper, L., & DiMillo, S. (2004). Cooperative and collaborative learning with 4–8 year olds: How does research support teachers' practice? *Journal of Institutional Psychology, 31,* 130–134.

Webre, E. C. (2005). Enhancing reading success with collaboratively created progress charts. *Intervention in School and Clinic, 40,* 291–295.

Weinstein, C., Curran, M., & Tomlinson-Clarke, S. (2003). Culturally responsive classroom management: Awareness into action. *Theory Into Practice, 42,* 269–276.

West-Olatunji, C. A., Frazier, K. N., Guy, T., Smith, A., Williams-Clay, L., & Breaux, W. (2007). The use of the racial/cultural identity development model (R/CID) to understand a Vietnamese American: A research case study. *Journal of Multicultural Counseling and Development, 34,* 77–88t.

Zhou, M., & Bankston, C. L. (1998). *Growing up American: How Vietnamese children adapt to life in the United States.* New York: Russell Sage Foundation.

Chapter 7

Achs, N. (1992). Exurbia. *American City & County, 107(7),* 64–72.

Berg, A. C., Melaville, A., & Blank, M. J. (2006). *Community and family engagement: Principals share what works.* Washington, DC: Coalition for Community Schools, Institute for Educational Leadership.

Blank, S. (2001). *Good works: Highlights of a study on the Center for Family Life.* Baltimore: Annie E. Casey Foundation.

Bloom, L. R. (2001). "I'm poor, I'm single, I'm a mom, and I deserve respect": Advocating in schools as/with mothers in poverty. *Educational Studies, 32(3),* 300–316.

Brooks-Gunn, J., Duncan, G., Klebanov, P. K., & Sealand, N. (1993). Do neighborhoods influence child and adolescent development? *American Journal of Sociology, 99(2),* 353–395.

Caspe, M., Traub, F., & Little, P. (2002). *Beyond the head count: Evaluating family involvement in out-of-school time.* (Issues and Opportunities in Out-of-School Time Evaluation Brief No. 4). Cambridge, MA: Harvard Family Research Project.

Caughy, M. O., & Franzini, L. (2005). Individual and neighborhood correlates of cultural differences in perceived effectiveness of parent disciplinary tactics. *Parenting: Science and Practice, 5(2),* 119–151.

Chase-Landale, P. L., Gordon, R., Brooks-Gunn, J., & Klebanov, P. K. (1997). Neighborhood and family influences on the intellectual and behavioral competence of preschool and early school-age children. In J. Brooks-Gunn, G. Duncan, and J. L. Aber (Eds.), *Neighborhood poverty: Context and consequences for children* (Vol. 1, 79–118). New York: Russell Sage Foundation.

Comer, J. (1998). *Waiting for a miracle: Why schools can't solve our problems and how we can.* New York: Plume.

Comer, J., & Haynes, N. M. (1991). Parent involvement in schools: An ecological approach. *Elementary School Journal, 91(3),* 271–277.

Cook, T. D., Herman, M. R, Phillips, M., & Settersten, R. A., Jr. (2002). Some ways in which neighborhoods, nuclear families, friendship groups and schools jointly affect changes in early adolescent development. *Child Development, 73(4),* 1283–1309.

Cooper, C. R., Chavira, G., Mikolyski, D., Mena, D., & Dominguez, E. (2004). Bridging multiple worlds: Building pathways from childhood to college. Retrieved July 28, 2007 from Harvard University, Harvard Family Research Project, Family Involvement Network of Educators, www.gse.harvard.edu/hfrp/projects/fine/ resources/research/minority.html.

Delgado-Gaitan, C. (1990). *Literacy for empowerment: The role of parents in children's education.* New York: Falmer.

Dryfoos, J., & Maguire, S. (2002). *Inside full-service community schools.* Thousand Oaks, CA: Corwin Press.

Edelman, M. W. (1992). *The measure of our success: A letter to my children and yours.* Boston: Beacon Press.

Epstein, J. (2001). *School, family and community partnerships: Preparing educators and improving schools.* Oxford, UK: Westview Press.

Fetto, J. (1999). Wide open spaces. *American Demographics, 21(10),* 44, 45.

Gephart, M. (1997). Neighborhoods and communities as contexts for development. In J. Brooks-Gunn, G. Duncan, and J. L. Aber (Eds.), *Neighborhood poverty: Context and consequences for children* (Vol. 1, 1–43). New York: Russell Sage Foundation.

Gold, E., Simon, E., & Brown, C. (2002a). *Strong neighborhoods, strong schools: Successful community organizing for school reform.* Chicago: Cross City Campaign for Urban School Reform.

Gold, E., Simon, E., & Brown, C. (2002b). *Strong neighborhoods, strong schools: The indicators project on education organizing.* Chicago: Cross City Campaign for Urban School Reform.

Gonzales, P. B. (1993). Historical poverty, restructuring effects, and integrative ties: Mexican American neighborhoods in a peripheral Sunbelt economy. In J. Moore & R. Pinderhughes (Eds.), *In the barrios: Latinos and the underclass debate* (pp. 149–171). New York: Russell Sage Foundation.

Gorman-Smith, D., Henry, D. B., & Tolan, P. H. (2004). Exposure to community violence and violence perpetuation: The protective effects of family functioning. *Journal of Clinical Child and Adolescent Psychology, 33(3),* 439–449.

Gutman, L. M., McLoyd, V. C., & Tokoyawa, T. (2005). Financial strain, neighborhood stress, parenting behaviors and adolescent adjustment in urban African American families. *Journal of Research on Adolescence, 15(4),* 425–449.

Halpern, R. (1995). *Rebuilding the inner city: A history of neighborhood initiatives to address poverty in the United States.* New York: Columbia University Press.

Halpern, R. (1999). *Fragile families, fragile solutions: A history of supportive services for families in poverty.* New York: Columbia University Press.

Halpern, R. (2002). A different kind of child development institution: The history of after-school programs for low-income children. *Teachers College Record, 104(2),* 178–211.

Heimerl, M. (2007). Somewhere special, New Mexico. *Sun Monthly, 282(1),* 26–35.

Jarrett, R. L. (1992). A family case study: An examination of the underclass debate. In J. Gilgun, G. Handel, & K. Daly (Eds.), *Qualitative methods in family research* (pp. 172–197). Newbury Park, CA: Sage.

Jarrett, R. L. (1994). Living poor: Family life among single-parent African-American women. *Social Problems, 41(1),* 30–49.

Jarrett, R. L. (1999). Successful parenting in high-risk neighborhoods. *Future of Children, 9(2),* 45–50.

Jarrett, R. L. (2000). Neighborhood effects models: A view from the neighborhood. *Research in Community Sociology, 10,* 305–323.

Jarrett, R. L., & Jefferson, S. R. (2003). "A good mother got to fight for her kids": Maternal management strategies in an urban housing project. *Journal of Children & Poverty, 9(1),* 21–39.

Johnson, V. R. (1993). *Parent/family centers in schools: Expanding outreach and promoting collaboration.* Baltimore: Center on Families, Communities, Schools and Children's Learning John Hopkins University.

Johnson, V. R. (1994). *Parent centers in urban schools: Four case studies* (Center Report 23). Baltimore: Center on Families, Communities, Schools and Children's Learning John Hopkins University.

Keith, N. Z. (1996). Can urban school reform and community development be joined? *Education and Urban Society, 28(2),* 237, 238, 243, 251.

Kretzmann, J. P., & McKnight, J. L. (1993). *Building communities from the inside out: A path toward finding and mobilizing community assets.* Evanston, IL: Institute for Policy Research.

Lipman, P. (2002). Making the global city, making inequality: The political, economic and cultural politics of Chicago school policy. *American Educational Research Journal, 39(2),* 379–419.

Livezey, L. (2001). Communities and enclaves: Where Jews, Christians, Hindus and Muslims share the neighborhoods. *Cross Currents, 51(1),* 45–70.

Lopez, M. E. (2003). *Transforming schools through community organizing: A research review.* Cambridge, MA: Harvard Family Research Project. Retrieved August 4, 2007, from *www.gse.harvard.edu/hfrp/projects/fine/resources/research/lopez.html.*

Marshall, N. L., Noonan, A. E., McCartney, K., Marx, F., & Keefe, N. (2001). It takes an urban village: Parenting networks in urban families. *Journal of Family Issues, 22(2),* 163–182.

Matthews, D. (1996). *Is there a public for public schools?* Dayton, OH: Kettering Foundation.

McCaleb, S. P. (1994). *Building communities of learners: A collaboration among teachers, students, families, and community.* New York: St. Martin's Press.

Moynihan, D. P. (1965). *The Negro family: The case for national action.* Washington, DC: Office of Policy Planning and Research, U.S. Department of Labor.

National Coalition of Advocates for Students. (1997). *Unfamiliar partners: Asian parents and U.S. public schools.* Boston: Author.

Neito, S. (1996). *Affirming diversity: The sociopolitical context of multicultural education* (2nd ed.). New York: Longman.

Nevarez-La Torre, A. (1997). Influencing Latino education: Church-based community programs. *Education and Urban Society, 30(1),* 58–74.

O'Neil, R., Parke, R. D., & McDowell, J. J. (2001). Objective and subjective features of children's neighborhoods: Relations to parental regulatory strategies and children's social competence. *Applied Developmental Psychology, 2(2),* 135–155.

Pager, D. (2003). The mark of a criminal record. *American Journal of Sociology, 108(5),* 937–976.

Purdy, J. (1999). The new culture of rural America. *The American Prospect, 11(3),* 26–31.

Putnam, R. (2000). *Bowling alone: The collapse and revival of American community.* New York: Simon & Schuster.

Ran-Kim, J., Chan, W., Settersten, R. A., & Teitler, J. O. (1999). How do neighborhoods matter? In F. F. Furstenberg, T. D. Cook, J. Eccles, G. H. Elder, & A. Sameroff (Eds.), *Managing to make it: Urban families and adolescent success* (pp. 145–170). Chicago: The University of Chicago Press.

Schorr, L. (1997). *Common purpose: Strengthening families and neighborhoods to rebuild America.* New York: Anchor.

Schutz, A. (2006). Home is a prison in the global city: The tragic failure of school-based community engagement strategies. *Review of Educational Research, 76(4),* 691–743.

Shirley, D. (1997). *Community organizing for urban school reform.* Austin, TX: University of Texas Press.

Turnbull, A., & Turnbull, R. (2005). *Families, professionals and exceptionality: A special partnership* (4th ed.). Upper Saddle River, NJ: Pearson/Merrill-Prentice Hall.

Tutwiler, S. (2005). *Teachers as collaborative partners: Working with diverse families and communities.* Mahwah, NJ: Erlbaum.

U.S. Census Bureau. (2002). *Census 2000 special report: Demographic trends in the 20th century.* Washington, DC: U.S. Department of Commerce, U.S. Government Printing Office.

Weiss, H., Mayer, E., Kreider, H., Vaughan, M., Dearing, E., Hencke, R., & Pinto, K. (2003). Making it work: Low-income mothers' involvement in their children's education. *American Educational Research Journal, 40(4),* 879–901.

Weiss, H., Kreider, H., Lopez, M. E., Chatman, C. M. (2005). *Preparing educators to involve families: From theory to practice.* Thousand Oaks, CA: Sage.

Wilson, W. J. (1997). *When work disappears: The world of the new urban poor.* New York: Vintage.

Chapter 8

Beghetto, R. A. (2001). Virtually in the middle: Alternative avenues for parental involvement in middle-level schools. *Clearing House, 75,* 21–25.

Christenson, S., & Hirsch, J. (1998). Facilitating partnerships and conflict resolution between families and schools. In K. C. Stoiber & T. R. Kratchowill (Eds.), *Handbook of group intervention for children and families* (pp. 307–344). Boston: Allyn & Bacon.

Colbert, R. D. (1996). The counselor's role in advancing school and family partnerships. *The School Counselor, 44,* 100–104.

Dodd, A. (2000). Making schools safe for all students: Why schools need to teach more than the 3 R's. *NASSP Bulletin, 84,* 25–31.

Elias, M., Bruene-Butler, L., Blum, L., & Schuyler, T. (1997). How to launch a social and emotional learning program. *Educational Leadership, 54,* 15–20.

Epstein, J., & Sheldon, S. (2002). Present and accounted for: Improving student attendance through family and community involvement. *Journal of Educational Research, 95,* 308–318.

Erford, B. T. (2007). Consultation, collaboration, and parent involvement. In B. Erford (Ed.), *Transforming the school counseling profession* (2nd ed., pp. 211–235). Upper Saddle River, NJ: Pearson Education.

Glesne, C. (1999). *Becoming qualitative researchers* (2nd ed.). New York: Longman.

Hundt, T. A. (2002). Videotaping young children in the classroom: Parents as partners. *Teaching Exceptional Children, 34(3),* 38–43.

Ivey, A. E., & Ivey, M. B. (2006). *Intentional interviewing and counseling: Facilitating client development in a multicultural society* (6th ed.). Pacific Grove, CA: Brooks/Cole.

Kyle, D., McIntyre, E., Miller, K., & Moore, G. (2002). *Reaching out: A K-8 resource for connecting families and schools.* Thousand Oaks, CA: Corwin Press.

Lawrence-Lightfoot, S. (2003, fall). *Questions and answers.* FINE Forum e-Newsletter. *Harvard Family Research Project.* Retrieved September 28, 2007 from www.gse.harvard.edu/hfrp/projects/fine/fineforum/forum7/questions.html.

Madden, M., & Rainie, L. (2003). *The changing picture of who is on line and what they do.* Pew Internet and American Life Project. Retrieved June 16, 2007 from www.pewinternet.org/report_display.asp?r-106.

McCaleb, S. P. (1994). *Building communities of learners: A collaboration among teachers, students, families and community.* New York: St. Martin's Press.

Perry, N. (2007). Reaching out: Involving parents and community members in the school counseling program. In J. Wittmer & M. A. Clark (Eds.), *Managing your school counseling program: K-12 developmental strategies* (3rd ed.). Minneapolis: Educational Media Corporation.

Roeser, R. W., Midgley, C., & Urdan, T. C. (1996). Perceptions of the school psychological environment and early adolescents' psychological and behavioral functioning in school: The mediating role of goals and belonging. *Journal of Educational Psychology, 88,* 408–422.

Stone, C., & Dahir, C. (2006). *The transformed school counselor.* Boston & New York: Houghton Mifflin.

Swap, S. W. (1993). *Developing home–school partnerships: From concept to practice.* New York: Teachers College Press.

Weiss, H., Caspe, M., & Lopez, M. E. (2006, spring). Family involvement in early childhood education. *Harvard Family Research Project.* Retrieved September 28, 2007 from www.gse.harvard.edu/hfrp/projects/fine/resources/ research/earlychildhood.html.

Weiss, H., & Edwards, M. (1992). The family–school collaboration project: Systemic interventions for school improvement. In S. Christenson & J. Conoley (Eds.), *Home–school collaboration: Enhancing children's academic and social competence* (pp. 215–243). Silver Spring, MD: National Association of School Psychologists.

Wittmer, J., & Clark, M. A. (2002a). *Teaching children to respect and care for others.* Minneapolis: Educational Media Corporation.

Wittmer, J., & Clark, M. A. (2002b). *Teaching children to respect and care for others. Instructor's guide.* Minneapolis: Educational Media Corporation.

Zins, J. E., Bloodworth, M. R., Weissberg, R. P., & Walberg, H. J. (2004). The scientific base linking social and emotional learning to school success. In J. Zins, R. Weissberg, M. Wang, & H. J. Walberg (Eds.), *Building academic success on social and emotional learning: What does the research say?* (1–22). New York: Teacher's College, Columbia University.

Chapter 9

Amatea, E. (2007) Handout from Workshop on Family and Community Involvement in Education. Gainesville, FL: University of Florida.

Au, K., & Jordan, C. (1981). Teaching reading to Hawaiian children: Finding a culturally appropriate solution. In H. Trueba, G. Guthrie, & K. Au (Eds.), *Culture in the bilingual classroom: Studies in classroom ethnographies* (139–152). Rowley, MA: Newbury House.

Auerbach, E. (1997). Family literacy. In V. Edwards & D. Corson (Eds.), *Encyclopedia of Language and Education* (Vol. 2, 153–161). Boston: Kluwer Academic Publishers.

Auerbach, E. (2001). Toward a sociocultural approach to family literacy. In S. W. Beck & L. N. Oláh (Eds.), *Perspectives on language and literacy: Beyond the here and now* (pp. 381–397). Cambridge, MA: Harvard Educational Review Reprint Series No. 35.

Ayers, M., Fonseca, J. D., Andrade, R., Civil, M. (2001). Creating learning communities: The "build your dream house" unit. In E. McIntyre, A. Rosebery & N. González (Eds.), *Classroom diversity: Connecting curriculum to students' lives.* Portsmouth, NH: Heinemann.

Barrera, R. M. (2005). Dispelling the myth. In A. Lopez (Ed.), *Latino early literacy development: Strategies for lifelong learning and success.* Washington, DC: National Council of La Raza (pp. 5–16). Retrieved September 1, 2007 from www.nclr.org/content/publications/download/34207.

Bennett, C. (2003). *Comprehensive multicultural education: Theory and practice* (5th ed.). Boston: Allyn & Bacon.

Center for Research on Education, Diversity, and Excellence (CREDE). (2006). Contextualization. Retrieved October 7, 2007 from http://crede.berkeley.edu/standards/3cont.shtml.

Coady, M. (2001). *Policy and practice in bilingual education: Gaelscoileanna in the Republic of Ireland.* Unpublished doctoral dissertation. University of Colorado, Boulder.

Coady, M. (2008). "Solamente libros importantes": Literacy practices and ideologies of migrant farm-working families in north central Florida. In G. Li (Ed.), *Multicultural Families, Home Literacies and Mainstream Schooling.* Albany, NY: SUNY Press.

Coady, M., & Escamilla, K. (2005). Audible voices, visible tongues: Exploring social realities in Spanish-speaking students' writing. *Language Arts 82,* 462–471.

Cummins, J. (2001). *Negotiating identities: Education for empowerment in a diverse society* (2nd ed.). Los Angeles: California Association for Bilingual Education.

Cummins, J., Cohen, S., Leoni, L., Bajwa, M., Hanif, S., Khalid, K., & Shahar, T. (2006). A language for learning: Home languages in the multilingual classroom. *Contact, 32,* 52–71.

Freire, P. (1998). Pedagogy of the oppressed. In A. M. Araújo Freire & D. Macedo (Eds.), *The Paulo Freire reader.* New York: Continuum.

Geertz, C. (1973). *The Interpretation of cultures.* New York: Basic Books.

González, N., & Moll, L. (1995). Funds of knowledge for teaching in Latino households. *Urban Education, 29,* 443–470.

Gudykunst, W. B., & Kim, Y. Y. (2003). *Communicating with strangers: An approach to intercultural communication.* New York: McGraw-Hill.

Heath, S. B. (1983). *Ways with words: Language, life, and work in communities and classrooms.* Cambridge, MA: Cambridge University Press.

Hoover-Dempsey, K., Battiato, A., Walker, J., Reed, R., DeJong, M., & Jones, K. (2001). Parental involvement in homework. *Educational Psychologist 36,* 195–209.

Krashen, S., & McField, G. (2005). What works? Reviewing the latest evidence on bilingual education. *Language Learner 1,* 7–10.

McCaleb, S. (1994). *Building communities of learners: A collaboration among teachers, students, families, and community.* New York: St. Martin's Press.

McIntyre, E., Rosebery, A., & González, N. (2001). *Classroom diversity: Connecting curriculum to students' lives.* Portsmouth, NH: Heinemann.

Moll, L. C., Amanti, C., Neff, D., & González, N. (1992). Funds of knowledge for teaching: Using a qualitative approach to connect homes and classrooms. *Theory Into Practice, 31,* 132–141.

Moll, L., & González, N. (1993). Lessons from research with language minority children. *Journal of Reading Behavior, 26,* 439–456.

New London Group. (1996). A pedagogy of multiliteracies: Designing social futures. *Harvard Educational Review, 66,* 60–92.

Nieto, S. (2004). *Affirming diversity: The sociopolitical context of multicultural education* (4th ed.). Boston: Allyn & Bacon.

Pappamihiel, E. (2004). The legislation of migrancy: Migrant education in our courts and government. In C. Salinas & M. Fránquiz (Eds.), *Scholars in the field: The challenges of migrant education.* Charleston, W. VA: ERIC Clearinghouse on Rural Education and Small Schools.

Riley, N. (2002). *Florida's migrant workers.* Gainesville, FL: University of Florida Press.

Shockley, B., Michalove, B., & Allen, J. (1995). *Engaging families, connecting home and school literacy communities.* Portsmouth, NH: Heinemann.

Taylor, D. (1983). *Family literacy: Young children learning to read and write.* Portsmouth, NH: Heinemann.

Tharp, R. G., Estrada, P., Dalton, S., & Yamauchi, L. (2000). *Teaching transformed: Achieving excellence, fairness, inclusion and harmony.* Boulder, CO: Westview Press.

Villenas, S. (2002). Reinventing *educación* in new Latino communities: Pedagogies of change and continuity in North Carolina. In S. Wortham, E. G. Murillo Jr., & E. T. Hamann (Eds.), *Education in the new Latino diaspora* (pp. 17–35). Westport, CT: Ablex.

Chapter 10

Atwell, N. (1998). *In the middle* (2nd ed.). Portsmouth, NH: Heinemann.

Austin, T. (1994). *Changing the view: Student-led conferences.* Portsmouth, NH: Heinemann.

Bailey, J. M., & Guskey, T. R. (2001). *Implementing student-led conferences.* Thousand Oaks, CA: Corwin Press.

Benson, B., & Barnett, S. (1999). *Student-led conferencing using showcase portfolios.* Thousand Oaks, CA: Corwin Press.

Costa, A., & Kallick, B. (2000). *Assessing and reporting on habits of mind.* Alexandria, VA: Association for Supervision and Curriculum Development.

Davies, A., Cameron, C., Politano, C., & Gregory, K. (1992). *Together is better: Collaborative assessment, evaluation and reporting.* Winnipeg, Canada: Peguis.

Gardner, H. (1983). *Frames of mind: The theory of multiple intelligences.* New York: Basic Books.

Gardner, H. (1999). *Intelligence reframed: Multiple intelligences for the 21st century.* New York: Basic Books.

Graves, D., & Sunstein, B. (1992). *Portfolio portraits.* Portsmouth, NH: Heinemann.

Herbert, E. (1998). Lessons learned about student portfolios. *Phi Delta Kappan, 79(8),* 583–585.

Little, A. W., & Allan, J. (1989). Student-led parent–teacher conferences. *Elementary School Guidance and Counseling, 23(3),* 210–218.

Picciotto, L. (1996). *Student-led parent conferences.* New York: Scholastic.

Porter, C., & Cleland, J. (1995). *The portfolio as a learning strategy.* Portsmouth, NH: Heinemann.

Quiroz, B., Greenfield, P., & Altchech, M. (1999). Bridging cultures with a parent–teacher conference. *Educational Leadership, 56,* 68–70.

Tomm, K. (1987). Interventive interviewing: Reflexive questioning as a means to promote self-healing. *Family Process, 26,* 167–183.

Chapter 11

Amatea, E., Daniels, H. D., Bringman, N., & Vandiver, F. (2004). Strengthening counselor–teacher–family connections: The family–school collaborative consultation project. *Professional School Counseling, 8,* 47–55.

Barth, R. S. (1990). *Improving schools from within.* San Francisco: Jossey-Bass.

Christenson, S., & Hirsch, J. (1998). Facilitating partnerships and conflict resolution between families and schools. In K. C. Stoiber & T. R. Kratchowill (Eds.), *Handbook of group intervention for children and families* (307–344). Boston: Allyn & Bacon.

Dupraw, M., & Axner, M. (1997). *Working on common cross-cultural communication challenges.* Retrieved July 10, 2007 from www.wwcd.org/action/ampu/crosscult.html.

Finders, M., & Lewis, C. (1994). Why some parents don't come to school. *Educational Leadership, 51(8),* 50–54.

Fisher, R., & Ury, W. (1991). *Getting to yes: Negotiating agreement without giving in.* New York: Penguin Books.

Gandara, P. C. (1995). *Over the ivy walls: The educational mobility of low-income Chicanos.* Albany, New York: State University of New York Press.

Lawrence-Lightfoot, S. (2003). *The essential conversation: What parents and teachers can learn from each other.* New York: Ballantine Books.

O'Hanlon, B. (1999). *Do one thing different: Ten simple ways to change your life.* New York: Harper.

Okagaki, L., & Sternberg, R. J. (1993). Parental beliefs and children's school performance. *Child Development, 64,* 36–56.

Quiroz, B., Greenfield, P. M., & Altchech, M. (1999). Bridging cultures with a parent–teacher conference. *Educational Leadership, 56,* 68–70.

Silverstein, J., Springer, J., & Russo, N. (1992). Involving parents in the special education process. In S. Christenson & J. Conoley (Eds.), *Home–school collaboration: Enhancing children's academic and social competence* (pp. 215–243). Silver Spring, MD: National Association for School Psychologists.

Trumbull, E., Rothstein-Fisch, C., Greenfield, P. M., & Quiroz, B. (2001). *Bridging cultures between home and school: A guide for teachers.* Mahwah, NJ: Erlbaum.

Weiss, H., & Edwards, M. (1992). The family–school collaboration project: Systemic intervention for school improvement. In S. Christenson & J. Conoley (Eds.), *Home-school collaboration: Enhancing children's academic and social competence* (pp. 215–243). Silver Spring, MD: National Association for School Psychologists.

Winslade, J., & Monk, G. (1999). *Narrative counseling in schools: Powerful and brief.* Thousand Oaks, CA: Corwin Press.

Chapter 12

Bailey, D. B., Palsha, S. A., & Simeonsson, R. J. (1991). Professional skills, concerns, and perceived importance of work with families in early intervention. *Exceptional Children, 58,* 156–165.

Bailey, D. B., Buysse, V., Edmondson, R., & Smith, T. M. (1992). Creating family-centered services in early intervention: Perceptions of professionals in four states. *Exceptional Children, 58,* 298–310.

Bailey, D. B., McWilliam, R. A., & Winton, P. J. (1992). Building family-centered practices in early intervention: A team-based model for change. *Infants and Young Children, 5,* 73–82.

Bailey, D. B. (2001). Evaluating parent involvement and family support in early intervention and pre-school programs. *Journal of Early Intervention, 24,* 1–24.

Barrera, M. E. (1991). The transactional model of early home intervention: Application with developmentally delayed children and their families. In K. Marfo (Ed.), *Early intervention in transition: Current perspectives on programs for handicapped children* (pp. 109–146). New York: Praeger.

Bennett, T., Deluca, D., & Bruns, D. (1997). Putting inclusion into practice: Perceptions of teachers and parents. *Exceptional Children, 64,* 115–131.

Berry, J. O. (1995). Families and deinstitutionalization: An application of Bronfenbrenner's social ecology model. *Journal of Counseling and Development, 73,* 379–383.

Beverly, C. L., & Thomas, S. B. (1999). Family assessment and collaboration building: Conjoined processes. *International Journal of Disability, Development, and Education, 46,* 179–197.

Bjorck-Akesson, E., & Granlund, M. (1995). Family involvement in assessment and intervention: Perceptions of professionals and parents in Sweden. *Exceptional Children, 61,* 520–535.

Boone, H. A., & Crais, E. (1999). Strategies for achieving family-driven assessment and intervention planning. *Young Exceptional Children, 3,* 2–11.

Bronfenbrenner, U. (1979). *The ecology of human development.* Cambridge, MA: Harvard University Press.

Bronfenbrenner, U. (1997). Ecology of the family as a context for human development: Research perspectives. In J. L. Paul, M. Churton, H. Rosselli-Kostoryz, W. Morse, K. Marfo, C. Lavely, & D. Thomas (Eds.), *Foundations of special education: Basic knowledge informing research and practice in special education.* Pacific Grove, CA: Brooks/Cole.

Brotherson, M. J., Cook, C., Cuonconan-Lahr, R., & Wehmeyer, M. L. (1995). Policy supporting self-determination in the environments of children with disabilities. *Education and Training in Mental Retardation and Developmental Disabilities, 30,* 3–14.

Bruder, M. B. (2000). Family-centered early intervention: Clarifying our values for the new millennium. *Topics in Early Childhood Special Education, 20,* 105–115.

Cho, S., Singer, G., & Brenner, M. (2000). Adaptation and accommodation to young children with disabilities: A comparison of Korean and Korean American parents. *Topics in Early Childhood Special Education, 20,* 236–250.

Dinnebeil, L. A., Hale, L. M., & Rule, S. (1996). A qualitative analysis of parents' and service coordinators' descriptions of variables that influence collaborative relationships. *Topics in Early Childhood Special Education, 16,* 322–347.

Duchnowski, A., Dunlap, G., Berg, K., & Adiegbola, M. (1995). Rethinking the participation of families in the education of children: Clinical and policy issues. In J. Paul, D. Evans, & H. Rosselli (Eds.), *Restructuring special education* (pp. 105–118). New York: Harcourt Brace Jovanovich.

Dunst, C. (1985). Rethinking early intervention. *Analysis and Intervention in Developmental Disabilities, 5,* 165–201.

Dunst, C. J., Johanson, C., Trivette, C. M., & Hamby, D. (1991). Family-oriented early intervention policies and practices: Family-centered or not? *Exceptional Children, 58,* 115–126.

Dunst, C. J., Leet, H. E., & Trivette, C. M. (1988). Family resources, personal well-being, and early intervention. *Journal of Special Education, 22,* 108–116.

Dunst, C. J., & Trivette, C. M. (1988). An enablement and empowerment perspective of case management. *Topics in Early Childhood Special Education, 8,* 87–102.

Dunst, C. J., & Trivette, C. M. (1996). Empowerment, effective help-giving practices and family-centered care. *Pediatric Nursing, 22,* 334–337, 343.

Dunst, C. J., Trivette, C. M., Hamby, D., & Pollock, B. (1990). Family systems correlates of the behavior of young children with handicaps. *Journal of Early Intervention, 14,* 204–218.

Dunst, C. J. (2002). Family-centered practices: Birth through high school. *Journal of Special Education, 36(3),* 139–147.

Durlak, C., Rose, E., & Bursuck, W. (1994). Preparing high school students with learning disabilities for the transition to post-secondary education: Teaching the skills of self-determination. *Journal of Learning Disabilities, 27,* 51–59.

Education for All Handicapped Children Act (1986). PL 99–457, 100 Stat. 1145.

Ferguson, P. M. (1994). Abandoned to their fate: Social policy and practice toward severely retarded people in America, 1820–1920. Philadelphia: Temple University Press.

Ferguson, P. M. (2002). Critical issues in research on families. *Journal of Special Education, 36(3),* 124–154.

Fiese, B. H., & Sameroff, A. J. (1989). Family context in pediatric psychology: A transactional perspective. *Journal of Pediatric Psychology, 14,* 293–314.

Gray, D. (1995). Lay conceptions of autism: Parents' explanatory models. *Medical Anthropology, 16,* 99–118.

Grigal, M., Neubert, D. A., Moon, M. S., & Graham, S. (2003). Self-determination for students with disabilities: Views of parents and teachers. *Exceptional Children, 70,* 97–112.

Harry, B. (2002). Trends and issues in serving culturally diverse families of children with disabilities. *Journal of Special Education, 36,* 131–138, 147.

Harry, B., Allen, N., & McLaughlin, M. (1995). Communication versus compliance: African-American parents' involvement in special education. *Exceptional Children, 61,* 364–377.

Heward, W. L. (2003). *Exceptional children: An introduction to special education* (7th ed.). Upper Saddle River, NJ: Merrill/Prentice Hall.

Hoffman, A., & Field, S. (1995). Promoting self-determination through effective curriculum development. *Intervention in School and Clinic, 30,* 134–141.

Hopfenberg, W., Levin, H., Chase, C., Christensen, S., Moore, M., Soler, P., Brunner, I., Keller, B., & Rodriguez, G. (1993). *The accelerated schools resource guide.* San Francisco: Jossey-Bass.

Howe, S. G. (1976). Remarks on the causes of idiocy. In M. Rosen, G. Clark, & M. Kivitz (Eds.), *The history of mental retardation: Collected papers* (Vol. 1, pp. 31–60). Baltimore: University Park Press. (Originally published in 1848)

Kaczmarek, L. A., Goldstein, H., Florey, J. D., Carter, A., & Cannon, S. (2004). Supporting families: A preschool model. *Topics in Early Childhood Special Education, 24,* 213–226.

Kaiser, D., & Abell, M. (1997). Learning life skills management in the classroom. *Teaching Exceptional Children, 30,* 70–75.

Katz, M. (1983). *Poverty and policy in American history.* New York: Academic Press.

Keith, N. Z. (1999). Whose community schools? New discourses, old patterns. *Theory into Practice, 38,* 225–336.

Lamorey, S. (2002). The effects of culture on special education services: Evil eyes, prayer meetings, and IEPs. *Teaching Exceptional Children, 34,* 67–71.

Lindsay, G., & Dockrell, J. E. (2004). Parents' concerns about the needs of their children with language problems. *Journal of Special Education, 37,* 225–235.

Magnusson, D., & Allen, V. L. (1983). An interactional perspective for human development. In D. Magnusson & V. L. Allen (Eds.), *Human development: An interactional perspective* (pp. 3–31). New York: Academic Press.

Mahoney, G., & Bella, J. M. (1998). An examination of the effects of family-centered early intervention on child and family outcomes. *Topics in Early Childhood Special Education, 18,* 83–94.

Mahoney, G., & Filer, J. (1996). How responsive is early intervention to the priorities and needs of families? *Topics in Early Childhood Special Education, 16,* 437–457.

Mahoney, G., & O'Sullivan, P. (1990). Early intervention practices with families of children with handicaps. *Mental Retardation, 28,* 169–176.

Mahoney, G., O'Sullivan, P., & Dennebaum, J. (1990). A national study of mothers' perceptions of family-focused early intervention. *Journal of Early Intervention, 14,* 133–146.

Mahoney, G., O'Sullivan, P., & Fors, S. (1989). The family practices of service providers of young handicapped children. *Infant Mental Health Journal, 10,* 75–83.

Mardiros, M. (1989). Conception of childhood disability among Mexican-American parents. *Medical Anthropology, 12,* 55–68.

Marfo, K. (1996). *A field in transition: Early intervention's accomplishments and future challenges.* Keynote Address Delivered at the Second National Conference of the Australian Early Intervention Association. Melbourne, Australia.

Marfo, K., & Cook, C. (1991). Overview of trends and issues in early intervention theory and research. In K. Marfo (Ed.), *Early intervention in transition: Perspectives on programs for handicapped children* (pp. 3–40). New York: Praeger.

Martin, E. J., & Hagan-Burke, S. (2002). Establishing a home–school connection: Strengthening the partnership between families and schools. *Preventing School Failure, 46,* 62–65.

Martin, J. E., Van Dycke, J. L., Greene, B. A., Gardner, J. E., Christensen, W. R., Woods, L. L., & Lovett, D. L. (2006). Direct observation of teacher-directed IEP meetings: Establishing the need for student IEP meeting instruction. *Exceptional Education, 72,* 187–200.

Mason, C., Field, S., & Sawilowsky, S. (2004). Implementation of self-determination activities and student participation in IEPs. *Exceptional Children, 70,* 441–451.

McBride, S. (1999). Family-centered practices. *Young Children, 54,* 62–68.

McNaughton, D. (1994). Measuring parent satisfaction with early childhood intervention programs: Current practice, problems, and future perspectives. *Topics in Early Childhood Special Education, 14,* 26–48.

McWilliam, P. J., & Bailey, D. B. (1993). *Working together with children and families: Case stories in early intervention.* Baltimore: Paul H. Brookes.

McWilliam, R. A., Lang, L., Vandiviere, P., Angell, R., Collins, L., & Underdown, G. (1995). Satisfaction and struggles: Family perceptions of early intervention services. *Journal of Early Intervention, 19,* 43–60.

McWilliam, R. A., Tocci, L., & Harbin, G. L. (1998). Family-centered services: Service providers' discourse and behavior. *Topics in Early Childhood Special Education, 18,* 206–221.

Murphy, D. L., Lee, I. M., Turnbull, A. P., & Turbiville, V. (1995). The family-centered program rating scale: An instrument for program evaluation and change. *Journal of Early Intervention, 19,* 24–42.

Muscott, H. S. (2002). Exceptional partnerships: Listening to the voices of families. *Preventing School Failure, 46,* 66–69.

Nelson, L. G. L., Summers, J. A., & Turnbull, A. P. (2004). Boundaries in family–professional relationships: Implications for special education. *Remedial and Special Education, 25,* 153–165.

Olubanji, D. (1981). Traditional attitudes to the handicapped. Annual general meeting and conference of the Nigerian Society for Handicapped Children. Owerri, Nigeria: Alvan Ikoku College of Education.

Powell, D. S., Batsche, C. J., Ferro, J., Fox, L., & Dunlap, G. (1997). A strength-based approach in support of multi-risk families: Principles and issues. *Topics in Early Childhood Special Education, 17,* 1–26.

Pretti-Frontczak, K., Giallourakis, A., Janas, D., & Hayes, A. (2002). Using a family-centered preservice curriculum to prepare early intervention and early childhood special education personnel. *Teacher Education and Special Education, 25,* 291–297.

Romer, E. F., & Umbreit, J. (1998). The effects of family-centered service coordination: A social validity study. *Journal of Early Intervention, 21,* 95–110.

Rothman, D. J. (1971). *The discovery of the asylum: Social order and disorder in the new republic.* Boston: Little Brown.

Rupiper, M., & Marvin, C. (2004). Preparing teachers for family centered services: A survey of preservice curriculum content. *Teacher Education and Special Education, 27,* 384–395.

Ryan, A., & Smith, M. (1989). Parental reactions to developmental disabilities in Chinese-American families. *Child and Adolescent Social Work, 6,* 283–299.

Sameroff, A. J. (1987). The social context of development. In N. Eisenberg (Ed.), *Contemporary topics in developmental psychology* (pp. 273–291). New York: John Wiley & Sons.

Serna, L., & Lau-Smith, J. (1995). Learning with PURPOSE: Self-determination skills for students who are at risk for school and community failure. *Intervention in School and Clinic, 30,* 142–146.

Shonkoff, J. P., & Meisels, S. J. (1990). Early childhood intervention: The evolution of a concept. In S. J. Meisels & J. P. Shonkoff (Eds.), *Handbook of early childhood intervention* (pp. 3–31). New York: Cambridge University Press.

Simeonsson, R. J., & Bailey, D. B. (1991). Family-focused intervention: Clinical, training, and research implications. In K. Marfo (Ed.), *Early intervention in transition: Current perspectives on programs for handicapped children* (pp. 91–108). New York: Praeger.

Smith, S. (2005). Teaching family-centered practices on-line and on-campus. *Journal of Special Education Technology, 20,* 74–76.

Summers, J. A., Hoffman, L., Marquis, J., Turnbull, A., Poston, D., & Nelson, L. L. (2005). Measuring the quality of family–professional partnerships in special education services. *Exceptional Children, 72,* 65–81.

Tam, K. Y., & Heng, M. A. (2005). A case involving culturally and linguistically diverse parents in pre-referral intervention. *Intervention in School & Clinic, 40,* 222–230.

Thompson, L., Lobb, C., Elling, R., Herman, S., Jurkiewicz, T., & Hulleza, C. (1997). Pathways to family empowerment: Effects of family-centered delivery of early intervention services. *Exceptional Children, 64,* 99–113.

Turnbull, A. P., & Turnbull, H. R. (1997). *Families, professionals and exceptionality: A special partnership* (3rd ed.). Upper Saddle River, NJ: Merrill.

Turnbull, A., & Turnbull, H. R. (2001). *Families, professionals, and exceptionality: Collaborating for empowerment.* Upper Saddle River, NJ: Prentice-Hall.

U.S. Department of Education. (2001). *Twenty-third annual report to Congress on the Implementation of the Individuals with Disabilities Act.* Washington, DC: Author.

Wehmeyer, M. (1996). Student self-report measure of self-determination for students with cognitive disabilities. *Education and Training in Mental Retardation and Developmental Disabilities, 31,* 282–293.

Werts, M. G., Mamlin, N., & Pogoloff, S. M. (2002). Knowing what to expect: Introducing preservice teachers to IEP meetings. *Teacher Education and Special Education, 25,* 413–418.

White, K. R., Taylor, M. J., & Moss, V. D. (1992). Does research support claims about the benefits of involving parents in early intervention programs? *Review of Educational Research, 62,* 91–125.

Winton, P. (1986). The developmentally delayed child within the family context. *Advances in Special Education, 5,* 219–255.

Chapter 13

Adelman, H., & Taylor, L. (2000). Addressing barriers to student learning and promoting healthy development: A research-base for Success4. Los Angeles: UCLA, Mental Health in Schools Center. Retrieved August 18, 2007, from www.state.ia.us/educate/ecese/cfcs/success4/doc/centerbrief.pdf.

Black, M., & Krishnakumar, A. (1998). Children in low income, urban settings: Interventions to promote mental health and well-being. *American Psychologist, 53,* 635–646.

Boston Children's Institute. (2000). Boston excels full service schools. Briefing paper. Author. Retrieved from www.thehome.org/site/pdf/excels_briefing.pdf on August 18, 2007.

Boyd-Franklin, N. (1989). *Black families in therapy: A multi-systems approach.* New York: Guilford Press.

Boyd Webb, N. (2003). *Social work practice with children* (2nd ed.). New York: Guilford Press.

Brewin, C. (2001). Cognitive and emotional reactions to traumatic events: Implications for short-term intervention. *Advances in Mind-Body Medicine, 17,* 163–169.

Cassidy, J. (1998). The nature of the child's ties. In J. Cassidy & P. Shaver (Eds.), *Handbook of attachment: Theory, research, and clinical applications* (pp. 3–21). New York: Guilford Press.

Chow, J., Jafee, K., & Snowden, L. (2003). Racial/ethnic disparities in the use of mental health services in poverty areas. *American Journal of Public Health, 93,* 792–797.

Dryfoos, J. (1994). *Full service schools: A revolution in health and social services for children, youth, and families.* San Francisco: Jossey-Bass.

Dryfoos, J. (2000). The mind-body building equation. *Educational Leadership, 57,* 14–17.

Durose, M., Harlow, C., Langan, P., Motivans, M., Rantala, R., & Schmitt, E. (2002). *Family violence statistics.* Bureau of Justice Statistics reports. Washington, DC: U.S. Department of Justice.

Ebrahim, S., & Gfroerer, J. (2003). Pregnancy related substance use in the United States during 1996–1998. *Obstetrics and Gynecology, 101,* 374–379.

Epstein, J. L. (2005). Developing and sustaining research-based programs of school, family, and community partnerships: Summary of five years of NNPS research. Johns Hopkins University: Center on School, Family and Community Partnerships, National Network of Partnership Schools (NNPS). Retrieved from www.csos.jhu.edu/P2000/Research%20Summary.pdf on September 11, 2006.

Fuller, M., & Tutwiler, S. (1998). Poverty: The enemy of children and families. In M. Fuller & G. Olson (Eds.), *Home school relations: Working successfully with parents and families* (pp. 257–264). Boston: Allyn & Bacon.

Gibson, P., & Abrams, L. (2003). Racial differences in engaging, recruiting, and interviewing African American women in qualitative research. *Qualitative Social Work, 2,* 457–476.

Gil, E. (1991). *The healing power of play.* New York: Guilford Press.

Graham-Bermann, S. A., & Seng, J. (2005). Violence exposure and traumatic stress symptoms as additional predictors of health problems in high risk children. *Journal of Pediatrics, 146(3),* 309–319.

Jaffe, P., & Sudermann, M. (1995). Child witness of women abuse: Research and community response. In S. Stith & M. Straus (Eds.), *Families in Focus Series, Vol. II.* Understanding partner violence: prevalence, causes, consequences, and solutions (pp. 213–222). Minneapolis: National Council on Family Relations.

Kagan, R. (2004). *Rebuilding attachments with traumatized children.* Binghamton, NY: Haworth Maltreatment and Trauma Press.

Karen, R. (1998). *Becoming attached: First relationships and how they shape our capacity to love.* New York: Oxford.

Karr-Morse, R., & Wiley, M. (1997). *Ghosts from the nursery: Tracing the roots of violence.* New York: Atlantic Monthly Press.

Kirschke, J., & van Vliet, W. (2005). How can they look so happy? Reconstructing the place of children after Hurricane Katrina. *Children, Youth, & Environments, 15,* 378–391.

Kreider, R. M., & Fields, J. (2005). Living arrangements of children: 2001. In *Current Population Reports* (U.S. Census Bureau, 70–104). Washington, DC: U.S. Census Bureau.

Kübler-Ross, E. (1997). (Reprint). *On death and dying.* New York: Scribner.

Loue, S. (2003). *Diversity issues in substance abuse treatment and research.* New York: Kluwer.

Moses, P., & Coltoff, P. (1999). Organizational change to promote psychosocial and academic development. In R. Tourse & J. Mooney (Eds.), *Collaborative practice: Social and human service partnerships.* Westport, CT: Praeger.

National Association of School Psychologists. (2005). *Hurricane Katrina: Helping children cope.* Bethesda, MD: NASP.

Piaget, J. (2001). *Language and thought of the child* (2nd ed., Rev.). London: Routledge.

Raphael, S. (2005). Poverty and children are a lethal combination. *Journal of Child & Adolescent Psychiatric Nursing, 18,* 36.

Sheldon, S. B. (2003). Linking school–family–community partnerships in urban elementary schools to student achievement on state tests. *Urban Review, 35,* 149–165.

Somerfield, M. (1996). Beyond the ivory tower. *Education Week, 35.*

Steinhausen, H., & Spohr, H. (1998). Long-term outcome of children with fetal alcohol syndrome: Psychopathology, behavior and intelligence. *Alcoholism: Clinical & Experimental Research, 22(2),* 334–338.

The Office of the Press Secretary, U. W. H. (2001, November 9). National Alcohol and Drug Addiction Recovery month proclamation. Washington, DC.

U.S. Department of Education. (2002). *Annual report to Congress on the implementation of the Individuals with Disabilities Act.* Washington, DC: Author.

U.S. Department of Justice. (June 12, 2005). *Press release: Family violence statistics.* Retrieved August 25, 2007 from U.S. Department of Justice, www.ojp.usdoj.gov.bjs/pub/press/fvspr.htm.

U.S. Department of Health and Human Services. (1990). *Fetal alcohol syndrome and other effects of alcohol on pregnancy.* Rockville, MD: USDHHS.

U.S. Census Bureau. (2005). *Relationship fact sheet.* Retrieved October 24, 2007 from http://factfinder.census.gov/servlet/ACSSAFFPeople?_event=&geo_id=01000US&_geoContext=01000US&_street=&_county=&_cityTown=&_state=&_zip=&_lang=en&_sse=on&ActiveGeoDiv=&_useEV=&pctxt=fph&pgsl=010&_submenuId=people_11&ds_name=ACS_2005_SAFF&_ci_nbr=&qr_name=&reg=%3A&_keyword=&_industry=.

United Way of America. (1999). One community at a time: The United Way, local communities and school success. Alexandria, VA: Author.

Vogel, C. (2006). Building a strong community partnership. *District Administration, June 2006,* 66–72.

Whalen, S. (2002). The Polk Bros. Foundation's Full Service Schools Initiative: Synopsis of evaluation findings (1996–1999). Chicago: The Polk Bros. Foundation. Retrieved from www.polkbrosfdn.org/full_service_schools_initiative.htm on August 15, 2007.

Chapter 14

Acock, A. C., & Demo, D. H. (1994). *Family diversity and well-being.* Thousand Oaks, CA: Sage.

Adams, K. S., & Christenson, S. L. (1998). Differences in parent and teacher trust levels: Implications for creating collaborative family–school relationships. *Special Services in the Schools 14(1–2),* 1–22.

Amatea, E., & Vandiver, F. (2004). Expanding the school leadership team: Using counselors to facilitate teacher collaboration with families. *Journal of School Leadership, 14,* 327–344.

Balli, S. J., Demo, D. H., & Wedman, J. F. (1998). Family involvement with children's homework: An intervention in the middle grades. *Family Relations 47(2),* 149–157.

Berends, M., Chun, J., Schuyler, G., Stockly, S., & Briggs, R. J. (2002). *Challenges of conflicting school reforms: Effects of New American Schools in a high-poverty district.* Santa Monica, CA: RAND.

Berends, M., Kirby, S. N., Naftel, S., & McKelvey, C. (2001). *Implementation and performance in New American Schools: Three years into a scale-up.* Santa Monica, CA: RAND.

Binns, K., Steinberg, A., & Amorosi, S. (1997). *The Metropolitan Life survey of the American teacher, 1998: Building family–school partnerships: Views of teachers and students.* New York: Louis Harris and Associates.

Bronfenbrenner, U. (1991). What do families do? Part 1. *Teaching Thinking and Problem Solving, 13(4),* 1, 3–5.

Christenon, S. L. (2004). The family–school partnership: An opportunity to promote the learning competence of all students. *School Psychology Review, 33(1),* 83–104.

Christenson, S. L., & Sheridan, S. (2001). *Schools and families: Creating essential connections for learning.* New York: Guilford Press.

Clark, R. (1993). Homework-focused parenting practices that positively affect student achievement. In N. F. Chavkin (Ed.), *Families and schools in a pluralistic society* (pp. 53–71). Albany: State University of New York Press.

Collignon, F. F., Men, M., & Tan, S. (2001). Finding ways in: Community-based perspectives on Southeast Asian family involvement with schools in a New England state. *Journal of Education for Students Placed at Risk 6(1–2),* 27–44.

Comer, J. P. (1985). Empowering black children's educational environments. In H. P. McAdoo and J. L. McAdoo (Ed.), *Black children: Special, educational, and parental involvement* (pp. 123–138). Newbury Park, CA: Sage.

Dalton, S. S., & Moir, E. E. (1992). Evaluating limited English proficient (LEP) teacher training and in-service programs. In *Proceedings of the second national research symposium on limited English proficient student issues: Focus on evaluation and measurement* (pp. 415–445). Washington, DC: U.S. Department of Education, Office of Bilingual Education and Minority Languages Affairs.

Dalton, S. S., & Moir, E. E. (1996). Text and context for professional development of new bilingual teachers. In M. McLaughlin & I. Oberman (Eds.), *Teacher learning: New policies, new practices.* New York: Teachers College Press.

Dalton, S. S. (1998). *Pedagogy matters: Standards for effective teaching practice.* Center for Research on Education, Diversity, and Excellence. Santa Cruz: University of California.

Darling-Hammond, L., & Falk, B. (1997). Using standards and assessments to support student learning. *Phi Delta Kappan, 79(3),* 190–199.

Deal, T., & Peterson, K. (1999). *Shaping school culture.* San Francisco: Jossey-Bass.

Desimone, L. (2002). How can comprehensive school reform models be successfully implemented? *Review of Educational Research, 72,* 433–479.

Dornbusch, S. M., & Ritter, P. L. (1988). Parents of high school students: A neglected resource. *Educational Horizons, 66,* 75–77.

Eccles, J. S., & Harold, R. D. (1993). Family involvement in children's and adolescents' schooling. In A. Booth & J. F. Dunn (Eds.), *Family-school links: How do they affect educational outcomes?* (3–34). Mahwah, NJ: Erlbaum.

Edmonds, R. R. (1979). Some schools work and more can. *Social Policy, 9,* 28–32.

Epstein, J. L. (1991). Effects on student achievement of teacher practices of parent involvement. In S. Silvern (Ed.), *Advances in reading/language research: Literacy through family, community, and school interaction* (Vol. 5, pp. 261–276). Greenwich, CT: JAI Press.

Epstein, J. L. (2001). *School, family, and community partnerships: Preparing educators and improving schools.* Boulder, CO: Westview.

Epstein, J. L. (2005). A case study of the partnership schools comprehensive school reform (CSR) model. *Elementary School Journal, 106(2),* 151–170.

Epstein, J. L., & Hollifield, J. H. (1996). Title I implementations for comprehensive school–family–community partnerships. *Journal of Education for Students Placed at Risk, 1(3),* 263–278.

Epstein, J. L., Salinas, K. C. (1995). *Manual for teachers and prototype activities: Teachers Involve Parents in Schoolwork (TIPS) in the elementary and middle grades.* Baltimore: Johns Hopkins University, Center on School, Family, and Community Partnerships.

Epstein, J. L., Sanders, M. G., Simon, B. S., Salinas, K. C., Jansorn, N. R., & Van Voorhis, F. L. (2002). *School, family, and community partnerships: Your handbook for action* (2nd ed.). Thousand Oaks, CA: Corwin.

Epstein, J. L., & Sheldon, S. B. (2002). Present and accounted for: Improving student attendance through family and community involvement. *Journal of Educational Research, 95,* 308–318.

Garbarino, J. (1997). *Adolescent development: An ecological perspective.* Columbus, OH: Merrill.

Garcia Coll, C., Akiba, D., Palacios, N., Bailey, B., Silver, R., DiMartino, L., & Chin, C. (2002). Parental involvement in children's education: Lessons from three immigrant groups. *Parenting, Science, and Practice, 2(3)*, 303–324.

Gonzalez, N., Andrade, R., Civil, M., & Moll, L. (2001). Bridging funds of distributed knowledge: Creating zones of practice in mathematics. *Journal of Education of Students Placed at Risk, 6(1–2)*, 115–132.

Graue, E., & Brown, C. P. (2003). Preservice teachers' notions of families and schooling. *Teaching and Teacher Education, 19*, 719–735.

Griffith, J. (1996). Test of a model of the organizational antecedents of parent involvement and satisfaction with public education. *Human Relations, 49(12)*, 1549–1571.

Griffith, J. (1998). The relationship of school structure and social environment to parent involvement in elementary schools. *Elementary School Journal, 99(1)*, 53–80.

Grolnick, W. S., Benjet, C., Kurowski, C. O., & Apostoleris, N. H. (1997). Predictors of parent involvement in children's schooling. *Journal of Educational Psychology, 89(3)*, 538–548.

Grolnick, W. S., Kurowski, C. O., Dunlap, K. G., & Hevey, C. (2000). Parental resources and the transition to junior high. *Journal of Research on Adolescence, 10(4)*, 465–488.

Harry, B. (1992). *Cultural diversity, families, and the special education system: Communication and empowerment.* New York: Teachers College Press.

Hoover-Dempsey, K. V., Barriato, A. C., Walker, J. M. T., Reed, R. P., DeJong, J. M., & Jones, K. P. (2001). Parental involvement in homework. *Educational Psychologist, 36*, 195–209.

Hoover-Dempsey, K. V., Bassler, O. C., & Brissie, J. S. (1992). Explorations in parent–school relations. *Journal of Educational Research, 85*, 287–294.

Hoover-Dempsey, K. V., & Sandler, H. M. (1995). Parental involvement in children's education: Why does it make a difference? *Teachers College Record, 97*, 310–331.

Hoover-Dempsey, K. V., & Sandler, H. (1997). Why do parents become involved in their children's education? *Review of Educational Research, 67(1)*, 3–42.

Hoover-Dempsey, K. V., Walker, J. M. T., Jones, K. P., & Reed, R. P. (2002). Teachers involving parents (TIP): Results of an in-service teacher education program for enhancing parental involvement. *Teaching and Teacher Education, 18(7)*, 843–867.

Hoover-Dempsey, K. V., Walker, J. M. T., Sandler, H., Whetsel, D., Green, C. L., Wilkins, A. S., & Closson, K. (2005). Why do parents become involved? Research findings and implications. *Elementary School Journal, 106(2)*, 105–130.

Hoover-Dempsey, K. V., Wilkins, A. S., Sandler, H., & O'Connor, K. J. (2004). *Parental role construction for involvement: Interactions among theoretical, measurement, and pragmatic issues in instrument development.* Paper presented at the annual meeting of the American Educational Research Association, San Diego, California.

Horvat, E. M., Weininger, E. B., & Lareau, A. (2003). From social ties to social capital: Class differences in relations between schools and parent networks. *American Educational Research Journal, 40(2)*, 319–351.

Keith, P. B., & Lichtman, M. V. (1994). Does parent involvement influence the achievement of Mexican-American eighth graders? Results from a national education longitudinal study. *School Psychology Quarterly, 9*, 256–272.

Kirby, S. N., Berends, M., & Naftel, S. (2001). *Implementation in a longitudinal sample of New American Schools: Four years into scale-up.* Arlington, VA: Rand Education.

Knapp, M. S. (1997). Between systemic reforms and the mathematics and science classroom: The dynamics of innovation, implementation, and professional learning. *Review of Educational Research, 67*, 227–266.

Kohl, G. O., Lengua, L. J., & McMahon, R. J. (2000). Parent involvement in school: Conceptualizing multiple dimensions and their relations with family and demographic risk factors. *Journal of School Psychology, 38(6)*, 501–523.

Levin, I., Levy-Shiff, R., Appelbaum-Peled, T., Katz, I., Komar, M., & Meiran, N. (1997). Antecedents and consequences of maternal involvement in children's homework: A longitudinal analysis. *Journal of Applied Developmental Psychology, 18*, 207–222.

Machida, S., Taylor, A. R., & Kim, J. (2002). The role of maternal beliefs in predicting home learning activities in Head Start families. *Family relations, 51(2)*, 176–184.

McNamara, K., Telzrow, C., & DeLamatre, J. (1999). Parent reactions to implementation of intervention-based assessment. *Journal of Educational and Psychological Consultation, 10(4)*, 343–362.

Merttens, R., & Woods, P. (1994). *Parents' and children's assessment of math in the home: Towards a theory of learning congruence.* Paper presented at the Annual Meeting of the American Educational Research Association, New Orleans.

Miedel, W. T., & Reynolds, A. J. (1999). Parent involvement in early intervention for disadvantaged children: Does it matter? *Journal of School Psychology, 31(4),* 379–402.

Moll, L. C., Amanti, C., Neff, D., & Gonzalez, N. (1992). Funds of knowledge for teaching: Using a qualitative approach to connect homes and classrooms. *Theory into Practice, 31(2),* 132–141.

Morris, V. G., & Taylor, S. I. (1998). Alleviating barriers to family involvement in education: The role of teacher education. *Teaching and Teacher Education, 14(2),* 219–231.

Musti-Rao, S., & Cartledge, G. (2004). Making home an advantage in the prevention of reading failure: Strategies for collaborating with parents in urban schools. *Preventing School Failure, 48(4),* 15–21.

National Commission on Teaching and America's Future. (1996). *What matters most: Teaching for America's future.* New York: Author.

National Research Council. (1996). *National science education standards.* Washington, DC: National Academy Press.

Newmann, F. M., King, M. B., & Youngs, P. (2000). Professional development that addresses school capacity: Lessons from urban elementary schools. *American Journal of Education, 108,* 259–299.

Pang, I. W., & Watkins, D. (2000). Towards a psychological model of teacher–parent communication in Hong Kong primary schools. *Educational Studies, 26(2),* 141–163.

Pena, D. C. (2000). Parent involvement: Influencing factors and implications. *Journal of Educational Research, 94(1),* 42–54.

Phelan, P., Davidson, A. L., & Yu, H. C. (1998). *Adolescents' worlds: Negotiating family, peers, and schools.* New York: Teachers College Press.

Pianta, R., & Walsh, D. J. (1996). *High-risk children in schools: Constructing sustaining relationships.* New York: Routledge.

Schein, E. H. (2004). *Organizational culture and leadership* (3rd ed.). San Francisco: Jossey-Bass.

Senechal, M., & LeFevre, J. (2002). Parental involvement in the development of children's reading skills: A five-year longitudinal study. *Child Development, 73(2),* 445–460.

Sheldon, S. B. (2005). Testing a structural equation model of partnership program implementation and parent involvement. *Elementary School Journal, 106(2),* 171–187.

Shumow, L., & Harris, W. (2000). Teacher thinking about home–school relations in low-income urban communities. *School Community Journal, 10,* 9–24.

Soodak, L. C., & Erwin, E. J. (2000). Valued member or tolerated participant: Parents' experiences in inclusive early childhood settings. *Journal of the Association for Persons with Severe Handicaps, 25(1),* 29–41.

Swap, S. M. (1993). *Developing home–school partnerships: From concepts to practice.* New York: Teachers College Press.

Swick, K. J., & McKnight, S. (1989). Characteristics of kindergarten teachers who promote parent involvement. *Early Childhood Research Quarterly, 4,* 19–29.

Van Voorhis, F. L. (2000). *The effects of interactive (TIPS) and non-interactive homework assignments on science achievement and family involvement of middle grade students.* Unpublished doctoral dissertation, University of Florida, Gainesville.

Walker, J. M. T., Wilkins, A. S., Dallaire, J. P., Sandler, H. M., & Hoover-Dempsey, K. V. (2005). Parental involvement: Model revision through scale development. *Elementary School Journal, 106,* 85–104.

Wang, M. C., Haertel, G. D., & Walberg, H. J. (1997). Fostering educational resilience in inner-city schools. In R. P. Weissberg, O. Reyes, & H. J. Walberg (Eds.), *Urban children and youth* (pp. 135–142). Thousand Oaks, CA: Sage.

Weiss, H. B., Mayer, E., Kreider, H., Vaughan, M., Dearing, E., Hencke, R., & Pinto, K. (2003). Making it work: Low-income working mothers' involvement in their children's education. *American Educational Research Journal, 40(4),* 879–901.

Index